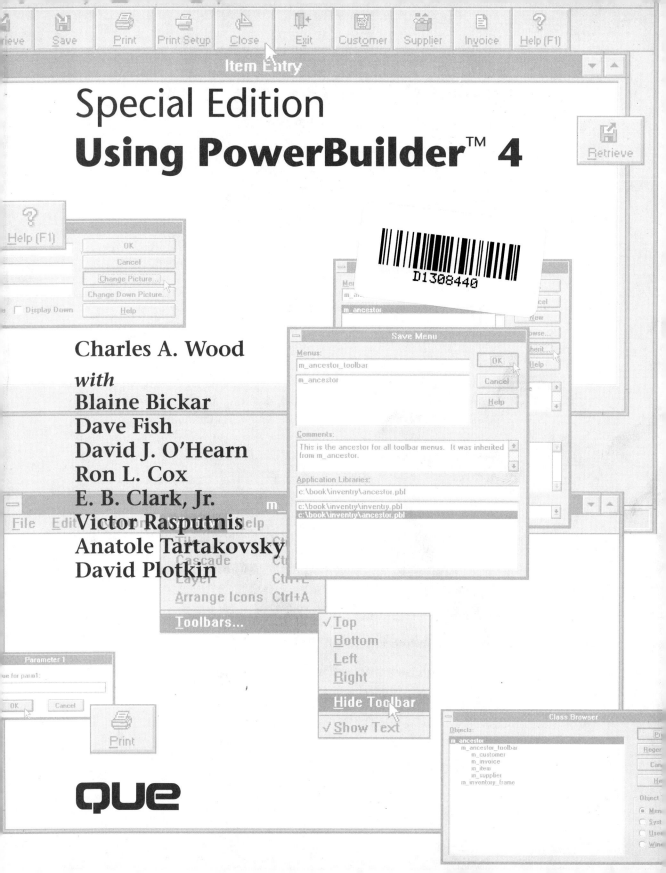

Special Edition
Using PowerBuilder™ 4

Charles A. Wood

with
Blaine Bickar
Dave Fish
David J. O'Hearn
Ron L. Cox
E. B. Clark, Jr.
Victor Rasputnis
Anatole Tartakovsky
David Plotkin

que

Special Edition Using PowerBuilder 4

Copyright © 1995 by Que® Corporation

All rights reserved. Printed in the United States of America. No part of this book may be used or reproduced in any form or by any means, or stored in a database or retrieval system, without prior written permission of the publisher except in the case of brief quotations embodied in critical articles and reviews. Making copies of any part of this book for any purpose other than your own personal use is a violation of United States copyright laws. For information, address Que Corporation, 201 W. 103rd St., Indianapolis, IN 46290.

Library of Congress Catalog No.: 94-069624

ISBN: 07897-0059-X

This book is sold *as is*, without warranty of any kind, either express or implied, respecting the contents of this book, including but not limited to implied warranties for the book's quality, performance, merchantability, or fitness for any particular purpose. Neither Que Corporation nor its dealers or distributors shall be liable to the purchaser or any other person or entity with respect to any liability, loss, or damage caused or alleged to have been caused directly or indirectly by this book.

97 96 95   6 5 4 3 2

Interpretation of the printing code: the rightmost double-digit number is the year of the book's printing; the rightmost single-digit number, the number of the book's printing. For example, a printing code of 95-1 shows that the first printing of the book occurred in 1995.

Publisher: David P. Ewing

Associate Publisher: Don Roche, Jr.

Associate Publisher—Operations: Corinne Walls

Managing Editor: Michael Cunningham

Credits

Acquisitions Editor
Jenny L. Watson

Product Director
Lisa D. Wagner

Product Development
Bob Hulett, Software Synergy, Inc.

Technical Editors
Mike Causey, Software Synergy, Inc.
Jim Rang

Production Editors
Lisa M. Gebken
Nancy E. Sixsmith

Editors
Elsa Bethanis
Charles K. Bowles
Susan M. Dunn
Patrick Kanouse
Julie A. McNamee
Theresa Mathias
Nicole L. Rodandello
Linda Seifert

Technical Specialist
Cari Ohm

Operations Coordinator
Patricia J. Brooks

Acquisitions Assistant
Tracy M. Williams

Editorial Assistant
Jill L. Pursell

Book Designer
Paula Carroll

Cover Designer
Dan Armstrong

Production Team
Stephen Carlin
Amy Cornwell
Maxine Dillingham
Chad Dressler
Bob LaRoche
Elizabeth Lewis
Stephanie Mineart
Alan Palmore
Kaylene Riemen
Caroline Roop
Clair Schweinler
Kris Simmons
Jonathan Swain
Donna Winter
Jody York

Indexer
Rebecca Mayfield

Composed in *Stone Serif* and *MCPdigital* by Que Corporation

About the Authors

Charles Wood is a senior programmer analyst at Indiana Farm Bureau Insurance. He graduated with bachelor's degrees in Computer Science and Finance from Ball State University in 1986. Along with developing software in PowerBuilder, C++, COBOL, and QuickBasic, Wood has instructed in C and C++ at Indiana Vocational Technical College. He is currently pursuing his MBA at Butler University.

Blaine Bickar is an independent consultant, operating as Grey Matter Systems. He is a Certified PowerBuilder Developer and a Certified PowerBuilder Instructor. Bickar has extensive experience with PowerBuilder, having built several systems ranging in size from individual applications utilizing local database-management systems to enterprise-wide client/server applications utilizing mainframe and mid-range database management systems. He has mentored many people in PowerBuilder, graphical design, regression testing, and general client/server architecture issues. Bickar graduated from Carnegie-Mellon University with a B.S. in Industrial Management.

Dave Fish is a Certified PowerBuilder Developer who has been designing and developing database applications for nine years. He has worked with DBMSs on mainframes, VAX, UNIX, and PC networks. He has been developing client/server Windows and Motif applications for two years, and has written several PowerBuilder applications using Oracle, Sybase, and MS SQL Server. His most recent application was a document-tracking system for a U.S. government agency, which supports over 100 concurrent users. Dave resides in Washington, D.C., and can be reached on CompuServe at 73503,3151 or on the Internet at 73503,3151@compuserve.com.

David O'Hearn graduated from Harding University in 1986 with a bachelor's degree in Computer Science. O'Hearn has worked as a computer programmer and systems analyst in the insurance industry for the past six years. He is currently working as a consultant for Computer Horizons Corporation. O'Hearn resides in Plainfield, Ind., with his wife Amy.

Ron L. Cox is a Project Manager with Computer People Unlimited in Milwaukee, Wisc. He focuses on client/server consulting, and he is a Certified PowerBuilder Developer. Cox lives with his wife, Jean, in Waukesha, Wisc. He can be reached on CompuServe at 71621,1551.

E. B. Clark, Jr. has been working with small computers for more than a dozen years, and has worked in virtually all facets of programming. Ben is a Novell-certified Network System Administrator and a Certified PowerBuilder Developer. He is the president of The Gryphon Alliance, an investment company, and is president of Avant-Garde Technologies, a microcomputer consulting and services company based in Texas. Ben likes to spend his spare time with his wife, Jeanne, and three children, Maeghan, Emily, and Jeromy.

Victor Rasputnis has a Ph.D. in Computer Science from the Moscow Institute of Robotics. He is the cofounder of CTI, a software development and consulting company in New York, which specializes in client/server, multimedia, and other emerging technologies. Rasputnis is a Certified PowerBuilder Developer, and has over 12 years of software development and consulting experience with financial and manufacturing companies. He leads development of CTI PowerBase Class Library for PowerBuilder, and can be contacted on CompuServe at 74643,1755.

Anatole Tartakovsky graduated from Kharkov University in 1986, with an M.S. degree in Math, and has a Ph.D. in Computer Science from the Moscow Institute of Robotics. He is the cofounder of CTI, a software development and consulting company in New York, specializing in client/server, multimedia, and other emerging technologies. Tartakovsky is a Certified PowerBuilder Developer, and has over 10 years of software development and consulting experience with financial and manufacturing companies. He leads a number of projects, including the development of imaging add-ons, custom controls, and application framework libraries for PowerBuilder. Tartakovsky can be contacted on CompuServe at 74250,1550.

David Plotkin is a Business Area Analyst with Integral Systems in Walnut Creek, Calif. He has extensive experience in designing and implementing databases, both at the desktop and on client/server systems. He writes extensively for various computer periodicals, and his favorite editor is his wife, Marisa.

Acknowledgments

I want to thank the Power Team of Dave O'Hearn, Michelle G. Lehman, Don Doty, Blaine Bickar, Jim Rang and John R. Zebrowski for all their help and advice, and Tom Gardner and Bruce Newcome for helping coordinate the project. Special thanks to Michelle Lehman, James W. Rang of NewMedia, Inc., and Ron Cox for their eleventh-hour technical reviews of the text.

Thanks to Don Roche, Jenny Watson, Nancy Sixsmith, Tracy Williams, and both Lisas (Gebken and Wagner) for their tireless efforts to get this book done.

Thanks to Marv Taylor and the management of Farm Bureau Insurance of Indiana for giving me the time off to write this book.

Kudos to Tony Navarra from Anatec for putting me in touch with knowledgeable people.

Most of all, thanks to my wife, Lyn, for her infinite patience and understanding while this book was being written. I couldn't have done it without you.

— Charles A. Wood

Trademarks

All terms mentioned in this book that are known to be trademarks or service marks have been appropriately capitalized. Que cannot attest to the accuracy of this information. Use of a term in this book should not be regarded as affecting the validity of any trademark or service mark.

Contents

2 Understanding Analysis, Design, and Databases   45

II Using PowerScript   121

5 Using Events, Functions, and the
PowerScript Language   123

III Using DataWindows   205

8 Creating DataWindows   207

9 Enhancing DataWindows   235

10 Manipulating Data Using DataWindows   267

11 Creating Reports   295

IV Delivering the Final Product   337

12 PowerBuilder Libraries   339

13 Pulling It All Together in an Application   351

19 Exploiting the Power of Inheritance   445

20 Using dwShareData Functions   461

D Getting Help with Your PowerBuilder Applications   597

E Using C++ in Your PowerBuilder Application   613

F Third-Party Products and Support (What's on the CD?)   627

Introduction

Windows development is usually considered to be difficult and tedious. With all the aspects of a graphical user interface to consider, Windows developers were usually forced to develop in hard-to-learn text-based languages. PowerBuilder has changed all that.

PowerBuilder is quickly becoming the premier Windows development tool. The capabilities of PowerBuilder have upped the ante on all Windows development, and programmers are starting to develop PowerBuilder applications in droves! Companies realize that PowerBuilder is an excellent way to develop in Windows, while consulting firms can't hire enough PowerBuilder programmers. (All the more reason to buy this book, right?)

Special Edition Using PowerBuilder 4 provides two functions. First, it leads the beginning PowerBuilder programmer through an entire application. Second, it serves as a one-stop resource for intermediate and advanced PowerBuilder developers.

The Emerging Client/Server Environment

In recent years, people have discovered the need to share information with each other through the PC. Instead of passing disks around with needed information, companies have turned to the *client/server environment*. A client/server environment allows several PCs (called *clients*) to access one centralized database (or databases) on one centralized PC (called a *server*).

Part of PowerBuilder's popularity relies on the demand for client/server applications. Typical databases will support client/server technology. Because of its extensive database support, PowerBuilder developers have easy access to client/server technology. Simply put, since databases address problems like distributed access, security, and multiple user access, and since PowerBuilder interfaces *easily* to these databases, the PowerBuilder developer is able to concentrate on functionality.

Trends in Application Development

Software developers (the readers of this book) are now expected to make their applications graphical, usually much to their dismay! As the DOS market shrinks and the Windows market grows, demand for graphical programs increases.

Add to this the incredible need for faster development. Many programming shops are years behind in development. Clearly, older methods of development have to be replaced.

What this means to you, the developer, is that your newly developed programs are supposed to be better than before, and you're supposed to develop them in less time! It's fortunate that PowerBuilder came along to help you accomplish these heavy demands.

What To Expect Using PowerBuilder 4

Using PowerBuilder 4, developers can expect several benefits:

■ *Rapid Development.* The time it takes to develop an application will decrease dramatically. Typical client/server Windows applications that took years can now take months or even weeks! You can now design a program as you write it. Maintenance will also be much easier due to the object-based nature of PowerBuilder 4. You'll be able to concentrate on program analysis and design without worrying about hours and hours of tedious coding.

■ *Less Training Time.* Remember when you first learned to program? Unless you were a prodigy, it usually took you months to learn the language and *years* to get up to speed. (If you don't believe me, try dusting off some of those first programs and take a look!) With PowerBuilder, you can begin quality client/server Windows development immediately. Your typical "up to speed" training time takes about three months of normal working days.

■ *Professional Windows Programs.* Even with such quick development and less training time, you can develop great Windows single-user or client/server applications. You'll be astounded at the high quality of code that such little effort can produce.

How This Book Is Organized

If you know Windows, this book will help you become a PowerBuilder developer. Throughout this book, you will go step by step through the development of an Inventory Tracking system. (You'll also find it on the CD-ROM included with this book.)

Part I: Introducing PowerBuilder

In Part I, you learn the basics about the PowerBuilder application and how it works:

- Chapter 1, "Introducing PowerBuilder," introduces windows, menus, libraries, and painters. It's a must-read for the beginning PowerBuilder developer.

- Chapter 2, "Understanding Analysis, Design, and Databases," gives a detailed description of the database painter and setting up tables in your database.

- In Chapter 3, "Exploring Windows," you learn more about the main thrust of today's graphical user interface development, and different ways you can use windows in your applications.

- Chapter 4, "Defining Menus," shows how to define menus for your window and how to associate a menu with a window.

Part II: Using PowerScript

Part II introduces you to PowerBuilder's powerful programming language:

- Chapter 5, "Using Events, Functions, and the PowerScript Language," describes basic PowerScript programming. It's a must for the beginner.

- Chapter 6, "Programming in PowerScript," describes the best way to implement PowerScript from within your application.

- In Chapter 7, "Using SQL in PowerBuilder," you learn how to incorporate SQL into your application.

Part III: Using DataWindows

Part III teaches you the techniques you need to know to design powerful DataWindows and use them in your applications:

- Chapter 8, "Creating DataWindows," shows how to choose and create the DataWindow you want.

■ Chapter 9, "Enhancing DataWindows," goes beyond creating DataWindows and delves into field manipulation and edit styles, such as radio buttons and drop-down DataWindows.

■ Chapter 10, "Manipulating Data Using DataWindows," explains the ways in which you can use SQL to define a DataWindow. In this chapter, you learn more about the SQL toolbox and the SQL syntax behind a DataWindow.

■ Chapter 11, "Creating Reports," shows how to use your DataWindows as reports. This chapter also describes grouping and graphing data, as well as some new PowerBuilder 4 features.

Part IV: Delivering the Final Product
In Part IV, you fit all the pieces of the puzzle together to finalize the application and get it ready for distribution:

■ Chapter 12, "PowerBuilder Libraries," teaches you how to build and use PowerBuilder libraries, which PowerBuilder uses to store all of its objects.

■ Chapter 13, "Pulling It All Together in an Application," shows you how to finalize your application before you compile.

■ Chapter 14, "Debugging Your Application," reminds you that no programming is finished until it's been fully tested and debugged.

■ Chapter 15, "Delivering an Executable," describes how to compile the application you developed and how to distribute the compiled application.

Part V: Techniques from the Pros
In Part V, industry experts share secrets they've learned, offer you their advice, and coach you through some advanced tips and techniques:

■ In Chapter 16, "Using Modify and Describe to Get the Most of DataWindows," an industry expert explains in simple terms how to improve the performance of your DataWindows through the use of dwDescribe and dwModify functions.

■ Chapter 17, "Using the Data Pipeline," shows you how to transfer data from one database to another using the data pipeline.

- Chapter 18, "DataWindows Tips and Tricks," provides you with secrets about DataWindows that might otherwise take you years to discover.

- Chapter 19, "Exploiting The Power of Inheritance," shows you how to increase your productivity as a developer by taking advantage of PowerBuilder's "reusable object" programming features.

- Chapter 20, "Using dwShareData Functions," explores this often-overlooked family of functions to speed up your development time.

Part VI: References

If you already develop in PowerBuilder, this book will become an invaluable reference. Contained in Part VI are short descriptions of all PowerBuilder functions and attributes. No longer will you have to sift through numerous manuals to find that needed reference. This book will be your best way to find an obscure function or attribute. The references include the following chapters:

- Chapter 21, "Function & Event Quick Reference," lists all the functions allowed in PowerBuilder. It can be helpful when reviewing available DataWindow functions.

- Chapter 22, "Enumerated Data Types Quick Reference," puts all these data types in one easy-to-find place.

- Chapter 23, "Attribute Quick Reference," provides you with a list and short definition of the attributes and events available for each PowerBuilder object and control.

- Chapter 24, "Message Quick Reference," gives you the meaning of those cryptic PowerBuilder and Watcom error messages and provides advice on how to deal with them.

Appendixes

At the end of the book, you'll find some valuable appendixes:

- Appendix A, "Using Naming Conventions," contains some basic standard naming conventions that should be followed with every PowerBuilder application. Proper naming conventions will assist you during debugging, and they make future maintenance easier.

■ Although Watcom SQL is included with every edition of PowerBuilder, I was hard pressed to find any external documentation on the database. The run-time version of Watcom is not documented very well in the PowerBuilder documentation. Appendix B, "Using Watcom Database and Watcom SQL," will alleviate this situation.

■ Appendix C, "Implementing Advanced Procedures," is a brief overview of advanced topics not covered in this book. If you want to try something tricky using PowerBuilder, this appendix will hopefully set you on the right track.

■ Appendix D, "Getting Help with Your PowerBuilder Applications," details how to get help on the system you are working on. There are many resources available to a PowerBuilder developer.

■ Appendix E, "Using C++ in Your PowerBuilder Application," gives you an in-depth look at this powerful new capability of PowerBuilder 4.

■ Finally, you'll find out what is included on the CD-ROM in Appendix F, "Third-Party Products and Support (What's on the CD?)."

Conventions Used in This Book

PowerBuilder enables you to use both the keyboard and the mouse to select menu and dialog box items. You can press a letter, or you can select an item by clicking it with the mouse. Letters you press to activate menus, choose commands in menus, and select options in dialog boxes are printed in boldface type: **F**ile, **O**pen.

Names of dialog boxes and dialog box options are written with initial capital letters. Messages that appear on-screen are printed in a special font: Document 1. New terms are introduced in *italic* type. Text that you are to type appears in **boldface**.

The following example shows typical command sequences:

Open the **F**ile menu and choose **C**opy, or press Ctrl+Ins.

Power Builder provides toolbars for your convenience. By clicking on a button from the toolbar, you can execute a command or access a dialog box. Chapters in this book contain button icons in the margins, indicating which button you can click to perform a task.

Throughout *Special Edition Using PowerBuilder 4*, you see shaded boxes labeled **Syntax-at-a-Glance.** These boxes explain important elements of the PowerBuilder language, with concise descriptions of the appropriate format for using these functions, statements, methods, and events, along with one or two short code examples. You can always jump back to these quick reference boxes as you move forward in your PowerBuilder programming. A sample Syntax-at-a-Glance box follows:

Syntax-at-a-Glance

Open(*window_name*, {*parent_window*})

Open opens your window. *parent_window* is never needed and is used only with pop-up or child windows. If you omit parent_window on a pop-up or child window, the current active window is assumed to be the parent window.

In addition to Syntax-at-a-Glance boxes, you find five other visual aids that help you on your PowerBuilder journey: **Notes**, **Tips**, **Cautions**, **Trouble-shooting**, and **TrackNotes**.

Note

This paragraph format indicates additional information that may help you avoid problems or that should be considered in using the described features.

Tip
This paragraph format suggests easier or alternative methods for executing a procedure.

Caution

This paragraph format warns the reader of hazardous procedures (for example, activities that delete files).

Troubleshooting

This paragraph format provides guidance on how to find solutions to common problems. Specific problems you may encounter are shown in italic. Possible solutions appear in the paragraph(s) following the problem.

> ### TrackNote
>
> TrackNotes are comments or other information from the author specifically related to the sample application you are building throughout the book.

Special Edition Using PowerBuilder 4 uses margin cross-references to help you access related information in other parts of the book. Right-facing triangles point you to related information in later chapters. Left-facing triangles point you to information in previous chapters.

If you are an experienced PowerBuilder user and are mostly interested in what's new to PowerBuilder 4, look for this icon. It points out places where new features are discussed.

Discussion that relates to exercises or files you can find on the *SE Using PowerBuilder 4* CD-ROM is noted by this icon.

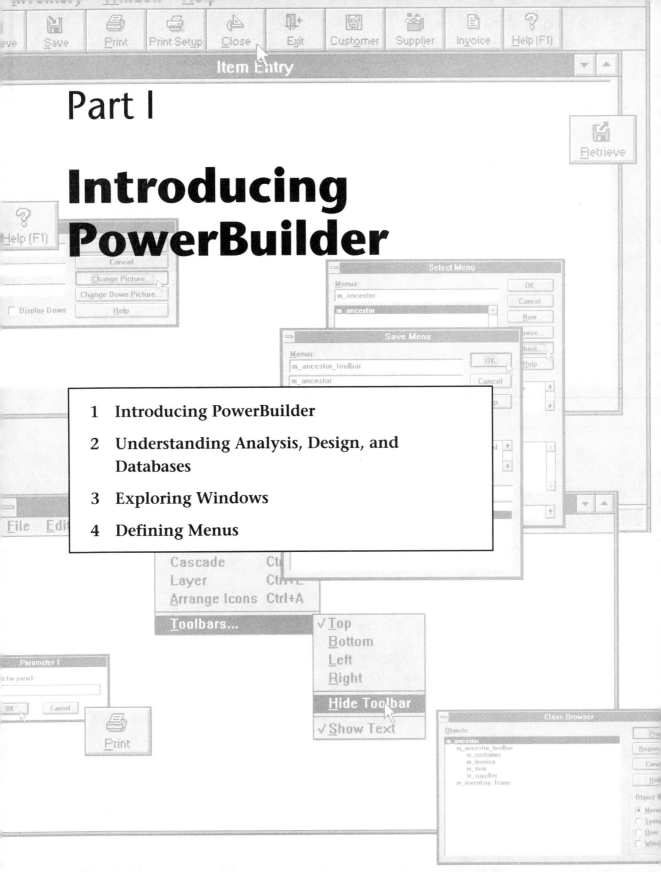

Part I

Introducing PowerBuilder

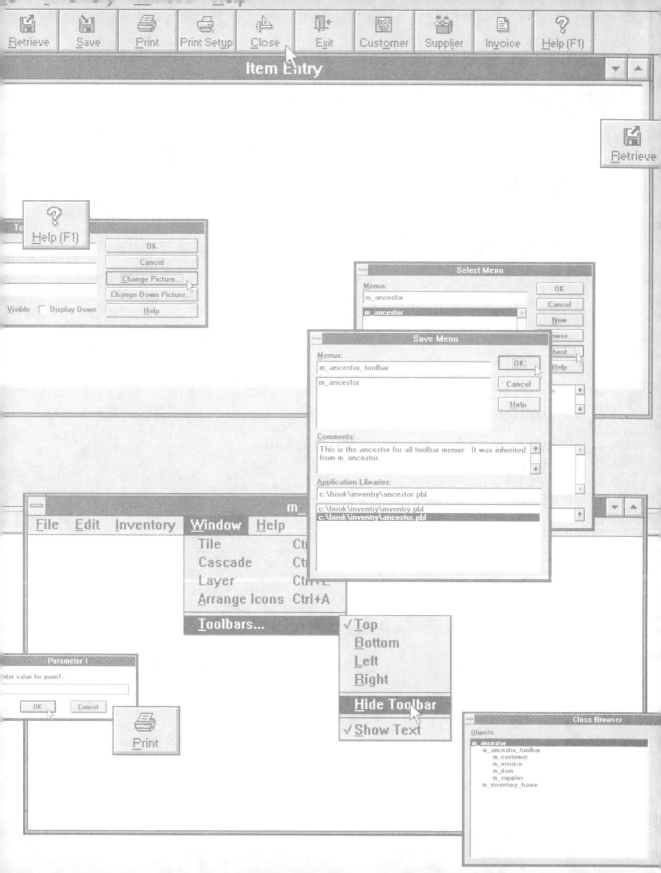

Introducing PowerBuilder

Fig. 1.1
PowerBuilder allows you to customize your toolbar to meet your individual preferences.

Using PowerBuilder as an Object-Based Environment

A lot could be said about object-oriented programming (OOP). To put it simply, object-oriented languages consist of three primary ways of doing things. First, every function and group of related functions (called *classes*) should not be allowed to affect the data values in other functions; this is called *encapsulation*. Second, the language should allow you to reuse much of your code in similar functions instead of the old-style way of copying your old code and making changes. Third, functions that inherit from each other should be allowed to customize themselves if necessary; this is called *polymorphism*.

The object-oriented *paradigm* (or way of doing things) is difficult for some to adjust to. Once implemented, OOP greatly facilitates iterative design. *Iterative design*, described in detail in this section, is a design that can be added to later with little work.

PowerBuilder is considered an *object-based environment*, which means it implements many of the features found in object-oriented environments. Some of these features include inheritance (discussed later in this chapter) and iterative design.

Using Visual Design

As you will soon see, PowerBuilder is visual in a way that other "visual" development environments can't match. You don't *program* your application; you *paint* it. If any programming is needed, it's implemented behind the painted objects. This may seem a little odd right now, but soon you will be using painters to develop your application.

Using Iterative Design

Iterative design is designing a little bit of your application at a time. Iterative design (also called *phased design*) is a by-product of object-oriented development. Iterative design enables you to develop your application in "chunks" from start to finish. While one chunk is being evaluated and tested, you can add to previous work easily.

Iterative design is different from old school design in that, using non-object languages, modifying existing code is difficult and perilous! Previously, analysis, design, and development each were separated into sections, and each had to be completed before another began, as if each were separated by a brick wall (see fig. 1.2).

Fig. 1.2

Moving between phases of development was very difficult—it was as if a wall existed between phases.

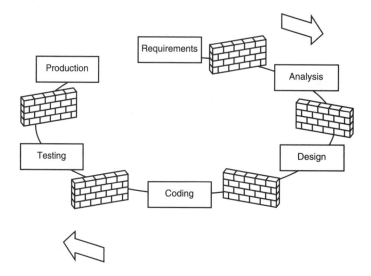

It was expensive and difficult to go back to a previous phase, and often the application suffered for it. Maintenance was a nightmare, and a program could not keep up with its environment. Eventually, systems became so out-of-date that a whole new system needed to be written from scratch! Data processing departments fell literally years behind in development as a result. (Indeed, some are still years behind!)

Clearly something had to be done. PowerBuilder and iterative design are answers to this dilemma. Not only can you return to the analysis phase, but you can easily modify your application to evolve with your work environment! In this chapter, you see iterative design (of sorts) by developing a working application in Chapter 1 and adding to it throughout the book until you develop a more fully-featured Inventory Tracking application. You'll find that iterative design allows the developer to move freely between design phases, as represented in figure 1.3.

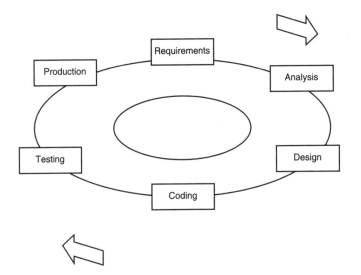

Fig. 1.3
Using iterative design, movement between phases is easily done.

Installing PowerBuilder

PowerBuilder's installation is simple and straightforward. Follow these steps:

1. Insert Disk 1, and then choose **F**ile, **R**un in Program Manager.

2. Enter **D: SETUP** and click OK.

3. Answer the questions that follow. (If you need any help, see the Getting Started manual provided with your PowerBuilder documentation.)

4. Double-click on the PowerBuilder icon in your Windows 3.x environment to start the application.

Using PowerBuilder Libraries

PowerBuilder puts all of its objects (such as windows and menus) into a library. This library always has a .PBL extension. PowerSoft put libraries into PowerBuilder to help you organize your work. Every library is a single DOS file ending in .PBL. (Hence, every PowerBuilder library is called a *pibble*.) Every library has members that you can access through PowerBuilder. These members are PowerBuilder objects that you develop while making your application.

To enter the library painter, click on the Library icon on the PowerBar. This icon might not have text depending on how you set your preferences, but the picture still appears.

Creating a Library

To create a library, click on the crane-like Create Library icon on the PainterBar. The Create Library dialog box appears (as shown in fig. 1.4). PowerBuilder then asks you what you want to name the PBL. After that, it creates the PBL in the current directory. Be sure that the number of characters in the name before the .PBL is no more than eight because this is a DOS file. When you are finished, click on OK or press the Enter key.

> **Note**
>
> Your default directory will be \PB4. To avoid cluttering your \PB4 directory, you probably want to change your default to another directory for each system. First, create a directory through File Manager. Then click on the proper directory in the library painter before creating your PBL.

Fig. 1.4
The Create Library dialog box appears every time you create a library.

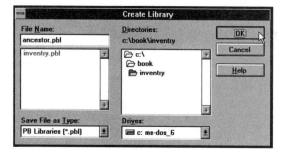

Now the Modify Library Comments dialog box opens, as seen in figure 1.5. Here, you enter the comments for the library you just created.

Fig. 1.5
The Modify Library Comments dialog box lets you add comments to a library.

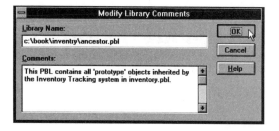

Tip
Comments should be entered every time PowerBuilder asks for them!

> **TrackNote**
>
> In the Inventory Tracking system, create two PBLs called ancestor and inventry. As discussed before, click on the Create Library icon on the PainterBar, type **ancestor,** and click on OK. Repeat the process for inventry.

> **Note**
>
> Using the Comments area, enter a description of what you are creating every time you create an object. Comments not only help those who are lucky enough to work on your system later, but they'll also help you when you look at old code a year from now!

Tip
You cannot move a PBL from one subdirectory to another using PowerBuilder. Instead, use the File Manager that comes with Windows 3.x.

▶ See "Power-Builder Libraries," p. 339

Using Libraries

Libraries cannot be used to create new objects. (To do this, you need to use the PowerBar.) However, they can be used to navigate around existing objects in the PowerBuilder environment. The more I use PowerBuilder, the more I tend to use libraries to work with existing objects.

To work on another object in the PowerBuilder Library, simply double-click on that member. This causes the proper painter to come up with that member ready to be worked on.

Using PowerBuilder Application Painter and Applications

To get into the application painter, either access the application through the library painter or click on the Application icon in the PowerBar. The application painter is unique among PowerBuilder objects in several ways:

- You always start a new project by defining an application.

- You always create your executable program in the application painter.

- You can only work with one application at a time, whereas with most painters, you can access several at a time.

- You are always attached to an application.

- The application is always executed when the program runs.

For more information, see Chapter 15, "Delivering an Executable."

Selecting Your Application

When you first enter PowerBuilder, you are in the Sample Application. You need to change your application to the application you are working on. This is done by selecting the Open icon pictured at the start of this section. Clicking on the Open icon opens the Select Application Library dialog box, shown in figure 1.6. Using this dialog box, you choose PBL where the application does (or will) reside.

Fig. 1.6
Select the
application's PBL
in the Select
Application
Library dialog box.

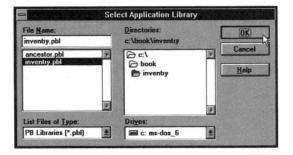

This allows you to choose a different application or to create a new one using the dialog box shown in figure 1.7.

Fig. 1.7
The Select
Application dialog
box allows you to
switch from one
application to
another or to
create a new
application.

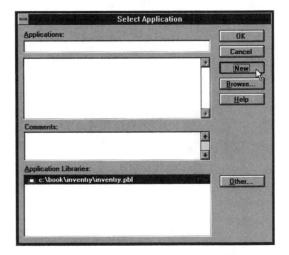

To create a new application, simply click on the **N**ew button in the dialog box pictured in figure 1.7, which opens the Select New Application Library dialog box, shown in figure 1.8. Here, you select the PBL where the new application will reside. When you're finished selecting the PBL for the new application, click on OK.

Now the Save Application dialog box opens, pictured in figure 1.9. Within this dialog box, you can create new applications and store them in the appropriate PBL.

After saving your application, PowerBuilder displays a message box, shown in figure 1.10, asking if you would like PowerBuilder to generate an Application template. If you click on **Y**es, PowerBuilder will build a minor application framework for you to work with, consisting of an MDI window and menu, a main window, and an About window. You can use this handy shourtcut later, but for now, choose **N**o.

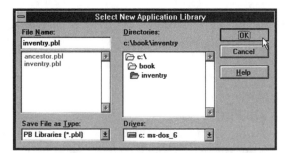

Fig. 1.8
Choose the PBL of the new application in the Select New Application Library dialog box.

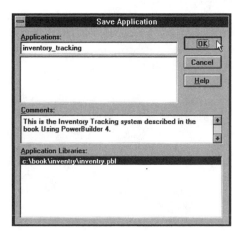

Fig. 1.9
The Save Application dialog box appears when you choose **N**ew in the Select Application dialog box.

Fig. 1.10
PowerBuilder always asks if you want to generate a template when developing a new application.

While this may suit your needs, often you will find the need to develop your own framework customized to your own system, as you do with the Inventory Tracking system. However, there's nothing wrong with letting Power-Builder do the work for you if you can.

TrackNote

Notice that the application is saved with the name `inventory_tracking`. This is the name used throughout the book for this application.

Troubleshooting

I know I created a PBL, but can't seem to find it in the library painter. Why is this?

If you can't find the PBL with your application in it, you are probably viewing the wrong directory. This window allows you to change your drive and directory and search other areas on your hard drive.

Using Default Fonts

To standardize your application, you should choose a default font that you are comfortable with. The default for all text, data, headings, and labels is Arial 10 point. However, you can adjust this to suit your own needs. By clicking on the Font icon, you open the Select Default Fonts dialog box, shown in figure 1.11. From here, you can choose the way your fonts look throughout your application. You can also differentiate between how text, data, headings, and labels look in your application.

Fig. 1.11
The Select Default Fonts dialog box is used for setting the default fonts in the major objects in PowerBuilder.

Tip
Set defaults that consistently apply throughout the application. That way, all your windows will look consistent since they all have the same font style and font size.

Caution

Nearly every end user will be using VGA monitors with Windows 3.x applications. Although you may be tempted to use color throughout your application, be careful that your target audience does not use black-and-white screens, such as those that come with many laptops. Colors may not look as clear on gray-scale monitors. At the very least, test your color choices with gray-scale monitors to make sure they are usable!

For those who have color monitors, some color combinations clash and may have a detrimental effect on your application. Color choice is important and should be considered during development and testing.

TrackNote

In the Inventory Tracking system, you will use the default fonts of Arial 10 point for all of your windows. Therefore, no changes are needed.

Specifying a Library Path

Every PowerBuilder application searches its own path for any references to windows or PowerBuilder objects. Sometimes, however, you may want to split your work up into multiple PBLs. For this, PowerBuilder created the Library Path icon, which pulls up the Select Libraries dialog box (see fig. 1.12) and in turn allows you to tell PowerBuilder which PBLs to search so you can find members.

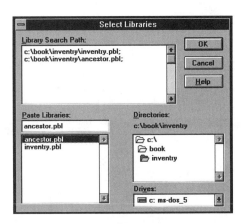

Fig. 1.12
The Select Libraries dialog box lets you choose which libraries are searched (which library search path is used) in order to run the program.

TrackNote

Be sure that both the inventry and ancestor PBLs are in the search path for the application. Since our application object (inventory_tracking) is already in inventry.pbl, you will find that inventry.pbl is already in the search path. You should double-click on `ancestor.pbl` in the **P**aste Libraries box so that both are included in the search path for the application. As always, click on OK when finished.

Using Menu Options in PowerBuilder Painters

Each PowerBuilder painter has its own menu. Some menu items you will find consistent in most of the PowerBuilder painters. The following sections discuss those menu items that you'll use most often.

Saving Your Work

After you complete your work, you'll need to save it. To do this, you need to open the **F**ile menu and choose **S**ave (see fig. 1.13). This saves your application with the new settings.

Fig. 1.13
To save work in a PowerBuilder painter, choose File, Save.

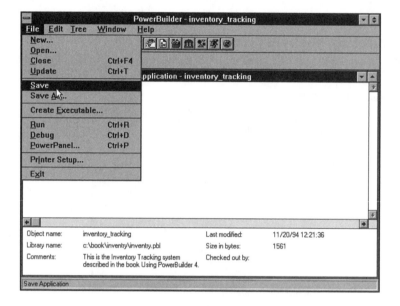

Closing the Painters

You'll want to close your painter after working with it. This not only frees up more memory, but also allows for easier movement between the painters you use. To close the painter you are currently working on, open the **F**ile menu and choose **C**lose (see fig. 1.14). This closes your current painter. If you have made changes but have not saved them, PowerBuilder asks if you want to save your changes before completely closing the painter.

Exiting PowerBuilder

To exit PowerBuilder completely, open the **F**ile menu and choose **E**xit. Before exiting, PowerBuilder closes all open painters and asks if you want to save any unsaved changes, as seen in figure 1.15. Here, answer **Y**es to save changes and exit, **N**o to exit without saving changes, and Cancel to not exit at all.

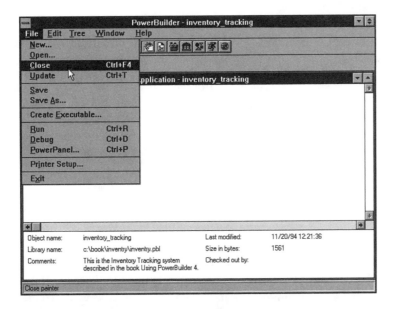

Fig 1.14
To close a
PowerBuilder
painter, choose
File, Close.

I

Introducing PowerBuilder

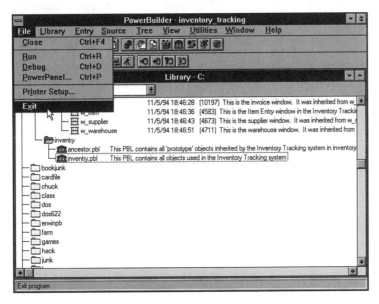

Fig. 1.15
To exit
PowerBuilder,
choose File, Exit.

Using Control Menu Boxes

There is a difference between the *sheet* (or *painter*) control menu box and the *frame* (or *application*) control menu box. The frame control menu box appears as a little square on the upper left corner of your screen when PowerBuilder is running. (The square looks like it has a big minus sign in the middle of it.) The sheet control menu box is the smaller box down from the frame control menu box. (It also has a little minus sign in the middle of it.)

By double-clicking on the sheet control menu box, you close that painter. If you have made changes in the painter, PowerBuilder asks if you want to save your changes (see fig. 1.16).

Fig. 1.16
PowerBuilder developers take the easy way out of a painter by double-clicking on the Control menu box.

Tip
To free up memory, navigate more easily, and to run more efficiently, you should periodically close all your painters so that just the PowerBar is showing.

By double-clicking on the frame control menu box, you close the entire PowerBuilder application. Any open painters automatically close (and ask if you wish to save any unsaved changes). PowerBuilder asks you if you really want to exit. If you answer OK, PowerBuilder ends. You can double-click on either the sheet control menu box or the frame control menu box, rather than go through the menu.

I use the toolbars and control menu boxes instead of the menus for saving and exiting. You will find that this way is easier and quicker. However, you should use the menu to save your work without exiting. This is a good idea if you have a large task before you inside a painter.

Using Menus

Menu

▶ See "Defining Menus," p. 103

Menus, which appear at the top of applications, are important for navigating between windows and for performing certain tasks. To get to the menu painter, click on the Menu icon. This displays the Select Menu window, shown in figure 1.17.

To create a new menu, click on the **N**ew button. This opens the menu painter shown in figure 1.18.

Making Your Menu

Now you decide what to put on your menu. On the top menu bar, you should include the following:

- **F**ile for file and exit options

- **E**dit for undoing, cutting, and pasting

- **I**nventory for inventory-related functions

- **W**indow for any window-related functions

- **H**elp to pull up on-line help

These items are called *menu bar items.* For now, limit your options under **F**ile to **S**ave, **C**lose, and E**x**it. You can add other options later.

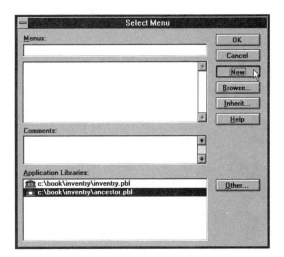

Fig. 1.17
The Select Menu window is similar to the Select Window window. It allows you to either view/update an existing menu or create a new menu.

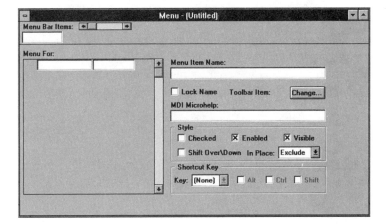

Fig. 1.18
In the menu painter, enter your menu bar choices and menu options.

TrackNote

Most developers allow you to run their Windows 3.x applications without ever using a mouse. At first, this may seem ridiculous to some of you. ("You can't run Windows without a mouse, can you?") Actually, you can! There are several reasons for allowing this:

- Some end users actually prefer using a mouse as little as possible, especially those that learned DOS pretty well.

- Sometimes using a mouse is inconvenient or annoying. This is particularly the case with some laptops.

- In a desire to save space, some laptops have excluded a mouse or have substituted a pointing device (such as a trackball, trackpoint [eraser], or trackpad) that mouse users don't like. Also, the placement of many trackballs sometimes makes them almost painful to use!

- On some laptop LCD (Liquid Crystal Display) screens, a mouse pointer is easy to lose (the gray-scale, lower-quality displays of some laptops cause users to lose track of the mouse pointer). An alternative way of moving around would be useful.

- It is a good idea to have an alternate way of conveying information, especially for exiting an application. This comes in handy if your mouse is acting up.

Because of this, try to make your application completely usable with or without the mouse. Always assign Alt keys to your menu items and command buttons, and make sure the tab order of your fields makes sense. You'll be happier with fewer complaints, and your end users will admire your talents even more than before!

▶ See "Tab Order," p. 92

For each menu item underneath the main options, PowerBuilder allows you to enter shortcut keys and accelerators. This is a great help if you use a keyboard, and a quick way to execute a function without a lot of mouse maneuvering.

Also notice that MDI MicroHelp is included. The MicroHelp is displayed every time the cursor passes over the menu item or the menu's toolbar item (while the left mouse button is held down). This is a very handy way to make your programs more user-friendly without a lot of work.

  To create the file, type **&File** in the first Menu For text box. Then type **&Save**, **&Close**, and **E&xit** in the following text boxes to create **S**ave, **C**lose, and E**x**it. Use the Insert icon each time to insert a new row. (The Insert icon is the icon on the far left on the PainterBar.) Notice how inserting a row option adds the row above the current option. If you want to rearrange your menu items, use the Move icon (the icon that looks like a hand) to position your options how you want them.

> **Note**
>
> So what's the difference between a shortcut key and an accelerator? A shortcut key allows the user to execute the menu function immediately without accessing the menu at all (for example, press F1 for help, or Alt+X for exit). To access the menu bar using the keyboard, you always use a shortcut key (for example, Alt+F opens the **F**ile menu bar item).
>
> An accelerator key is implemented when the user is in the menu list already. Pressing a key will highlight or execute the option with that accelerator key. For instance, when you have the **F**ile menu bar pulled down, pressing **C** will execute the **C**lose function.

To add another column, left-click on the scroll bar that the mouse pointer is sitting on in figure 1.19, or click on the right arrow, or press the Tab key. This blanks out your screen and allows you to type both the next menu bar item and your options for the next menu bar item (see fig. 1.20). Don't worry if what you just typed disappears. It reappears once you click on the left side of the scroll bar or the left arrow or press backtab, or Shift+Tab (see fig. 1.21). Add additional menu bar items **E**dit, **I**nventory, **W**indow, and **H**elp. (Make sure that these items are added to the menu bar, not as options on a single menu bar item.) You'll add more menu bar items and options to menus later in the book.

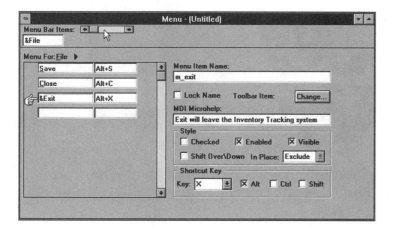

Fig. 1.19
Notice how **Save**, **Close**, and **Exit** are typed underneath **F**ile. For each menu option, you also should assign an accelerator, a shortcut key (also called a *hot key*), and MDI MicroHelp.

Fig. 1.20
Notice how adding
a new menu bar
item appears to
clear out the
previous menu bar
item. Click on the
left side of the
scroll bar next to
Menu Bar Items to
make previous
entries reappear.

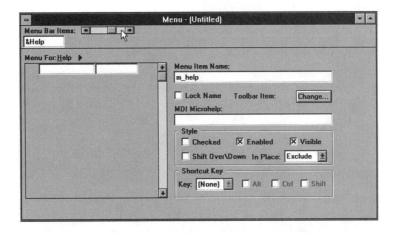

Fig. 1.21
See? The other
menu items are
still there. You can
see these again by
clicking on the left
side of the scroll
bar or the left
arrow where the
pointer is now.

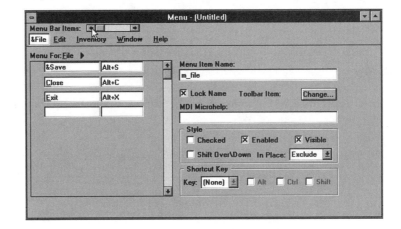

Saving Your Menu

As within other painters, when you want to save your menu, choose File,
Save. This opens the Save Menu dialog box, pictured in figure 1.22. Now you
can save your window.

▶ See "Imple-
   menting
   Window
   Inheritance,"
   p. 96

▶ See "Imple-
   menting Menu
   Inheritance
   and Toolbars,"
   p. 109

TrackNote

In the Inventory Tracking system, you will create one menu and call it **m_ancestor**.
It will go into ancestor.pbl and become a menu ancestor. *Menu ancestors* are prototypes for other menus. (Windows can also have ancestors.) You'll learn more about
ancestors and what else you can do with menus in the menu chapter later in this
book.

Introducing PowerBuilder

Fig. 1.22
The Save Menu
dialog box is
identical to the
Save Window
dialog box. As
always, don't forget
the comments.

Using Windows

A *window* is a rectangular box that appears on your screen when you run a
Windows 3.x program. You may already know what a window is, but you
may not know that there are several types of windows and lots of different
ways to program for them.

▶ See "Exploring
Windows,"
p. 77

To define a window, click on the Window icon. This opens the Select Window dialog box, shown in figure 1.23.

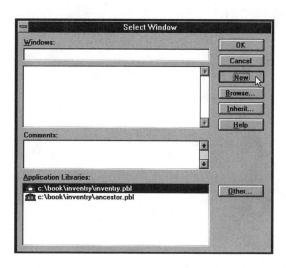

Fig. 1.23
The Select
Window dialog
box allows you
to either view or
update an existing
window or create a
new window.

To create a new window, click on **N**ew. This opens the window painter,
shown in figure 1.24.

Fig. 1.24
In the window painter, the rectangular box in the upper left corner represents the window that will appear.

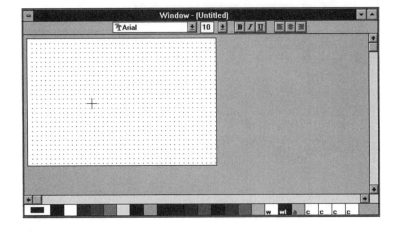

By double-clicking on the rectangle in the upper left corner of the window, you should see the Window Style dialog box, as seen in figure 1.25. Change the title appropriately. Also, notice that in figure 1.25, MDI Frame with MicroHelp is selected in the Window Type area.

Fig. 1.25
In the Window Style dialog box, notice how you can change the title, attributes, and window type of the PowerBuilder window all in one area.

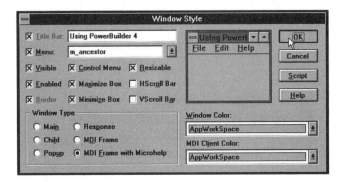

TrackNote

I changed the **W**indow Color to match the MDI Client Color. This is personal preference only.

Comparing SDI vs. MDI Frame

Notice you can choose MDI Frame and MDI Frame with MicroHelp as the window type in the Window Style dialog box (see fig. 1.25). MDI stands for *Multiple Document Interface*. (As you probably guessed, SDI stands for *Single Document Interface*.) Most Windows 3.x applications are MDI applications.

With an MDI application, all windows (called *sheet windows*) are opened "inside" a master window. This master window is called an MDI Frame. All sheet windows opened can reference each other easily, and movement between sheet windows is clean. SDI is typically used for single-window applications. The sample Inventory Tracking system is MDI; therefore, an MDI Frame must be created to hold the other windows in the Inventory Tracking system.

Associating Your Menu to Your Window

Now you need to attach a menu to the MDI frame. (In Version 4, MDI frame windows are no longer allowed to be saved without a menu associated with the frame.)

By clicking on the **M**enu check box in the Window Style dialog box in figure 1.25, a drop-down list of available menus appears. Since you only created one menu, you get one choice. Remember, you must click on the **M**enu check box in order to pull down the menu selections.

Using MicroHelp

MicroHelp messages are short help messages that can appear at the bottom of an MDI frame. These messages are a good way to communicate an idea to the user (such as Save was successful or Enter a numeric field) without having to stop the program with a response window (often called a *dialog box*). Since MicroHelp is only available with MDI programs, most of your programs will be developed using MDI Frame with MicroHelp, instead of only an MDI Frame (without MicroHelp).

> **Note**
>
> Figure 1.26 shows an MDI frame window with a sheet window inside of it. This set of windows is not part of the Inventory Tracking system, but was made to explain frame windows, sheet windows, and MicroHelp.

▶ See "Using MDI Frames and MDI Frames with Micro-Help," p. 80

▶ See "Opening a Window Sheet," p. 98

Saving Your Window

When you want to save your window within the application painter, choose **F**ile, **S**ave. This opens the Save Window dialog box, pictured in figure 1.27; from there you can save your window. In the **W**indows text box, enter the name of your window (**w_inventory_frame**). Provide the appropriate comments, click on the appropriate application library (inventry.pbl), and click on OK.

Fig. 1.26
Inside the MDI
frame, you can
place other
windows. The
MicroHelp
message is located
at the bottom of
the window.

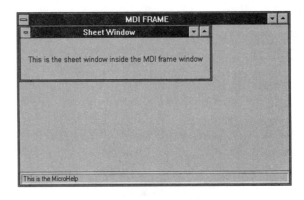

Fig. 1.27
After creating your
window, you need
to save it. This is
similar to other
save windows
you've seen so far.
Don't forget the
comments!

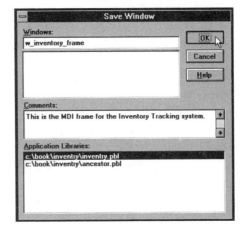

▶ See "Using
Naming Con-
ventions,"
p. 551

Pulling It Together with PowerScript and Events

▶ See "Using
Events, Func-
tions, and the
PowerScript
Language,"
p. 123

PowerScript is the language of PowerBuilder; it is how you control the flow of your application and how you code for certain events.

Exploring PowerBuilder Events

Event programming is the main area in which Windows 3.x programs differentiate from old-style MS-DOS and mainframe applications. In older operating systems, sequential programming (in which steps needed to follow a set of procedures) was necessary. This caused programs and procedures to be set in action sequentially. When these programs were finished running, they would typically set other programs or procedures in motion. This continued until processing was done.

Soon it became apparent that most businesses did not do their business functions sequentially, but rather in response to events that take place. Programs that attempted to mirror businesses were hard to develop, hard to maintain, and often cumbersome to run.

Event programming allows the programmer to program for a specified event. Examples of typical events are mouse clicks, starting or ending the application, opening or closing a window, pressing the Enter key, or choosing a menu item. Windows 3.x programmers program for these and other events.

Programming in PowerScript

In PowerBuilder, events control the flow of an application. Specific PowerScript is executed every time a corresponding event occurs. In the following section, you can code three events in PowerScript.

Application Events

> **Note**
>
> Using the library painter, you can pull up your existing PowerBuilder objects. Pull up the library by clicking on the Library icon. The library painter will automatically display the members (also known as entries) of the current application's PBL, although you can open other directories and PBLs by double-clicking on them as they appear in the painter.
>
> By double-clicking on an entry (like the application, as seen in fig. 1.28), you automatically open that entry in its proper painter (much like the Windows 3.x File Manager starts the associated program with a file on the disk drive).

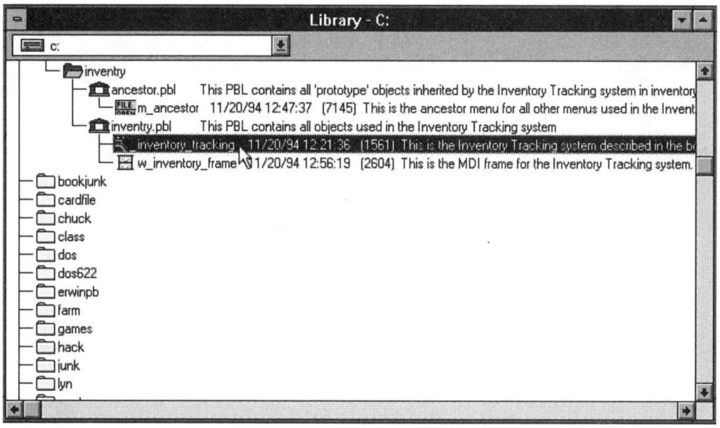

Tip
When you saved the window, the name you saved it under started with a **w_**. This is not required by PowerBuilder, but naming conventions in PowerBuilder make your code easier to use and debug. See Appendix A for a list of suggested naming conventions.

▶ See "Programming in PowerScript," p. 167

Library

Introducing PowerBuilder

Fig. 1.28
By double-clicking on an entry in the library painter, you automatically open that entry in its proper painter.

Using the Library or the Application icon, run the application painter for the Inventory Tracking application. Now, click on the Script icon to enter the script painter. Your screen should now look like the one in figure 1.29.

Fig. 1.29
The script painter is a full-screen editor that lets you type your PowerScript.

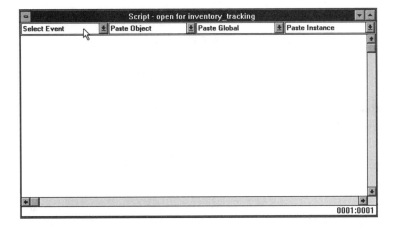

Notice how the script painter for your application automatically opens with the application open event. PowerBuilder does a reasonably good job of determining which event you want to code first. If you want to code for another event, PowerBuilder gives you four events in the application that you can code for: open, idle, systemerror, and close (as shown in fig. 1.30). You can select an event by clicking the Select Event box and clicking the event you want to code for.

Fig. 1.30
When you click on the Select Event box, all the available events for the PowerBuilder object you're coding for are displayed.

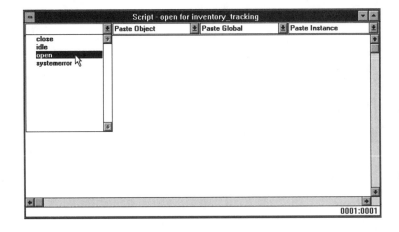

Be sure the open event is selected. Without coding for the open event in the application, your application cannot run! In the application painter, the open event is executed when the application opens. Right now, just code an open statement for your window. Do this by simply typing **open(w_inventory_frame)** in the PowerScript editor (see fig. 1.31).

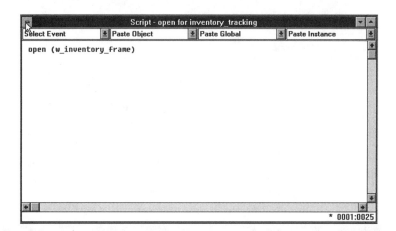

Fig. 1.31
With the PowerScript painter, simply enter your commands. Here, you want to open your MDI frame window as soon as the application opens.

Syntax-at-a-Glance

Open(*window_name*, *{parent_window}*)

Open opens your window. *parent_window* is never needed and is used only with pop-up or child windows. If you omit parent_window on a pop-up or child window, the current active window is assumed to be the parent window.

To close, use the menu or double-click on the Script Control menu box (where the arrow is pointing in fig. 1.29). PowerBuilder asks if you want to keep your changes. Click on Yes. Now close the application painter.

▶ See "Using Child Windows," p. 79

▶ See "Using Pop-up Windows," p. 79

Menu Events

One of the first actions pre-Windows 3.x developers learned was to always code the exit first. (That way, you can always get out of your program!) With Windows 3.x, that is no longer such a great concern (because you can always terminate a task), but old habits die hard, so code the Close and Exit events in the menu.

When you built your menu (m_ancestor), you told PowerBuilder what you wanted the choices to be, but not what to do when the choices were selected. This is done through PowerScript.

Click on the Menu icon to run the menu painter and select m_ancestor. Within the menu painter (not on the menu bar), click on **F**ile, and then on E**x**it in the Menu For: **F**ile area. Now click on the Script icon (see fig. 1.32).

Fig. 1.32
Choose which event you want to code for, and then click on the Script icon (where the pointer is) to enter PowerScript for that event.

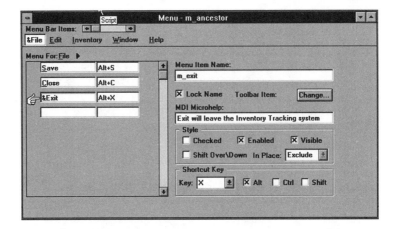

> ### Note
>
> When you click on **F**ile and E**x**it, be sure you are doing this in the menu painter, not on PowerBuilder's menu bar. Clicking **F**ile and E**x**it on the menu bar makes you exit out of PowerBuilder.

This brings you into the script painter for the Exit event. Type **Halt Close** in the script painter, as seen in figure 1.33. Halt immediately terminates your application; Halt Close executes the close event of the application and then terminates.

Fig. 1.33
This code immediately executes the application close event and then exits the application.

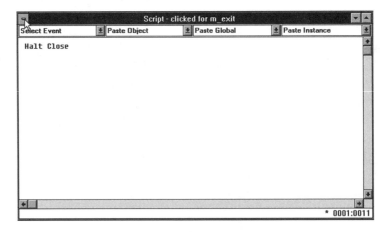

Syntax-at-a-Glance

Halt {Close}

Halt by itself immediately terminates the application. Halt Close first executes the close event of the application, then terminates the application.

After coding PowerScript for your E**x**it event, leave the script painter and repeat the process for **C**lose. Here, instead of entering Halt Close, type **Close (ParentWindow)**, as shown in figure 1.34. This closes whatever window the menu is attached to, but usually does not close the application. However, if there are no more windows open in the application, the application closes. Now exit out of the script painter and out of the menu painter.

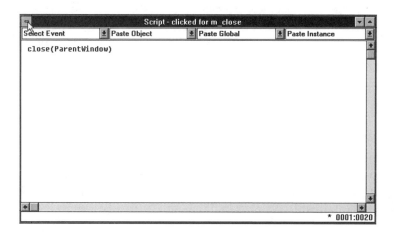

Fig. 1.34
Here is the code to close the window that the menu is attached to.

Syntax-at-a-Glance

Close(window_name)

Close closes your window. If window_name is ParentWindow, then the window that is attached to this object is closed. The use of ParentWindow is only valid in menus and on command buttons.

Other Events

You have just scratched the surface of available events. Every PowerBuilder object can use PowerScript to enhance it.

▶ See "Program-
ming in
PowerScript,"
p. 167

> **Note**
>
> PowerBuilder is not case-sensitive. Therefore, Halt Close, halt close, HALT CLOSE, and hAIT CIOsE all do the same thing. Perhaps capitalizing functions may make them more readable, but it's really a matter of preference.

▶ See "Under-
standing
Analysis, De-
sign, and Data-
bases," p. 45

Using the Database Interface

One of PowerBuilder's strong points is its capability to interface with many databases. These database interfaces are transparent to the end user and (for the most part) also transparent to the developer.

You'll find that the database cannot be accessed through the library. It can only be accessed through the Database icon on the PowerBar. The database interface is coded through the open event of the application. (The next chapter explains this process.)

Using DataWindows

After defining the database, DataWindows are used as data-entry screens and reports connected to these databases. They are an integral part of PowerBuilder and are covered in detail in the DataWindow chapters (Chapters 8 through 11). You won't create any DataWindows until after you go through the database.

Using On-line Help

PowerBuilder's on-line help is extraordinary! All functions, attributes, and ways to do things can be found in the on-line help. You'll find yourself using PowerBuilder's help quite often. To access help, click on the **H**elp menu bar item. (In the next section, "Customizing Your PowerBuilder Toolbars," you'll see how to get an icon for searching help added to your PowerBar.)

> **Note**
>
> To get help on a specific command in the PowerScript painter, type that command, position your cursor in the middle of that command, and press Shift+F1. To open the help table of contents, press F1.

Note

Before you dive into the reams of documentation that come with PowerBuilder, try searching through on-line help. In most cases, you can save a lot of time with an on-line search, as opposed to a manual one.

I find it much easier to pull up the on-line help and immediately perform a search (by clicking on the Search button) for the desired topic, rather than reading through the table of contents.

Customizing Your PowerBuilder Toolbars

Depending on what painter you are in, you can have up to four toolbars:

- *The PowerBar* runs all of the time in PowerBuilder. It allows you to navigate between most of the painters, and it contains some tools (such as the Run Current Application icon, which runs your program).

- *The PainterBars* are different for each painter. They contain tools that you'll want to use when inside that painter.

- *The StyleBar* is for text manipulation. With the StyleBar, you can change any text's size, font, or style. The StyleBar is not customizable.

- *The ColorBar* allows you to select colors when you are in a window or DataWindow painter.

Before you go any further, open your w_inventory_frame window in the window painter. The window painter gives you access to all the toolbars.

Using the Toolbars Dialog Box

To get to the Toolbars dialog box, open **W**indow and choose T**o**olbars. The Toolbars dialog box controls the toolbars (see fig. 1.35). From here you can hide or show toolbars, move the toolbars to a desired location, control the text display within the toolbar, or customize the toolbar by adding or deleting icons from it.

Fig 1.35
The Toolbars dialog box allows you to manipulate your toolbars.

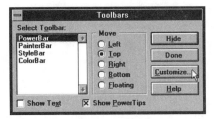

Note

There are many ways to manipulate toolbars. If you don't want to go through the menu, try right-clicking a toolbar. This opens a pop-up menu that is functionally equivalent to the Toolbars dialog box (see fig. 1.36). From here, you can do anything that could be done through the Toolbars dialog box. Try it and see which one you like better.

Fig. 1.36
You can get to this toolbar pop-up menu by right-clicking any toolbar.

Positioning Toolbars

By clicking on the appropriate toolbar and then choosing how you want that toolbar displayed, PowerBuilder moves the toolbar to your desired location. You can also hide a toolbar completely if you wish.

Troubleshooting

I'm trying to hide my ColorBar and my StyleBar to give me more viewing area, but no matter what I click on, they still are showing. Why is that?

The ColorBar must be hidden by choosing **O**ptions, **H**ide. The StyleBar can't be hidden. If you try to hide them using the pop-up menu, they instead become part of the window painter sheet (as opposed to part of the PowerBuilder frame). You can also control where they are displayed through the **O**ptions menu.

The StyleBar and ColorBar can only be moved to the top or the bottom of the screen. PowerBuilder lets you indicate that you want to move either one to the right, left, or floating positions; but PowerBuilder won't accept your choice.

> **Note**
>
> PowerBuilder lets you drag the PowerBar and PainterBar to the position of your choice. Simply click an empty area on the toolbar, hold down the left mouse button, and drag the toolbar to where you want them to go.

Showing PowerTips

PowerTips are new to PowerBuilder 4, and are used both in the PowerBuilder environment and in any application you develop. When ShowText for a menu is turned off, PowerTips appears if your mouse cursor sits on a toolbar item for about two seconds.

In figure 1.37, the mouse is stationary on the Library icon. After a few seconds, the PowerTip appears, describing what that icon is used for.

Fig. 1.37
PowerTips are displayed when ShowText is off and the mouse cursor is stationary on an icon for about two seconds.

PowerTips make the PowerBuilder environment and any applications you develop more friendly, especially for beginning users.

Showing Text

When you first start using PowerBuilder, you may want to display text underneath your toolbar icons. Although this makes PowerBuilder easier to use, it makes the icons on the toolbar take up a lot more space. Most experienced developers eventually turn off the text on the toolbars.

To toggle the toolbar text on and off, click on or off the Show Text check box in the Toolbars dialog box, as seen in figure 1.38.

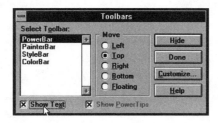

Fig. 1.38
Although the toolbar is more user-friendly, text makes each icon take up a lot more space. With Show Text selected, fewer icons fit on the window.

Adding, Deleting, and Rearranging Icons

By clicking on the **C**ustomize button in the Toolbars dialog box, you arrive at the Customize dialog box, which lets you place icons on a toolbar, take them off a toolbar, or rearrange icons on a toolbar. Simply find the icon you want and drag it where you want it, as shown in figure 1.39. You can only customize the PowerBar and the PainterBar.

Fig. 1.39

The Customize dialog box shows the Run Window icon being dragged from the selected palette to the current toolbar.

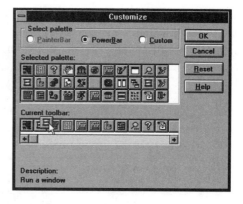

Note

Are you confused about what all those icons do? If you don't know what an icon's function is, look at the bottom of the window at PowerBuilder's MicroHelp. Every time you click on an icon, its MicroHelp is displayed.

Note

Although I leave most PainterBars alone, I like to add four icons to the PowerBar:

- *Run Window* (the little gray window) allows you to run a window without running the entire application. I put this icon right next to the Window Painter icon (the little blue window).

- *Search* (the magnifying glass) runs the help search. I put this icon right next to the Help icon (the question mark).

- *Run Report Painter* and *Run Report Painter* (*Run mode Only*) help with reports. These icons resemble the DataWindow icon, except that they resemble reports a little more closely. I put these icons right next to the DataWindow icon.

Again, it's personal preference. If you find yourself frequently using a function that PowerBuilder has provided an icon for, then put that icon on one of the toolbars. It'll save you loads of mouse wear and tear!

Running Your PowerBuilder Application

To run your application, click on the Run icon, which opens your window and first application. Of course, right now you can't do much with it except open the File menu and choose either Exit or Close, both of which do the same thing. Still, it's an important start. Chapter 2, "Understanding Analysis, Design, and Databases," discusses what you want the application to do and tells you why these initial building blocks are important.

From Here...

By now, you should know how to build a small application in PowerBuilder. You've also gone over the concepts of visual and iterative design and most of the PowerBuilder components including PowerBuilder Libraries (PBLs), windows, and menus.

One of the many great things about PowerBuilder is its ability to build on existing work. Use what you started in this chapter; in the following chapters, you'll examine the components in more detail as you come closer to finishing the Inventory Tracking system.

This chapter serves as an introduction to the rest of the book, and all other chapters reference and build on this chapter. Some related information could also be found in the following user guides:

- *The PowerBuilder User's Guide*
- *The PowerBuilder Getting Started Guide*

Introducing PowerBuilder

Chapter 2

Understanding Analysis, Design, and Databases

Although database and program analysis and design chapters are usually discussed last in most books, they are probably the most important parts of any project. Because you're designing a system as you learn PowerBuilder, it is wise to define what you are developing. Here is your crash course in analysis and design.

This chapter has something for every level of experience. It is one of the most complex chapters in *Using PowerBuilder 4*, yet it covers concepts so vital to an application that everyone should be aware of the techniques discussed herein.

In this chapter, you will:

- Analyze what is needed in an application

- Design what you've analyzed using the PowerBuilder database painter

- Create, maintain, and administer the database

- Access and update data in your database tables using the database painter

Exploring Analysis: Catching All the Objects

> **Note**
>
> Experienced developers know that there are many different analysis methodologies. In addition, each methodology is implemented slightly different from developer to developer. The methodology I use is a hybrid of several different methodologies, and is well-suited for system analysis by hand into PowerBuilder if no CASE (Computer Aided Software Engineering) tool is available.
>
> The analysis methodology mentioned in this chapter is designed to give developers without an analysis tool a methodology which they can evolve (or mutate) to meet their specific needs.
>
> Keep in mind that your analysis methodology should be flexible enough to support iterative design, and should organize your system in such a way so that you can deliver a quality system with a minimum amount of time.
>
> If possible, use a CASE tool; it helps with analysis and system documentation.

◄ See "Using Iterative Design," p. 13

In the analysis phase of a project, the language you're using (PowerBuilder), the operating system (Windows), and the computer you're using (a PC) are not considered. *Analysis* deals only with description of the current business activities and the software that needs to be developed. Therefore, the analysis discussion in this chapter does not deal with PowerBuilder in detail. (Don't worry, though—in the following parts of the chapter, you'll see how to implement design using PowerBuilder and you'll get into the database painter!)

Finding the Entities

The first step in analysis is finding all the entities in a system (an *entity* is someone or something associated with a system). In the Inventory Tracking system, there are several entities, as shown in figure 2.1.

Fig. 2.1
Here you see every entity in a box.

Eventually, each entity you find turns into a database table. Using analysis, you need to define which tables you'll need.

> **Note**
>
> Remember that entities are always nouns! If you write down an entity that is not a person, place, or thing, what you have written down it is not an entity. (However, it could be an entity relationship. See the next section for details.)

> **Caution**
>
> You could name about 80 percent of the entities in any system in a few minutes. The last 20 percent, however, require some in-depth research. Be prepared for a long and laborious process of interviews, research, and analysis to name all of the entities.

Determining Relationships

After determining the entities, you must find out how the entities relate to each other. This is done with *functions*. In other words, entities relate to each other by doing some action. Draw arrows with words on them between the entities to show the relationship, as seen in figure 2.2.

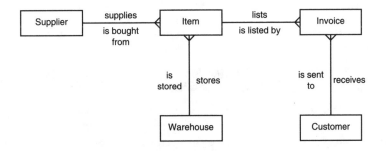

Fig. 2.2
Now you see the relationships between the entities.

> **Note**
>
> Remember that functions are always verbs! If you write down a relationship between two entities that is not an action, rethink your entities.

In a traditional language such as C, COBOL, or BASIC, each relationship translates into a function, subroutine, or paragraph. Using PowerBuilder, you can also code relationships as functions, as command buttons on a window, or as menu bar items.

Notice that the relationship, or function, of the left (or top) entity is listed above (or on the left side of) the line connecting the entities, as shown in figure 2.3. The relationship of the right (or bottom) entity is listed below (or on the right side of) the line connecting the entities. Therefore, you can read the relationship between supplier and item in figure 2.3 as "The Supplier supplies the Item" and "The Item is bought from the Supplier."

Fig. 2.3
When displaying relationships, connect the two entities with a line and describe the relationship.

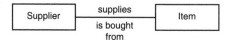

Showing Ordinality

After you define the entities and relationships, you need to define *ordinality*, which describes the number of entities that can exist with another entity. For example, how many Warehouses can exist for each Item? (The answer is one—and only one—Warehouse can exist for each Item.) How many Items can exist for each Warehouse? (The answer is zero to many Items can exist for each Warehouse.)

Tip
Two entities can have more than one relationship between them. Don't be afraid to draw more than one relationship, and don't feel forced to choose between two valid relationships.

Thus, Items and Warehouses have a one-to-many relationship, or a one-to-many ordinality.

> **Note**
>
> I have heard many people use *cardinality* as opposed to *ordinality* in design when referring to relationships, but I think ordinality fits the definition better. If you look up *ordinal number* vs. *cardinal number* in the Random House College Dictionary like I did, you'll see that:
>
> ■ A *cardinal number* is defined as any of the numbers that express amount, such as one, two, three, and so on.
>
> ■ An *ordinal number* is defined as any of the numbers that express degree, quality, or position in a series, such as first, second, third, and so on.
>
> You could argue that relationships like "one-to-one" are cardinal in nature, while relationships like "many-to-many" are ordinal in nature. However, I think "ordinality" fits a little better than "cardinality" since ordinal numbers seem more relational-, degree-, and series-oriented than cardinal numbers, which are isolated and stand alone.

In figure 2.4, Item has a many-to-one relationship with Supplier. Item has a many-to-many relationship with Invoice. Item has a many-to-one relationship with Warehouse. Finally, Customer has a one-to-many relationship with Invoice.

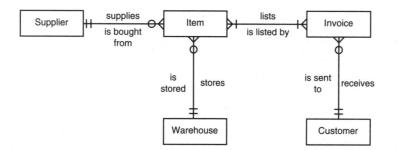

Fig. 2.4
Now you add all of the lines and ordinalities.

Note

Notice how the Inventory Tracking system seems to revolve around the Item. You should try to find out which entities your system revolves around, and (in the Inventory Tracking system) ask, "How do my entities revolve around Item?" (instead of trying to find all entities that relate to any other entity). This is a good way to limit the size of your system, and to avoid programming for entities that really have no place in your system.

Did you notice the new type of lines drawn in figure 2.4? This is one way of identifying your ordinality. Figures 2.5 through 2.8 identify the symbols used to denote notation.

Figure 2.5 indicates that each instance of Entity One can have no (zero) corresponding instance of Entity Two, or can have one corresponding instance of Entity Two. (This is referred to as a *none-or-one relationship*. None of these exist in the Inventory Tracking system.)

Fig. 2.5
Entity One has a none-or-one relationship with Entity Two.

The symbol shown in figure 2.6 indicates that each instance of Entity One can have one and only one corresponding instance of Entity Two. This is referred to as a *one-and-only-one relationship*.

Fig. 2.6
Entity One has a
one-and-only-one
relationship with
Entity Two.

In this Inventory Tracking system, an Item entry must be stored in only one Warehouse.

Figure 2.7 indicates that each instance of Entity One can have no (zero) corresponding instance of Entity Two, but can have many corresponding instances of Entity Two. This is referred to as a *zero-through-many relationship*.

Fig. 2.7
Entity One has a
zero-through-
many relationship
with Entity Two.

In this Inventory Tracking system, a warehouse can be empty (not have any item entries), but a warehouse also can store many items (and therefore have several item entries).

Figure 2.8 indicates that each instance of Entity One must have at least one corresponding instance of Entity Two, but can have many corresponding instances of Entity Two. This is referred to as a *one-through-many relationship*.

Fig. 2.8
Entity One has a
one-through-
many relationship
with Entity Two.

In this Inventory Tracking system, each invoice must list at least one item. However, an invoice might list several items.

Eliminating Unwanted Relationships

Some relationships, while they exist in the real world, are difficult to implement in a system. Such relationships should be replaced with more manageable relationships during analysis. This must be done carefully. The more manageable relationship in the analysis should preserve the functionality of the difficult real world relationship.

Eliminating Triangular Relationships

You should eliminate *triangular relationships*, which occur when three entities relate to each other. The following three relationships exist in figure 2.9:

1. The Customer requests an Item.

2. The Customer issues an Invoice.

3. The Invoice orders an Item.

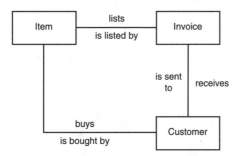

Fig. 2.9
Triangular relationships should be avoided.

Although all three relationships are valid, such a triangle adds much complexity to the system. If instead you say that a Customer issues an Invoice to request an Item, as seen in figure 2.10, the triangle is resolved and your system is easier to implement.

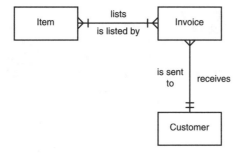

Fig. 2.10
Often, eliminating triangular relationships is as simple as not allowing that relationship. In this case, the only way a Customer can get an Item is through an Invoice.

Eliminating Many-to-Many Relationships

Many-to-many relationships can't be represented on a database very easily. For this reason, many-to-many relationships need to be eliminated before you start defining tables. To eliminate a many-to-many relationship, add an entity between them.

In the Inventory Tracking system, notice that Item and Invoice have a many-to-many relationship. An Item can have many Invoices, and an Invoice can list many Items. To resolve this situation, you can use the Invoice_line entity.

Invoice_line is called an *associative entity*. Associative entities are introduced into a system to get rid of many-to-many relationships. Invoice_lines are lines on the Invoice, each listing one item. Although an Invoice can have many Invoice_lines, each Invoice_line can only have one Invoice. Similarly, although an Item can be listed on an Invoice_line several times, each Invoice_line can list only one Item. Now there are no more many-to-many relationships.

The process of eliminating all many-to-many relationships is necessary because it will make your analysis cleaner, as well as help design, development, and implementation.

▶ See "Under-
standing
Events," p. 123

> **Note**
>
> You still have to add *event analysis* (an important part of object-oriented analysis) to the Inventory Tracking system. (You learn about event analysis when you get deeper into the PowerScript language and event programming.)

> **Note**
>
> You've really just scratched the surface on analysis, and limited it to defining your Inventory Tracking system. If all of this seems foreign to you, probably additional reading and/or classes are in order. If you decide to do more research on analysis, concentrate on *object-oriented analysis* (OOA) because it lends itself to PowerBuilder really well! Be careful, though, because OOA has reached buzzword levels; many books and software packages claiming to be object-oriented fall short.

Designing a System with the PowerBuilder Database Painter

"So," you ask, "all this analysis stuff is really great, but how do I put it into PowerBuilder?" After you decide what your entities are and how they relate, implement your analysis inside the database painter. This allows you to "draw" your entities into your PowerBuilder system. PowerBuilder's database painter lets you identify instances of entities (with primary keys) and assign relationships to other entities (with foreign keys). Primary and foreign keys will be covered in this section.

As you learn about the database painter, you will continue to learn more database concepts. To get into the database painter, click on the Database icon.

Creating a Database

As soon as you click on the Database icon for the first time, you see the PowerSoft Demo DB appear (as shown in fig. 2.11). This is the database that PowerBuilder uses for its sample application. (Of course, it's not the database you need—you must create a new database.)

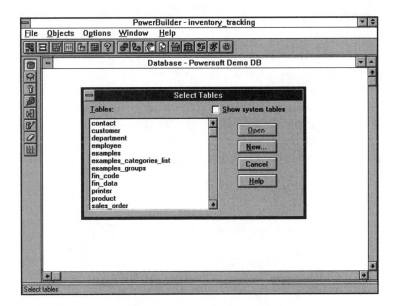

Fig. 2.11
The first database that opens when you click on the Database icon is not the database you need, so you need to create a new database.

To create a new database, click on the Cancel button (see fig. 2.11). Then choose File, Create Database, as shown in figure 2.12.

Introducing PowerBuilder

Fig. 2.12
In the database
painter, open File
to find Create
Database.

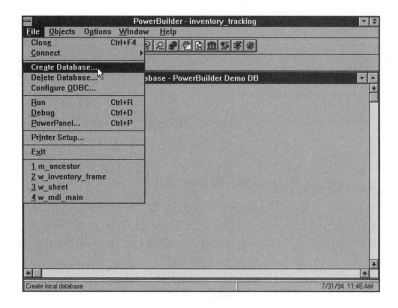

The Create Local Database dialog box appears (see fig. 2.13). You must type the full path of your database name. It is a good idea to end it with a .db extension; remember that the first part of the name must not contain more than eight characters (hence the name Inventry for Inventory Tracking). The user ID defaults to DBA and the password to SQL. You should change these if security is an issue. Finally, the start command defaults to db32w -d when using a Watcom database. The start command tells PowerBuilder which program to run to start the database engine.

▶ See "Using
DB32W.EXE,
DBSTARTW.EXE,
RT32W.EXE, and
RTSTARTW.EXE,"
p. 561

Fig. 2.13
Use this dialog
box to create your
database.

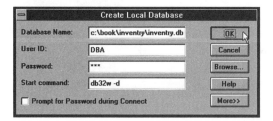

After this step, your database is created.

Connecting and Customizing Your Database

Even though you can't create databases with names longer than eight characters, your database can be renamed with a longer and more descriptive name by using the profile setup. By choosing **F**ile **C**onnect, and then **S**etup in the database painter, as seen in figure 2.14, you allow PowerBuilder to edit your database profiles.

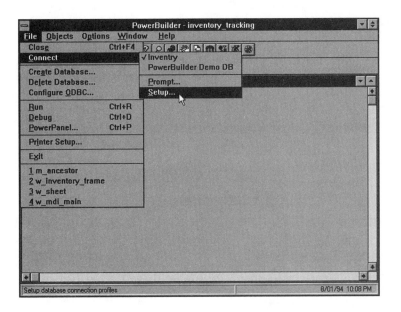

Fig. 2.14
You can help configure your database by choosing File, Connect and then Setup.

PowerBuilder now displays all valid database profiles for you to choose from in the Database Profiles dialog box, as shown in figure 2.15. Pick Inventry and click on **E**dit.

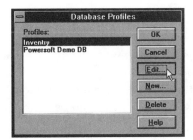

Fig. 2.15
The Database Profiles dialog box allows you to choose which profile you want to edit, or to create or delete database profiles.

The Database Profile Setup dialog box appears (see fig. 2.16). In the Profile Name field, you can change the name to **Inventory Tracking.** Type the name, the user ID, and the password, and click on OK.

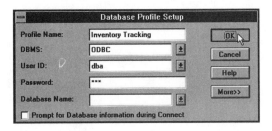

Fig. 2.16
You can change the name in the Database Profile Setup dialog box.

> ### Note
>
> PowerBuilder allows you to type in a user ID and a password into the Database Profile Setup dialog box. This defaults in PowerBuilder to a user ID of dba and a password of sql. If you assign the user ID and password when you connect to your database, your users will not be forced to enter a user ID and password every time they use your system.

Fig. 2.17
Inventory
Tracking now
shows in the
Profile Name field.

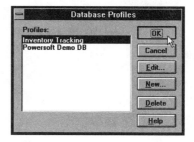

The Database Profiles dialog box appears after you click on OK (see fig. 2.17). Notice that Inventory Tracking appears. By clicking on OK here, Inventory Tracking will be brought up in the database painter.

Creating Tables

Right now, you have an empty database. That is, you have a database that contains no *tables,* which are groups of data inside a database. Think of a database as a file cabinet; each table represents a file within that file cabinet. In any system, the entities developed in analysis track directly to each table. Therefore, you will have a supplier table, an item table, a customer table, and so on.

To create a table, either click on the Open icon (the one that looks like a canister) and click on the **N**ew button, or click on the New Table icon.

This opens the Create Table dialog box, as seen in figure 2.18. Enter the name of your table (in this case, **Item**). The table and field (column) names can be entered in lower-case letters only.

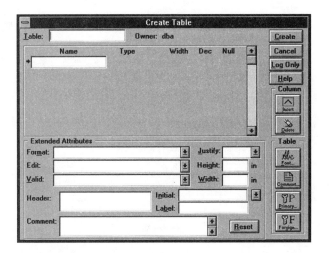

Fig. 2.18
The Create Table
dialog box is
where you create
tables for the
database.

Determining a Table's Columns

Using database terminology, a *column* is a field on a table. Although determining a table's columns is done in the analysis of a project, this process can be automated to go right into the design of your system. When dealing with PowerBuilder applications, do all database-column analysis in the database painter.

In database terminology, a *row* is a record on a table. Two different types of items have two corresponding rows on the Item table.

Use the following guidelines to help you determine which columns to put in your database:

- Any variable that changes from row to row that you want to report. For instance, the cost a Supplier charges for an Item is important to record and report. Include **order_price** in each row to report this.

- A column (or set of columns) that makes this row unique from other rows (this is called a *primary key*). For instance, item_number is unique to each item row.

- A column (or set of columns) indicating that rows have either a zero or one, or a one-and-only-one correspondence to a row in another table (this is called a *foreign key*). For instance, because each Item is stored in one and only one Warehouse, you can include warehouse_number in every Item row.

Your columns for items are shown in the Create Table dialog box (see fig. 2.19).

Fig. 2.19
Now enter all the columns needed for the item table.

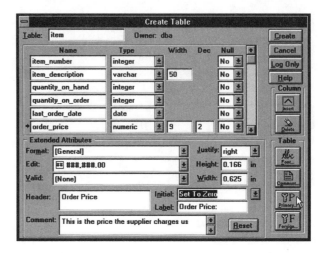

▶ See "Using the Database Painter to Define Different Column Attributes," p. 257

Here you enter all your fields; their data type (such as character, integer, and date); width (if applicable); number of decimals (if applicable); and whether or not you allow NULLs in your database for this field.

▶ See "Understanding NULL," p. 197

Caution

In the database painter, the database data types are the same as the ones used in the database. They are not the same data types as in PowerBuilder. Furthermore, little checking is performed to make sure numbers are still within the range for a data type.

For instance, in Watcom SQL, *integer* is defined as any value from -2,147,483,648 through 2,147,483,647. In PowerBuilder, integer is defined as any value from -32,768 through 32,767. If you were to read an integer from Watcom into an integer in PowerBuilder, a wrap-around might occur, and you would end up with a random number some of the time. This is a hard bug to catch. (By the way, if you define an integer in Watcom, make sure that any values do not exceed the PowerBuilder limit or use a long data type in PowerBuilder. A long data type in PowerBuilder has the same range as an integer data type in Watcom.)

> **Note**
>
> *NULLs* are not zeros; they are empty columns in a row on your database. (An empty column contains nothing—no zeros, no spaces, no anything!) Most columns require some entry, so most databases allow you to define a column as Not NULL when you create it. By declaring a column Not NULL, you force the database to not allow an update when the column in question is NULL.

If you're following along on your computer as you're reading this, do not click on the Create button yet! You still have a little work to do on this database.

Picking Primary Keys

After entering all of your fields into your table, you need to tell your database what sets every row in a table apart from each other. For this you need a *primary key*, a unique indicator that allows you to address individual table entries. Every table needs to have a primary key defined.

Click on the **P**rimary button on the lower right corner of the window. This opens the Primary Key Definition dialog box for your table. Choose the field (or fields) that you want for your primary key for this table by clicking on the appropriate field name. In figure 2.20, by choosing item_number as your primary key, you are saying that item_number can't ever be duplicated on the item table. Now you can use item_number to identify an item.

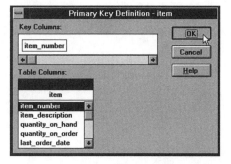

Fig. 2.20
Choose
`item_number` as
your primary key.

When you're finished, click on OK to return to the Create Table dialog box. Click on OK again in the Create Table dialog box to return to the database painter. Notice that you now have a table window containing the column name and comments of the item table. This window can be resized, especially if you want to display several table windows at a time (see fig. 2.21).

Fig. 2.21
You now have a
resizable table
window describing
your item table.

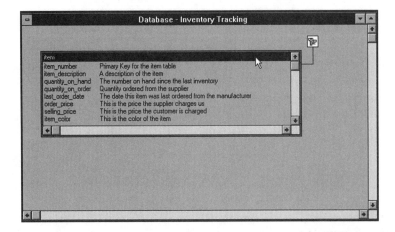

TrackNote

A lot can be added to this inventory system to make it more fully featured. (For
example, backorders, order points, economic order quantities, items supplied by
several suppliers and stored in several warehouses, and so on, could all be added.)
Keep in mind that your goal is to learn PowerBuilder, and that you are merely using a
scaled-down inventory system to illustrate all your points.

Note

A table sometimes will have more than one primary key (known as a *composite key*).
In the invoice_line table, the primary key invoice_number tells you which invoice this
invoice_line is a part of, as seen in figure 2.22. Invoice_line tells you which line of the
invoice this table entry represents.

Notice that you can also name a field with the same name as the table. (Although
you should usually avoid such ambiguity, in this case it is the best way to identify the
field.)

Tip
Use your scroll
bars on the table
windows to see
any columns that
may have
scrolled off.

Fig. 2.22
The invoice_lines
table has two
fields for a
primary key!

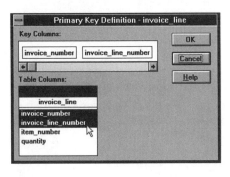

Now repeat the process of creating tables for the rest of the Inventory Tracking system. This has been done for you, as seen in table 2.1 and figure 2.23.

> **TrackNote**
>
> If you're following along, you may want to see what data types all of these have. Table 2.1 shows all of the data types used. Note that all columns don't allow NULLs.

Table 2.1   Table Definitions for the Inventory Tracking System

Table	Column Name	Data Type	Width	Decimals
*customer	customer_number	integer		
	customer_name	varchar	50	
	customer_contact	varchar	50	
	customer_address1	varchar	30	
	customer_address2	varchar	30	
	customer_city	varchar	16	
	customer_state	char	2	
	customer_zip	char	10	
	customer_phone	varchar	12	
invoice	invoice_number	integer		
	invoice_date	date		
	miscellaneous_charges	numeric	9	2
	sales_tax	numeric	9	2
	freight	numeric	9	2
	invoice_comments	varchar	200	
	customer_number	integer		
invoice_line	invoice_number	integer		
	invoice_line_number	integer		
	item_number	integer		

(continues)

Table	Column Name	Data Type	Width	Decimals
	quantity	integer		
item	item_number	integer		
	item_description	varchar	50	
	quantity_on_hand	integer		
	quantity_on_order	integer		
	last_order_date	date		
	order_price	numeric	9	2
	selling_price	numeric	9	2
	item_color	char	10	
	item_size	char	1	
	obsolete	char	1	
	supplier_number	integer		
	warehouse_number	integer		
supplier	supplier_number	integer		
	supplier_name	varchar	50	
	supplier_contact	varchar	50	
	supplier_address1	varchar	30	
	supplier_address2	varchar	30	
	supplier_city	varchar	16	
	supplier_state	char	2	
	supplier_zip	char	10	
	supplier_phone	varchar	12	
	supplier_comments	varchar	200	
warehouse	warehouse_number	integer		
	warehouse_name	varchar	50	
	warehouse_manager	varchar	30	

Table 2.1 Continued

Table	Column Name	Data Type	Width	Decimals
	warehouse_address1	varchar	30	
	warehouse_address2	varchar	30	
	warehouse_city	varchar	16	
	warehouse_state	char	2	
	warehouse_zip	char	10	
	warehouse_phone	varchar	12	1

*Customer comments are to be added in the "Modifying Tables" section later in this chapter.

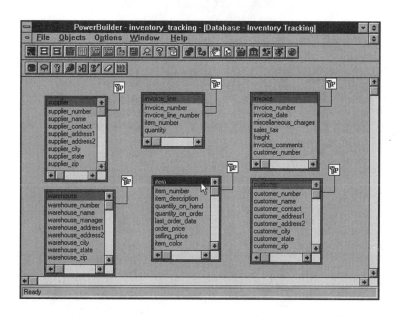

Fig. 2.23
All of the fields have been entered on all of the tables, and all of the primary keys have been chosen.

To close a table, right-click on the table name and choose Close from the pop-up menu.

Adding Foreign Keys

Now that you have defined all of the primary keys, you can start working on your foreign keys. As mentioned previously, a *foreign key* is a field (or set of fields) indicating that table entries have either a zero or one, or a one-and-only-one correspondence to a table entry in another table. Foreign keys are defined by taking the corresponding table's primary key and duplicating it in the related table.

Introducing PowerBuilder

For example, because every entry in the Item table has one and only one corresponding Warehouse entry, and because every entry in the Item table has one and only one corresponding Supplier entry, Item will have foreign keys to Warehouse and Supplier.

To add a foreign key, you must first double-click on one of the open tables in your database painter, which opens the Alter Table dialog box. Now click on For**e**ign to open the Foreign Key Selection dialog box for your table. To add a foreign key, click on **N**ew, as shown in figure 2.24. Often, foreign keys stop you from making a grievous error and help you track down bugs caused by database irregularities.

Fig. 2.24
It's important to relate the tables together with a foreign key.

The Foreign Key Definition dialog box opens for your table. To define a foreign key, perform the following steps:

1. Enter a foreign key name. (This will probably be a name ending in **_key**.)

2. Choose the columns you want to relate by clicking on a column in the Select Columns list box.

3. Choose the table you want to relate in the Primary Key Table drop-down list box. (The primary key of the Primary Key Table is shown automatically. See fig. 2.25.)

4. Choose the type of referential integrity you want to enforce in the On Delete of Primary Table Row group box. Your choices are as follows:

    ■ You cannot allow a primary key table row to be deleted if a foreign key table row (dependent row) exists. This is called *Restrict* referential integrity.

    ■ You can delete dependent rows if a primary key table row is deleted. This is called *Cascade* referential integrity.

    ■ You can set the foreign keys to NULL if the foreign keys reference a deleted row. This is called *Set NULL* referential integrity.

Tip
Some databases allow referential integrity on SQL Updates as well as Deletes. Check the user's guide of your database to see if your database supports cascading updates.

Caution

If you use Set NULL referential integrity, make sure you did NOT define your column as NOT NULL when you created it. Otherwise, you'll receive an error.

---

5. Click on OK to return to the Foreign Key Selection dialog box.

6. Click on Done to return to the Alter Table dialog box.

7. Click on Alter to save your changes to this table. Now you have established a foreign key.

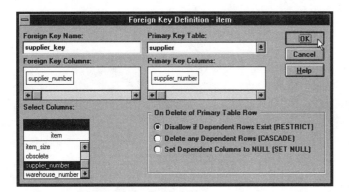

Fig. 2.25
Supplier_number is chosen as one of the foreign keys for the item table.

Establishing a foreign key in PowerBuilder enforces a somewhat complicated universal database concept called referential integrity. *Referential integrity* implies that if you have a foreign key in table 1 referencing a primary key in table 2, that primary key will definitely be in table 2, or you will not be allowed to add your table entry in table 1. Furthermore, you will not be able to delete your entry in table 2 until all corresponding foreign keys in table 1 have been either deleted or changed to another entry in table 2.

For example, suppose that you have several entries in your supplier table (table 2). If you try to add an Item entry in the Item table, Watcom (or other databases) automatically makes sure that the supplier_number you entered in the Item table corresponds to an existing entry in the Supplier table. Otherwise, Watcom (or other databases) will not allow the item to be added, and will return an error to PowerBuilder giving some cryptic message that referential integrity has been violated.

If you try to delete an entry in your Supplier table and that entry has a corresponding supplier_number in the item table, Watcom (or other databases) will not allow you to delete the Supplier and return another referential integrity error to PowerBuilder.

In any case, using foreign keys is a good way to catch your errors during development and ensures that future developers do not make mistakes that can mess up your database. Foreign keys also maintain the integrity of your database for your users and any third-party database packages that can alter the contents of your database.

Now you're finished defining foreign keys. When you return to the database painter, foreign keys will be noted, as seen in figure 2.26.

Fig. 2.26
Barring any future changes, you have defined your database, and all foreign keys have been noted.

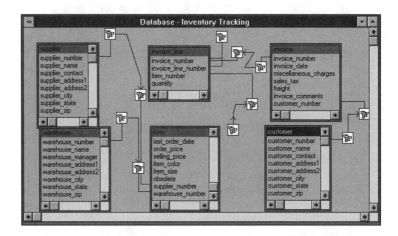

> **Note**
>
> Although the screen in figure 2.26 looks complicated, it is even more so when you first open it. After opening all of the tables, the foreign key lines looked like spaghetti! It took a lot of time to resize the tables windows and move the tables windows and key boxes around so that the window was more readable. You should not pull up more than three tables at a time if you want to check out foreign key relationships.

Modifying Tables

Now you can create tables. As development goes on, however, you need to modify your tables. A general rule is that you can't make a table smaller, but you can increase it. You can increase the size of variables or add new variables, but you can't decrease the size of variables or delete exiting fields.

Opening and Modifying a Table

To open an existing table, you use the Select Tables dialog box, as shown in figure 2.27. It automatically displays when you enter the database, or when you select the Open Table icon. Although several tables can be opened at once, right now only the customer table will be opened.

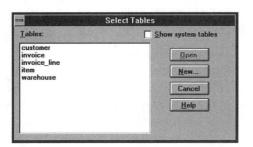

Fig. 2.27
By using the Select Tables dialog box, you can modify your database.

The customer table appears in the database painter. To alter the table, choose **O**bjects, **E**xtended Definition. The Alter Table dialog box appears (see fig. 2.28).

Note

Like most PowerBuilder menu bar functions, there are several ways to open the Alter Table dialog box. You can double-click on the customer table shown in the database painter. You can also right-click on the table name and choose Definition. This may be preferable to some, though probably less intuitive. Finally, you can choose **O**bjects, **E**xtended Definition from your menu to open the Alter Table dialog box.

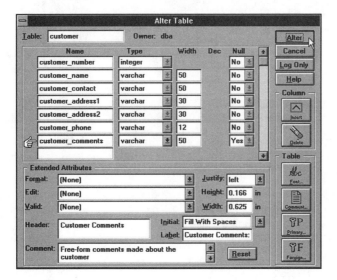

Fig. 2.28
You can add customer comments to the customer table in the Alter Table dialog box.

The database painter now reflects the changes made in the Alter Table dialog box.

Using Table Indexes

Sometimes, you'll want to look up data using criteria other than the primary or foreign key. For instance, even though you have declared customer_number for your primary key, you are more likely to look up people by name. Hence, you should probably have names indexed.

Indexing speeds up data retrieval immensely! If you often use a field to look up data, an index on that field speeds things up. To index a field, open a table (as described in the last section), and click on the Index icon on your PainterBar. This opens the Create Index dialog box (as shown in fig. 2.29), in which you choose the field or fields you want indexed, the index name, whether you want the index ascending or descending, and whether or not the index should be unique.

Fig. 2.29
Clicking on the Index (Key) icon opens the Create Index dialog box. Here you can define another key for your table.

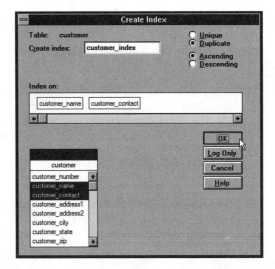

Note

Indexes decrease querying time in a database, so you can retrieve records faster using an index. However, indexes increase the time needed to update or add to your tables, so use them only when you need them.

Also, the longer the key, the longer both queries and updates are, so try to keep your keys reasonable in length. For instance, if you only need customer_name and customer_contact as keys, don't also include customer_phone.

Because graphical applications tend to run slower than old-style text-based applications, you should do what you can to speed things up!

> **Caution**
>
> Although PowerBuilder will let you, you should never define an index for your primary or foreign key. Databases do this for you. Indexes increase the time it takes to add or update your data. Use them, but only when you need to.

Manipulating Data in a Table

Now that you've created the table, you need to know how to get data inside it. Normally, this is done through the application in either a DataWindow or through PowerScript. However, PowerBuilder gives you two ways to access and alter data in your PowerBuilder environment: through the Data Manipulation window, and through the database administrator painter and SQL.

Using the Data Manipulation Dialog Box

You get to the Data Manipulation window (as shown in fig. 2.30) through the database painter. Click on the Preview icon, which opens the Data Manipulation window for the table you selected.

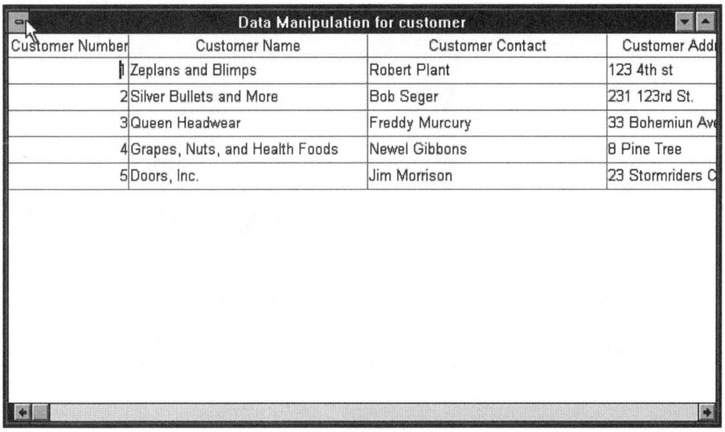

Customer Number	Customer Name	Customer Contact	Customer Addr
1	Zeplans and Blimps	Robert Plant	123 4th st
2	Silver Bullets and More	Bob Seger	231 123rd St.
3	Queen Headwear	Freddy Murcury	33 Bohemiun Ave
4	Grapes, Nuts, and Health Foods	Newel Gibbons	8 Pine Tree
5	Doors, Inc.	Jim Morrison	23 Stormriders C

Data Manipulation for customer

Fig. 2.30
In the Data Manipulation window for your table, you can add, change, or delete table entries.

This window contains the following utilities for quick updates to your table:

- *Retrieve*. Retrieve lets you re-retrieve your data in your table. It's handy if you want to start over on your manipulations.

- *Update Database*. Update Database lets you write any changes you've made to your table.

- *Insert Row*. Insert Row lets you add a new row to your database.

■ *Delete Row.* Delete Row lets you delete the current row from your database.

■ *Scroll to First Page.* Scroll to First Page allows you to go to the beginning of your table.

■ *Scroll to Last Page.* Scroll to Last Page brings you to the end of your table.

■ *Scroll to Previous Page.* Scroll to Previous Page pages up for you.

■ *Scroll to Next Page.* Scroll to Next Page pages down for you.

In addition to the PainterBar commands, you will find the menu bar commands very helpful. Within **F**ile, you will find many commands that help you print your table. Within **R**ows, you have two commands that are particularly helpful—**F**ilter and **S**ort.

Clicking on **R**ows, **F**ilter opens up the Specify Filter dialog box, as shown in figure 2.31. The Specify Filter dialog box screens out certain rows so that you're only working with the rows you want.

Fig. 2.31
By opening Filter and choosing Rows, you can specify which rows on your table you want to work with. Here you choose to display those rows that don't have NULL in the comments field.

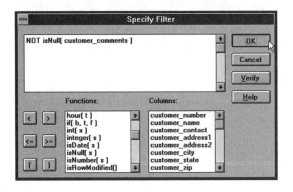

Clicking on **R**ows, **S**ort opens the Specify Sort Columns dialog box, as shown in figure 2.32. Using your mouse, drag each field from the Source Data area to the Columns area. The Specify Sort Columns dialog box displays the rows in any order you want.

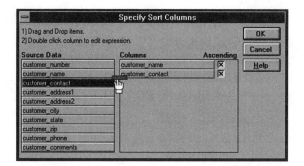

Fig. 2.32
In the Specify Sort Columns dialog box, you can specify the row order in which you want to display your table.

Troubleshooting

I'm trying to change or delete a row on a table, but my database and PowerBuilder won't let me. I keep getting this cryptic Foreign keys attached to primary keys *message. How do I drop a row I don't want?*

Sometimes you will try to delete or alter a primary key on a table that has foreign keys attached to it. This can be maddening because you can have several tables with corresponding foreign keys to your table's primary key. All foreign keys must be tracked down before you make any alterations to a primary key.

To do this quickly in the database painter, maximize the table you are working on (so that the fields and keys are all displayed). Then right-click on the primary key box. A pop-up menu appears with an Open Dependent Tables selection, as shown in figure 2.33. If you click on this choice, all tables that have foreign keys that relate to this primary key are displayed, as shown in figure 2.34.

You need to reassign or delete all foreign keys that reference the primary key of the row you are trying to delete before you can delete that row.

Fig. 2.33
Open Dependent
Tables opens any
table with a
foreign key that
relates to a table.

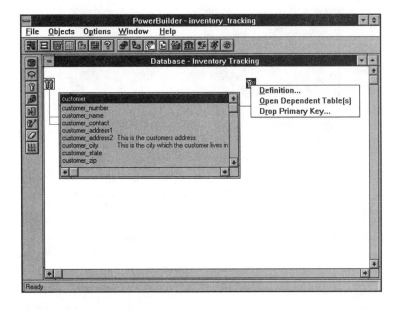

Fig. 2.34
After clicking on
Open Dependent
Tables, all tables
that relate to the
primary key you
right-clicked on
will open.

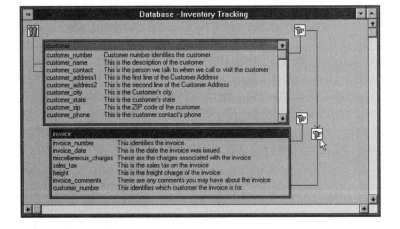

Using the Database Administration Painter and SQL

▶ See "Under-
standing SQL
Syntax," p. 190

If you know SQL pretty well, you will spend a lot of your development time
in the database administration painter, which allows you to issue SQL
commands to your database. To enter the database administration painter
pictured in figure 2.35, click on the Admin icon. You'll learn about SQL commands in Chapter 7, "Using SQL in PowerBuilder."

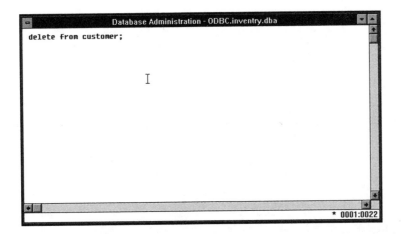

Fig. 2.35
From the Database Administration window, you can alter any table in the database you are connected to. For example, you can delete all records from the customer table.

Syntax-at-a-Glance

DELETE FROM table_name {WHERE condition};

Delete is an SQL statement that deletes all the records in your table denoted by table_name. If you specify a WHERE condition (for example, where customer_name = "Smith"), only those records that fit the criteria are deleted. Note that SQL statements such as delete require a semicolon (;) at the end.

Tip
The database administration painter is good for massive operations on huge tables that would be impractical using the Data Manipulation window.

Implementing Database Changes with a Spreadsheet

It may be easier to implement changes into a database by going outside of PowerBuilder, especially in a spreadsheet. This is done using the following steps:

1. Back up your database! This is probably the most important step. That way, if all your manipulation destroys needed data, you'll have a backup to return to.

2. Drop all foreign keys. This can be done several ways, but the easiest is to pull up your table; open dependent tables, as shown in figure 2.22; and then drop the foreign keys.

3. Go into the Data Manipulation window and choose File, Save Rows As. This allows you to save your database rows in several popular formats (see fig. 2.36). If you select Include Headers, the headers are displayed for easier manipulation.

Tip
Use the data manipulation painter to do minor data manipulation, and use SQL to do major data manipulation.

Fig. 2.36
In the Save Rows
As dialog box, you
can save your
table in several
formats, such as
the Lotus .WK1
format.

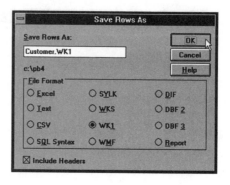

4. Go to the database administration painter and type a delete command to delete all rows off the table, as shown in figure 2.35.

5. Work on your data in the spreadsheet. After you complete your changes, save the data in tab-delimited format. (You can also use dBASE II or dBASE III format. These are the only formats that PowerBuilder imports.)

6. Go to the Data Manipulation window. Choose **R**ows, **I**mport. The Select Import File dialog box appears, in which you can enter the name of your new file, as shown in figure 2.37. Save from the spreadsheet into tab-separated format.

Fig. 2.37
You import the
data in this dialog
box.

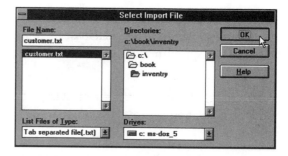

7. Finally, go back to your Alter Table window, as shown in figure 2.28, and reassign all your foreign keys.

If you mess up during this process, restore immediately! This seven-step process will help out if you are proficient with a spreadsheet, and your data manipulation will go faster in a spreadsheet than in the database painter.

Dropping a Table

Of course, there will be times when a table is no longer needed. Click on the Drop icon to drop a table from your database.

Exploring PowerBuilder Database Independence

One of the nice things about PowerBuilder is its database independence. Using the fields you defined, you can use any database you want to implement or (usually with little effort) switch between them. If you are using Oracle at work with the PowerBuilder Enterprise Edition, you could work at home on the same application using Watcom with the PowerBuilder Desktop Edition. Similarly, if you are using DB2 but want to change your database to Oracle, such a change is accomplished relatively easily by editing your database profile.

> **Caution**
>
> Although switching between databases is, in theory, transparent, not all databases support the same data types. Before you switch databases, be sure that you are using datatypes that exist in both databases.
>
> Also, some databases implement a "nonstandard" form of SQL. Sometimes, minor syntax changes can be a problem. For instance, Sybase has to have strings in double quotes; Watcom has them in single quotes.

From Here...

This chapter is the most complex chapter in *Using PowerBuilder 4*. However, once you understand the techniques discussed, the rest of development will become *much* easier.

Analysis and design normally should take roughly twice as long as the actual development; but done properly, analysis and design will mean the difference between a mediocre application and a *great* application. If you've mastered analysis and design, you'll be worth your weight in gold to your company.

For more information about analysis, design, and the database painter, see the following chapters:

- Chapter 1, "Introducing PowerBuilder," mentions iterative design, which speeds up PowerBuilder development considerably.

- Chapter 7, "Using SQL in PowerBuilder," shows how to incorporate SQL into your application.

- Appendix B, "Using Watcom Database and Watcom SQL," shows how you can use Watcom to implement your application. Also covered in this chapter are Watcom SQL functions and SQL commands not allowed inside the PowerBuilder environment.

Chapter 3

Exploring Windows

The biggest push in application development today is the need for a *graphical user interface*, or *GUI*. The main thrust of GUI development centers around the window.

This chapter describes much of what you can do with a window in the Windows development. You've already touched on windows in the first chapter, so this chapter will add to what you've already learned.

In this chapter, you should be able to:

- Describe and differentiate between different window types
- Set window attributes through the window painter
- Add and implement window controls
- Implement window inheritance

Defining Window Attributes

You've seen a little bit of windows attributes when w_inventory_frame was defined. The following sections discuss the other types of windows and why you would use them.

Defining Window Types

◀ See "Using Windows," p. 29

Window type has been covered somewhat: w_inventory_frame is defined as an MDI frame with MicroHelp, which is a window type. In Chapter 1, you pulled up the Window Style dialog box by double-clicking on the window displayed on the screen while running the window painter. Although most developers pull up the Window Style dialog box in this manner, you can also get to the Window Style dialog box by using the menu bar. By clicking on **D**esign, **W**indow Style, as shown in figure 3.1, you can also get into the Window Style dialog box. (The Window Style dialog box can be seen in fig. 3.2.)

Fig. 3.1
Open the Window Style dialog box by double-clicking on the displayed window or by using the PowerBuilder menu.

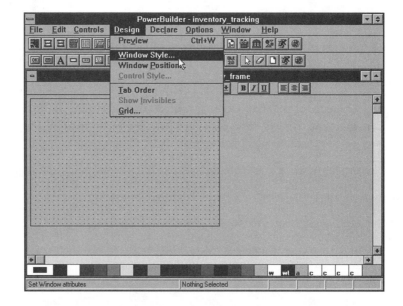

Fig. 3.2
From the Window Style dialog box, you can change the window type attributes.

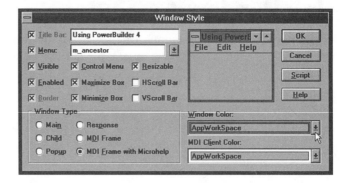

Using Main Windows

You will probably use main windows more than any other type. *Main windows* are stand-alone windows (unless inside an MDI frame). If you aren't using an MDI frame, the first window opened will be a main window.

> **Note**
>
> Even in a simple Windows application, you may find yourself wanting to use MDI frame with MicroHelp as a "shell" for all your main windows. MicroHelp is great for displaying short messages to the user, and MDI frames look more professional than stand-alone main windows.
>
> Inside your MDI frame, all your major sheet windows will probably end up being main windows.

Using Pop-up Windows

Pop-up windows are usually opened from within another window (they have a parent window). Although the pop-up window can't be overlaid by its parent window, it *can* extend beyond the boundaries of its parent window. When the parent window is closed or minimized, the pop-up window is also closed or minimized.

Pop-up windows are commonly used as support windows. For example, if you were asked to enter a customer number, a pop-up window could display all customer numbers with names for you.

> **Note**
>
> Pop-up windows are a good way to tie one window to another window, but be careful not to overuse them. An application with tons of pop-up windows is usually a sign that an MDI frame should have been used, especially if the windows don't seem to relate to each other.

Using Child Windows

Child windows are also opened from within another window and also have a parent window. There are some strong differences, however:

- Child windows can never exist outside of the parent window.

- Child windows are never considered active.

- When a child window is maximized, it only fills the space of the parent window.

- Child windows can't have menus.

▶ See "Program-
ming for Win-
dows Events,"
p. 185

Although child windows aren't used that often, they can be a type of pop-up window if you want to avoid activating and deactivating your parent window because of some PowerScript you have written.

Using Response Windows

Response windows are a type of pop-up window. They differ from pop-up windows in that they are *application modal* (no other window in the application can be accessed until the response window is closed).

Response windows are often called dialog boxes. You'll use response windows often. For example, they are useful if you don't want the user to continue with your application until some questions have been answered. If your changes have not been saved, a response window appears and asks if the changes should be saved. The user won't be able to continue until the question has been answered.

Using MDI Frames and MDI Frames with MicroHelp

◀ See "Compar-
ing SDI vs.
MDI Frame,"
p. 30

An MDI frame is a window (called a *frame*) which contains other windows (called *sheets*). You only have one frame per application but can have many sheets within your frame.

In any complex (and usually any simple) Windows application, you should use an MDI frame. The MicroHelp works well as an easy way to convey a message to the user (`Save was successful!`, `Performing Calculations. Please wait.`, and so on) without stopping your application.

> **Note**
>
> Most books start you with an SDI application, claiming that MDI is too advanced. This is simply not so! PowerBuilder has done a fine job implementing MDI, and using MDI allows you more freedom in development. Also, your final project will be more professional.
>
> You should be careful about suggesting an SDI application. You may wish you hadn't. MDI offers MicroHelp and easy interaction between windows for the user that SDI applications can't match. All this is done with very little extra effort from the developer.

Tip
If you use an MDI frame, you should use it with MicroHelp. (MicroHelp is easy to use; it won't noticeably impact your application's performance.)

> **Note**
>
> If you already defined your window as a certain type and then later change your mind and want it to be a different type, go into the Window Style dialog box and simply choose a new type. This may cause some difficulty if you're changing from an SDI application to an MDI application, but otherwise there should be little problem.

Color

You can also change the background color of your window in the Window Style dialog box. In the **W**indow Color drop-down list box seen in figure 3.3, you can choose the color you want for your main window. If your window is an MDI frame, the MDI Client Color drop-down list box can control the background color of all your sheet windows.

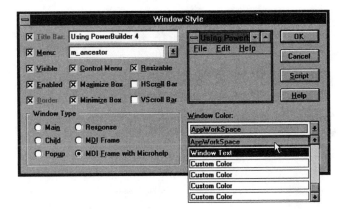

Fig. 3.3
Click on the **W**indow Color box (or the MDI Client Color box) to change the color of a window or the color of the individual sheets.

Other Attributes in the Window Style Dialog Box

As you can see in figures 3.2 and 3.3, there are other attributes you can set in your Window Style dialog box:

- **T**itle Bar. The title bar is the bar at the top of a dialog box with the title in it. The title bar also contains the Control menu box (called **C**ontrol menu in this dialog box), Ma**x**imize box, and Mini**z**ize box. If any of these are active, the title bar is also active.

> **Note**
>
> The title of the MDI Frame (or the main window in an SDI application) is also the name of the application. The title will be displayed when you pull up your task list in Windows by pressing Ctrl+Esc.

I

Introducing PowerBuilder

- **M**enu. The menu option tells PowerBuilder which menu to attach to the window. Because you have created only one menu, m_ancestor, that's the one you'll have to use for now.

- **V**isible. The **V**isible indicator tells whether you want this window shown when it's pulled up. This indicator may seem a little odd—you may ask why create a window and then make it invisible? Sometimes it's more expedient to hide a window by making it invisible and only show it when it's needed.

TrackNote

All windows in the Inventory Tracking system will be visible.

- **E**nabled. Sometimes you will want to display a window but not allow entry into it. Clicking this off disables a window.

TrackNote

All windows in the Inventory Tracking system will be enabled.

Note

The visible and enabled attributes are most often handled using PowerScript. If you want to make a window or window control invisible, use the windowname.Hide( ) command. If you want to make a window or window control visible, use the windowname.Show() command.

It should also be noted that instead of using Hide and Show commands, it's faster to directly assign the window attribute:

```
windowname.visible = TRUE
windowname.enabled = FALSE
```

Using the enabled attribute is the only way to choose whether or not a window is enabled or disabled. Note that all these attributes can be affected by setting the proper attribute. Chapter 23, "Attribute Quick Reference," lists all of the attributes for all of the objects and controls in PowerBuilder.

- **B**order. **B**order controls whether a border surrounds the window. Main and MDI windows must have borders. Getting rid of a border on a window creates the illusion of one window, when in fact there are two.

- **C**ontrol Menu. The Control menu box is the box in the upper left hand corner of your window with a minus sign in it. This controls whether you have a Control menu box on your window.

Note

It's easy to get confused when discussing the Control menu with other Windows users. The Control menu box is also called the *Control box*. The **C**ontrol menu appears when you click once on the Control box, as shown in figure 3.4. PowerBuilder groups the Control menu box and the Control menu into one and calls it the **C**ontrol menu.

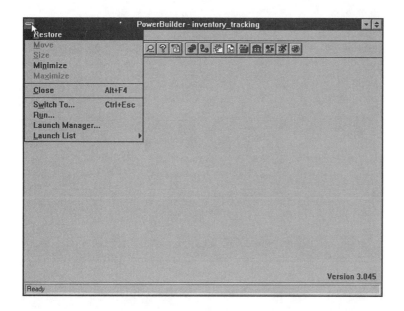

Fig. 3.4
Clicking on the Control menu box pulls up the **C**ontrol menu.

- Ma**x**imize Box. The Maximize box is the box in the upper-right hand corner of your window. It acts as a toggle between full-screen and its normal area.

- Minimi**z**e Box. The Minimize box is the box in the upper-right hand corner of your window. It reduces your window to an icon. (Icons are discussed later in this chapter.)

- **R**esizable. Clicking on **R**esizable resizes the window.

- HScr**o**ll Bar. A horizontal scroll bar puts a scroll bar at the bottom of your window. This lets you "shift" the window over, in case your information is wider than your window.

■ VScroll Bar. A vertical scroll bar puts a scroll bar on the right side of your window. This lets you "shift" the window down, in case your information is longer than your window.

Position

When you ran your application after Chapter 1, the MDI frame took up a small section of the screen. You probably want to change it so the MDI frame takes up the whole screen. To do this, open **D**esign and choose Window **P**osition, as shown in figure 3.5.

Fig. 3.5
Under **D**esign, you can choose Window **P**osition to change the size and opening position of your window.

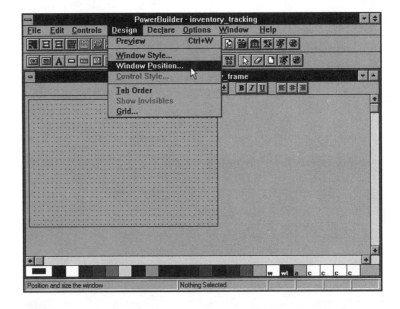

Tip
When changing the size of your window, click on **C**enter Horizontally and **C**enter Vertically. This will help you center your window on-screen and make it easier to implement increases and decreases in window size.

Note

There's often no need to go to the menu bar. By right-clicking on the window, a pop-up menu appears, as shown in figure 3.6. This pop-up menu not only allows you to duplicate much of what was entered on the Window Style dialog box, but you also can alter the position, pointer, and icon.

The Window Position dialog box appears (as seen in fig. 3.7). In this dialog box, you not only define the size and position of your window, but you also define the way your window will scroll, and what the initial state of your window will be. (The *initial state* can be **M**aximize, **M**inimize, or **N**ormal.)

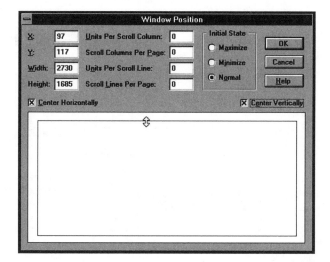

Introducing PowerBuilder

Fig. 3.6
By right-clicking on the window, a pop-up menu appears which allows you to change your window attributes.

Fig. 3.7
The Window Position dialog box allows you to control the opening position and size of your window. For an MDI frame, a full screen works best.

Icon

If your window is minimized, an icon representing your window will appear. This icon defaults to the Application! icon. If you want to change your icon to another, right-click on the window inside the window painter (refer to fig. 3.6) and choose **I**con. This brings up the Select Icon dialog box shown in figure 3.8.

If you want to use a different icon for your minimized window, this is the place to do so.

Tip
MDIs look best when they're full-screen. Adjust the size of the frame window so there is no "bleeding" application on either side of it. Your user won't be distracted while running your application.

Fig. 3.8
Select an icon to represent your window if your window is minimized. The default is the Application! icon.

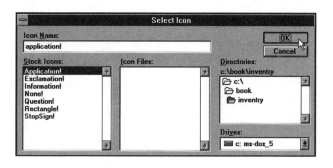

Pointer

Usually, you want to keep the default pointer icon when the mouse pointer moves over your window. However, there may be times you want to change that by using the Select Pointer dialog box, as seen in figure 3.9. To open the Select Pointer dialog box, right-click on the window you're painting (refer to fig. 3.6), and choose **P**ointer.

Fig. 3.9

Use the Select Pointer dialog box to see a different pointer when the pointer is over your window.

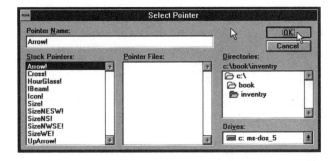

> ### Note
>
> PowerBuilder comes with many icons and several pointers, but you can't create new icons or pointers within PowerBuilder. These are created by using third-party Windows development toolkits.
>
> Watcom Image Editor comes with the PowerBuilder Enterprise Edition, and is available as a stand-alone product.

Adding Window Controls

A *window control* is anything you put in a window. The window PainterBar mostly contains different controls you can place on your window. Controls are necessary for every window—without controls, a window is simply a box with no functionality displayed on your screen.

Types of Controls

There are several different types of controls you can choose from. Most of the controls are shown in figure 3.10. The icon for each control precedes each control description in the following sections.

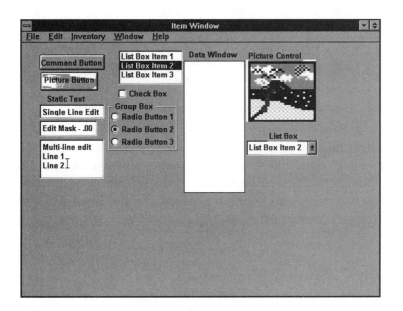

Fig. 3.10
Many different
window controls
are displayed here,
but usually you
have only one or
two types of
window controls
at a time.

Command Buttons

Command buttons look like buttons on your window. When clicked, command buttons give a pushed-in look while the mouse button is depressed. To put a command button on your window, click on the Command Button icon and then click on the window where you want the command button to go in the window you are defining.

When command buttons are "pushed" (clicked on), PowerScript defined in command button events is executed. Command buttons are often not used on a window where a menu toolbar is available. However, command buttons are often used on response windows since the menu is inoperable when a response window is active.

▶ See "Adding an About Window," p. 352

Note

Controls are named by PowerBuilder. For instance, this command button was called cb_1 at first. When you start accessing these controls, cb_1 is hard to work with because it's not intuitive and not very maintainable.

To pull up a dialog box to set the attributes of any control, double-click on that control. In figure 3.11, the command button's name is changed. (You can also change what is displayed on the button and certain attributes regarding that button.) You should rename all your controls to better fit their descriptions. By renaming this command button to cb_OK, you and your coworkers now know that you are dealing with the OK command button.

Fig. 3.11
By double-clicking on any control in the window painter, you can see a dialog box of information about the window control.

Picture Buttons

Picture buttons are just like command buttons except they have pictures on them. Pictures can make the words on the picture button hard to read, but there are times when a picture button can enhance the presentation quality of an otherwise nondistinct window.

To put a picture button control on your window, click on the Picture Button icon and then click where you want the picture button to go in the window you are defining. When you double-click on a picture button, you can select the picture you want to display (see fig. 3.12).

Fig. 3.12
When adding a picture button or picture control, the Select Picture dialog box automatically appears.

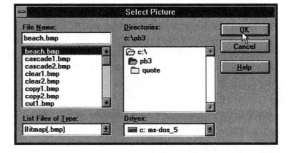

Static Text

Static text is a phrase or description displayed on your window. To put a static text control on your window, click on the Static Text icon and then click where you want the static text to go. By clicking on the static text, you can type the text you want displayed in the window you are defining.

Static text is handy for describing controls (such as pictures), or for using multiple lines on a controls (such as a check box) that only allow a single line of descriptive text to be displayed.

DataWindows

To put a DataWindow control on your window, click on the DataWindow icon and then click where you want the DataWindow to appear in the window you are defining.

DataWindows are PowerBuilder's answer to data-entry screens. DataWindows are very handy to use when trying to tie your application to a database, and are integral to development in PowerBuilder. Also, DataWindows have several advanced editing features.

You'll notice that the DataWindow pictured in figure 3.10 is a white blank screen. This is because you've told PowerBuilder you want a DataWindow control on your window, but you haven't specified which one. (Actually, none have been defined yet.) DataWindows are discussed at length in the chapters listed in Part III, "Using DataWindows."

Multi-line Edits

To put a multi-line edit control on your window, click on the Multi-Line Edit icon and then click where you want the multi-line edit to go in the window you are defining.

Unlike single-line edits (discussed later in this section), which only allow one line of text to be entered or viewed, *multi-line edits* are controls that allow several lines of text to be entered by the user. Multi-line edits are often used for free-form comments. With many editing features built in (such as cut and paste and arrow movement), multi-line edits are indispensable when entering large amounts of data in a field. However, multi-line edit controls are often not used since enhanced functionality can be achieved through a DataWindow column.

Pictures

To put a picture control on your window, click on the Picture icon and then click where you want the picture to go in the window you are defining.

Pictures are controls that reference bit maps to be displayed in a window. Like static text, pictures are only used for displaying information (except in the form of pictures, not words). Usually, nothing more is done with these.

> **Note**
>
> Although not commonly used this way, picture objects can be used as buttons. When you code for the clicked event, picture objects behave identically to buttons except they don't give the appearance of being pressed down. Usually, if you want to press on a picture, you use a picture button as opposed to a picture object.

Single-line Edits

To put a single-line edit control on your window, click on the Single-Line Edit icon and then click where you want the single-line edit to go in the window you are defining.

Single-line edits are data-entry fields that you can put in a window to enter a single line of text. Single-line edit controls usually aren't used because most data entry is done on a DataWindow.

Edit Masks

To put an edit mask control on your window, click on the Edit Mask icon and then click where you want the edit mask to go in the window you are defining.

Edit masks are a type of single-line edit that allow you to specify the formatting required upon entry. This formatting is defined when you first add the edit mask control using the Edit Mask dialog box, seen in figure 3.13. Like single- and multi-line edits, edit mask window controls are often not used since enhanced functionality is provided by DataWindows.

Fig. 3.13
When defining an edit mask control, the Edit Mask dialog box automatically appears.

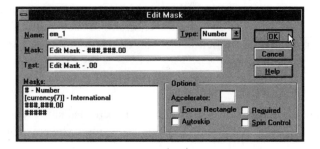

List Box

To put a list box control on your window, click on the List Box icon and then click where you want the list box to go in the window you are defining.

List boxes are a type of single-line edit that gives the user several choices for the right answer. Scroll bars can be used if there are a lot of choices that can be made. Like many other window controls dealing with data entry, list box window controls are often not used since enhanced functionality is provided by DataWindows.

Drop-Down List Box

To put a drop-down list box control on your window, click on the Drop-Down List Box icon and then click where you want the drop-down list box to go in the window you are defining.

Drop-down list boxes do not usually display choices unless the user presses the down arrow to display them (although they can be configured to always display their list). Like many other window controls dealing with data entry, drop-down list box window controls are often not used since enhanced functionality is provided by DataWindows.

Check Box

To put a check box control on your window, click on the Check Box icon and then click where you want the check box to go in the window you are defining.

Check boxes are yes-no questions that can be clicked on or off. Internally, a code table describes the data value returned when a check box is clicked on or off. Like many other window controls dealing with data entry, check box window controls are often not used since enhanced functionality is provided by DataWindows.

Radio Buttons and Group Boxes

To put a radio button control on your window, click on the Radio Button icon and then click where you want the radio button to go in the window you are defining. To put a group box control on your window, click on the Group Box icon and then click where you want the group box to go in the window you are defining.

A *radio button* is a type of check box. Several radio buttons are grouped together inside a group box. These radio buttons, like check boxes, are either on or off, but only one radio button inside a group box can be clicked at one time.

Note

Usually you won't use single-line edits, multi-line edits, edit masks, list boxes, drop-down list boxes, check boxes, radio buttons, or group boxes in a window. Instead, you'll find it easier to use a DataWindow with these type of controls and attach the DataWindow to your window through a DataWindow control. Database fields can then be directly linked to your window through the DataWindow control. You'll find out how to use DataWindows and these controls in Part III, "Using DataWindows."

Manipulating Window Controls

Often, you'll want to manipulate your controls. By double-clicking on your control, some basic information (such as control name) is displayed (refer to fig. 3.11). By right-clicking on your control, a menu of possible actions for that control is shown (see fig. 3.14).

Fig. 3.14
By right-clicking on most controls, a pop-up window appears, showing options for that control.

Tab Order

You can use the keyboard instead of the mouse. To move between controls, the user must press the Tab key. However, the tab order of the window controls defaults to the order in which those controls were added.

To change the tab order in a window, open **D**esign and choose **T**ab Order (see fig. 3.15), which displays the tab order of each control, incremented by 10. To change the tab order, simply renumber your controls. Then choose **D**esign, **T**ab Order again to turn off the tab order.

> **Note**
>
> When you pull up the tab order, PowerBuilder automatically renumbers the tabs by 10 for you. For example, assume that when you pull up tab orders, you have the following buttons with the following tab orders:
>
> | Button | Tab Order |
> | --- | --- |
> | ■ BUTTON_A | 10 |
> | ■ BUTTON_B | 30 |
> | ■ BUTTON_C | 20 |

With this tab order, you go from BUTTON_A to BUTTON_C to BUTTON_B. If you want to change the order to BUTTON_A, BUTTON_B, and BUTTON_C, change the BUTTON_B tab order to 15. Now you have the following tab orders:

Button	Tab Order
■ BUTTON_A	10
■ BUTTON_B	15
■ BUTTON_C	20

Now your buttons are numbered 10, 20, and 15. If you leave tab order and get back in, you'll see that PowerBuilder renumbered the buttons by 10 so you'll have the following tab order:

Button	Tab Order
■ BUTTON_A	10
■ BUTTON_B	20
■ BUTTON_C	30

As you can see, PowerBuilder keeps the tab orders numbered for you with enough space between numbers so you can easily reorder your tabs.

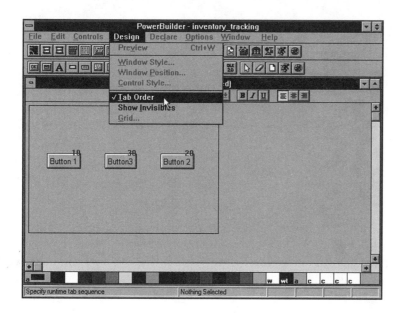

Fig. 3.15
By choosing **D**esign, **T**ab Order, you can change the order when tabbing through your window.

I

Introducing PowerBuilder

Starting a Data Entry Window

◄ See "Using
Windows,"
p. 29

Now, you are going to add another window, but you need to define a prototype for the data entry windows. First, create a new window as you did in Chapter 1. Then add a DataWindow control.

> **Note**
>
> Most data entry DataWindows take up the whole window, so expand your DataWindow to cover almost the entire window. For a good effect, leave a little room around the edges, right-click on the window, and choose Border, **3D** Lowered, as shown in figure 3.16. This gives your DataWindow a three-dimensional look.

Fig. 3.16
Right-clicking on the data window pulls up a menu. Choose Border, **3D** Lowered for a three-dimensional look.

► See "Associating
DataWindow
Controls with a
DataWindow
Object," p. 231

As mentioned previously, you should name your data window control appropriately. Double-click on the DataWindow; the Select DataWindow dialog box appears, as seen in figure 3.17. Because you have not yet defined any DataWindows, you can't select one. (In this case, you probably wouldn't ever want to select a DataWindow because this is a prototype for all other data entry windows. You will see the Select DataWindow window again in Chapter 8, "Creating DataWindows.") Click on OK.

Now the DataWindow dialog box appears. Rename `dw_1` to `dw_data`, as seen in figure 3.18. Now all other windows that use this data entry window prototype have a DataWindow called dw_data.

Now save this window in the ancestor.pbl, as shown in figure 3.19. (I called it **w_datawindow_ancestor**.) Because this window is a prototype for other windows, save it as **w_datawindow_ancestor** in the ancestor.pbl. by clicking on ancestor.pbl under **A**pplication Libraries.

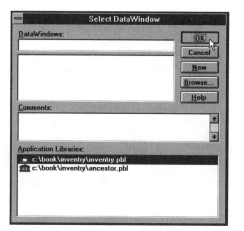

Fig. 3.17
The Select
DataWindow
dialog box allows
you to tie a
DataWindow
object to a
DataWindow
control.

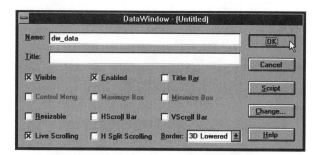

Fig. 3.18
You can change
the name of your
DataWindow
object in the
DataWindow
window.

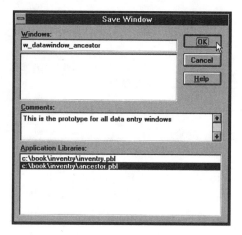

Fig. 3.19
This window will
now be a proto-
type for other data
entry windows.

Implementing Window Inheritance

Inheritance is the way we use our prototypes in PowerBuilder. By using inheritance, the *child* object takes all the controls, PowerScripts, and attributes from the *ancestor* object. Any further changes to the ancestor object are automatically made in the child object. The child object can then add to or modify what it has inherited. Windows and menus can be inherited.

> **Note**
>
> Only windows, menus, and user objects can be inherited. User objects are, for the most part, beyond the scope of this book. You can find more about user objects in Appendix C, "Implementing Advanced Procedures."

To inherit a window, click on the Window icon on the PowerBar. This pulls up the Select Window dialog box. However, instead of clicking on **New** as before, click on Inherit, as shown in figure 3.20.

Fig. 3.20
To inherit from a window, pull up the Select Window dialog box and click on Inherit.

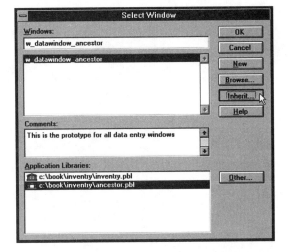

The Inherit From Window dialog box appears. Click on the ancestor.pbl, choose w_datawindow_ancestor, and click on OK. (Ancestor.pbl and w_datawindow_ancestor may be selected already by PowerBuilder.)

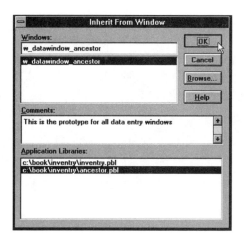

Fig. 3.21
Use the Inherit
From Window
dialog box to tell
PowerBuilder what
window you want
to inherit from.

Notice that this pulls up a window that looks exactly like the
w_datawindow_ancestor window, as seen in figure 3.22. This new
window has been inherited from w_datawindow_ancestor.

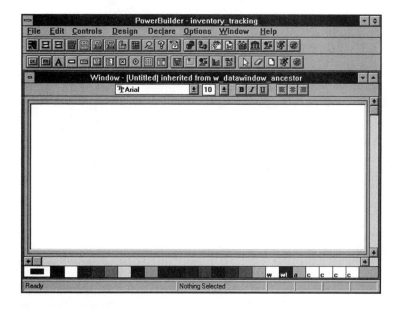

Fig. 3.22
When you first
start developing a
child window, it is
identical to its
ancestor.

Now pull up the Window Style dialog box for your new window, as seen in
figure 3.23, by double-clicking on the window you are defining (but not the
DataWindow), or by choosing **D**esign, **W**indow Style from the menu bar.
Because you need to enter items in an inventory system, you can make this
the Item Entry window. You can also attach m_ancestor to the window until
you make other menus.

Fig. 3.23
Using the Window Style dialog box, you differentiate it from other "children."

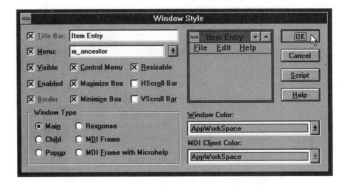

Finally, save this window as **w_item** in the inventry.pbl, as seen in figure 3.24. (Because w_item is not an ancestor, don't save it in the ancestor.pbl.)

Fig. 3.24
Now save your window as **w_item** in the inventry.pbl.

Opening a Window Sheet

This chapter discussed window frames and sheets, and you learned how to open a window frame. To open a sheet within a window, you use the OpenSheet command, typically in the open event of the frame window, as shown in figure 3.25. To get to the open event, open the window and click on the Script icon. (As an added bonus, the MicroHelp has been set to welcome the user to your system.)

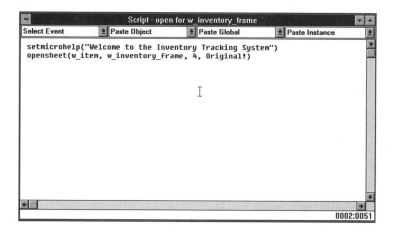

Introducing PowerBuilder

Fig. 3.25
As you code the
open event for
w_inventory_frame,
OpenSheet is used
to open a window
sheet inside the
frame window,
and SetMicroHelp
sets the
MicroHelp.

Syntax-at-a-Glance

OpenSheet(sheet,{window_name},frame,{position{, arrangeopen}})

OpenSheet opens a sheet window within a frame.

- *sheet* is the window name of the sheet.

- *window_name (optional)* is a string containing the name of the window type you want opened. For our purposes, window_name is not needed.

- *frame* is the window name of the MDI frame.

- *position* is the menu item in which all open sheets are displayed. You can read more about this item in Chapter 4, "Defining Menus."

- *arrangeopen* is a PowerBuilder enumerated data type that tells you how you want the sheet opened. Valid values are:

  Cascaded! (default). Cascade the sheet when it is opened.

  Layered!. Layer the sheet when it is opened.

  Original!. Open the sheet in its original size and cascade it.

Note the exclamation points on the arrangeopen parameter. All PowerBuilder enumerated data types end in an exclamation point.

▶ See "Listing
Open MDI
Sheets," p. 117

Syntax-at-a-Glance

MDIFrame.SetMicroHelp(helpstring)

SetMicroHelp sets the MicroHelp on an MDI frame window. *MDIFrame* is the name of the frame containing the MicroHelp. If this command is done within an MDI frame window event (as this one was), MDIFrame is not needed and is assumed to be the MDIFrame containing the event. *helpstring* is the string you want displayed in the MicroHelp.

What's To Come

Once more, you can run your application. With a full-screen MDI frame and an open sheet inside it, you can see the development toward a professional Windows application (see fig. 3.26). Have you noticed how you've added so easily onto existing work? This is one aspect of PowerBuilder's easy iterative design.

Fig. 3.26

With a full-screen MDI frame and a sheet inside the frame, it's looking a lot more like a professional Windows application.

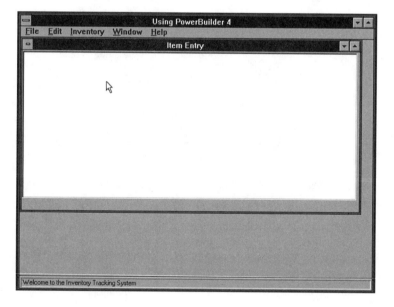

From Here...

In this chapter, you've seen different types of windows and different types of window controls. You have learned about inheritance and how an MDI application can look. The importance of windows can't be understated in a PowerBuilder application. Windows are the cornerstone of an application and how the application interfaces with the end user.

Further information on windows and window controls can be found in the following chapters:

- Chapter 1, "Introducing PowerBuilder," introduces windows and the window painter. It's a must-read for the beginning PowerBuilder developer.

- Chapter 4, "Defining Menus," shows how to define menus for your window and how to associate a menu with a window.

- Chapter 6, "Programming in PowerScript," discusses window events and how to program for windows. You also see how inheritance affects programming for windows.

- Chapter 8, "Creating DataWindows," teaches you how to create a DataWindow object to attach to your DataWindow control.

Chapter 4

Defining Menus

Menus are an important part of any Windows 3.x application. Menus issue commands, trigger events, and control the flow of an application.

You've already been exposed to menus somewhat when m_ancestor was created in Chapter 1. Now you can increase your understanding of menus in this chapter by learning how to:

- Use the menu painter

- Use inheritance to build a menu

- Enhance an existing menu

- Code for menu events

Designing Your Menu

Before you design your menu, it's important to have an idea of what you want your menus to look like. Using a spreadsheet, a word processing table, or a piece of paper, sketch what you want contained in all your menus. It may be helpful to look at other Windows 3.x applications to see what they have in their menus.

To keep your menus consistent, develop one menu with all of your menu options instead of designing several different menus. (As you'll soon see, it's also a lot easier to maintain and code if you use a consistent layout.) This master menu (called m_ancestor) will be used as a prototype for other menus. The menu design you'll be using for the Inventory Tracking system is shown in table 4.1.

Table 4.1 Menu Prototype (m_ancestor) for Inventory Tracking System

File	Edit	Inventory	Window	Help
New	Undo	Item Entry...	Tile	Table of Contents...
	-	Customer Entry...	Cascade	Search...
Save	Cut	Supplier Entry...	Layer	-
-	Copy	Invoice Entry...	Arrange Icons	Introduction...
Print	Paste	Warehouse Entry...	-	-
Print Setup...	-	Toolbars...	About...	
-	Insert		[Top]	
Close	Delete		[Bottom]	
Exit			[Left]	
			[Right]	
			[-]	
			[Hide Toolbar]	
			[-]	
			[Show Text]	
			-	
			{Open Sheets}	

You'll notice in the menu that there are several dividing lines (-) within menu bar options. Most Windows 3.x menus use these to group related menu bar options. Also notice the ellipses (...) at the end of several menu bar options. Added by the developer, this tells the user that another screen or menu will pop up if this option is chosen. The {Open Sheets} entry under Window is where you list all open sheets within the MDI frame. Finally, brackets ([ ]) indicate that these options are part of a cascading menu that pops up when the menu bar option above them is chosen.

Developing Your Menu

In Chapter 1, you started your ancestor menu, which serves as the prototype for all menus in the Inventory Tracking system. To enhance what was already begun in the m_ancestor menu, click on the Menu icon to pull up the Select Menu dialog box, shown in figure 4.1. Click on ancestor.pbl, and then click on m_ancestor. Finally, click on OK to pull up the menu painter.

◀ See "Using Menus," p. 24

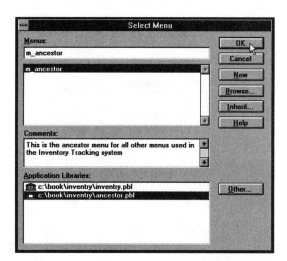

Fig. 4.1
Use the Select Menu dialog box as the first step toward creating new menus or editing existing menus.

In the first chapter, only **S**ave, **C**lose, and E**x**it were added to the menu. Now you will make a complete menu for your Inventory Tracking system, which will serve as a prototype for all other menus in the Inventory Tracking system.

Adding Options

As you saw by the design in table 4.1, you need to add several items to your menu structure. PowerBuilder gives you the following three tools to do that:

Icon	Name	Description
Insert	Insert	Insert a new menu option between two other menu options.
Move	Move	Move an option or menu bar item to another position.
Delete	Delete	Delete menu bar items and menu options.

You can add to the rest of your menu by using these icons or use the Enter key to add menu options to the bottom of the list. When you're done with File, continue with Edit, Inventory, and so on until the rest of the menu items are added.

To add the separator line, use a hyphen (-) as the option name. Several separators will cause PowerBuilder to display the Invalid Menu Item Name dialog box, as seen in figure 4.2. This is telling you that you have two menu items (but in this case, menu separators) with the same name, and that PowerBuilder is automatically renaming one of them. Click on OK to continue.

Fig. 4.2
Often, the Invalid Menu Item Name dialog box appears when you add separators to a menu.

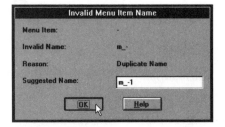

> **Note**
>
> Placing an ampersand (&) before a menu bar item allows the user to access that menu bar item with Alt + the letter after the ampersand. (This is called a *hot key* or *shortcut key*.)
>
> An ampersand before an option under a menu bar item allows the end user to press the letter after the ampersand to execute that option if the menu bar item is pulled down. (This is called an *accelerator*.)

Using Shortcut Keys

To make your application easier to use, PowerBuilder gives you the ability to assign a shortcut key to a menu option. As shown in figure 4.3, you can assign any key combination using the Alt, Ctrl, and Shift keys (and any letter) to execute a menu option. In figure 4.3, Alt+U executes the Print Setup menu option.

You can even use function keys, Ins, and Del to act as shortcut keys. In figure 4.4, Alt+Ins executes the Insert option; Alt+Del executes the Delete option.

I

Introducing PowerBuilder

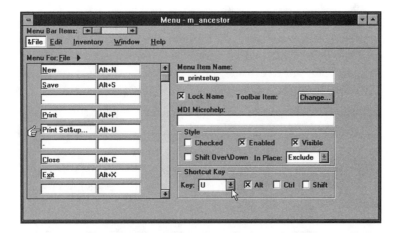

Fig. 4.3
Alt+U executes the
Print Setup menu
option.

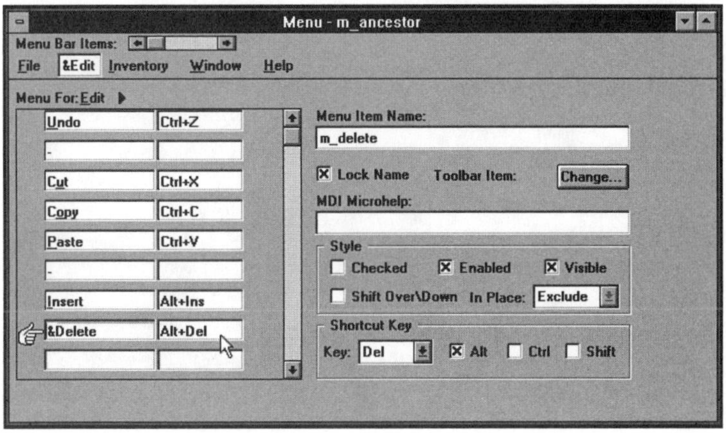

Fig. 4.4
You can also use
the function keys,
Ins, and Del to act
as shortcut keys.

Using shortcut keys is a must for any quality program. Not only do they allow the user to avoid using a mouse when desired, they can also be much
faster—the user can use a quick key combination instead of going through
the menu.

> **Caution**
>
> Be sure not to mask over one of your menu bar items or one shortcut key with an-
> other shortcut key. For example, because Alt+I pulls down the Inventory menu bar,
> assigning another Alt+I to an option as a shortcut key disables the quick keyboard
> access to your menu bar. It's also very confusing to the end user.

Using Cascading Menus

Sometimes, you want your menu options to pull down other menus. These pull-down menus are called *cascading menus*. To form a cascading menu, click on the option you want to cascade and then click on the Next Level icon on the painter bar. This brings up a new menu list in which you enter your menu choices. Also, notice that the Menu For: statement at the top of the painter shows the parent menu item.

By clicking on the Prior Level icon, you return to the first drop-down level under your menu bar. As seen in figure 4.5 (where the mouse is pointing), Toolbars has a right arrow displayed right next to it. This denotes that there is a cascading menu under Toolbars.

Fig. 4.5
Returning to **T**oolbars from the cascaded menu, you see the right arrow right next to **T**oolbars, denoting that it has a cascading menu beneath it.

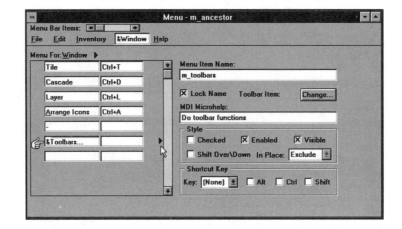

Tip
You can add a shortcut key before defining it as a cascading menu, but the key will not function. You cannot define it as cascading and then add a shortcut key.

Previewing Your Menu

You can preview your menu while you're working on it or after you're finished by clicking on **D**esign, Previe**w** (see fig. 4.6). You can check out your work, as seen in figure 4.7.

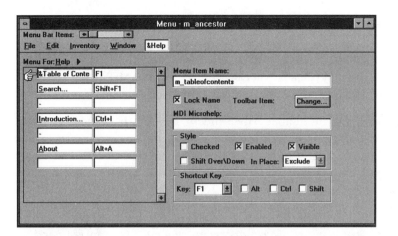

Fig. 4.6
To preview your menu, click on **D**esign Previe**w**, or press Ctrl+W.

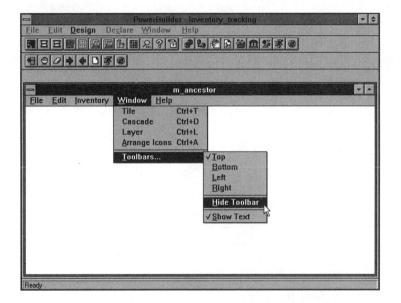

Fig. 4.7
A cascading menu appears in the menu preview.

Tip
The MicroHelp and shortcut keys are not implemented in a preview. They will show when the program is run.

Implementing Menu Inheritance and Toolbars

Like windows, menus can be inherited from other menus and changed some-what. This is especially useful for menus because every menu in a system is usually similar to every other menu in the system. Having one parent menu allows the developer to go to just one place to find the code for all the menus.

◄ See "Implement-ing Window Inheritance," p. 96

Using Toolbars and Inheritance

Menu inheritance and toolbars are discussed together because you will be using a toolbar ancestor menu that inherits from m_ancestor. A *toolbar* is a set of icons that (usually) appear at the top of your MDI Frame window. In PowerBuilder, these toolbars correspond to menu entries.

Similar to the PowerBuilder environment, an MDI application can have two toolbars—one toolbar for the frame window and one for the sheet window. All menus in the Inventory Tracking system are inherited from m_ancestor. If you use a toolbar with the MDI frame menu, you unnecessarily duplicate your toolbar icons.

Here comes the confusing part. Because you don't want to duplicate your toolbar icons, two ancestors are implemented—m_ancestor and m_ancestor_toolbar. The frame menu will inherit from m_ancestor; the sheet menus (or system menus) will inherit from m_ancestor_toolbar. Actually, m_ancestor_toolbar is inherited from m_ancestor, thereby making m_ancestor the "grandparent" of the system menus. This is shown graphically in figure 4.8.

Fig. 4.8
The system menus get all the benefits of the m_toolbar_ancestor, as well as the m_ancestor through inheritance.

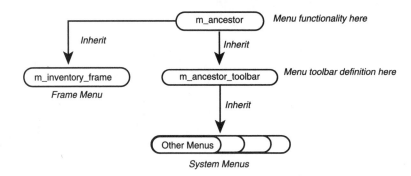

Implementing Inheritance

To inherit a new menu from an existing menu, click on the Menu icon to pull up the Select Menu dialog box, as shown in figure 4.1, and click on Inherit.

Note

You don't need to choose an existing menu in the Select Menu dialog box before clicking on Inherit. The menu you inherit from is chosen from the Inherit From Menu dialog box, shown in figure 4.9.

Clicking on the Inherit button pulls up the Inherit From Menu dialog box, shown in figure 4.9. Choose the PBL and the menu you wish to inherit from. When you've made your choice, click on OK.

Fig. 4.9
The Inherit From Menu dialog box is used to choose which menu you're inheriting from.

Now you're in the menu painter again. Notice on the title bar that the menu is inherited from m_ancestor. Also notice that this menu seems to be a copy of m_ancestor. Inheritance fills up the new menu with the entries in m_ancestor, but any future changes to m_ancestor will automatically be reflected in this menu.

Making a Toolbar

Now you need to add a toolbar by assigning pictures to each menu item you want displayed on the toolbar. On the menu painter, click on the Change button (refer to fig. 4.6), which pulls up the Toolbar Item dialog box, shown in figure 4.10. This dialog box lets you define your toolbar icons. Click on Change Picture to add an icon to the toolbar.

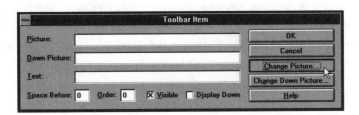

Fig. 4.10
In the Toolbar Item dialog box, you can enter information about your toolbar.

Now, the Select Toolbar Item Picture dialog box (see fig. 4.11) is pulled up. Choose the picture you want on your toolbar, and click on OK. You return to the Toolbar Item dialog box.

You can also define a down picture in the Toolbar Item dialog box (your toolbar icons change pictures while they are pressed down). Adding or changing your down picture also pulls up the Select Toolbar Item Picture dialog box (see fig. 4.11). Once more, pick the picture you want displayed when your toolbar icon is pressed down, and click on OK.

Fig. 4.11
The Select Toolbar Item Picture dialog box allows you to select a toolbar picture for a menu item.

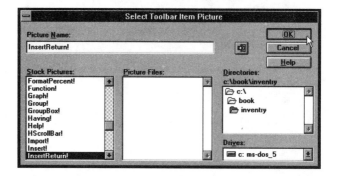

Now you are back in the Toolbar Item dialog box. Type in some text in the **T**ext area, which will be displayed on the bottom of your toolbar icon. When you are finished, click on OK.

Caution

Don't type too much text in the Toolbar Item dialog box. Large amounts of text in a toolbar icon won't fit on the icon during run time and will be truncated. (Eleven characters should be the maximum for a toolbar icon.)

Tip
Similar to the menu bar, you can use an ampersand (&) before a letter on the toolbar to underline the letter that corresponds to the hot key.

Note

You can use the **S**pace Before to place space holder before your icon if the toolbar text is turned off. You can also control the order of your icons so that the ones you want to appear first do so by using the **O**rder control.

Now you return to the menu painter. This time, the toolbar picture appears on the menu painter (see fig. 4.12).

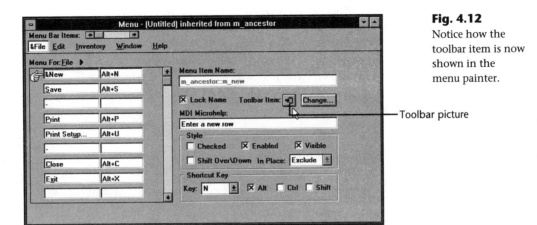

Fig. 4.12
Notice how the toolbar item is now shown in the menu painter.

—Toolbar picture

TrackNote

Repeat the process of selecting toolbars for all items that will have an icon. Table 4.2 lists the pictures that were selected for the Inventory Tracking system.

You are now finished with this menu; it will be the ancestor to all system menus. When exiting the menu painter, save this menu as **m_ancestor_toolbar,** as seen in figure 4.13. Be sure to save it in the ancestor PBL.

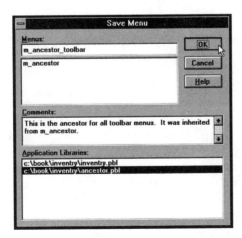

Fig. 4.13
You have created the m_ancestor_toolbar—your second ancestor menu.

Inheriting Your Frame Menu

Remember that you only wanted one toolbar appearing at the top of the frame window. To do this, each sheet within a frame has a specialized menu with a toolbar, but a frame that contains multiple sheets has a specialized menu without a toolbar. Hence, the menu for the w_inventory_frame window inherits from m_ancestor; the system menus on each sheet inherit from m_toolbar_ancestor.

Click on the Menu icon to create a new menu, and click Inherit to open the Inherit From Menu dialog box. Choose the ancestor.pbl and m_ancestor, and click on OK (refer to fig. 4.9). Now you are in the menu painter with a new menu inherited from m_ancestor, as shown in figure 4.14.

The frame menu will be active only when no sheets with menus are open. You aren't allowed to delete ancestor members from your inherited menu. To suppress and hide options that make no sense from the frame, deselect the Enabled and Visible options, as shown in figure 4.14.

Fig. 4.14
Disabling and making invisible are good ways to customize your inherited menu.

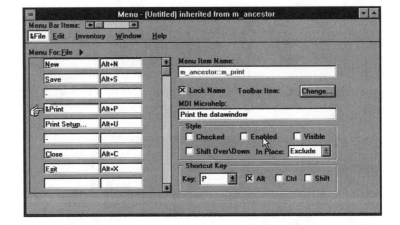

For the new inventory frame, you only need **C**lose and **E**xit (under **F**ile). Because you can't cut, copy, or paste anything from here, you can't inherit or delete from here, and you can't undo anything from here, the entire **E**dit menu bar selection has been disabled and made invisible. Because no sheet windows are open, there is no need for sheet window manipulation, so the entire **W**indow menu bar selection has been disabled and made invisible. The rest of the options will stay. After you're done disabling options you don't want, save this menu as **m_inventory_frame** (in the inventory.pbl).

Inheriting a System Menu

Follow the same process, as shown in figures 4.10 and 4.11, to make each sheet menu that is within the inventory frame. For these, however, inherit from m_toolbar_ancestor instead of m_ancestor, as before.

For each sheet, the entire menu will stay except for the menu option, which calls up the sheet. (How can you pull up your sheet if it already has been pulled up?) In w_item's case, w_item's menu will be identical to m_toolbar_ancestor, except that there will be no Ite&m Entry option under **I**nventory. Disable the entry and make it invisible, as seen in figure 4.14.

Unlike previous inheritance, you must also make the toolbar item invisible if you want to avoid displaying a toolbar icon for your disabled menu option. To disable a toolbar icon, click on Change in the menu painter, which pulls up the Toolbar Item dialog box (refer to fig. 4.10). Now, however, you see m_toolbar_ancestor's default options for the toolbar item. Deselect **V**isible and save this menu as **m_item** in inventory.pbl.

Table 4.2 lists the attributes for the m_ancestor and m_ancestor_toolbar menus.

TrackNote

For those of you following along on your computer, table 4.2 lists all menu bar items and attributes in the Inventory Tracking system.

Table 4.2 Inventory Tracking Menu Bar Items and Attributes

Menu Bar Item	Option Name	Menu Item Name	Picture*	Toolbar Text*	Shortcut Key
&File		m_file			Alt+F
	&New**	m_new	CheckIn!	&New	Alt+N
	&Save	m_save	Custom008!	&Save	Alt+S
	-	m_-			
	&Print	m_print	Print!	&Print	Alt+P
	Print Set&up	m_printsetup	Custom074!	Print Set&up	Alt+U
	-	m_-1			
	&Close	m_close	Custom041!	&Close	Alt+C
	E&xit	m_exit	Exit!	E&xit	Alt+X
&Edit		m_edit			Alt+E
	&Undo	m_undo			Ctrl+Z
	-	m_-2			
	&Cut	m_cut			Ctrl+X
	C&opy	m_copy			Ctrl+C

(continues)

Menu Bar Item	Option Name	Menu Item Name	Picture*	Toolbar Text*	Shortcut Key
	&Paste	m_paste			Ctrl+V
	-	m_-3			
	&Insert	m_insert	Insert!	&INSert	Alt+Ins
	&Delete	m_delete	Clear!	&DELete	Alt+Del
&Inventory		m_inventory			Alt+I
	Ite&m Entry	m_itementry	UserObject!	Ite&m	Alt+M
	Cust&omer Entry	m_customerentry	Picture!	Cust&omer	Alt+O
	Supp&lier Entry	m_supplierentry	CreateRun time!	Supp&lier	Alt+L
	In&voice Entry	m_invoiceentry	ScriptYes!	In&voice	Alt+V
	Wa&rehouse Entry	m_warehouseentry	Structure!	Wa&rehouse	Alt+R
&Window		m_window			Alt+W
	&Tile	m_tile			Ctrl+T
	&Cascade	m_cascade			Ctrl+D
	&Layer	m_layer			Ctrl+L
	&Arrange Icons	m_arrangeicons			Ctrl+A
	-	m_-5			
	&Toolbars...	m_toolbars			Alt+T
	&Top	m_top			
	&Bottom	m_bottom			
	&Left	m_left			
	&Right	m_right			
	-	m_-4			
	&Hide Toolbar	m_hidetoolbar			
	-	m_-6			
	&Show Text	m_showtext			
&Help		m_help			Alt+H
	&Table of Contents	m_tableofcontents	Help!		Help (F1)
	&Search...	m_search			Shift+F1
	-	m_-7			
	&Introduction	m_introduction			Ctrl+I
	-	m_-8			
	&About	m_about			Alt+A

* *m_ancestor_toolbar only*
***New uses InsertReturn! as a drop-down picture. There are no other drop-down pictures defined.*

Associating a Menu with a Window

◀ See "Defining Window Type," p. 78

You've completed the first step of forming your menus; now you need to attach them to your windows. This way, every time you switch sheets, the menu and toolbar will automatically switch.

Attaching Your Menu to a Window

To attach a menu to a window, open the window (w_inventory_frame) in the window painter. Double-click on the Window; the Window Style dialog box appears. Choose your menu from the drop-down list, as shown in figure 4.15. Attach the inventory frame menu (m_inventory_frame) to the inventory frame window (w_inventory_frame). After you choose the appropriate menu, save your choices and exit the window painter. Repeat this process for the item menu (m_item) and the item window (w_item).

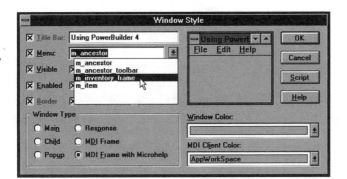

Fig. 4.15
You can hook a menu to a window by using the Window Style dialog box.

TrackNote

Perform the same process with other menus (for example, m_customer, m_supplier, and m_invoice). Then attach m_customer, m_supplier, m_warehouse, and m_invoice to w_customer, w_supplier, w_warehouse, and w_invoice, as you did with m_item and w_item.

Running Your Application with a Toolbar

Click on the Run icon on the PowerBar to run your application (see fig. 4.16). Look at the improvements you made. In figure 4.16, you can see the Item Entry dialog box activate with a set of toolbar icons at the top of the frame.

Listing Open MDI Sheets

In figure 4.17, notice that all your open sheet windows are listed. (In this case, Item Entry is currently the only open sheet.) With an MDI application, PowerBuilder appends the name of the open sheets to the next-to-last menu item in the menu bar. A check mark appears next to the current active sheet. You can control which menu option the open sheets appear under by using the OpenSheet command (discussed in Chapter 3).

◀ See "Opening a Window Sheet," p. 98

Fig. 4.16
When running
your program, the
toolbar(s) display
at the top of the
frame window.

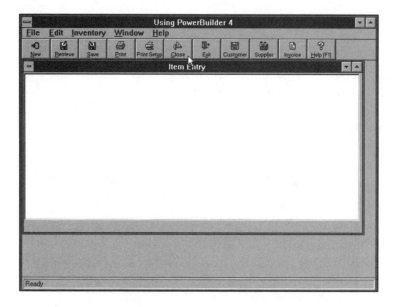

Fig. 4.17
Using the
OpenSheet
command, you
can control where
the open sheet
windows are
displayed.

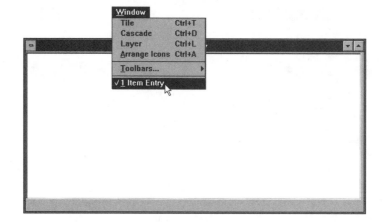

Viewing the Frame Menu

▶ See "Enumer-
ated Data Type
Quick Refer-
ence," p. 509

When you click on the **C**lose icon (see fig. 4.16), you end up with just the
inventory frame showing with no sheets open. Notice in figure 4.18 how the
menu is scaled down to allow only those choices that made sense for the
frame window to show. As you can see, there aren't as many functions available for just the frame window.

Syntax-at-a-Glance

OpenSheet(sheet {, window_name}, frame,{position{, arrangeopen}})

OpenSheet opens a sheet window within a frame.

- *sheet* is the window name of the sheet.

- *windowname* is a string containing the name of the window type you want opened. For our purposes, window_name is not needed.

- *frame* is the window name of the MDI frame.

- *position* is the menu item in which all open sheets are displayed. If omitted, PowerBuilder lists open sheets in the next-to-last menu bar item.

- *arrangeopen* is a PowerBuilder enumerated data type that tells the way you want the sheet opened. Valid values are as follows:

    Cascaded! Cascade the sheet when it is opened.

    Layered! Layer the sheet when it is opened.

    Original! Open the sheet in its original size and cascade it

    Note the exclamations on the arrangeopen parameter. All PowerBuilder enumerated data types end in an exclamation point.

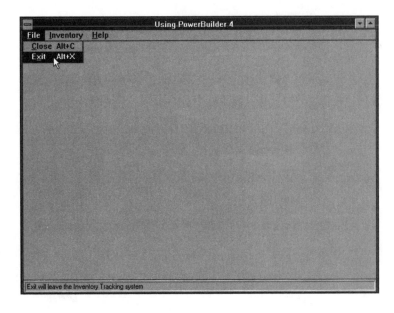

Fig. 4.18
With all sheet windows closed, the menu reverts to the frame menu.

From Here...

From this chapter, you should have learned how to create, edit, and display menus. You also examined menu inheritance and toolbars. If you need to review what was already discussed, or you want to discuss menus further, refer to the following chapters:

- Chapter 1, "Introducing PowerBuilder," is a must for beginners and introduces menus and menu programming.

- Chapter 5, "Using Events, Functions, and the PowerScript Language," teaches you how to implement PowerScript within your events. Menu programming is covered extensively.

- *PowerBuilder User's Guide*, Chapter 9, "Working with Menus."

Part II

Using PowerScript

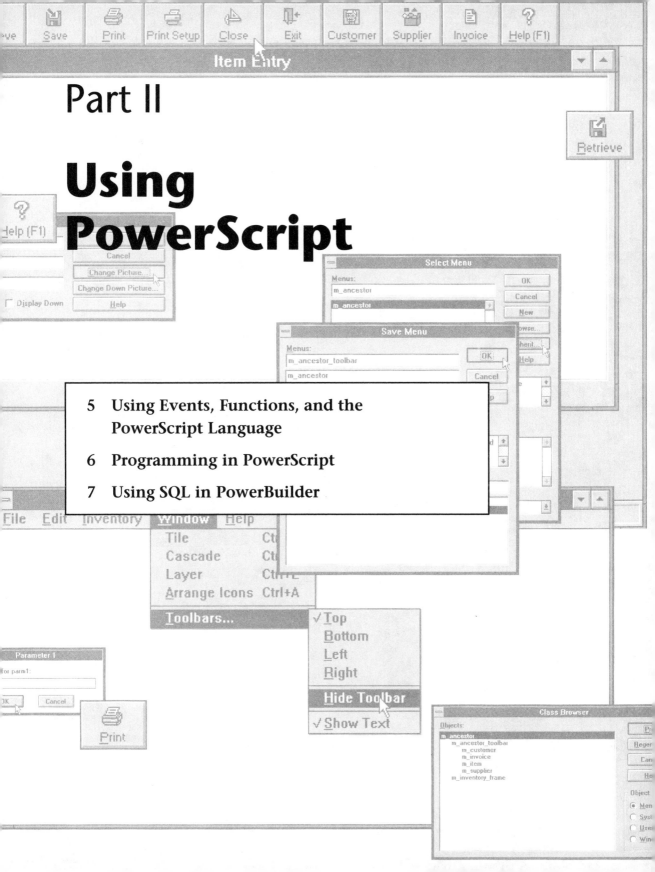

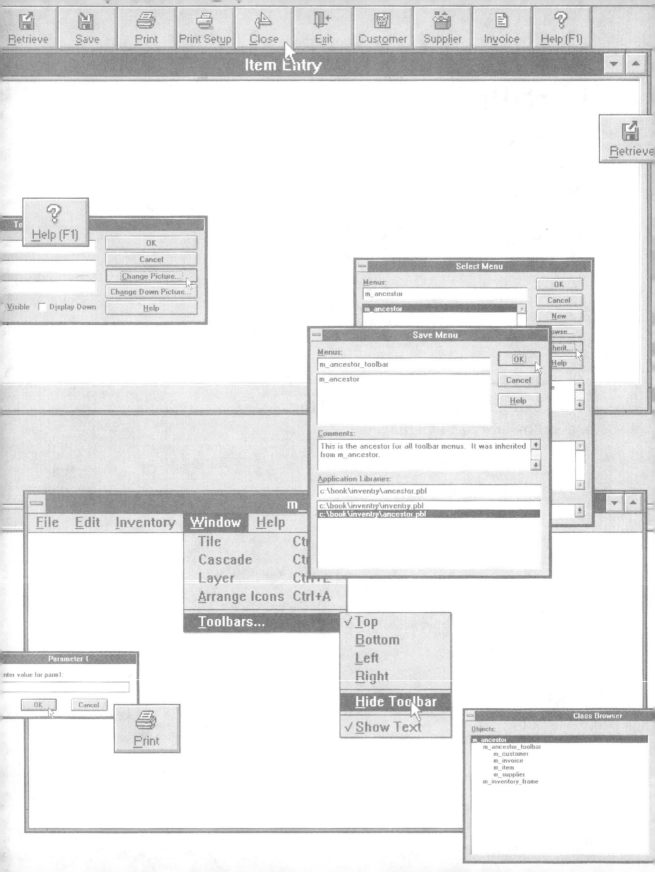

Chapter 5

Using Events, Functions, and the PowerScript Language

As the programming language of PowerBuilder, PowerScript controls the flow of a program, updates databases, displays information and error messages, and ends the program.

It's important that the PowerBuilder developer have a good working knowledge of PowerScript. In this chapter, you learn how to:

- Use the PowerBuilder script painter

- Have a complete understanding of events

- Use the PowerScript variable types

- Understand structures, objects, and controls and how to access them

- Understand variable scope

Understanding Events

Event programming is a relatively new concept in software development. Traditional programming is sequential in nature—every function can be traced to a previous statement. However, in the real world, most business functions are event-driven instead of sequential.

Event-driven functions are functions that don't follow a logical sequence. Rather, certain events cause the functions to be executed. (For example, you order new supplies when your inventory is low, you play solitaire when you double-click on the solitaire icon, and so on.) Consequently, software development was difficult because programmers tried to map the event-driven world onto their sequential programs.

PowerBuilder codes for events. For example, if you click on an icon, certain PowerScript in an event is executed. If a window loses focus (a new window pops up), other PowerScript in another event is executed. Event programming is better suited to the way an end user will use your application. Event programming is one of the many strengths of PowerBuilder.

Entering the PowerBuilder Script Painter

A PowerBuilder *object* is an entity you develop usually by using the PowerBar. Windows, menus, DataWindows, and applications are all examples of objects.

PowerBuilder *controls* are constructs that attach to objects. Command buttons, pictures, and DataWindows are all examples of controls.

> **Note**
>
> There is a difference between DataWindow objects and DataWindow controls. It is discussed in Chapter 8, "Creating DataWindows."

▶ See "Associating Data-Window Controls with a DataWindow Object," p. 231

Each control and each object can have PowerScript (also called script). To code script for an object or control, follow these steps:

1. Click the Script icon. (Every painter, except the library painter and the database painter, has a script icon.)

2. Choose the window that needs PowerScript in its events. In this case, start with the w_ancestor window.

3. Click on the Window icon, click on ancestor.pbl, and pull up w_datawindow_ancestor.

4. Now click on the Script icon to pull up the script painter, as shown in figure 5.1.

5. Now you can type any PowerScript commands you want for the open event of w_datawindow_ancestor.

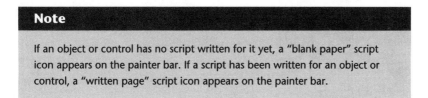

> **Note**
>
> If an object or control has no script written for it yet, a "blank paper" script icon appears on the painter bar. If a script has been written for an object or control, a "written page" script icon appears on the painter bar.

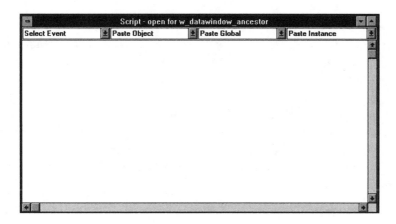

Fig. 5.1
The script painter appears every time you click on the Script icon.

Using the Event List Box

Each object and control has many different events for which you can code. By clicking on Select Event in the upper left corner of the painter window (see fig. 5.2), you see the event list box. Using the event list box, you select which event you want to code for that window (open, close, activate, and so on).

Using PowerScript

II

Fig. 5.2

The script painter automatically opens for the first time in the open event.

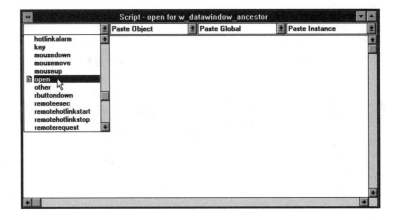

Whenever the event you code for is triggered, the script you've written for that event is executed. This is vastly different from traditional programming techniques, in which code always has to be written to check for events as well as react to the event.

Implementing User-Defined Events

PowerBuilder does an excellent job predetermining what events you'll need to code for. However, you may need to define your own events if a special event is needed that PowerBuilder has not provided for. To define your own events, follow these steps:

1. On the menu bar, open the Declare menu and choose User Events, as shown in figure 5.3. The Events dialog box appears.

2. Enter a unique event name and a unique event ID from the Paste Event ID: data list. As you can see in figure 5.4, three events were added to your normal event list: print, save, and retrieve.

3. After you're done adding events, click on OK to save it and return to your painter.

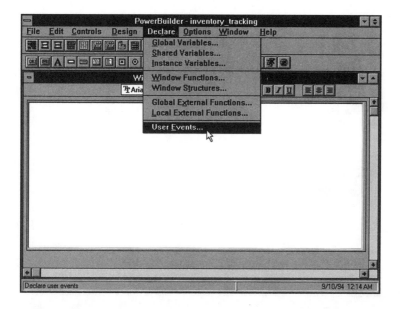

Fig. 5.3
To declare a user event, open Declare and choose User **E**vents.

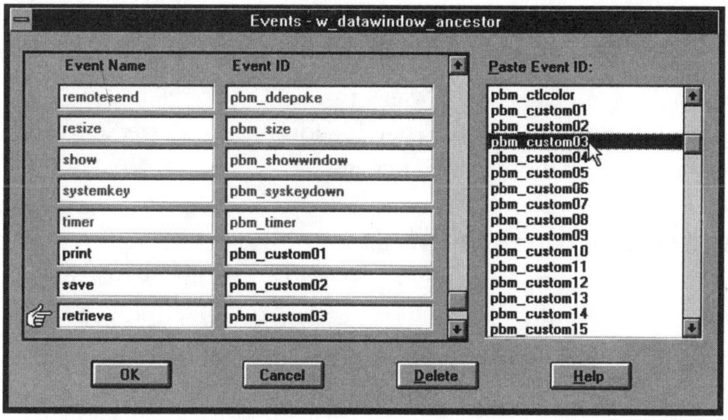

Fig. 5.4
In the Events dialog box, you can add customized events.

II

Using PowerScript

Now when the event list box displays in the painter, you can see the new events at the bottom, as shown in figure 5.5.

Fig. 5.5
Any new events are listed at the bottom of the event list box.

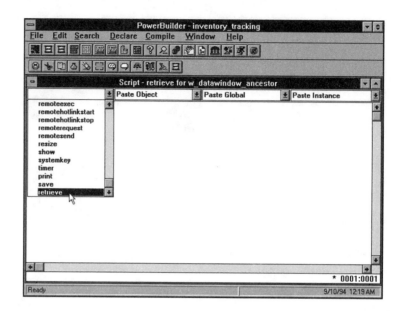

Discussing the Scripting Language

Tip
In this example, user events are added to the window; you can add them to any window or window control by using this method.

You saw some examples of the PowerScript when you opened w_inventory_frame and w_item. There's a lot more to PowerScript, however—it is a fully functional language.

PowerScript Fundamentals

It seems that every computer language treats comments, white space, and multiline statements differently. Before coding PowerScript, you need to know some fundamental information about the language that will resolve these issues.

Comments

Comments are an important part of any development. Comments are not executed or compiled, but serve as notes to future developers about what a script is doing, who wrote a script, why a script is needed, and so on. Well-commented PowerScript will save hours (or longer!) in future maintenance.

A double slash (//) makes the rest of the line comments. Enclosing a set of text (even several lines) in /* and */ also works well for commenting.

In the following example, notice how you can use a // to comment a line after a command:

```
a = b        // This part after the double slash is a comment
```

Now you can see how a comment can span several lines (without the need for continuation characters) by using /* and */ to enclose the comment:

```
/*  This is
also a long series
of contiguous comments */
```

Continuation Character

Sometimes a line goes off the window, which can make debugging, printing, or viewing the PowerScript difficult. You can type in the continuation character **&** (ampersand) at the end of the line to tell PowerBuilder to continue on to the next line.

The following example uses the continuation character:

```
string Gaddress

Gaddress = "Four score and seven years ago our fathers brought" &
      + " forth, upon this continent, a new nation, conceived in" &
      + " Liberty, and dedicated to the proposition that all men" &
      + " are created equal...."
```

White Space

White space, or spaces between variables, constants, and commands, is ignored in PowerScript except inside a string variable. You can put as many spaces between commands as you like.

Using Variables

As with any language, PowerScript allows you to use variables to hold values. Some of these variables you declare; others are declared for you by PowerBuilder.

Data Types

Every variable has a *data type*, which tells the developer what kind of information is stored in the variable, and tells PowerBuilder the amount of storage to set aside and how to handle the variable. The following is syntax for a variable declaration:

```
data type variable_name
```

Tip

Remember, the Enter key (a carriage return) is not considered white space. Carriage returns are only ignored when inside of comments.

For example, to declare the integer loop_counter, you use the following statement:

```
int loop_counter
```

Table 5.1 lists commonly used data types, their ranges, and a short comment on their uses.

Table 5.1	Commonly Used Data Types	
Data Type	**Range**	**Comments**
Boolean	TRUE or FALSE	Often used as a return value from a function.
Character	Single Character	Can be abbreviated as char.
Date	01-01-1900 through 12-31-3000	Date is in mm-dd-yyyy format. Blanks are not allowed.
DateTime	01-01-1900 00:00:00:0000 23:59:59:9999	Usually used as a database timestamp holder.
Decimal	Up to 18 digits (all significant)	The decimal point can occur anywhere within the 18 digits. The sign and decimal point are not counted as digits. Can be abbreviated as dec.
Integer	-32,768 through 32,767	Can be abbreviated as int.
Long	-2,147,483,648 through 2,147,483,647	
String	Up to 60,000 characters	All ASCII characters.
Time	00:00:00:0000 - 23:59:59:9999	Time is incremented in milliseconds.

Some data types are not commonly used, but PowerBuilder gives you access to them. These data types are listed in table 5.2.

Table 5.2 Data Types Not Commonly Used

Data Type	Range	Comments
Blob		Unbound data type that stands for binary large object. Usually used to hold pictures in a database.
Double	2.23E-308 through 1.78E+308 —15 digits of precision	
DragObject		Contains the dragged object type. Values include all dragable objects with controls (but no drawing objects).
Object		Contains the enumerated type of a PowerBuilder object. Values include all windows and controls.
PowerObject		Any PowerBuilder object including structures. Usually used with the OpenWithParm commands.
Real	1.18E-38 to 3.40E+38 — 6 digits of precision	
UnsignedInteger	0 through 65,535	Can be abbreviated as unsignedint or uint.
UnsignedLong	0 through 4,294,967,295	Can be abbreviated as ulong.

Caution

All number data types include ranges for that data type. Also, some number data types include digits of precision (or significant digits). If you do a calculation that loses significant digits, PowerBuilder won't tell you, so be careful!

Also, if you exceed the data type's range, rollover occurs. *Rollover* happens when a number exceeds one range and starts over at the other side of the range. For example, if you stored 32,766 in an integer and added five, the integer would contain –32,765 in the field. (In other words, you rolled over by four.) Now you have a corrupt value in your integer. No error message will occur if this happens.

Variable Scope

In old languages, such as COBOL and BASIC, every variable could be accessed everywhere in the application. Now, most languages support the concept of variable *scope*. Scope describes where a variable can be used.

The concept of *variable scope* is important. Scope allows one user to write a function or event without writing over the variables in another area of the application, even if the variables have the same name. There are four levels of scope in PowerBuilder.

Local Scope. *Local scope variables* (or just local variables) are variables you declare inside your script. Most user-defined variables you use are local variables, which exist only inside the event or function in which they are declared.

For example, you can declare int loop_counter in the window open event and also declare int loop_counter in the window close event. Now you have two versions of loop_counter; each is separate from the other. If you increment loop_counter in the open event, loop_counter in the close event is not affected.

Furthermore, no other event or function has access to the loop_counter variables. For instance, you can't access either loop_counter variable from the activate event.

Troubleshooting

I set a local variable in a script, but every time I go back into the script, the value is reset to 0 or "". What can I do?

Local variables go out of scope when their function or event is finished. When a variable goes out of scope, no function or event has access to it any more, and the memory where the variable was stored is freed up for other functions and variables to use. If you re-enter the event or function later, all local variables will be reset.

If you want to keep a value in a script, try using an instance, shared, or global variable.

Instance Scope. *Instance variables* are variables that the entire object has access to. If you declare a variable to be an instance variable of an object, then every event, function, or control of that object has access to the variable.

To declare an instance variable, open **D**eclare and choose **I**nstance Variables.

Type in your instance variable's data type and name, as shown in figure 5.6. When you're finished, click on OK.

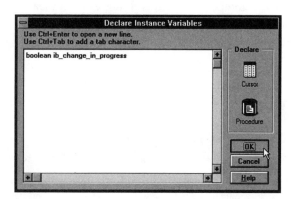

Fig. 5.6
In the Declare Instance Variables dialog box, you declare the instance variable used in your object.

Instance variables go out of scope when their control is closed, and get reset if the control is reopened.

Shared Scope. With an MDI application, you can open more than one window of the same type. (In other words, two w_item windows can be open at the same time.) These multiple versions of the same window are called *instances* of that window. *Shared variables* are variables that are allowed to be shared by every event, function, and control of every instance of an object.

To declare a shared variable, open **D**eclare and choose **S**hared Variables. Now type in your shared variables.

Global Scope. *Global variables* are accessed by the entire application. They never go out of scope until the application is closed.

You should not use global variables if another variable type will do. Using a lot of global variables violates the principle of encapsulation. In other words, if you set a global variable in an event, another event can reset it without your event knowing it.

To declare a global variable, open **D**eclare and choose **G**lobal Variables. Now type in your global variables.

▶ See "Object Functions," p. 555

Encapsulation. Encapsulation is a term used often in object-oriented programming. When a function or event is *encapsulated*, it means that it stands alone. The encapsulated function can't have its variables changed from outside itself. The encapsulated function also does not access variables outside of itself.

The beautiful part of encapsulation is that a function, object, or control can be used in many systems *without modification*! You should keep encapsulation in mind while you develop any system.

Caution

Local, instance, shared, and global variables can all share the same name. However, if you access a variable that shares its name with a variable of another scope, you may not be able to anticipate the results.

To search for variables, PowerBuilder follows this series of procedures:

1. First, PowerBuilder looks for a local variable with the name you're using.

2. If PowerBuilder can't find a local variable, it searches for a shared variable with the name you're using.

3. If PowerBuilder can't find a local or shared variable, it searches for a global variable with the name you're using.

4. Finally, if PowerBuilder can't find any other variable scope with the name you're using, it searches for an instance variable with the same name.

This is different than the variable search path that most languages (such as C++ and Smalltalk) use, so be careful! By the way, none of this needs to concern you if you use the naming conventions outlined in Appendix A.

Encapsulation is a matter of degrees. To encapsulate a system as much as possible, follow these tips:

- All your variable declarations should be local, if possible, because this is the best way to encapsulate your data from corruption by other functions and events. At this highest level of encapsulation, a function or event can be placed in any object and still work properly.

- If a local variable won't work because you need to preserve a value or access the variable from other areas in your object, try an instance variable or (if that won't work) a shared variable. In PowerBuilder, other events and functions can access your instance and shared variables, so any degree of protection from other developers is lost. However, many developers will resist setting an instance or shared variable in a different object. At this level of encapsulation, a window, menu, or user object can be moved to another system and still function properly.

- If no other course of action is possible, try a global variable. Global variables can be altered or redefined by any object or function in an application, so you have to assume that your global variable can be changed at any time. At this level of encapsulation, when you copy any script or object to another application, you must also copy the global variable to the new area.

- The very lowest form of encapsulation is when an object accesses one instance or shared variable of another object. Not only can this set a variable "owned" by another object, but now your objects must travel together. At this level, reusability is lost.

> **Note**
>
> If you need to set an instance variable in another object, try writing a function or user defined event in one object for the other object to access. For example, instead of setting object B's variable from object A like this:
>
> ```
> B.variable = NEW_VALUE          // Don't set variables this way
> ```
>
> try instead writing a function inside object B to set the variable and access it from object A by passing the NEW_VALUE like this:
>
> ```
> B.set_variable(NEW_VALUE)        // Set variables this way
> ```
>
> This way, although these two functions still must travel together, you at least leave object B in full control of its own variables. Any future maintenance to B will not involve looking at A.

▶ See "Implementing User Defined Functions," p. 171

Troubleshooting

I set a variable and it gets reset somehow but is NOT going out of scope. How does that happen?

Your variable probably is declared as an instance, shared, or global variable, and another script or function that you invoke in the middle of your function is resetting your variable.

When you use a variable type that another script can access, you violate the principle of encapsulation.

Using Objects and Controls

Often, you'll need to refer to one control from within another control. (For example, the open event of the application object issued a command to open the wf_ancestor_frame window object.) You also need to be able to tell one object or control to perform a function, or to set an attribute of one object or control from within another object or control.

Every control and object has *attributes*, or variables that control the functionality and appearance of an object or control. You access the attributes of an object or control with dot notation:

```
control.attribute
object.attribute
```

Tip

TRUE and FALSE are Boolean constants provided by PowerBuilder to set or test other Boolean variables.

Setting Attributes with Dot Notation. To set an attribute, you simply refer to the control or object the attribute is in, followed by a *dot* (period) and the attribute name. For example, most objects and controls have a Boolean attribute called *visible* that sees whether the object or control can be seen on the screen. To set this for your DataWindow dw_data in the w_item window, use the following notation:

```
w_item.dw_data.visible = FALSE
```

Through inheritance, you have many DataWindows called dw_data. w_item tells which window dw_data is in. In this case, the entire name (also called the *fully qualified* name) of the control is *w_item.dw_data*. The visible attribute is set to FALSE using this statement, which makes the DataWindow invisible.

You can also check to see if something is visible by using the following if statement:

```
        if w_item.dw_data.visible then
{perform some function}
        end if
```

Visible

Visible is an attribute on most objects and controls. It determines and describes whether or not a control or object can be seen.

```
If condition-1
    command-set-1
ElseIf condition-2
    command-set-2
ElseIf condition-3
    command-set-3
  .
  .
  .
Else
    command-set-n
End If
```

The If tests a condition. If the condition is true, a command or set of commands is executed. ElseIf is always accompanied by an If. ElseIf tests a condition if all previous If and ElseIf conditions have failed. If the tested condition is true, a command set is executed. Else executes a command set if all previous If and ElseIf conditions have tested false. Finally, End If ends an If statement.

Executing a Function with Dot Notation. You also use the dot notation to execute functions. Every object and control has a set of functions that can run within it. Some functions (such as open for opening a window) don't need to be qualified with an object or control name.

The Hide function is shared by most controls and objects, and it sets the visible attribute. To hide the dw_data DataWindow by using a function instead of an attribute, use the following function:

```
w_item.dw_data.hide()
```

II

Using PowerScript

Note

Using a function to set another object's attributes is considered more object-oriented than actually setting the attribute. For instance,

```
w_item.dw_data.visible = FALSE          // Not very encapsulated
```

is not as encapsulated as

```
w_item.dw_data.hide()                   // More encapsulated
```

The idea behind encapsulation is to let each object set its own variables.

Syntax-at-a-Glance

```
objectname.Hide()
objectname.Show()
```

Hide() makes a control or object referred to by objectname invisible. Show() makes an object visible again.

Using Dot Notation with Menus. Menus have a unique structure. To access a menu item, you need to give the menu name, followed by the tree structure of the menu. For instance, to use the TriggerEvent function to make PowerBuilder "pretend" that the user opened the **W**indow menu and chose Display, **T**ile in the m_item menu, you use the following syntax:

```
m_item.m_window.m_display.m_tile.TriggerEvent(Clicked!)
```

Syntax-at-a-Glance

```
objectname.TriggerEvent(PowerBuilder enumerated variable)
objectname.TriggerEvent(event_name_string)
```

You can use the TriggerEvent function in PowerBuilder to force PowerBuilder to execute that event. TriggerEvent uses one argument. That argument can either be a string containing the event name or a PowerBuilder enumerated data type describing the event.

Syntax-at-a-Glance

Clicked!

Clicked! is an enumerated data type describing a clicked event.

Tip
For more information, refer to Chapter 22, "Enumerated Data Types Quick Reference."

Using Structures

Structures are used to create your own data type. Structures contain several different related variables of different types and group them under a single name. Structures allow you to move data around and refer to the data under a single name instead of using several names.

Creating a Structure. To create a structure, follow these steps:

1. Click on the Struct icon. This will pull up the Select Structure window shown in figure 5.7.

2. Click on New to start creating a new structure. The New Structure dialog box appears (see fig. 5.8).

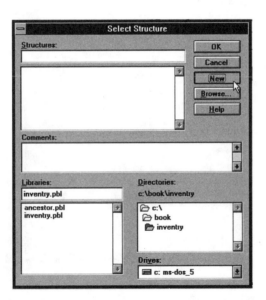

Fig. 5.7
By clicking on the Struct icon, you pull up the Select Structure window. Click on New to start a new structure.

II

Using PowerScript

Fig. 5.8

Using the New Structure dialog box, you can define your structure by typing in structure variable names and their data types.

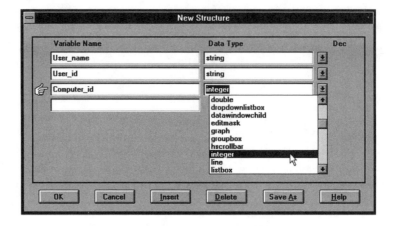

3. Type in your variable names and data types. When you're finished, click on OK.

4. After you define your structure, PowerBuilder asks if you want to save your work (see fig. 5.9). Pick a PBL (PowerBuilder Library), type in a name, and click on OK.

Fig. 5.9

After you're done defining your structure, the Save Structure dialog box allows you to save your work in a PBL.

Updating a Structure. To update your structure, follow these steps:

1. Click on the Struct icon and pull up the Select Structure dialog box.

2. Now click on the PBL containing the structure you want to edit, click on the structure, and then click on OK. The Modify Structure dialog box appears (see fig. 5.10).

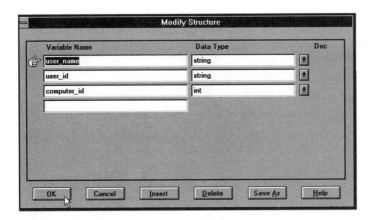

Fig. 5.10
You can edit an existing structure using the Modify Structure dialog box.

3. Make any adjustments to the variable name or data type, and delete or insert any fields you need. When you're finished, click on OK.

Developing Local Structures. So far, the structures that have been discussed are global structures, which, like global variables, can be used by any event or function in your application.

PowerBuilder also allows you to declare *local structures,* which can only be accessed in the object where they were created.

To create a local structure, pull up one of your windows, open Declare and choose Window Structures.

This pulls up the Select Structure in Window dialog box (seen in fig. 5.11). This dialog box is identical in function to the Select Structure dialog box, except that it only selects or creates local structures.

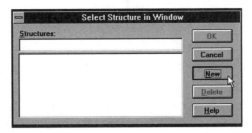

Fig. 5.11
The Select Structure in Window dialog box appears if you want to modify or create a local window structure.

II

Using PowerScript

Depending on whether you choose to edit an existing structure or create a new structure, you see either the New Structure dialog box or the Modify Structure dialog box. When you're finished creating a new structure, the Save Structure in Window dialog box appears, as seen in figure 5.12, which enables you to save your local window structure.

Fig. 5.12
The Save Structure in Window dialog box allows you to save your work.

You just created a local window structure. You can also create a local structure for most PowerBuilder objects (menus, applications, and so on) by using the same technique.

Accessing a Structure. You're done creating your structure, but remember that a structure is a data type—not a variable. You still have to declare variables using your structure, and then use dot notation to access the variables within a structure. The following PowerScript code assigns values to your structure:

```
string name              // name is a variable of type string
s_login login_info       // login_info is a variable of type s_login

name = "C Wood"                    // Assign a value to name
login_info.user_name = name        // Assign user name to name
login_info.user_id = 123-45-6789   // Assign a constant to user_id

login_info.computer_id = 12  // Assign computer number to computer_id
```

Notice how you have to declare login_info, just as name is declared. After a variable is declared for the structure, you can access the structure's variables using dot notation.

> **Note**
>
> The Inventory Tracking system doesn't use any structures—although when dealing with a group of variables, there are several cases in which using structures dramatically decreases workload (for example, sorting groups of different variables or moving a group of variables).

Enumerated Data Types

Enumerated data types are constants that PowerBuilder provides which are related to certain functions and usually act as parameters or attribute values. TRUE and FALSE are examples of enumerated constants.

With the exception of TRUE and FALSE, enumerated constants end in an exclamation point (!). Clicked! is an example of an enumerated data type. All enumerated data types are listed in Chapter 22, "Enumerated Data Types Quick Reference."

Arrays

Arrays are series of indexed variables of the same data type. Think of an array as a numbered variable.

You declare an array by putting a number in brackets behind a data declaration. In figure 5.13, you see that declaring an integer sets up a single integer cell in memory. By adding [10] to the integer declaration, you now have declared 10 integers. Arrays can be accessed using the array name, followed by a bracketed number.

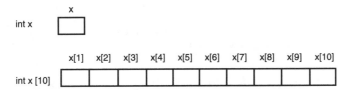

Fig. 5.13
By declaring an array, you create a group of like variables of a single data type, as opposed to a single variable.

If you use the following statements, 15 cells of x are reserved, and the number 1492 is placed in cell 5:

```
int x[15]
x[5] = 1492
```

Multi-Dimensional Arrays. *Multi-dimensional arrays* are also hard to understand. If an array declaration has more than one set of numbers following it, a multi-dimensional array has been declared.

A good example of a multi-dimensional array is a program that keeps track of bowling scores (tracking every frame of every match). Suppose, for example, you have five bowling matches per season. You can store all the bowling scores in a 5 × 10 multi-dimensional array, as shown in figure 5.14.

II

Using PowerScript

Fig. 5.14

You can see the difference in storage between single- and multi-dimension arrays.

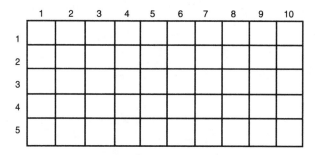

int bowling_match [10]

int bowling_season[5,10]

The following is an example of how to code such an array:

```
int bowling_season[5, 10]      // Declare a multi-dimensional array
int score = 200                // Set an average score
int match = 3                  // Declare the game counter
int frame = 7                  // Declare the frame counter
// Set the bowling array to the score for the given frame and match
bowling_season[match, frame] = score
```

This code puts a score of **200** into row 3, column 7 of the bowling season array.

Caution

You can do more than two dimensions in an array, but be careful. Nothing grabs available memory more than a huge multi-dimensional array. It can cause your Windows application to fail.

For example, suppose you want to keep bowling scores for your entire high school team for a four-year period. There are 20 members on your bowling team, and they bowl 10 frames per match, five matches a night, 50 times per year. Your four-dimensional array declaration looks like this:

```
// Declare 20 team members for 4 years, 50
// nights per year, 5 matches per night, 10
// frames per match.
int bowling_life[20, 4, 50, 5, 10]
```

Because an integer takes up two bytes, you have just declared 400,000 (2 * 20 * 4 * 50 * 5 * 10) bytes of storage with this declaration. That alone may cause Windows to send an application error.

Variable Arrays. *Variable arrays* are arrays whose size is not set upon declaration. To declare a variable array, leave the number out of the brackets when declaring your array. The size of the array is set with the first access to that array. The following code shows the use of the variable array:

```
string months[ ]                        // Setting up a variable array

// Set the upper array bound to 12 and fill it in
months[12] = "December"
```

Caution

Variable arrays aren't used much in PowerBuilder and should probably be avoided because of the way variable arrays set their upper bounds. The following code produces an error:

```
// Setting up a variable array
string months[ ]
// Set the upper array bound to 1
months[1] = "January"
// Now you exceed your array upper bound
months[2] = "February"
```

Remember, the first access to a variable array sets the upper bound. Furthermore, this error is not caught until run time.

Object Data Types (Instances)

The objects you declare are themselves a data type. These special kind of data types are called *instances* of your object (not to be confused with instance variable scope).

The main use of instance variables is to open multiple versions of the same window in an MDI frame. For instance, if you wanted to open two w_item windows, you could use the following code:

```
w_item window1        // Declare the first instance of w_item
w_item window2        // Declare the second instance of w_item

Open (window1, w_item)
Open (window2, w_item)
```

The previous syntax opens two windows. You can navigate between them by using the window list in the **W**indow menu. Also, because **C**lose (in the **F**ile menu) closes the parent window to the menu, you really don't need any special coding from here to use your windows.

The hard part of multiple windows arises when you have another set of windows coming from the multiple windows. (For instance, you open the supplier of each item.) Now you must keep track of which window was opened from where. This can get quite confusing.

You also have the problem of both windows trying to update the same database, and perhaps the same row, at the same time. The questions that arise are who gets to update and who doesn't?

Syntax-at-a-Glance

Open (window_var , window_type {, parent})

This open statement opens an instance of a window. The `window_var` is the variable name of the window. The `window_type` is a string containing the object name of the window. The parent defaults to the current window if your window is a child or pop-up window. Otherwise, it isn't needed.

Note

If you try to open a window that is already open, the window will simply appear. No new window will be opened.

TrackNote

In the Inventory Tracking system, multiple versions of the same window are not opened by using instances. It's much easier to navigate through windows if only one version of that window is open at a time. However, instances definitely have their place in MDI applications. If you are designing an MDI application, you should consider whether or not you want multiple copies of the same window open at one time.

Naming Conventions

It's important to follow naming conventions when writing your scripts, especially with instance variables, shared variables, and global variables that are not part of the script.

Do yourself and all your coworkers a favor—implement the naming conventions suggested in Appendix A, or develop your own. This saves time and trouble later during debugging.

Operators

There are four types of operators: arithmetic, string, logical, and grouping. *Arithmetic* operators are used for mathematical calculations. *Logical* operators are used for testing conditions. *String* operators perform functions on string variables. The only *grouping* operators are parentheses, which affect the order in which your operators will be executed.

Arithmetic Operators

Arithmetic operators can be divided into three categories: binary operators, unary operators, and combination operators.

Binary operators require two operators. (*Operators* are variables or constants.) The PowerBuilder binary operators are listed in table 5.3.

Table 5.3	Binary Arithmetic Operators		
Symbol	**Name**	**Example**	**Description**
^	Exponential	$a \wedge b$	Raises a to the bth power.
+	Addition	$a + b$	Adds a and b.
−	Subtraction	$a - b$	Subtracts b from a.
*	Multiplication	$a * b$	Multiplies a and b.
/	Division	a / b	Divides a by b.
=	Equals	$a = b$	Places the value of b into a.

Unary operators require one operator. The PowerBuilder unary operators are listed in table 5.4.

Table 5.4	Unary Arithmetic Operators		
Symbol	**Name**	**Example**	**Description**
-	Negative	$- a$	Symbolizes the negative value of a.
+	Positive	$+ a$	Symbolizes the positive value of a. (This is never needed.)
++	Increment	$a ++$	Increments a by one.
--	Decrement	$a --$	Decrements a by one.

II

Using PowerScript

> **Note**
>
> In PowerBuilder, the subtraction (–), unary negative (-), and decrement (--) operators must be surrounded by spaces.

C and C++ programmers will be happy to know that combination operators are included in PowerBuilder. *Combination operators* are binary operators that combine the functionality of two operators, equals and either addition or subtraction. Because combination operators are binary, they require two operators. The PowerBuilder combination operators are shown in table 5.5.

Table 5.5 Combination Operators

Symbol	Name	Example	Description
+=	Plus Equals	$a += b$	Sets a equal to $a + b$.
-=	Minus Equals	$a -= b$	Sets a equal to $a - b$.
*=	Times Equals	$a *= b$	Sets a equal to $a * b$.
/=	Divide Equals	$a /= b$	Sets a equal to a / b.
^=	Power Equals	$a ^= b$	Sets a equal to $a \wedge b$.

String Operators

The only string operator PowerBuilder uses is a plus sign (+) for concatenation. The following PowerScript shows how this is done:

```
string s1 = "Hi "
string s2 = "Mom!"
string s3
s3 = s1 + s2
```

The resulting value in s3 is "Hi Mom!"

Logical Operators

Logical operators test for a condition to be true or false. There are two types of logical operators: relational operators and conjunction operators.

Relational operators are always binary, and therefore require two operators. The PowerBuilder relational operators are seen in table 5.6.

Table 5.6   Logical Operators

Symbol	Name	Example	Description
=	Equal	$a = b$	Returns TRUE if a is equal to b.
>	Greater than	$a > b$	Returns TRUE if a is greater than b.
<	Less than	a < b	Returns TRUE if a is less than b.
>=	Greater than or equal	$a >= b$	Returns TRUE if a is greater than or equal to b.
<=	Less than or equal	$a <= b$	Returns TRUE if a is less than or equal to b.
<>	Not equal	$a <> b$	Returns TRUE if a is not equal to b.

Any relational operator that does not return TRUE returns FALSE.

Caution

In PowerBuilder, relational operators always try to evaluate both operands as numbers. However, if an operand can't be evaluated as a number, PowerBuilder treats it as text and performs a string comparison. For example, the following is evaluated as TRUE because 2 is less then 10.

```
2 < 10
```

The following statement, however, is treated as FALSE because "Paragraph 10" comes alphabetically before "Paragraph 2".

```
"Paragraph 2" < "Paragraph 10"
```

Conjunction operators have relational expressions as their operands. (*Relational expressions* are expressions using relational operators.) PowerBuilder's three conjunction operators are two binary operators, AND and OR, and one unary operator, NOT. Their functions can be seen in the truth table in table 5.7.

II

Using PowerScript

Table 5.7	Conjunction Operators			
a	**b**	**a AND b**	**a OR b**	**NOT a**
TRUE	TRUE	TRUE	TRUE	FALSE
TRUE	FALSE	FALSE	TRUE	FALSE
FALSE	TRUE	FALSE	TRUE	TRUE
FALSE	FALSE	FALSE	FALSE	TRUE

The first row can be read as "If *a* is TRUE and *b* is TRUE, then *a* AND *b* is TRUE, *a* OR *b* is TRUE, and NOT *a* is FALSE."

Precedence and Parentheses

Certain operations take precedence over each other. For instance, you may (incorrectly) think that the following equation evaluates to 27 because 5 + 4 = 9 and 9 multiplied by 3 is 27.

```
5 + 4 * 3
```

In actuality, this equation is evaluated to 17 because multiplication (*) takes precedence over addition (+). Therefore, 4 * 3 is evaluated first to 12, and then 5 is added to the result to make 17.

Parentheses change all that. Parentheses are the only grouping operators. To evaluate the statement to 27, group it as follows:

```
(5 + 4) * 3
```

Parentheses cause 5 + 4 to be evaluated first before multiplying by 3.

You can also nest parentheses. (*Nesting* means putting one inside of another.) The following expression evaluates the 7 + 3 first (because it's in the deepest nested parentheses) to 10:

```
NOT (8 > ((7+3)*12))
```

This is multiplied by 12 to get 120. Because 8 is not greater than 120, NOT (8 > 120) evaluates to TRUE.

Table 5.8 shows the order of operations (or precedence) in PowerBuilder.

Table 5.8 Precedence of Operators	
Operator	**Use**
( )	Grouping
^	Raising a number to a power
* /	Multiplication and division of numbers
+ –	Addition and subtraction of numbers / concatenation of strings
< > <= >= =	Logical operation for numbers / Arithmetic
<> += -= *= ^= /*	assignment
NOT	Negation of relational statements
AND	Logical AND
OR	Logical OR

Tip

For future maintenance, try to pick the "easiest" way to state your operation. (For instance, use a < b as opposed to NOT (a >= b).)

If a statement has two operators with the same precedence, the statement is evaluated from left to right.

Equivalent Statements

In English, there are several ways to say the same thing. In PowerBuilder, too, there are several ways to code the same logical or arithmetic statement, and have it mean the same thing. Table 5.9 lists some equivalent statements.

Table 5.9 Equivalent Logical and Arithmetic Statements	
Statement	**Equivalent Statement**
a = a + 1	a ++
a = a – 1	a --
a = a + b	a += b
a = a – b	a –= b
a <> b	NOT (a = b)
a <= b	NOT (a > b)
a < b	NOT (a >= b)

(continues)

II

Using PowerScript

| **Table 5.9 Continued** | |
Statement	Equivalent Statement
a = b	NOT (a <> b)
a AND b	NOT (a OR b)
a OR b	NOT (a AND b)

Using PowerBuilder Commands

The PowerScript Language contains two types of statements: built-in functions and commands. Although there are lots of built-in functions, there are only three major types of commands: *assignment commands,* which assign a value to a variable, *decision structures,* which consist of If statements and Choose Case statements, and *iterative* (or *looping*) structures, which consist of Do loops and For...Next loops.

Using Decision Structures

Decision structures are commands that evaluate variables. PowerBuilder supports two types of decision structures: the If...ElseIf...Else...End structure (or just the If structure) and the Choose Case structure.

Using the If Structure. The If statement evaluates variables. Based on that evaluation, the If statement takes some form of action. The following is an example of the simplest form of an If statement:

```
If a < b Then                      // First evaluate a logical
                                   // expression
    a command or set of commands   // Commands if expression is
                                   // true
End If                             // End the If statement
```

As you can tell by the comments, a logical expression is first evaluated. If that logical expression is true, then a set of commands is executed. Now we have a more complicated If statement. This time, the If statement contains an Else clause:

```
If a < b Then                  // First evaluate a logical
                               // expression
    command set 1              // Commands if expression is TRUE
Else
    command set 2              // Commands if expression is FALSE
End If                         // End the If statement
```

With this statement, one of the command sets gets executed, depending on the value of a and b.

The following is a third If statement, which contains an ElseIf:

```
If a < b Then                   // First evaluate a logical expression
    command set 1               // Commands if expression is TRUE
ElseIf a < c Then               // Commands if previous expression is
                                // FALSE
    command set 2               // and this expression is TRUE
Else                            // Commands if all previous expressions
                                // are FALSE
    command set 3
End If                          // End the If statement
```

The following is a fourth If statement, which contains two ElseIfs:

```
If a < b Then                   // First evaluate a logical expression
    command set 1               // Commands if expression is TRUE
ElseIf a < c Then               // Commands if previous expression is
                                // FALSE
    command set 2               // and this expression is TRUE
ElseIf a < d Then               // Commands if all previous expressions
    command set 3               // are FALSE and this expression is TRUE
Else                            // Commands if all previous expressions are
    command set 4               // FALSE
End If                          // End the If statement
```

You can have as many ElseIfs in an If statement as you want.

Using the If statement is a powerful way to control the flow of your program based on existing information.

Using the Choose Case Structure. In the previous example, *a* was compared to several other variables. In a situation such as this, it's better to use a *Choose Case statement,* which evaluates a single variable in several different ways. The format for the Choose Case statement is as follows:

```
Choose Case test_variable
    Case expression1
        command set 1           // Commands if expression1 is TRUE
    Case expression2            // Commands if expression2 is TRUE
        command set 2           // and previous expressions are FALSE
        ...
    Case expression3            // Commands if expression3 is TRUE
        command set 3           // and previous expressions are FALSE
    Case Else
        command set 4           // Commands if all expressions are FALSE
End Choose
```

In the previous statement, the test_variable is the variable you want to run several tests on. Each Case statement performs a test on the test_variable. At least one CASE clause is required.

Each expression can test many different situations. An expression can be a single value (such as variable2 or 5), a list of values separated by commas, a TO clause (such as 10 to 20) or a relational operator preceded by Is (such as Is < 50).

Following is a Choose Case statement that could be used at the Las Vegas blackjack tables (with a little more work, of course):

```
Choose Case card_total
    Case is > 21
        busted = TRUE
    Case 3 To 16
        hit_me = TRUE
    Case 21
        black_jack = TRUE
    Case 17, 18, 19, 20
        stick = TRUE
    Case Else                  // Only 2 is left
        double_down = TRUE
End Choose
```

Tip

Typically, a Choose Case command is more efficient than an equivalent If...ElseIf... ...Else...End If command.

As you can tell, a Choose Case statement is easier to write, easier to read, and more efficient to run than the equivalent If...ElseIf...Else...End If statement, but not as versatile.

Using Iteration (Looping) Structures

Looping structures are constructs that cause a series of commands to be executed a number of times. PowerScript has two looping structures: the Do Loop structure and the For...Next structure.

Using the Do Loop Structure. The Do Loop structure in PowerScript is a powerful way to implement a loop. Following are four different types of Do Loops and their functions.

```
Do While condition1       // Executes command set 1 While condition1 is
    command set 1         // TRUE
    Loop

Do Until condition2       // Executes command set 2 Until condition2 is
    command set 2         // TRUE
    Loop

Do                        // Executes command set 3 at least once
    command set 3         // until condition3 is TRUE
```

```
Loop Until condition3

Do                          // Executes command set 4 at least once
     command set 4          // while condition4 is TRUE
Loop While condition4
```

Suppose you want to search for the first space in an instance variable string named is_full_name. Use the following logic:

```
int count                      // Declare your string counter

count = 1                      // Initialize your count to one
// Now search the string using Mid.  Notice the continuation
// character
Do Until Mid(is_full_name, count, 1) = " " and &
               count <= len(is_full_name)
     count++
Loop
```

Syntax-at-a-Glance

Mid (string, start {, length})

Mid returns a portion of a string. The following arguments are used:

- string. The string you want to search.

- start. The starting position of your string.

- length. The maximum length of the string you want to return.

Syntax-at-a-Glance

Len (string)

The Len function returns the length of the passed string.

Using the For...Next Structure. The other type of loop construct is the *For...Next loop*, which combines iteration with incrementing a counter. It has the following format:

```
For numeric_variable = start  To  end { Step increment }
     command set
Next
```

Tip

Often, Step -1 is used with the For...Next statement to force the loop to decrement instead of increment.

II

Using PowerScript

In the above For command, `numeric_variable` is a variable (usually an integer) to be incremented during the loop. `start To end` tells what the numeric variable is to be initialized with and where it's supposed to go to until the loop ends. `Step increment` allows you to increment your loop during each iteration. If this step is skipped, 1 is assumed. `Next` symbolizes the end of the loop.

Caution

Any variable you use for incrementing during your loop will have its value altered.

Here's an example of a For...Next loop that resets an array:

```
int a                          // Loop Counter
int b[100]                     // Array to be reset
.
.              Additional processing here
.
For a = 1 to 100               // To reset your array, set a to go
                               // from 1 to 100
      b[a] = 0;                // Reset your array
Next                           // End loop
```

Nested Loops and Loop Statements. No discussion of PowerBuilder loops would be complete without mentioning the statements Continue and Exit. *Continue* is used to skip down to the bottom of the loop for another iteration; *Exit* is used to leave the loop completely.

Nested loops are loops inside of each other. Exit only leaves the current loop. The following code is the traditional (and a little inefficient) *bubble sort,* which is used to sort an array using a nested loop.

```
int sort_array[100]            // Declare an array to be sorted
int loop1                      // loop counter 1
int loop2                      // second loop counter
int last_change                // check up to this number + 1
int hold_number                // holder for the sort
int hold_last_change           // holder for last change
boolean changes_made       // Flag to see of changes were made
// .
// . Commands fill the array with values
// .
// Now begin the bubble sort
last_change = 99               // Check the entire array
for loop1 = 1 to 99            // Go through the entire array
    changes_made = FALSE       // Reset changes_made
    for loop2 = 1 to last_change // loop2 is nested
```

```
            if sort_array[loop2] < sort_array[loop2+1] // Check values
                continue            // Iterate loop2 again
            end if
            changes_made = TRUE     // set changes_made
            holder_last_change = loop2 - 1   // Go this far next loop2
            hold_number = sort_array[loop2]  // Swap array numbers
            sort_array[loop2] = sort_array[loop2 + 1]
            sort_array[loop2 + 1] = hold_number
        next                        // End loop2
    if NOT change_made then
        exit                        // Exit if sort is done
    end if
    last_change = holder_last_change   //set how far loop2 should go
next                                // End loop1
```

The previous example used a nested loop to perform a sort. You also can employ a Continue statement to skip to the next iteration of loop2. Finally, if the array is sorted, you can exit the loop.

Using Built-in Functions

In its PowerScript, PowerBuilder gives you a lot of built-in functions (such as the Mid function). *Built-in functions* are already declared and ready for use.

Also, every control and object has functions of its own. All built-in functions are listed in Chapter 21, "Function and Event Quick Reference."

Using Context-Sensitive Help

If you have any question about a command or PowerBuilder construct, PowerBuilder comes with an excellent on-line help. By pressing F1, you see the table of contents. By placing the cursor on a script command, and pressing Shift+F1, you'll pull up help for that command.

Using the PowerBuilder Script Painter

The PowerScript language comes with a very handy script painter. Properly used, this painter makes your job as a developer much easier.

Undoing What You've Done

You'll find that the Undo function will save you lots of time. When you've done something in a script that you shouldn't have, click on the Undo icon and put your script back the way it was.

> **Note**
>
> You can also access the Undo function by pressing Alt+Backspace or by clicking on **E**dit, **U**ndo.

Selecting Text

Often you'll find you need to select text before you can perform other actions, like commenting, cutting, or pasting text. There are many ways you can select text:

■ To select all your text, click on the Select All icon.

■ To select part of your text:

1. Position your mouse pointer to the start of your selection.

2. Press and hold the left mouse button.

3. Move your mouse pointer to the end of your selection.

4. Release the mouse button.

> **Note**
>
> You can also select text with the keyboard with the following steps:
>
> 1. Position your cursor at the beginning of your selection.
>
> 2. Hold down the Shift key while you use your arrows to move to the end of your selection.
>
> 3. Release the Shift key.

Commenting and Uncommenting

To comment or uncomment your text, click on the Comment or Uncomment icon. Clicking on these icons will add (or take away) the double slash (//) at the beginning of each line selected (or the current line, if no lines are selected). It's just a faster way to comment out a lot of code.

> **Note**
>
> PowerBuilder won't let you leave the script painter if you have any errors in your script. However, there are times you may want to leave your script painter anyway.
>
> To leave your painter with errors in the code, click on the Select All icon and then the Comment icon. This comments out all your code and allows you to leave your script.
>
> When you return, click on the Select All icon again and then the Uncomment icon. Your code will be as you left it.

Copying, Clearing, and Cutting Text

After you've selected text, you can copy the selected text to the Windows Clipboard by clicking on the Copy icon. If you click on the Clear icon, the selected text is deleted out of your script. Cutting text is a combination of the copy and clear functions. If you click on the Cut icon, the selected text is copied to the Clipboard and then deleted out of your script.

II

Pasting Text

If you have anything in the Windows Clipboard, you can paste it into your text by clicking on the Paste icon.

> **Note**
>
> In PowerBuilder, you can pull up any text file on your hard drive by pressing Shift+F6. Using the same icons, you can cut, copy, or paste from any file to any other file.

Using PowerScript

Pasting Statements

To paste a statement in your script painter, click on the Paste icon which has what looks like a flow chart on it. This pulls up the Paste Statement dialog box (see fig. 5.15).

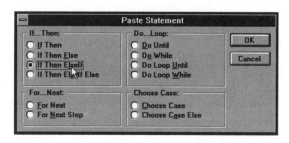

Fig. 5.15
You can paste the syntax for a PowerBuilder statement using the Paste Statement dialog box.

From here, click on the function you want, then click on OK. This pastes the syntax for the PowerBuilder statement, as shown in figure 5.16.

Fig. 5.16
This is the result of using the Paste Statement dialog box.

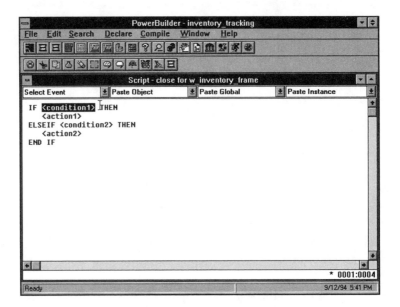

Now change the words surrounded in less-than and greater-than signs to appropriate syntax.

Pasting Functions

You can also paste functions by using the function painter. Click on **E**dit and choose Paste **F**unction (see fig. 5.17).

Now you should see the Paste Function dialog box, as shown in figure 5.18.

In the Paste Function dialog box, click on the function you want to paste (see fig. 5.19).

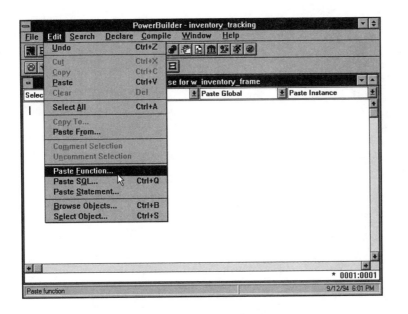

Fig. 5.17
Use the PowerBuilder menu to access the Paste Function dialog box.

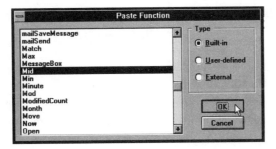

Fig. 5.18
The Paste Function dialog box allows you to choose a function and paste it back to your script painter.

II

Using PowerScript

Fig. 5.19
Now the function name is pasted in your window.

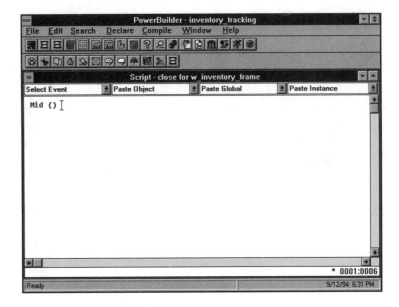

Now the function you've chosen is pasted onto the script painter. You'll notice that none of the arguments are included when you paste your function. You have to fill these in for yourself.

Using the Paste List Boxes

On the top of your script painter, you can see three *paste list boxes,* which allow you to quickly paste variables and objects that you often use while coding your script.

The Paste Instance list box, as shown in figure 5.20, pulls down all instance variable declarations. By double-clicking on an instance variable, it is pasted in your script.

The Paste Global list box, as shown in figure 5.21, allows you to paste any global variable (and system global variable) into your script.

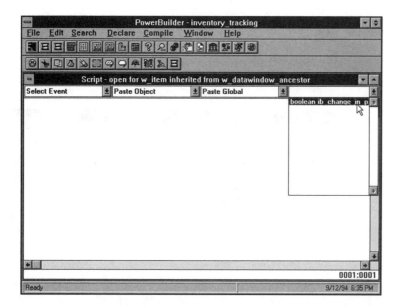

Fig. 5.20
The Paste Instance list box allows you to paste instance variables into your script.

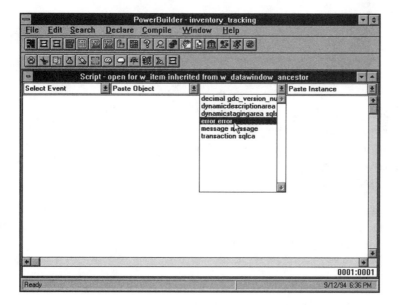

Fig. 5.21
The Paste Global list box allows you to paste global variables into your script.

Finally, the Paste Object list box allows you to paste objects that are related to the script you are writing. As you can see in figure 5.22, the DataWindow control name (dw_data) and the window name (w_item) are in the Paste Object list box.

Fig. 5.22
The Paste Object list box allows you to paste related object names into your script.

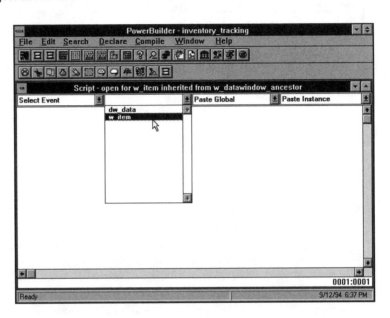

Tip
Shift+Del cuts your selected text. Shift+Ins pastes your script. Cut, copy, and paste can also be accessed by Ctrl+X, Ctrl+C, and Ctrl+V, respectively.

Using the Object Browser

Sometimes, you need to go outside what is provided in the paste boxes for areas in your script. However, keeping track of all the objects, their attributes and functions, and all the instance variables and events for each object can be mind-boggling.

To meet this need, PowerBuilder developed the *Object Browser*, which enables you to browse into any object, enumerated data type, function, or control. To get into the Object Browser, click on the Browse icon.

In the Object Browser (see fig. 5.23), click on the object type you want (in this case, **A**pplication), and choose the paste category of what you want to paste (in this case, Attri**b**utes). You'll then be given a list of paste values. Pick one, and click on OK to paste that value into your script painter.

As you can see in figure 5.24, the highlighted variable gets pasted into your script. Furthermore, the variable is fully qualified. Now just finish the statement and you're finished.

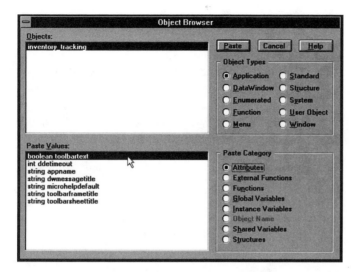

Fig. 5.23
You can scan all
the attributes
of your
inventory_tracking
application.

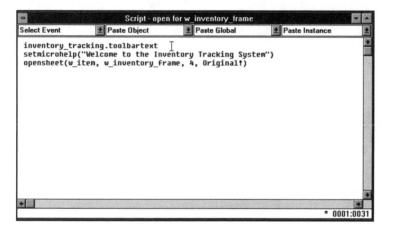

Fig. 5.24
The Browse Objects
pastes the appropri-
ate name into your
script painter.

II

Using PowerScript

From Here...

In this chapter, you learned a lot about the PowerScript language and
PowerBuilder's script painter. As with any language, the best way to learn
PowerScript is to practice it.

You can find more discussion on PowerScript in this book by reviewing the
following chapters:

- Chapter 6, "Programming in PowerScript," describes the best way to
  implement PowerScript from within your application.

- Chapter 7, "Using SQL in PowerBuilder," shows you how to access your database effectively within PowerScript.

- Chapter 21, "Function and Event Quick Reference," lists all the functions allowed in PowerBuilder.

PowerBuilder Documentation also discusses the PowerScript language in the *User's Guide*, Chapter 3, "Writing Scripts," which shows beginners how to write PowerScript.

Chapter 6

Programming in PowerScript

In the last chapter, you learned the basics on how to program in PowerScript. Now you get to apply your knowledge using the Inventory Tracking system.

In this chapter, much of the PowerScript coding for the Inventory Tracking system is complete. It is designed to give you a hands-on feel for PowerScript.

In this chapter, you learn how to:

- Define a database transaction
- Use the PowerScript language
- Program for PowerBuilder events and functions
- Avoid certain programming practices

Understanding Database Transactions

Transaction objects are used by PowerBuilder to communicate with a database. Before you use a database, you must define it in the transaction object. Although you can define your own transaction variable, PowerBuilder provides one for you: the SQLCA.

Exploring PowerBuilder's Transaction Objects

A transaction object (or structure) such as SQLCA has 15 fields. Ten of these fields need to be filled in by the developer; the other five are used for a return area after you make SQL calls. The structure is defined in tables 6.1 and 6.2.

Tip

Instead of trying to define your own transaction object, you should probably use the SQLCA transaction that is already defined.

Table 6.1 shows the elements of the SQLCA transaction object that are defined by the user.

Table 6.1	User-Defined Transaction Variables	
Attribute	**Data Type**	**Description**
DBMS	String	The name of the database type (for example, ODBC for Watcom).
Database	String	The name of the database to which you are connecting. In Watcom, use the file-name prefix (INVENTRY).
UserID	String	The UserID connecting to the database ("dba" in Inventory Tracking).
DBParm	String	DBMS-specific. (In Watcom, this is the connect string.)
DBPass	String	The password that will be used to connect to the database ("sql" in Inventory Tracking).
Lock	String	The isolation level (often not needed).
LogId	String	The name or ID of the user who will log on to the server (often not needed).
LogPass	String	The password used to log on to the server (often not needed).
ServerName	String	The name of the server on which the database resides (often not needed).
AutoCommit	Boolean	The automatic commit indicator. TRUE commits automatically after every database activity. FALSE (default) does not commit automatically.

Table 6.2 shows the elements of the SQLCA transaction object that are returned to the user by the database the user is working with. These values then can be accessed to give information about the previous SQL call, particularly to tell if the SQL code worked or what error occurred.

Table 6.2 Database Transaction Return Variables

Attribute	Data Type	Description
SQLCode	Long	The success or failure code of the most recent SQL operation: 0—Success 100—No result set returned −1—Error (use SQLDBCode or SQLErrText to obtain the details)
SQLNRows	Long	The number of rows affected. The database vendor supplies this number; therefore, the meaning may not be the same in every database.
SQLDBCode	Long	The database vendor's error code.
SQLErrText	String	The database vendor's error message.
SQLReturnData	String	DBMS-specific return data.

Caution

Before you can use the default transaction object (SQLCA) or any other transaction object, you must assign values to the attributes that will be used.

The user-defined transaction structure variables may vary from database to database.

Using Your Transaction in the Application Open Event

Probably the best place to code your database connection is in the application open. The following code is added before the w_inventory_frame open statement in the application open event:

```
// — — — Define the parameters necessary to connect to the database.
SQLCA.DBMS      = "ODBC"
SQLCA.Database  = "INVENTRY"
SQLCA.UserID    = "dba"
SQLCA.DBPass    = "sql"
SQLCA.DBParm    = "Connectstring='DSN=INVENTRY;UID=DBA;PWD=SQL'"

// — — — Once transaction object parameters are defined,
// — — — try connecting to the database
CONNECT USING SQLCA;

If SQLCA.SQLCode <> 0 Then
    MessageBox ("Database Connect", &
                "Unable to connect to the Inventory Database.~r~n" &
```

(continues)

```
                              + "DB Error Code: " + String (SQLCA.SQLDBCode ) &
                              + "~r~n" + "DB Error Message: " + SQLCA.SQLErrText, &
                        StopSign!, OK!, 1 )
          Halt
   End If

   open (w_inventory_frame)
```

Tip

To check the syntax of your script, press Ctrl+L or choose Compile, **S**cript.

As you can see, you didn't have to code every transaction variable. Now you are ready to start using SQLCA and your database in your application.

Always test the SQLCode (usually SQLCA.SQLCode) after making any SQL call. You'll want to know if it worked. Most databases don't display error messages automatically; instead, they return codes for the developer to test.

Tip

Always include a semicolon (;) after each SQL command in PowerBuilder.

Syntax-at-a-Glance

CONNECT {USING TransactionObject}

CONNECT is an SQL statement used to connect to the database using your transaction object. If you don't include a USING statement, the transaction object defaults to SQLCA.

Syntax-at-a-Glance

MessageBox(title,text{,button{,default}})

MessageBox displays a system MessageBox with the title, text, icon, and buttons you specify. MessageBox returns the number of the selected button (1, 2, or 3) if it succeeds; it returns -1 if an error occurs. (See Chapter 22, "Enumerated Data Types Quick Reference," for a list of icon and button enumerated data types.) The parameters are defined as follows:

- *title.* A string containing the caption you want to display in the title bar of the message box.

- *text.* The text you want to display in the MessageBox. The text can be a numeric data type, a string, or a Boolean value.

- *icon (optional).* An enumerated data type that indicates the icon you want to display on the left side of the MessageBox.

- *default (optional).* The number (1 to 3) of the button you want to be the default button. 1 is the default.

Syntax-at-a-Glance

~r~n

~r~n is used as a carriage return-line feed in many PowerBuilder strings (such as MessageBox).

Implementing User-Defined Functions

In addition to user-defined events, PowerBuilder also lets the developer write user-defined functions. A *user-defined function* can either be *global* (every object in the application has access to the function) or *local* (only the object the local function is defined in has access to that function).

Using the PowerBuilder Global Function Painter

To create a global function, click on the Function icon. The Select Function dialog box appears, as shown in figure 6.1.

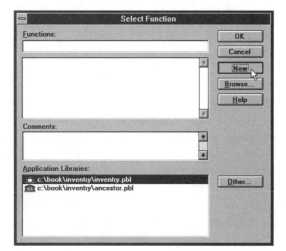

Fig. 6.1
The Select Function dialog box appears when you click on the Function icon.

Click on New in the Select Function dialog box. The New Function dialog box appears (see fig. 6.2).

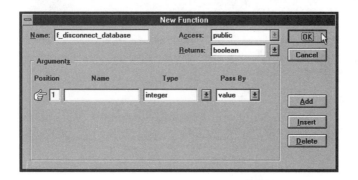

Fig. 6.2
The New Function dialog box is where you start defining your new function.

II

Using PowerScript

The following fields are available in the New Function dialog box:

■ The **N**ame field is where you type in the name of the function (the name other objects use to access your function).

■ The A**c**cess field tells who has access to this function. There are three types of access: public, private, and protected. *Public access* means that anyone can access the function. *Private access* means that only the object that the function is defined in has access to the object. *Protected access* means that only the object the function is defined in (and all the descendants of that object) have access to the function.

Global functions are only allowed to have public access because global functions aren't defined within an object. (You'll probably be using public access almost exclusively anyway.) Private or protected access are for those destructive, monetary, or secretive information functions that you don't want every developer calling from their object.

■ The **R**eturns field tells what data type of variable is returned by this function to the calling function. Valid values for a Boolean variable are TRUE and FALSE. Boolean variables usually make excellent return variables if you want to indicate to the calling program whether the function succeeded or failed.

Tip

When calling a function with a large structure, it's more efficient to pass it by reference as opposed to value, even if you don't intend to change the values in the structure.

■ Argument**s** fields allow you to pass arguments to your function. You can type in the name of your argument and choose the data type. You can also choose to pass the argument by *value* (which tells PowerBuilder that any changes you make to the argument won't be reflected in the calling script) or by *reference* (which tells PowerBuilder that any changes made to the argument variable during the function will be reflected in the calling script).

> **TrackNote**
>
> Your first function will be a function to disconnect the database when you leave the application. This function will be called by the close event and any other function that wants to disconnect the database.

When you're done defining your function, click on OK. This will pull up the function painter, as seen in figure 6.3.

```
// f_disconnect_database

if NOT g_disconnecting then
    g_disconnecting = TRUE
else
    return FALSE            // Already disconnected
end if

DISCONNECT USING SQLCA;
If SQLCA.SQLCode <> 0 Then
    MessageBox ( "Database Disconnect", "Unable to disconnect from the " +&
        "database.~r~n" + &
        "DB Error Code: " + String (SQLCA.SQLDBCode ) + "~r~n" + &
        "DB Error Message: " + SQLCA.SQLErrText, StopSign!, OK!, 1 )
    halt
End If
return TRUE                // Disconnect was successful
```

Fig. 6.3
The function painter is used to type PowerScript into a function.

The function painter is just like the script painter except for the paste list boxes. Because functions don't have events, there is no Paste Event list box—it is replaced with a Paste Argument list box that pastes any arguments you have defined. Global functions have no instance variable or objects they are attached to, so the function painter for global functions does not include these paste list boxes.

Type in your function script, and then save your function by choosing File, Save or by double-clicking the painter Control menu box and clicking on Yes when PowerBuilder asks if you want to save your changes. The Save Function dialog box appears, as seen in figure 6.4.

Tip
Always put the name of your function or event in comments at the top of your script. That way, when you print the function or event, you know which function or event it came from.

Fig. 6.4
The Save Function dialog box allows you to save changes to your function.

II

Using PowerScript

In the Save Function dialog box, the function name is already entered. Type in your comments, and choose which PBL to store the function in.

TrackNote

The source code for f_disconnect_database is as follows:

```
// f_disconnect_database

if NOT g_disconnecting then
     g_disconnecting = TRUE
else
    return FALSE                    // Already disconnected
end if

DISCONNECT USING SQLCA;
If SQLCA.SQLCode <> 0 Then
    MessageBox ( "Database Disconnect", &
    "Unable to disconnect from the " +&
    "Database. ~r~n" + &
    "DB Error Code: " + String (SQLCA.SQLDBCode ) + "~r~n" + &
    "DB Error Message: " + SQLCA.SQLErrText, StopSign!, OK!, 1 )
    halt
End If
return TRUE                        // Disconnect was successful
```

Note that you have to add a Boolean global variable, *g_disconnecting,* for this script to work.

Syntax-at-a-Glance

DISCONNECT {USING TransactionObject}

Disconnect is an SQL statement used to disconnect from the database using your transaction object. If you don't include a USING statement, the transaction object defaults to SQLCA (but it is included in the code anyway).

Syntax-at-a-Glance

return {value}

Return immediately ends the program. If you specified a return type in the **R**eturns area in the New Function dialog box (refer to fig. 6.2), you must include a variable of that data type to return to the calling script any time you exit the function.

Using the PowerBuilder Local Function Painter

You can also use *local functions* (functions tied to a specific PowerBuilder object). You can have local functions in applications, menus, and windows. (You can also have them in user objects, but user objects are beyond the scope of this book.) To access a local function painter, choose Declare and pick *objectname* Functions, in which *objectname* is the type of object function you're declaring (Application, Menu, or Window). This can be seen in figure 6.5.

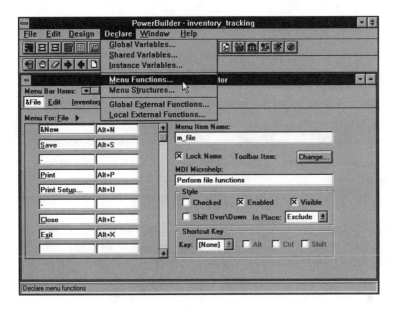

Fig. 6.5
To get into a local function painter, choose Declare, **M**enu Functions for the object you're in.

The local Select Function in Menu dialog box appears, as seen in figure 6.6.

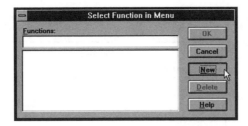

Fig. 6.6
The local Select Function in Menu dialog box allows you to modify an existing local function or create a new local function.

Click on **N**ew to pull up the New Function dialog box. This dialog box, shown in figure 6.7, is identical to that seen in figure 6.2.

Using Arguments

In figure 6.7, an argument is added to the local function you are declaring. Now, every script calling this function must also pass a character argument.

Fig. 6.7
The New Function dialog box is the same for local functions as it is for global functions.

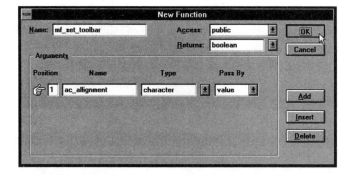

TrackNote

mf_set_toolbar will be used to manipulate the toolbar position in the Inventory Tracking system.

After you're done declaring your function, click on OK. This will pull up the local function painter, which is identical to the global function painter except that there's a Paste Instance window and a Paste Object window on the local function painter. (This is understandable—global functions have no instance variables or connected objects like local functions have.)

Because you declared an argument in figure 6.7, you can access the Paste Argument list box, as seen in figure 6.8.

Fig. 6.8
To paste your argument into your function painter, access the Paste Argument list box.

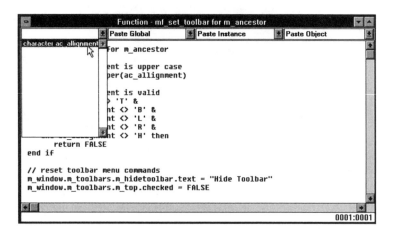

Figure 6.9 shows the completed local function. When you're done, exit the painter. Although PowerBuilder will ask you if you want to save, because this is a local function, you can't specify a PBL or comments as in a global function.

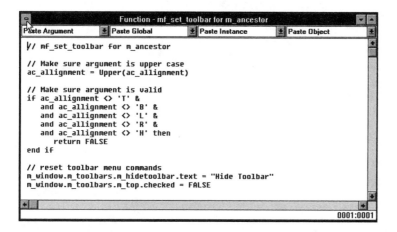

```
        Function - mf_set_toolbar for m_ancestor
Paste Argument      Paste Global      Paste Instance      Paste Object

// mf_set_toolbar for m_ancestor

// Make sure argument is upper case
ac_allignment = Upper(ac_allignment)

// Make sure argument is valid
if ac_allignment <> 'T' &
    and ac_allignment <> 'B' &
    and ac_allignment <> 'L' &
    and ac_allignment <> 'R' &
    and ac_allignment <> 'H' then
        return FALSE
end if

// reset toolbar menu commands
m_window.m_toolbars.m_hidetoolbar.text = "Hide Toolbar"
m_window.m_toolbars.m_top.checked = FALSE

                                            0001:0001
```

Fig. 6.9
Here's the finished local function to adjust the toolbar.

II

Using PowerScript

TrackNote

The mf_set_toolbar function handles all of your toolbar needs. The complete PowerScript listing is as follows (note that *ib_visible_toolbar* is a Boolean instance variable.):

```
// mf_set_toolbar for m_ancestor

// Make sure argument is upper case
ac_alignment = Upper(ac_alignment)

// Make sure argument is valid
if ac_alignment <> 'T' &
    and ac_alignment <> 'B' &
    and ac_alignment <> 'L' &
    and ac_alignment <> 'R' &
    and ac_alignment <> 'H' then
        return FALSE
end if

// reset toolbar menu commands
m_window.m_toolbars.m_hidetoolbar.text = "Hide Toolbar"
m_window.m_toolbars.m_top.checked = FALSE
m_window.m_toolbars.m_bottom.checked = FALSE
m_window.m_toolbars.m_left.checked = FALSE
m_window.m_toolbars.m_right.checked = FALSE
choose case Upper(ac_alignment)
    case 'T'
```

(continues)

```
(continued)
        Parentwindow.ToolBarAlignment = AlignAtTop!
        m_window.m_toolbars.m_top.checked = TRUE
case 'B'
        Parentwindow.ToolBarAlignment = AlignAtBottom!
        m_window.m_toolbars.m_bottom.checked = TRUE
case 'L'
        Parentwindow.ToolBarAlignment = AlignAtLeft!
        m_window.m_toolbars.m_left.checked = TRUE
case 'R'
        Parentwindow.ToolBarAlignment = AlignAtRight!
        m_window.m_toolbars.m_right.checked = TRUE
case 'H'
   if ib_visible_toolbar then
        parentwindow.toolbarvisible = FALSE
        m_window.m_toolbars.m_hidetoolbar.text = "Show Toolbar"
        ib_visible_toolbar = FALSE
        return TRUE                      // Don't execute the rest of the code
   else
// Minor league recursion to set toolbar on top if it was hidden and
// now should be shown.
        mf_set_toolbar('T')
      end if
end choose

ib_visible_toolbar = TRUE
parentwindow.toolbarvisible = TRUE
return TRUE
```

Syntax-at-a-Glance

UPPER(string) or *UPPER(character)*

The Upper function converts any lowercase letters in the string or character to uppercase.

Syntax-at-a-Glance

The following attributes are used in the previous PowerScript:

- *text*. In this case, text is a string attribute of a menu selection. Text tells what is displayed when the menu is viewed.

- *toolbarvisible*. toolbarvisible is a Boolean window attribute describing whether or not the toolbar is displayed.

Programming for Specific Events

Now that you've declared and written some functions, you need to code for some application events and the myriad of menu events, and also declare and program for some window events.

Programming for Application Events

You have seen the programming for the open event of the application. As was mentioned before, unless you code for the open event of the application, nothing will happen in your application. Now you can program for other application events.

Coding for the Application Close

You should disconnect from the database upon exit, which can be done in the close event of the application. Fortunately, you've already written a global function to disconnect from the database. So, the entire code for your event consists of two comments and one function call:

```
// Close event of the Inventory Tracking system.
// Before application closes, disconnect database.

f_disconnect_database ( )
```

Although you've written functions, this is the first time you've called a user-defined function. See how easy it is?

System Errors

The systemerror event on the application is triggered when PowerBuilder encounters an error in a script it is executing. If it can, PowerBuilder will then call the systemerror event of the application.

You may want to format your messages a little differently than PowerBuilder formats them. You also may want to give an option to continue. The following code in PowerBuilder can accomplish this:

```
// Systemerror event in Inventory_tracking

int answer

answer=MessageBox("System Error","A system error has occurred."+&
     "~r~n~r~n    Powerbuilder error number: "+String(error.number)+&
     "~r~n    Error Message:         " + error.text + &
     "~r~n    Window/Menu in error: " + error.windowmenu + &
     "~r~n    Object in error:       " + error.object + &
     "~r~n    Event in error:        " + error.objectevent + &
     "~r~n    Line of error:         " + string(error.line) + &
```

(continues)

II

Using PowerScript

```
                    "~r~n~n Do you wish to continue?", StopSign!, YESNO!, 1 )

        if answer <> 1 then
            close (w_inventory_frame)
            halt close
        end if
```

In the above event, a message box appears with a yes or no question, telling the user about the error and asking the user if he or she wants to continue. If the answer isn't yes, the frame window closes and issues a halt close statement.

> **Syntax-at-a-Glance**
>
> You'll notice that what appears to be a structure called *error* is used. *error* is defined by PowerBuilder and contains valuable error messages in case a system error occurs.

Programming for Menu Events

The need for PowerScript is most apparent with menus. For every menu option or every toolbar button you click, some PowerScript needs to be executed. In this section, you'll program for every menu option except those options under **H**elp.

▶ See "Adding Help for Inventory Tracking," p. 351

Most event coding consists of one or two lines. Therefore, you can see each event script, in table form, listed in the following sections.

Using Window Inheritance with PowerScript

As said before, you probably want to do all of your coding in the ancestor menu and then inherit all the code to all other menus. This way, you have one place to go to add a menu item, and one place to modify the code.

Triggering Windows Events

Because you are using generic functions in your menu, you probably don't want to specifically name a sheet window in your processing. Therefore, all references to windows will use ParentWindow as the window name.

◀ See "Understanding Events," p. 123

Because you are using ParentWindow as your window name, you can't access DataWindows or other window controls. Therefore, you'll delegate functions that need access to a window control to the windows themselves by declaring user-defined window events and then triggering them from your window.

Table 6.3 and 6.4 list all the scripts in the **F**ile and **E**dit menu bar items of m_ancestor shown in figure 6.10 and figure 6.11. (Therefore, they will be inherited to all menus in the Inventory Tracking system.) For brevity, comments were left out of the table.

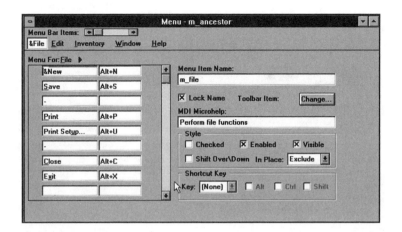

Fig. 6.10
Here is a list of all
items under **F**ile
in the Inventory
Tracking system
(except **E**xit, which
has scrolled off the
window).

Table 6.3   Menu Script for Items in the File Menu

Menu Option	PowerScript for Menu Option
&**N**ew	ParentWindow.TriggerEvent("new")
&**S**ave	ParentWindow.TriggerEvent("save")
&**P**rint	ParentWindow.TriggerEvent("print")
PrintSet&**up**	PrintSetup()
&**C**lose	Close(ParentWindow)
E&**x**it	Halt Close

Table 6.4   Menu Script for Items in the Edit Menu

Menu Option	PowerScript for Menu Option
&**U**ndo	ParentWindow.TriggerEvent("undo")
C&**ut**	ParentWindow.TriggerEvent("cut")
C&**o**py	ParentWindow.TriggerEvent("copy")
&**P**aste	ParentWindow.TriggerEvent("paste")
&**I**nsert	ParentWindow.TriggerEvent("newrow")
&**D**elete	ParentWindow.TriggerEvent("delrow")

II

Using PowerScript

Fig. 6.11

Here is a list of all items under **E**dit in the Inventory Tracking system.

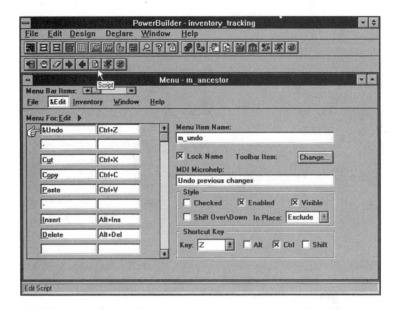

Syntax-at-a-Glance

objectname.TriggerEvent(event_name)
objectname.TriggerEvent(enumerated_data_type_event)

TriggerEvent automatically executes the event argument. This event can be a string containing the event name or an enumerated data type specifying the event.

If there is no objectname specified, TriggerEvent will trigger the event in the current object. Otherwise, TriggerEvent can trigger an event in a different object or control denoted by objectname.

Syntax-at-a-Glance

PrintSetup()

PrintSetup() automatically calls the pre-built print setup function in Windows.

TrackNote

Of course, now all of those events that have been triggered need to be defined. These windows events will be discussed later in this chapter.

Using OpenSheet Commands

In the **I**nventory menu bar item, all the commands relate to opening windows. The OpenSheet command is used for each option, as seen in table 6.5.

Table 6.5 Menu Script for Items under Inventory	
Menu Option	**PowerScript for Menu Option**
Ite&m Entry	opensheet(w_item, w_inventory_frame, 4, Layered!)
Cust&omer Entry	opensheet(w_customer, w_inventory_frame, 4, Layered!)
Supp&lier	opensheet(w_supplier, w_inventory_frame, 4, Layered!)
In&voice Entry	opensheet(w_invoice, w_inventory_frame, 4, Layered!)
Wa&rehouse Entry	opensheet(w_warehouse, w_inventory_frame, 4, Layered!)

Arranging Sheets and Icons

Table 6.6 shows that most of the menu items in this category share the same command. Each of these commands arranges your window a little differently, depending on the enumerated variable passed to the windows function ArrangeSheets.

> **Note**
>
> You can actually name the window in this category since the window is a frame window.

Table 6.6 Menu Script for Items under Window	
Menu Option	**PowerScript for Menu Option**
&Tile	w_inventory_frame.ArrangeSheets (Tile!)
Casca&de	w_inventory_frame.ArrangeSheets (Cascade!)
&Layer	w_inventory_frame.ArrangeSheets (Layer!)
&Arrange Icons	w_inventory_frame.ArrangeSheets (Icons!)
Toolbars...	Not Applicable since Toolbars is a cascaded menu

II

Using PowerScript

Syntax-at-a-Glance

framewindow.ArrangeSheets(arrangement)

Arrangesheets is an MDI frame window command that arranges all open sheet windows, depending on the value of arrangement. For the valid parameters, consult Chapter 22, "Enumerated Data Types Quick Reference."

Changing the Toolbar

Remember the long mf_set_toolbar function? Here's where that pays off. Because of writing one function, you can coordinate all functions that affect the appearance of the toolbar—all with a single call to that function.

Table 6.7 shows the commands needed to write each toolbar function now that you have mf_set_toolbar.

Table 6.7   Menu Script for Items under Toolbars

Menu Option	PowerScript for Menu Option
&Top	mf_set_toolbar('T')
&Bottom	mf_set_toolbar('B')
&Left	mf_set_toolbar('L')
&Right	mf_set_toolbar('R')
&Hide Toolbar	mf_set_toolbar('H')

&Show Text	if checked = FALSE then
	checked = TRUE
	inventory_tracking.toolbartext = TRUE
	else
	checked = FALSE
	inventory_tracking.toolbartext = FALSE
	end if

Now you have a menu script more than one line long. Remember that mf_set_toolbar is a user-defined function.

Syntax-at-a-Glance

checked

Checked is a Boolean attribute of a menu item. It describes whether or not a check mark is next to the menu text.

II

Using PowerScript

Syntax-at-a-Glance

toolbartext

Toolbartext is a Boolean application attribute. It describes whether or not your toolbars in your system have text under them.

Programming for Window Events

Developing applications by using PowerBuilder windows events makes your windows programming easier than with any other windows development tool. Remember all those events you typed in while programming your ancestor menu? Well, now you have to declare them, as seen in figure 6.12. This is best done, again, in w_datawindow_ancestor. That way, the PowerScript extends down to the individual windows as it did with the menus.

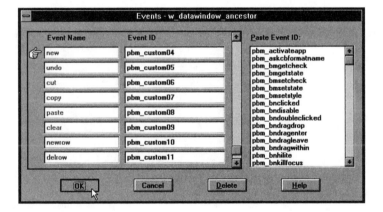

Fig. 6.12
You have to declare many events because of the way the menus were created.

Again, PowerScript makes programming for events fairly easy. Table 6.8 lists events and the script (without comments) that goes with each event.

Note

Instead of listing lots of Syntax-at-a-Glance entries, table 6.8 has a syntax description.

Table 6.8 Events in w_datawindow_ancestor

Window Event	PowerScript for Window Event	Syntax Description
new	int rownum	

	// delete all active rows
	rownum = dw_data.getrow()
		getrow() returns the current row in a DataWindow.

	do while dw_data.getrow() > 0 dw_data.deleterow(0) loop	DeleteRow(n) deletes row n in a DataWindow. If n is 0, the current row is deleted.

	// clear all connections
	// with the database
	// and the DataWindow
	dw_data.reset()
		Reset() clears all connections between the database and the DataWindow.

	// Insert a new row
	dw_data.insertrow(0)
		InsertRow(n) inserts a new row in that DataWindow before row n. If n is 0, a row is inserted before the current row.

retrieve	dw_data.retrieve(long (string(message. doubleparm)))	Retrieve fills a DataWindow from a database. Long(n) converts string n to a long. String(num) converts a number to a string. Message is a predefined global structure that PowerBuilder uses for passing parameters.
save	dw_data.update()	Update() updates the database from the DataWindow.
print	dw_data.print()	Print prints the current DataWindow.
undo	dw_data.undo()	Undo reverses the last action taken in a DataWindow.
cut	dw_data.cut()	Cut cuts selected data into the Clipboard from a DataWindow.
copy	dw_data.copy()	Copy copies selected data into the Clipboard from a DataWindow.

Window Event	PowerScript for Window Event	Syntax Description
paste	dw_data.paste()	Paste pastes data from the Clipboard to the cursor position in a DataWindow.
newrow	dw_data.insertrow(0)	
delrow	dw_data.deleterow(0)	

TrackNote

In the retrieve event, you first needed to convert the doubleparm to a string and then to a long. PowerBuilder has no facility for converting decimals to longs.

Avoiding Trouble

PowerBuilder has incorporated many tools to help you develop your applications. Behind every one of these tools, PowerScript controls the flow of control and the implementation of the design. Following are some tips to help you prevent problems while coding in PowerScript.

- Use comments generously. Often, a developer thinks his or her code is self-documenting. When other developers start to work on this code or when the developer comes back to the code after a year, sometimes several days can be wasted as the flow of the code is deciphered.

  A well-placed comment, especially on a tricky or "really neat" piece of code, can help future developers maintain your code.

- Avoid bad coding constructs. A poorly written SQL SELECT statement or a deep, complicated nested loop can bring an application to its knees. If you find your application running slowly, try looking at your SQL SELECT statements and your loops to see if there's a way to improve them.

- Avoid excessive coding in PowerScript. PowerScript is necessary in PowerBuilder for every application. However, usually only a few lines of PowerScript are necessary for each event and menu item. If you find yourself coding scripts that are several pages in length (especially if no SQL or database-initialization calls were used), then you're *probably* being inefficient and/or using older COBOL-like and BASIC-like experience to code your PowerBuilder.

Try reviewing the code to see if there is any way to not code in PowerScript or to code less PowerScript to achieve the same ends. One of the major benefits of PowerBuilder is that it does a lot of work for you if you let it.

From Here...

This chapter shows you much about how to program for events and functions. If you need further help, consult the PowerBuilder on-line help. You could also read further in these areas:

■ Chapter 5, "Using Events, Functions, and the PowerScript Language," describes basic PowerScript programming. It's a must for the beginner.

■ Chapter 13, "Putting it All Together in an Application," discusses inheritance, on-line help, and how to make your Inventory Tracking system ready to deliver.

■ Chapter 14, "Debugging Your Application," reminds you that no programming is finished until it's been fully tested and debugged. Here, PowerBuilder expert Blaine Bickar shows how to debug an application.

■ Part VI, "References," serves as an excellent reference resource when you need to look up a function, an enumerated data type, an attribute, or an event.

Chapter 7

Using SQL in PowerBuilder

SQL (Structured Query Language) is a common language found in many databases. SQL was designed to give developers a common method for updating and retrieving data from tables on a database. SQL allows you to access your database from your PowerScript. There are many concepts common to most SQL implementations. Most of these commands (except the cursor commands) can be entered through the Database Administrator in the database painter.

This chapter discusses what you can do with SQL inside PowerBuilder. Notice all of the cautions in this chapter—when dealing with SQL, your application can either be accelerated or grind to a complete halt. SQL is a powerful tool, but be aware of its pitfalls.

In this chapter, you learn how to:

- Understand the SQL syntax of several SQL commands
- Understand the way databases handle NULLs
- Implement an SQL cursor
- Use the SQL painter and the cursor painter

Tip
Don't confuse *all* SQL with *Watcom* SQL. There is a Watcom SQL appendix with tips, notes, cautions, and utilities that are unique to Watcom. PowerBuilder's implementation of SQL works on any database PowerBuilder supports.

II

Using PowerScript

Understanding SQL Syntax

You'll first learn the SQL syntax that you are likely to run into when inside PowerBuilder.

> **Note**
>
> Because this chapter is about most of the SQL syntax you'll be using, the *Syntax-at-a-Glance* feature will be skipped in this chapter.

SELECT

SELECT is the command that lets you read from your tables. It is one of the most complex SQL commands. Its format is the following:

```
SELECT     { DISTINCT } ¦ select-list ¦
                        ¦  *          ¦
      INTO host_variable_list
      FROM table_list
      { WHERE search_condition }
      { GROUP BY column_name }
      { HAVING search_condition }
      { ORDER BY  field_list {DESC }};
```

The components of the SQL SELECT command are as follows:

- DISTINCT. If DISTINCT is specified, all duplicate rows are eliminated. Otherwise, all rows are returned.

> **Caution**
>
> Remember, DISTINCT only eliminates rows that are exact duplicates of each other. This is not the same as only selecting one row. If *any* columns are different between two rows, DISTINCT will report both rows.
>
> Embedded SQL can only retrieve one row at a time. Reporting more than one row could cause an SQL run time error.
>
> Also, using DISTINCT takes a lot of time. If possible, avoid using it.

- *select-list*. The select-list is the list of column names you want selected. An asterisk (*) in the place of the select-list will cause *all* columns to be selected.

> **Caution**
>
> Although coding an * for your select-list is much easier than typing every column in a table, if columns are added, deleted, or change order, your select statement may no longer work. It's better to bite the bullet and code in all of the field names.

- INTO *host_variable_list*. The *host_variable_list* is a list of variables in your application that will hold the retrieved columns.

> **Note**
>
> The INTO clause of the SELECT statement is required when you embed SQL into your PowerScript. However, the INTO clause is not allowed any other time, as with the Database Administrator in the database painter. Host variables cannot be declared or used in the Database Administrator. With no host variables, you can't make the host_variable_list required for the INTO clause.

> **Caution**
>
> Remember, not all database data types are the same as PowerBuilder data types. For instance, the Watcom integer has a range of –2,147,483,647 to 2,147,483,647; PowerBuilder's integer only has a range of –32,768 to 32,767. There's a lot of room for overflow when the two transact with each other. When overflow of this nature occurs, no error message is given, and your PowerBuilder integer has a corrupted value! Any overflow errors have to be caught during run-time testing!
>
> (If you are reading in a Watcom integer datatype, store it into a PowerBuilder long datatype and everything will be OK.)

- FROM *table_list*. The FROM clause allows the developer to specify which tables to SELECT data from.

- WHERE *search_condition*. The WHERE clause filters the incoming data based on the search_condition specified.

- GROUP BY *column_list*. The GROUP BY clause groups together multiple rows from the database, based on unique values found in your column_list.

■ HAVING *search_condition*. The HAVING clause must be accompanied by a GROUP BY clause. The search_condition of the HAVING clause filters the SELECT much like the WHERE clause, but unlike the WHERE clause, the HAVING clause is applied to the group data.

■ ORDER BY *field_list* {DESC}. The ORDER BY clause allows you to arrange the resulting columns of SELECT in a certain order, defined by field_list. The order is ascending unless DESC is specified.

Some SQL SELECT examples are shown in table 7.1.

Table 7.1 SQL SELECT Examples

SQL SELECT Statement	Description
SELECT * FROM *customer*;	This selects all columns and rows from the customer table.
SELECT *name,* *address,* *sales* FROM *customer* WHERE *purchase* > 1000 ORDER BY *sales*;	This selects the name, address, and sales from the customer table for all customers whose purchases are over 1,000. It puts these customers in sales order.
SELECT *territory,* SUM(*sales*) INTO :*sales_territory,* :*sales_total* FROM *customer* GROUP BY *territory* HAVING COUNT(*) > 10;	This sums the sales by territory for those territories with more than 10 customers. It puts these values into host variables sales_territory and sales_total.

SELECT *supplier.name,*
    item.name,
    item.cost
FROM   *item,supplier*
WHERE *item.cost* > 100 AND
supplier.supplier_number = item.supplier_number;
	This joins the item and supplier table by supplier number and selects supplier name, item name, and item cost for all items priced over $100.

Note

A *host variable* is a variable previously declared in PowerScript. These can be used inside most SQL commands. Notice in table 7.1 that they are always preceded by a colon (:). This indicates to your database that they are host variables and not table columns.

INSERT

INSERT puts additional rows into a table. Its format is the following:

```
INSERT INTO table_name {column_list} | VALUES values_list    |
                                     | SELECT command         |
```

The parts of the INSERT command are as follows:

- *table_name*. This is where you are going to insert new rows. It can be as fully qualified as your database allows.

- *column_list*. This is a list of columns that you are going to fill with your INSERT. If omitted, the INSERT command assumes all fields will be entered in the order they appear on your table.

> **Caution**
>
> Although *column_list* is not required in an INSERT command, you should be careful about omitting it. If you try to save some typing by not adding it and someone later adds fields to your table, your SQL statement may no longer work.

- *values_list*. This is a list of values (either constants or host variables) that you want to insert.

- SELECT_command. This is a SELECT command that returns values in the same order as the *column_list*.

Some examples of the INSERT command are shown in table 7.2.

Table 7.2   SQL INSERT Examples

SQL INSERT Statement	Description
INSERT INTO *customer* (*name, address*) VALUES ('Joe Schmoe', :*working_address*);	This inserts a row into the customer table with "Joe Schmoe" as the name and the contents of the host variable *working_address* as the address.
INSERT INTO *customer* (*name, address, phone*) VALUES (SELECT *prospect_name*, :*working_address*, '555-5555' FROM *prospect_table* WHERE *prospect_id* = :*new_client_id*);	This inserts a row into the customer table with the *prospect_name* from the *prospect_table* as the name, the host variable *working_address* as the address, and a constant "555-5555" as the phone number.

II

Using PowerScript

> **Note**
>
> Notice how you can mix host variables, constants, and table variables on the INSERT command when you use a SELECT command to retrieve your INSERT information.

UPDATE

The UPDATE command is used to update existing rows on a table with new data. Its format is as follows:

```
UPDATE table_name
SET   column_name1 = expression1,
      column_name2 = expression2,...
WHERE search_condition;
```

The *table_name* is the name of the table you wish to update. The *search_condition* in the WHERE clause is the same as in the SELECT statement. The *column_name* is a name of a column, and *expression* is the constant or host variable whose value will be placed inside the column.

Some examples of the UPDATE statement are shown in table 7.3.

Table 7.3 SQL UPDATE Examples

SQL UPDATE Statement	Description
UPDATE *my_table* SET *inactive_switch* = 'Y';	This sets *inactive_switch* to 'Y' for all rows in *my_table*.
UPDATE *my_table* SET *inactive_switch* = 'Y', *inactive_date* = :todays_date WHERE *last_name* = "SMITH";	This sets *inactive_switch* to 'Y' and *inactive_date* to the host variable *:todays_date* for all rows in *my_table* whose *last_name* is SMITH.

DELETE

The DELETE command is used to delete existing rows from a table. Its format is as follows:

```
DELETE FROM table_name
{WHERE search_condition};
```

The *table_name* is the name of the table in which you can delete rows. The *search_condition* in the WHERE clause is the same as in the SELECT statement.

Some examples of the DELETE statement are shown in table 7.4.

Table 7.4 SQL DELETE Examples

SQL DELETE Statement	Description
DELETE FROM *my_table*;	This deletes all rows from *my_table*.
DELETE FROM *my_table* WHERE *last_name* = "SMITH";	This deletes all rows from *my_table* whose last name is SMITH.

CONNECT and DISCONNECT

The CONNECT command connects the database transaction (*SQLCA*) to your application. The DISCONNECT command releases the database and frees up system resources used to keep the database connected to your application. The format for the two commands is as follows:

```
CONNECT {USING transaction};

DISCONNECT {USING transaction};
```

The *transaction* is usually *SQLCA*, although you can define new transactions in PowerBuilder. Table 7.5 shows some examples of CONNECT and DISCONNECT.

Table 7.5 SQL Connect and Disconnect Examples

SQL Statement	Description
CONNECT;	This connects to the database defined by *SQLCA*.
CONNECT USING *my_transaction*;	This connects to the database defined by *my_transaction*.
DISCONNECT;	This disconnects from the database defined by *SQLCA*.
DISCONNECT USING *my_transaction*;	This disconnects from the database defined by *my_transaction*.

Note

If you don't use *SQLCA*, you must add a USING clause every time you use a SQL statement. Most developers simply use *SQLCA* to avoid additional coding.

COMMIT and ROLLBACK

When you make changes to your table, the changes are not permanent until you use COMMIT to commit them to the table. If you later (in your application) decide against keeping the data, you issue a ROLLBACK statement to erase all changes to the database since the application started or since the last COMMIT statement. Table 7.6 shows examples of COMMIT and ROLLBACK.

Table 7.6 SQL Commit and Rollback Examples	
SQL Statement	**Description**
COMMIT;	This commits all work since the last COMMIT.
ROLLBACK;	This erases all work since the last COMMIT.

Using SQL Transactions and Testing Your SQLCode

◀ See "Understanding Database Transactions," p. 167

Depending on your database and how it's defined, not committing your work will eventually cause a slowdown in database performance. This is because the disk space and memory space that the database sets aside for non-committed work can grow to a size larger than what the database creators have optimized for. It's not a bad idea to commit your work every time you have a successful SQL function, thereby keeping the buffer organized and efficient.

To see if you have a successful SQL function, you should check *SQLCode* every time you access the database. If *SQLCode* is not 0, then you know you have a database error and can act on it. For example, the following code checks for errors that occurred during the CONNECT and COMMIT statements:

```
CONNECT;
If SQLCA.SQLCode = 0 Then
  COMMIT;
End If
If SQLCA.SQLCode <> 0 Then
    { error processing goes here }
End If
```

Troubleshooting

My program works fine on my system, but I can't CREATE, DROP, or ALTER anything on my Watcom database after I distribute. Why is that?

Certain Watcom SQL commands (such as CREATE commands, DROP command, and ALTER command) work fine inside your PowerBuilder environment, but don't work with the run-time version of Watcom SQL and your compiled program. The incompatibility between the developer and run-time versions will cause your application to work inside the PowerBuilder environment, but cause your application to fail upon distribution. Unfortunately, incompatibilities between the Watcom SQL development version and the Watcom SQL run-time version are only discussed in the Deployment and Development Kit that comes with PowerBuilder. (By the time you read the PowerBuilder documentation, some massive recoding may be necessary.)

If you are using the Watcom database, refer to Appendix B, "Using the Watcom Database and Watcom SQL," for some commands not seen inside the PowerBuilder documentation and for some distribution tips.

▶ See "Comparing the Run-Time Version and the Developer's Version," p. 658

▶ See "Listing Watcom ISQL Commands," p. 569

Understanding NULL

One of the most difficult concepts in databases is the concept of *NULL*. When a database field has a value of NULL, that means that nothing was entered into the field. NULL is not zero, nor is it an empty string—it means that nothing was entered.

Several SQL statements (such as SELECT) can cause hard-to-track errors if they encounter a NULL. *Update*s can also fail with a NULL in a field if the field was defined to have no NULLs allowed.

Using the SQL Painter

If you haven't guessed by now, SQL statements can be a pain to write. Not only do you have to know SQL syntax, but you have to know the columns of the tables you want to access.

PowerBuilder answers these concerns with its SQL painter. If you go into either a script painter or into the Database Administration painter, you can enter the SQL painter by choosing the SQL icon. The SQL Statement Type dialog box appears (see fig. 7.1).

Fig. 7.1

Clicking on the
SQL icon displays
the SQL Statement
Type dialog box.

Although you can paint other SQL commands, in this example, the SELECT
statement is chosen. In the SQL Statement Type dialog box, choose Select.
The Select Tables dialog box, shown in figure 7.2, appears. Select both item
and supplier, and choose **O**pen.

Fig. 7.2

The first step in
using the SQL
painter is to
choose the table(s)
you want to access
through the Select
Tables dialog box.

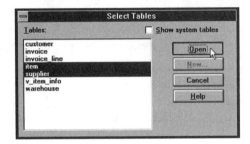

Now the painter pulls up the tables and shows you the two tables and how
they are related, as shown in figure 7.3. Using the icons in the SQL painter
PainterBar, you can choose any part of the SQL statement. Choose the
tab, also shown in figure 7.3, to specify a WHERE clause in your SELECT
statement.

Fig. 7.3

After choosing the
item and supplier
tables to SELECT
from, the SQL
painter appears.

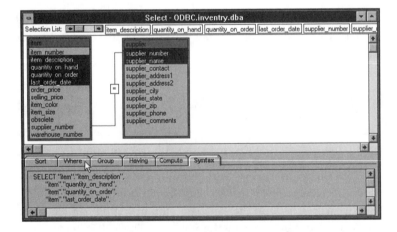

The Where Criteria tab now appears, as shown in figure 7.4. Here you can choose an SQL function or field, and then compare it to an expression (which would be a constant or host variable).

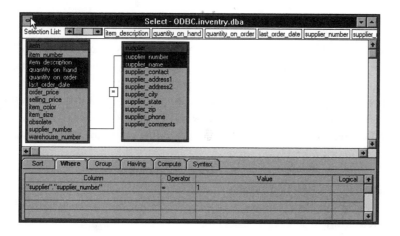

Fig. 7.4
In the Where Criteria tab, you can define the criteria for your WHERE statement.

Finally, exit out of the SQL painter. PowerBuilder then asks you if you want to paste your changes to your script or database administration. Click **Yes**, and the PowerScript painter in figure 7.5 pops up. Now you have a relatively complicated SQL statement on-screen.

▶ See "Using the SQL Toolbox," p. 277

```
          Database Administration - ODBC.inventry.dba

 SELECT "item"."item_description",
        "item"."quantity_on_hand",
        "item"."quantity_on_order",
        "item"."last_order_date",
        "supplier"."supplier_number",
        "supplier"."supplier_name"
   FROM "item",
        "supplier"
  WHERE ( "supplier"."supplier_number" = "item"."supplier_number" ) and
        ( ( "supplier"."supplier_number" = 1 ) )   ;
```

Fig. 7.5
Now you have a finished, flawless SQL statement.

II

Using PowerScript

This is easier than coding it yourself (unless you're a fast typist, you happen to be an SQL genius, *and* you're completely familiar with your database).

Using Cursors

In embedded SQL, you'll receive an SQL error if you try to retrieve more than one row from a table. However, there are times when you want to retrieve many rows that meet certain criteria. If this is the case, you need to use a cursor. A *cursor* is a temporary table set up by SQL that brings in all rows that meet certain criteria. These rows can then be accessed one row at a time. Unlike previous SQL commands, you will examine all cursor commands and then see syntax examples for them.

DECLARE

Before you use a cursor, you must first DECLARE it. The syntax for declaring a cursor is as follows:

```
DECLARE cursor_name CURSOR FOR select_statement;
```

With this syntax, the *cursor_name* is any valid PowerBuilder name, and the *select_statement* is any valid SELECT statement, except that it can't have an INTO clause. (The INTO clause is used for the FETCH statement, which is described in the following sections.)

The CURSOR Painter

As you recall, the SQL statement for the cursor is fairly lengthy. You can enter the Select SQL painter by entering the Declare Instance Variables dialog box from an event or function, and double-clicking on Cursor, as shown in figure 7.6. This puts you into an SQL painter so you can paint an SQL cursor statement as seen in the earlier figures. Your cursor now becomes an *instance variable*, a variable that PowerBuilder initializes with its default datatype when you open an object and ceases to exist when the object closes.

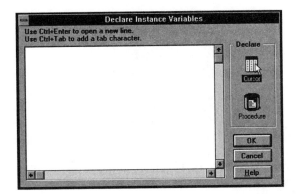

Fig. 7.6
Using the Declare
Instance Variables
dialog box, you
can paint your SQL
cursor.

OPEN

After you DECLARE your cursor, you must OPEN it. The OPEN applies the SELECT criteria and builds your temporary table with your rows in it. Its syntax is as follows:

```
OPEN cursor_name;
```

FETCH

After you are OPEN, you FETCH each row. FETCH allows you to sequentially process each row. Its syntax is as follows:

```
FETCH cursor_name

    INTO host_variable_list;
```

The INTO clause is identical to the INTO clause used in the SELECT statement.

CLOSE

When you are done with your cursor, you CLOSE it. Closing your cursor frees up any memory taken up by the temporary tables, or allows you to reopen your cursor with new criteria. Its syntax is as follows:

```
CLOSE cursor_name;
```

Tip
You might not like having SQL in your instance variables. You can use the **E**dit menu bar item to Cu**t** and **P**aste your cursor to the script in which you use it. This changes your cursor into a local variable.

II

Using PowerScript

UPDATE and DELETE (Positioned)

You can issue update or delete commands on a FETCHed row by using what are called *positioned* cursor commands. While you are fetching your rows, you can issue a positioned DELETE to the current row by the command:

```
DELETE {table_name} WHERE CURRENT OF cursor_name;
```

cursor_name is the name of the cursor defined in the declare statement. *table_name* is optional, but used most often with multiple-table cursors.

The positioned UPDATE command is very similar to the normal UPDATE command mentioned earlier. You can also issue a positioned UPDATE to the current row by the command:

```
UPDATE table_name
SET    column_name1 = expression1,
       column_name2 = expression2.
WHERE CURRENT OF cursor_name;
```

Example of a Cursor

In an event or function, table 7.7 shows how you would use a cursor.

Table 7.7 SQL CURSOR Examples	
SQL CURSOR Statement	**Description**
DECLARE *my_cursor* CURSOR FOR SELECT *name, address* FROM *customer;*	This statement tells the cursor to SELECT the name and address from the customer table of all the customers when the cursor is OPENed.
OPEN *my_cursor;*	This statement applies the SELECT described in the DECLARE statement. It builds a temporary table to store the results.
FETCH *my_cursor* INTO *:name, :address;*	This statement retrieves one row into the host variables *name* and *address*. Now the processing begins until the next FETCH statement.
CLOSE *my_cursor;*	This statement closes *my_cursor* and frees all the resources needed for the cursor.

From Here...

In this chapter, you've become familiar with several SQL commands and have learned how to work with them in PowerBuilder. This chapter has also shown you how databases handle NULLs, one of the most difficult concepts in databases. You've also examined all cursor commands and seen syntax examples for them.

SQL is necessary in PowerBuilder to do those tasks which are out of the ordinary. If you want to learn more about SQL, refer to the following chapters:

- Chapter 10, "Manipulating Data Using DataWindows," shows how SQL can be used to define a DataWindow. In this chapter, you learn more about the SQL toolbox and the SQL syntax behind a DataWindow.

- Appendix B, "Using Watcom Database and Watcom SQL," shows how you can use Watcom to implement your application. Also covered in this chapter are Watcom SQL functions and SQL commands not allowed inside the PowerBuilder environment.

II

Using PowerScript

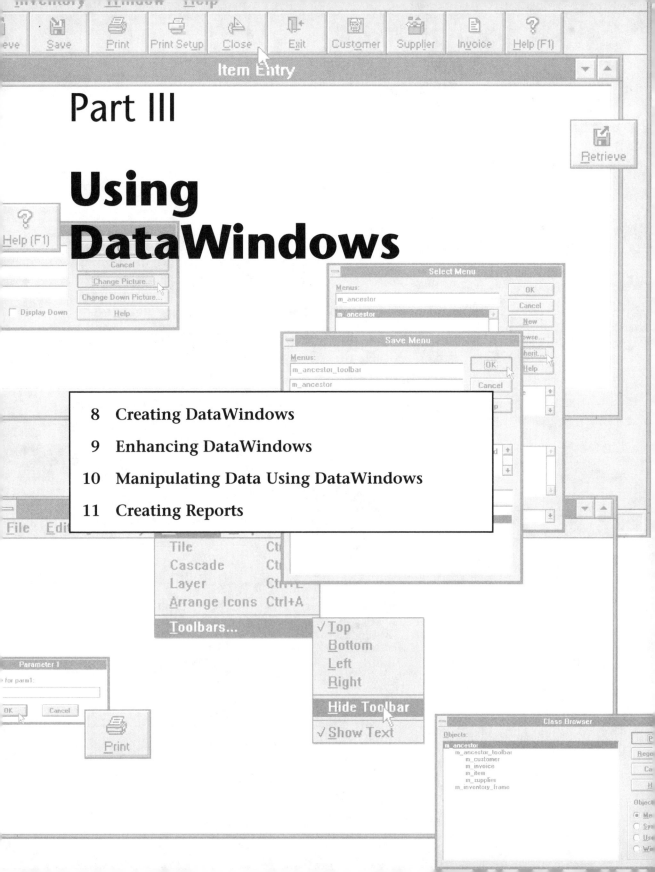

Part III

Using DataWindows

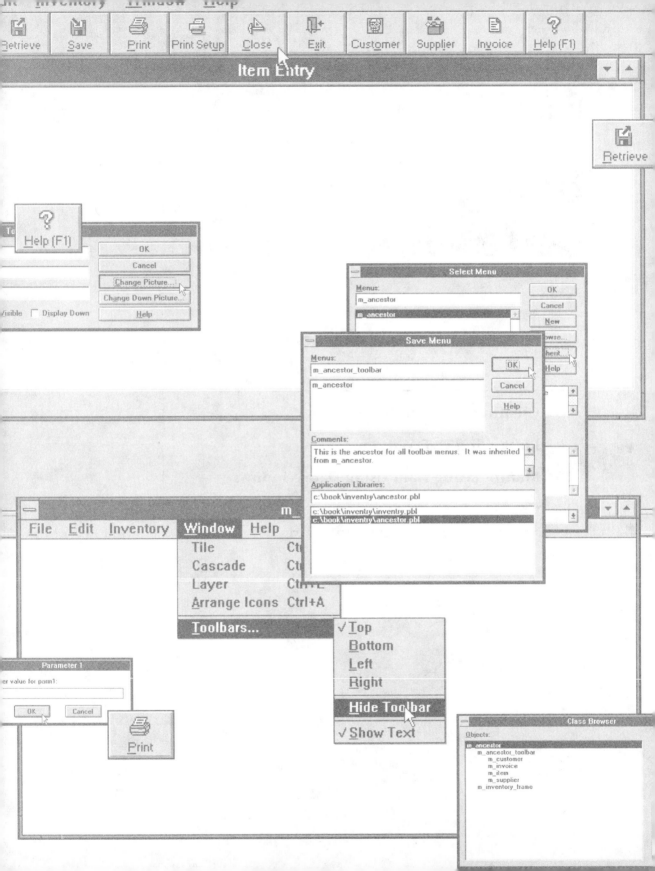

Chapter 8

Creating DataWindows

One of PowerBuilder's strongest features is DataWindows. DataWindows are data-entry screens that link a window to a database. They include several types of controls found on PowerBuilder windows.

The difference between DataWindows and data window screens found in other development environments is that DataWindow fields can be treated as individual columns or as single entities that consist of several rows. This makes updates to and retrieval from the database easier.

This chapter describes several DataWindow development techniques. You follow this by creating three DataWindows to use in your Inventory Tracking system. You then learn how to hook your DataWindows to your application.

In this chapter, you will do the following:

- Set and change default options for your DataWindow

- Differentiate between different data sources

- Differentiate between different presentation styles

- Use DataWindow controls

- Associate your DataWindow with a window

Using the DataWindow Painter

To get into the DataWindow painter, follow these steps:

1. Click on the DataWindow PowerBar icon. The Select DataWindow dialog box, shown in figure 8.1, appears.

Fig. 8.1
Click on the
DataWindow icon;
the Select
DataWindow
dialog box
appears.

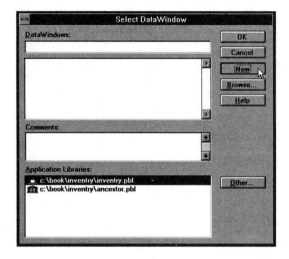

2. You can instruct PowerBuilder to either create a new DataWindow or
modify an existing DataWindow. For now, click on **N**ew to create a new
DataWindow. The New DataWindow dialog box appears (see fig. 8.2).

Fig. 8.2
In the New
DataWindow
window, you
choose your data
source and
presentation style.

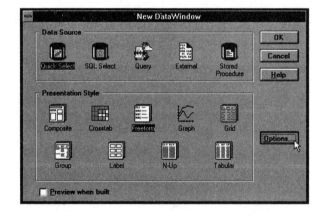

3. In the New DataWindow dialog box, you can define the Data Source,
the Presentation Style, and the Generation Options, as discussed in the
following sections.

In figure 8.2, Quick Select is chosen, which tells PowerBuilder to only use one
table to create the DataWindow; and Freeform is chosen to tell PowerBuilder
that you want a full screen with a single row represented. This also gives you
the freedom to position the fields (columns) where you want them on the
window.

Note

Notice in figure 8.2 that the **P**review when built check box is deselected. Choosing to **P**review when built only displays the DataWindow as PowerBuilder built it if there is data on the table chosen. You have no data on your tables, so choosing this only displays a confusing blank window. (Often you won't have any data on your tables when first creating your DataWindows because you'll probably use DataWindows to populate your tables.)

Understanding Generation Options

By clicking on the **O**ptions button in the New DataWindow dialog box, the Generation Options dialog box appears (see fig. 8.3).

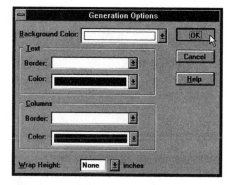

Fig. 8.3
The Generation Options dialog box lets you set default options for all DataWindows.

The following options can be set using the Generation Options dialog box, seen in figure 8.3:

- *Background Color.* This is the color of the DataWindow with no data on it.

- *Text Border.* This is the border of each field. Border choices are None, Underlined, Box, Shadowbox, 3D Raised, and 3D Lowered.

- *Text Color.* This is the color of any text on the DataWindow.

- *Column Border.* This is the border of each data entry field (column) on the DataWindow.

- *Column Color.* This is the color of each column on the DataWindow.

■ *Wrap Height*. New to Version 4.0, Wrap height allows the developer to start a new column after a given number of inches of fields have been placed on a free form DataWindow. Wrap height allows easier placement of columns on a DataWindow.

Understanding Data Sources

Tip
You may want to use Window Background and Window Text as your options for color. That way, the user can adjust the application's colors through Windows without you having to write a special setup module.

The *data source* is the database table (or tables) that you want to use to populate fields in your DataWindow. You can later change your mind on what your data sources are with little difficulty.

This chapter discusses the main data sources used in PowerBuilder: Quick Select and SQL Select.

Quick Select

Choosing Quick Select as your data source tells PowerBuilder that you want your DataWindow to retrieve from and write to a single table.

SQL Select

Choosing SQL Select as your data source tells PowerBuilder that the information on your DataWindow comes from multiple tables.

Determining Presentation Style

The *presentation style* tells PowerBuilder the way you want to present your data. Once chosen, the presentation style is hard to change. (You'll probably want to recreate your DataWindow if such a change is needed.)

The following lists the various types of presentation styles, why they should be chosen, and how to format them. Following the list are examples of DataWindows used in the Inventory Tracking system.

■ *Freeform*. Freeform DataWindows are used for data-entry screens of primary entities (such as Item, Warehouse, Supplier, Customer, and so on). Usually, freeform DataWindows show only one row at a time, and have no headers or summary information. You can see a completed freeform DataWindow in figure 8.13, later in the chapter.

■ *Tabular*. Tabular DataWindows typically show several rows of information at once. Usually, tabular DataWindows have a header row (instead of prompts as seen in the freeform DataWindow in fig. 8.5) and often have summary rows. An invoice is an excellent example of a tabular DataWindow. An invoice shows many rows (invoice lines) at once, and has header information (company and customer name and address, date, and so on), as well as summary information (tax and total amount owed).

- *Grid.* The best example of a grid DataWindow is a spreadsheet. Grids force the developer to keep detail entries on one line. They can have headings and summary information, but headings and summary information are part of the grid. Grids are best used for retrieval screens and when spreadsheet functionality is called for.

- *Label.* Label DataWindows are used for printing mailing labels (instead of data entry).

- *N-Up.* Like labels, N-Up DataWindows are usually not for data entry. N-UP DataWindows are typically used for reporting multiple rows across a report.

- *Groups, Graphs, and Crosstabs.* Groups allow you to group data for displaying, sorting and summarizing. Graphs graphically represent your data on a DataWindow. Crosstabs allow you to compare and contrast data values as they relate to two different columns. Groups, graphs, and crosstabs are complicated subjects. They will be explained later in the book.

▶ See "Using Crosstabs," p. 291

▶ See "Creating a Grouped Report," p. 300

▶ See "Creating Graphs," p. 320

Creating a Quick Select/Free Form DataWindow

The type of DataWindow you'll probably use most often is the quick select/free form DataWindow. This DataWindow is commonly used for single-table single-row data entry. All of our tables in the Inventory Tracking system will be this type.

Making the Item DataWindow

The first DataWindow you will create is the Item DataWindow. When you choose Quick Select and Freeform (refer to fig. 8.2), the Quick Select dialog box appears, as shown in figure 8.4.

III

Using DataWindows

Fig. 8.4

Populate your DataWindow by clicking on the columns you want represented or use the Add All button.

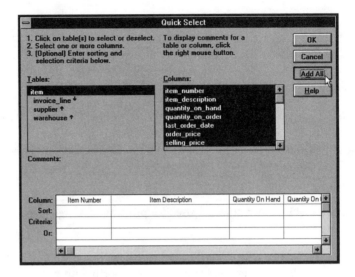

Hooking Your DataWindow to a Table

In the Quick Select dialog box, first select the table you want to use (in this case, the item table). Remember, you can only choose one table because you chose Quick Select.

After choosing your table, you can choose the fields you want on the DataWindow. You can choose one field at a time or add all of them with the Add All button. You can also choose the sort criteria or selection criteria. *Sort criteria* are the order you want your data appearing on a retrieval. Sort criteria are entered in each column in the Sort row. *Selection criteria* act as a filter for unwanted rows. You enter selection criteria in the Criteria row, and any additional criteria in the Or rows that follow. A sort is added in figure 8.4 to the DataWindow to sort by Item Description. When you've added all of the fields, and sort and selection criteria you desire, click on OK or press Enter.

Formatting Your DataWindow

After clicking on OK, the DataWindow painter appears. Initially (with freeform presentation style), all columns are displayed with their prompt beside them in a single column (or multiple columns if you use enough columns), as shown in figure 8.5. Using the mouse, simply drag the fields to where you want them to appear within the DataWindow.

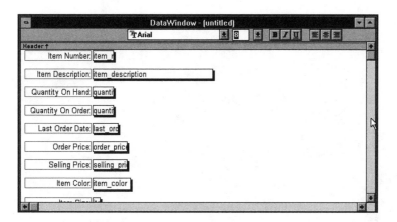

Fig. 8.5
Because you picked Freeform in the New DataWindow dialog box, you now can move the columns and text around.

Notice how hard it is to line up fields and prompts next to each other, and how difficult it is to evenly space between them using a mouse. Also, notice the way the size height of fields sometimes varies. PowerBuilder makes it easier by providing a way to align objects, evenly space between objects, and size objects identically. To format your DataWindow, perform the following steps:

1. Select at least two objects (to select an object, click on that object). A selected object has a dot in each corner. There are many different ways to select several objects at once—some of the most popular ways are listed as follows:

    ■ Hold down the left mouse key and drag the mouse pointer to "box" your objects in.

    ■ Click on your first object, and then hold down the control button while clicking on all other objects you want to select.

    ■ Open **E**dit and choose **S**elect. This activates a menu that allows you to select several different types of objects.

2. After selecting objects, open the **E**dit menu and choose the formatting action you want to accomplish. Choose A**l**ign to line all the objects up (as shown in fig. 8.6), **S**pace to evenly space between objects, or Si**z**e to make all selected objects either the same height or the same width. If you select numeric fields, you can also format them to be currency or percent by choosing **E**dit, F**o**rmat.

Tip
When moving selected items around your Data-Window, you can drag with your mouse for speed or use the arrow keys for more control.

III

Using DataWindows

Fig. 8.6
Use the **E**dit menu
to align objects,
select spacing, and
size the objects
appropriately.

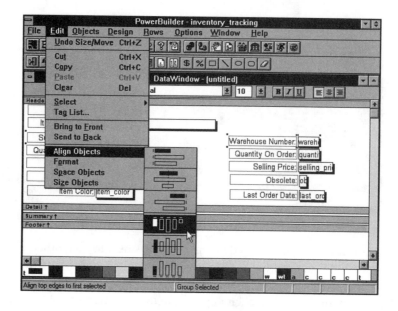

3. Once you've lined up the fields, you probably want to change the color
   so your DataWindow stands out a little more. Although it's easier to set
   the color in the Generation Options dialog box when the DataWindow
   is created, there are several ways to change the color of the
   DataWindow after it's been created. To change the color, double-click
   on any blank area in the DataWindow to pull up the DataWindow Style
   dialog box, as seen in figure 8.7. From here, you can change the background color of your DataWindow.

Fig. 8.7
By double-
clicking on the
DataWindow
(outside of any
columns), you
can change the
background color
of the DataWindow
through the
DataWindow
Style dialog box.

> **Note**
>
> You can also change the background of your window by right-clicking on the background area. A menu appears that allows you to quickly change the color, pointer, or measuring units of your DataWindow, as seen in figure 8.8.

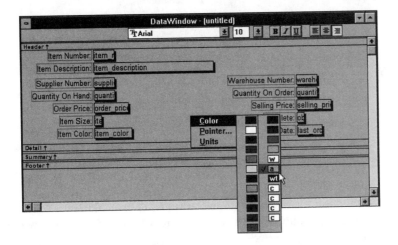

Fig. 8.8
Right-clicking on
the background
area of your
DataWindow
is an easy way
to change the
background color,
the units, and the
mouse pointer.

4. Next, you probably want to differentiate between your prompts and columns. There are several different ways to make your columns and prompts look different. For now, try a different background color and a different border. (You can do this by using the Generation Options dialog box, as discussed earlier, but for now you can see how to change your column attributes after creating your DataWindow.)

You can change column attributes one column at a time or change every column at once. To select every column at once, open **E**dit and choose Select **C**olumns, as shown in figure 8.9.

Fig. 8.9
Select all columns
by opening **E**dit
and choosing
Select **C**olumns.

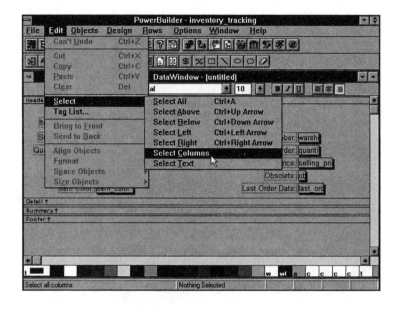

5. Now that all the columns are selected, you can change the background
color of each column, as shown in figure 8.10. Right-click on any of the
columns you've selected; a menu appears. Choose **C**olor **B**ackground,
and then pick the appropriate background color.

Fig. 8.10
On most
PowerBuilder
objects, right-
clicking on an
object activates a
menu window.

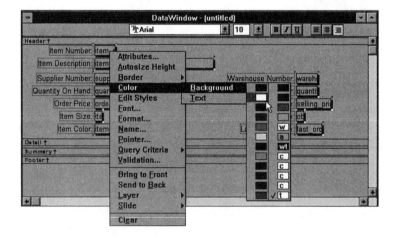

6. To further set your columns apart from your text, you can set the border of all selected columns. Once more, right-click on one of the selected columns, and choose **B**order 3D **L**owered (see fig. 8.11).

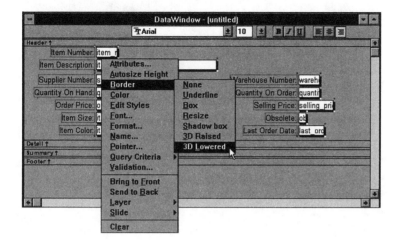

Fig. 8.11
You can individually select a border for a column or a group of columns by selecting and right-clicking on the columns you want to change.

7. Now you have finished formatting your screen. However, all the field moving has affected the order that you tab through your DataWindow. Open **D**esign and choose Tab **O**rder to put your DataWindow in Tab Order mode. Click on the red number above each field to set the tab order to flow with the layout of the DataWindow.

8. You won't be able to perform any other actions to your DataWindow until you leave tab order mode. When you're done ordering fields, choose **D**esign Tab **O**rder again to leave the tab order mode so you can save your DataWindow (see fig. 8.12).

You've finally finished your DataWindow (see fig. 8.13). Now you need to save your work. Double-click on the painter Control menu box. PowerBuilder will ask you if you want to save. Click on **Y**es. This pulls up the Save DataWindow dialog box shown in figure 8.14. Like other Save windows, click on the PBL where you want to store this DataWindow (inventry.pbl), and type in your DataWindow name (**d_item**). You'll continue defining DataWindows for the major entities in your Inventory Tracking system.

Fig. 8.12

Setting the tab order should be the last order of business before saving your DataWindow.

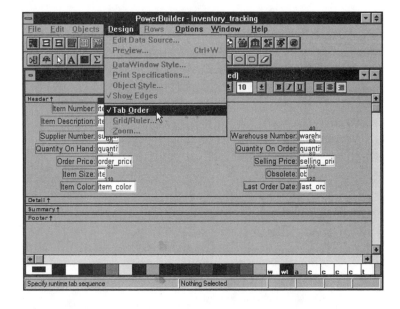

Fig. 8.13

After you're done formatting, your Item DataWindow should look like this.

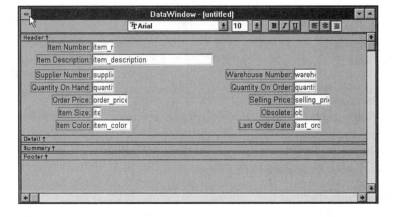

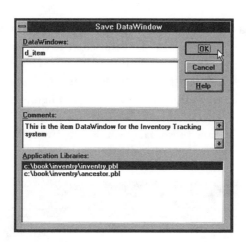

Fig. 8.14
Close the
DataWindow by
double-clicking on
the painter
Control menu
box, and save the
DataWindow in
the Save
DataWindow
dialog box.

Making the Customer DataWindow

Now you should make some of your other DataWindows. Click on the
DataWindow icon to start working with the Customer DataWindow. Activate
the Select DataWindow dialog box by clicking on the DataWindow icon.

Click on the New button to activate the New DataWindow dialog box.
Choose your options and click on Quick Select, Freeform, and then OK. Like
before, the Quick Select window displays. This time, instead of choosing
Item, select Customer (because this is the Customer DataWindow).

Next, format and align the DataWindow the way you want to see it. After
you're done, set the tab order. You should now have a DataWindow that
looks like figure 8.15. Notice how the customer_comments column is
stretched out into a multi-line edit.

Tip
Instead of
changing the
DataWindow
column color
and border later,
use the Generation
Options menu
(seen in fig. 8.3).

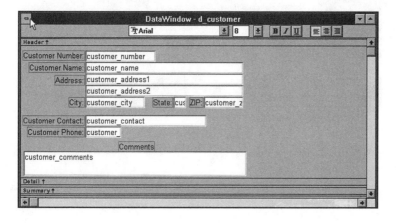

Fig. 8.15
Here is a sample
of the Customer
DataWindow.

III

Using DataWindows

Save your finished Customer DataWindow to d_customer in your inventry.pbl. You've now finished your work on the Customer DataWindow.

Making the Warehouse and Supplier DataWindows

Now create the Warehouse DataWindow, shown in figure 8.16, and the supplier DataWindow, shown in figure 8.17, just as you made the Item and Customer DataWindows. Save these DataWindows to d_warehouse and d_supplier.

Fig. 8.16
Using the same process you used with Item and Customer, develop the Warehouse DataWindow.

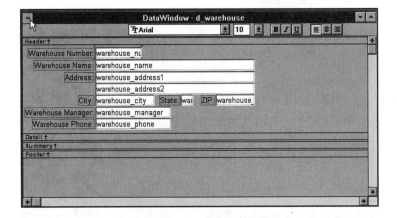

Fig. 8.17
Using the same process as with Item, Customer, and Warehouse, develop the Supplier DataWindow.

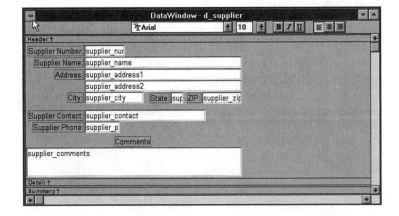

Making a SQL Select/Tabular DataWindow

Most of your data entry DataWindows will be Quick Select/Freeform. Quick Select/Freeform DataWindows are useful for single-table DataWindows that don't require much processing, but sometimes more complicated processing is needed.

Reviewing Invoice Design

A typical invoice has several components:

- *Header information.* Usually found at the top of the invoice, this information consists of invoice number, date, customer name and address, and headings for the invoice lines.

- *Detail information.* Consists of the line number, the item description, the quantity ordered, the unit price, and the total price. There can be several lines per invoice, each referring to a different order.

- *Footer information.* This information usually consists of some comments, miscellaneous charges, sales tax, freight, and a total amount owed.

To enter, display, or print an invoice, several tables need to be involved. Also, the DataWindow must be made to be a little more complicated than a straight single-row data entry.

Making the Invoice DataWindow

To start making your Invoice DataWindow, click on the DataWindow icon. As before, the New DataWindow dialog box appears. This time, select SQL Select and Tabular as your Data Source and Presentation Style, and choose OK (see fig. 8.18).

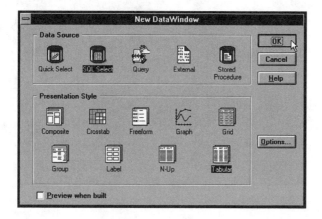

Fig. 8.18
To make a multiple-table DataWindow, choose SQL Select for the Data Source. A Tabular Presentation Style places the headings at the top of the DataWindow.

Choosing and Joining Tables

Now, the Select Tables dialog box appears. Choose all the tables that you need to make your DataWindow by clicking on them, as seen in figure 8.19. For an invoice, you need invoice and invoice_line. You also have customer and item information on the invoice, so those tables should be chosen also. When you are finished choosing all the tables you need for a DataWindow, click on **O**pen.

Fig. 8.19
The Select Tables dialog box appears when using the SQL Select Data Source. Choose all the tables for your DataWindow, and click on OK.

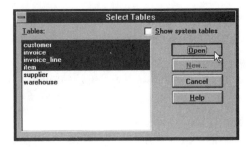

After you've picked your tables, the DataWindow SQL painter appears, as shown in figure 8.20. This painter lists all your tables and the way they are joined together (via the foreign keys you set up earlier). Pick the columns you want to be displayed as fields on your DataWindow. When you're done, click on the Design icon on the PainterBar.

Fig. 8.20
In the DataWindow SQL painter, you choose which columns will appear on your DataWindow.

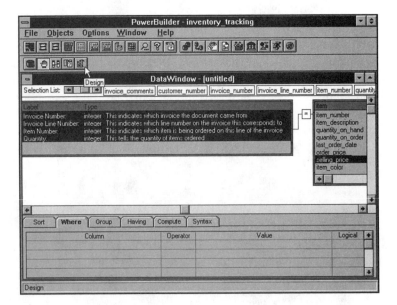

Formatting an Invoice Using DataWindow Bands

Now you are in the DataWindow painter. PowerBuilder has done something
different this time. Instead of all the information being displayed in one area
on the screen (in the Detail area) with a tabular presentation style, the
prompt information is now in the Header area; the column information is in
the Detail area, as shown in figure 8.21. These areas are called *bands*.

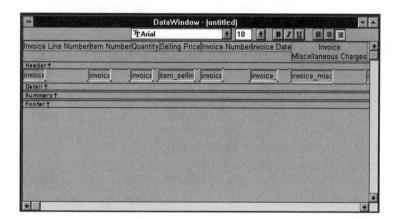

Fig. 8.21
With the tabular
presentation style,
prompts appear in
the header band;
column informa-
tion appears in the
detail band.

There are four bands to each DataWindow (although seldom are all used in
one DataWindow). They are as follows:

- *Header band.* This band appears at the top of your DataWindow. All
  fields that you want displayed only once per window go here.

- *Detail band.* The detail band is the second band. All repetitive information is stored here. The DataWindow displays as many detail bands on a
  DataWindow as it can, given the window space that you allocate for it.

- *Summary band.* In this third band, you summarize (usually via computed fields) the information in the Detail band. You can also move
  entry columns to this band that you want at the end of your detail
  information.

- *Footer band.* Fields and prompts in the footer band are displayed at the
  bottom of each DataWindow. On single-window or single-sheet
  DataWindows, often the footer band is used to display summary information at the bottom of the page. This is also a good place for page
  numbers, recurring footnotes, and so on.

Tip
Be sure to choose
the primary keys
for all tables you
will be updating
from your
DataWindow.

III

Using DataWindows

Although tabular presentation style places all of your columns in the detail band, don't be afraid to move them to other bands. For example, you only want one customer address on each invoice (as opposed to the same customer address repeating for each invoice line). Therefore, you should move customer prompts and columns to the header band. You probably want tax, charges, and freight at the bottom of each single-page invoice, so prompts and columns relating to such information should go to the footer area.

Examining DataWindow Controls

Like the window painter, the DataWindow painter allows you to add several different types of controls. Every column or static text (prompts) are considered controls. (You'll add some more controls to your Invoice DataWindow.)

After you're finished moving your prompts and columns where you want them, add a company name and address to the title invoice by clicking on the Text icon. Now, highlight any prompts that seem out of place and delete them. Finally, click on the Text icon again to add appropriate prompts to your system.

By clicking on the Picture icon and answering the appropriate questions, a bit map is added to your DataWindow (see fig. 8.22).

Fig. 8.22
By selecting the Picture icon, you can choose a bit map picture to add to your DataWindow.

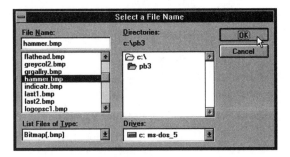

Before the bit map is added to the DataWindow, the Extended Bit Map Definition dialog box appears. Change the name to something appropriate, and click on OK.

In this example of a hardware store, hammer and screwdriver bit maps (included with PowerBuilder) were added to the invoice. You can see this invoice in figure 8.23.

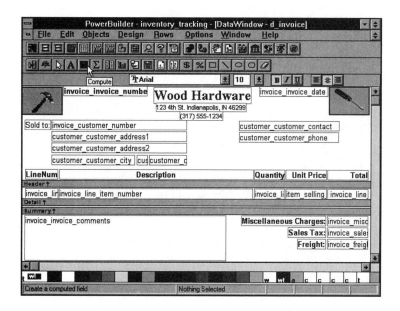

Fig. 8.23
The Invoice
DataWindow in
development has
most columns in
the header band.

Using Computed Fields

In figure 8.23, you see the Invoice DataWindow as it is defined so far. However, the Invoice layout is still incomplete. Although it lists quantity ordered and selling price, you still need to list the total amount owed for each invoice line (and the total amount owed for the entire invoice). These fields aren't stored on a table—they are *computed fields*.

To show a computed field on your DataWindow:

1. Click on the Compute icon on the PainterBar.

2. Click on the place where you want the computed field to go. This activates the Computed Field Definition dialog box, shown in figure 8.24.

3. Although PowerBuilder gives you many functions to choose from, you only need a simple equation to calculate your line total. Click on the quantity field in the Columns area. Then press the multiplication symbol (*). Finally, click on the selling price and then click on OK. The computed field of quantity * unit price will then appear. (Don't forget to add the appropriate prompt to the heading band.)

III

Using DataWindows

Fig. 8.24

The Computed Field Definition dialog box allows you to enter a computed field for your DataWindow.

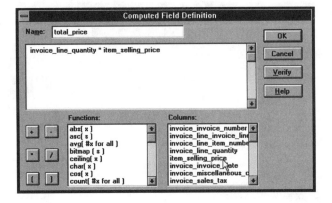

Summation is the most common computed field. The Invoice total amount owed is a summation of all line totals, and any miscellaneous charges, tax, and freight. Click on all of these columns by boxing them with your pointer, or click on one column and then press the Ctrl key as you click on the other columns. Then click on the Sum icon. A computed sum will appear in the summary band. Then supply the appropriate prompt. You can see a layout of the invoice in figure 8.25.

Fig. 8.25

The tab order is set to zero on several fields, making them display-only. Computed fields don't have tab orders—they are always display-only.

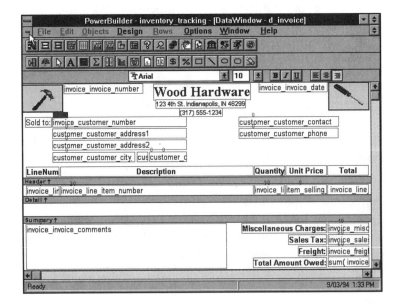

Most summations are placed in the footer or summary bands, since several detail rows can then be summarized. If you place a summation in a detail line, only one detail row can be summarized at a time.

Revisiting Tab Order

Now you can set the tab order of your DataWindow, as you did for the Item DataWindow, by opening **D**esign and choosing Tab **O**rder. However, the Invoice DataWindow is different from all previous DataWindows because there are some fields that are display-only.

> **Note**
>
> By setting the tab order to zero, you make a column display-only. The end user can't tab to or click on a column with a zero tab order (refer to fig. 8.25).

Specifying Update Characteristics

The last step to complete a DataWindow with an SQL Select data source is to specify the update characteristics. Because you are pulling from several tables, PowerBuilder doesn't know which table to update. Open **R**ows and choose **U**pdate, as seen in figure 8.26.

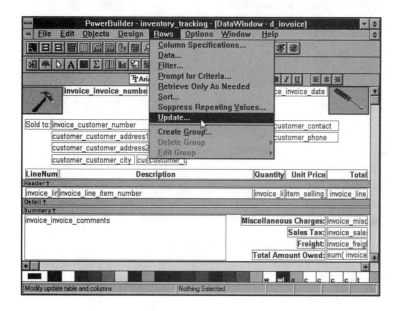

Fig. 8.26
To change the update characteristics, open **R**ows and choose **U**pdate.

III

Using DataWindows

The Specify Update Characteristics dialog box appears (see fig. 8.27).

Fig. 8.27

The Specify Update Characteristics dialog box tells PowerBuilder which table to update with this DataWindow.

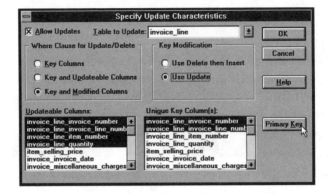

First, click on **A**llow Updates to allow this DataWindow to update a table. Then choose the table you want to update. You probably want to update two tables with this DataWindow (invoice and invoice_line) instead of one. Because you can only choose one table for the DataWindow to automatically update, it is better to update the detail table (invoice_line).

> **TrackNote**
>
> You will use SQL to update the Invoice table later. You should update the detail table because multiple rows are more complicated to update than single rows using PowerScript and SQL.

Next, click on the columns you want to update in the table you have chosen.

You also can choose the Where clause that the DataWindow will use for your updates and deletes from the DataWindow. This is useful in a multi-user situation, in which several users are updating a single set of tables at once. Clicking on Key and U**p**datable Columns or on Key and **M**odified Columns enhances security—one user can't write over another user's table. This way, if a row gets updated by one user while another is also attempting an update, one update will fail.

Under Key Modification, you have the options of issuing a Delete and Insert, or an Update to update the key if a user modifies a key. This can be useful (or problematic) in cascading updates and cascading deletes that some databases support. Using an Update to change the key is faster.

Finally, pick which key the table will be using. If you have already chosen your table, you can click on Primary **K**ey and let PowerBuilder pick your update key for you.

Click on OK to return to the DataWindow painter. Now save your DataWindow under d_invoice and exit the DataWindow painter.

> **TrackNote**
>
> Because the invoice_line table was chosen as the table to update, you want the invoice_line_number, the item_number on the invoice, and the quantity ordered to display. Now pick the primary key of the line number and the invoice_number as the key.

> **Caution**
>
> You won't be able to update any tables using an SQL Select or Query data source unless you use the Specify Update Characteristics dialog box (refer to fig. 8.27). This dialog box tells PowerBuilder which tables to update, and flags that the DataWindow is updatable.

Using Other Data Sources

There are other data sources than SQL Select and Quick Select. These other data sources aren't as popular since SQL Select and Quick Select are so versatile and meet most needs. However, you may find yourself using or running into them some day.

Queries

Using a *query* is a lot like creating a permanent SQL Select—even the windows are laid out the same way. The only difference between the two is that you can use queries as the predefined data source for several different DataWindows instead of recoding your SQL Select every time.

Queries aren't that popular because a change to a query is not reflected in the DataWindow that uses it. In fact, when you use a query for a data source, it is immediately converted to an SQL Select. If you only plan to use a query once, you should save yourself some time and space by using an SQL Select.

▶ See "Using Queries," p. 577

Queries are gaining acceptance with certain third-party software packages—they are being produced to use with PowerBuilder. Like many alternative development techniques, it's a matter of preference.

External Data Sources

You can populate your DataWindow by using PowerScript, but only by building a DataWindow using an external data source.

When you start building your DataWindow using an external data source, the Result Set Description dialog box will appear. You can determine which fields are to be used and what their data type and length are, as shown in figure 8.28. You can then continue to build your DataWindow as if you were using a Quick Select as your data source.

Fig. 8.28
Using an external source allows you to make a DataWindow, but populate the fields with a PowerScript statement after describing your fields.

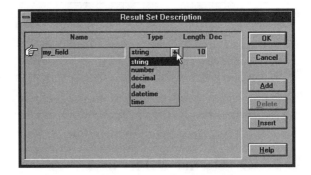

With the exception of stored procedures, external data sources are not popular, and with good reason. By taking away the database table from the DataWindow, you take away much of its functionality. Working with the data becomes extremely tedious. Your life will probably be easier if you instead consider using a temporary database table for your DataWindow.

Stored Procedures

Stored procedures are extremely popular for display-only DataWindows that you can use if your database supports them. Some databases have extremely efficient stored procedures. You can often improve the speed of your application by doing some of your SQL statements inside a stored procedure.

> **Note**
>
> Every database differs on how to declare a stored procedure, and not all databases support stored procedures. To find out if your database supports stored procedures, review your database documentation or contact your Database Analyst (DBA).

Associating Your DataWindow with a Window

Now that you've completed your DataWindows, you need to hook them to your windows so they can be used.

Hooking a DataWindow to an SQL Transaction

Before going further, you must tell PowerBuilder which database you want all your DataWindows to access. By putting the following code in w_datawindow_ancestor, you ensure that all your DataWindows are hooked up to SQLCA. In addition, you automatically do an insert on the DataWindow unless the window is opened with a parameter.

```
?dw_data.settrans(sqlca)
if message.doubleparm = 0 then
    dw_data.insertrow(0)
else
    triggerevent("retrieve")
end if
```

> **Syntax-at-a-Glance**
>
> *SetTrans(transaction)*
>
> SetTrans associates your DataWindow with the database defined by a transaction like SQLCA. This way, your DataWindow knows where to go to retrieve and update data. This is a DataWindow function—not an SQL statement. Although this is a DataWindow function, you'll usually see it inside the open event of your window.

Associating DataWindow Controls with a DataWindow Object

There is a difference between a DataWindow control and a DataWindow object. A DataWindow *object* is what has been defined in this chapter. A DataWindow *control* is a window control, such as a command button or a graph. Use DataWindow controls to communicate with DataWindow objects.

III

Using DataWindows

A DataWindow control, dw_data, has already been defined in the ancestor window (w_datawindow_ancestor). You must now point the control in each window to the appropriate DataWindow.

To associate a DataWindow object with a DataWindow control, activate a window with a DataWindow control (such as w_item). Right-click on the DataWindow area so that a menu displays, as shown in figure 8.29.

Fig. 8.29
By right-clicking on your data window, a pop-up menu appears.

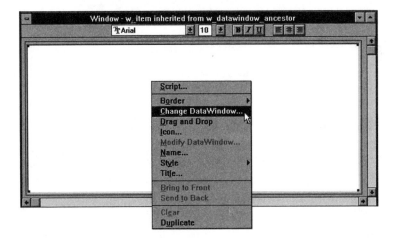

In this menu, click on **C**hange DataWindow. This option does not change an existing DataWindow. (For that, you would have had to pick **M**odify DataWindow.) Instead, this changes (or sets) the DataWindow object that this DataWindow control points to.

After you click on **C**hange DataWindow, the Select DataWindow window pops up listing all your DataWindows in your default PBL. From here, click on the appropriate PBL and choose the DataWindow you want associated with your window. (In this case you would pick d_item, as seen in fig. 8.30.)

Now a picture of your DataWindow object appears in the menu painter. Be sure to resize your DataWindow control to fit your DataWindow object, as seen in figure 8.31.

Fig. 8.30
The Select
DataWindow
dialog box allows
you to choose a
DataWindow
object to be
associated with
your DataWindow
control.

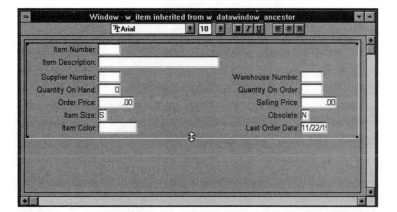

Fig. 8.31
Your DataWindow
control should be
resized to fit your
DataWindow
object as much as
possible.

Note

On freeform DataWindows, all the information is put in the detail band. Although it's
not necessary, most developers keep the information in the detail band. You must be
careful not to size your DataWindow so that more than one row appears on your
DataWindow (unless you have designed it that way). Otherwise, you'll have a multi-
row DataWindow when you wanted a single-row DataWindow.

III

Using DataWindows

Repeat this process for all DataWindows (d_item, d_supplier, d_invoice, and d_customer would attach to w_item, w_supplier, w_invoice, and w_customer, respectively).

Running Your Application

Once more, you are ready to click on the Run icon and run your application. All the windows have been pulled up and tiled. Notice that all the windows now have DataWindows attached to them.

From Here...

In this chapter, you learned how to create a DataWindow and how to hook a DataWindow object to a DataWindow control. If you want to find out more information, refer to the following chapters:

- Chapter 9, "Enhancing DataWindows," goes beyond creating DataWindows and delves into field manipulation and edit styles, like radio buttons and drop-down DataWindows.

- Chapter 10, "Manipulating Data Using DataWindows," describes how to use a DataWindow to convey information to and from a database.

- Chapter 11, "Creating Reports," shows how to use your DataWindows as reports. This chapter also describes grouping and graphing data, as well as some new PowerBuilder 4.0 features.

- Chapter 13, "Pulling It All Together in an Application," describes the final steps needed to finalize your application.

The PowerBuilder User's Guide also dedicates several chapters to DataWindows.

Chapter 9

Enhancing DataWindows

In the last chapter, you learned how to create DataWindows. Now you will see how to modify, enhance, and use your DataWindow. In this chapter, you will learn how to:

- Use edit styles

- Use validation rules

- Use display formats

- Set default values for your columns in the database painter

- Set default values for your columns in the DataWindow painter

Using Edit Styles

So far, you have been shown all columns as entry fields on the DataWindow. This section will show you how to enhance your DataWindow to include other edit styles such as drop-down lists, radio buttons, check boxes, and edit masks. You'll also learn how to include a DataWindow within a DataWindow.

To define or review an edit style, right-click on the column you want to modify or review. You will see a pop-up menu. Choose **E**dit Styles, and another pop-up menu appears showing you a list of possible edit styles for your field (see fig. 9.1).

Fig. 9.1
By right-clicking on a column and choosing **E**dit Styles, you can view or modify the edit style chosen. Edit is the default edit style.

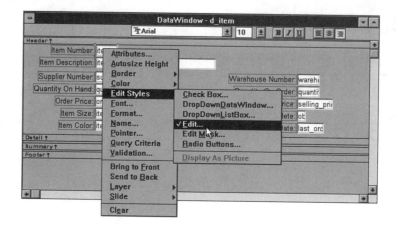

Edit

Edit is the default edit style. By clicking on **E**dit, the Edit Style dialog box appears, as shown in figure 9.2.

Fig. 9.2
The Edit Style dialog box allows you to set attributes on your field relating to this edit style.

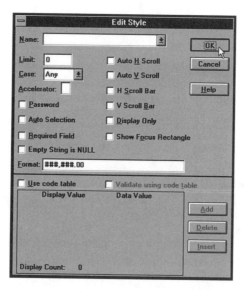

From the Edit Style dialog box seen in figure 9.2, you can define many aspects of your edit field.

Name

You can design your own edit styles from the database painter. Also, some edit styles (especially for numeric fields) are defined for you. If you want to use a predefined edit style, you put the name of the edit style here.

▶ See "Defining Your Own Edit Styles," p. 257

Limit

The **L**imit box is where you specify how many characters can be entered. If you specify 0, you can enter an unlimited amount of characters.

Case

You can specify upper or lowercase in the **C**ase box. The default is any case.

Accelerator

The **A**ccelerator key allows you to define a key or key sequence that will set focus on the column you are defining. (Remember, to set focus on a field or control means to bring the cursor to that field.)

Tip

As with menus, if you define an accelerator key for your DataWindow, underline the letter associated with the Accelerator key by placing an ampersand (&) before the letter.

Password

The **P**assword check box tells PowerBuilder to place asterisks (*) when the user types in this column (similar to a password).

Auto Selection

The **Au**to Selection check box, when clicked, tells PowerBuilder to highlight the column when it receives focus. Since the entire field is now selected, anything you type will take the place of the current contents of the field. If **Au**to Selection is not selected, the cursor will go to the beginning of the field when that field receives focus.

Required Field

The **R**equired Field check box does not allow the field to lose focus unless a value is entered.

Empty String is NULL

An empty string is not normally considered a NULL. If the Empty String NULL check box is selected, PowerBuilder converts any empty string entered into a NULL.

Auto H Scroll

If you type past the end of a data entry column, the Auto **H** Scroll check box automatically scrolls horizontally. The default is checked.

Auto V Scroll

To allow a column to automatically scroll vertically when needed, click on the Auto **V** Scroll check box. The default is not checked.

H Scroll Bar

Clicking on the H **S**croll Bar check box places a horizontal scroll bar on the field.

V Scroll Bar

Clicking on the V Scroll **B**ar check box places a vertical scroll bar on the field.

Display Only

To mark a field as Display Only, click on the **D**isplay Only check box. The default allows the user to edit the field. (You could also set a field to Display Only by using the Tab Order, as discussed in Chapter 8, "Creating DataWindows.")

Show Focus Rectangle

Clicking on the Show Focus Rectangle check box makes PowerBuilder display a faint rectangle around the field if it has focus.

Format

The **F**ormat box is usually used for numeric fields. Formatting allows an edit mask to be applied to the field after the field has been entered. For instance, if you typed **$#,###** in the Format box and the user typed **1234** in the field, as soon as the field lost focus, 1234 would be converted to $1,234.

Use Code Table

A **U**se Code Table in the Edit edit style tells PowerBuilder to convert a specific value entered into another value. For instance, you can click on the **U**se Code Table check box and then enter the following:

Display Value	Data Value
Indiana	IN
In	IN
indiana	IN
in	IN

If the user entered one of the display values, the field would be converted to IN internally.

Validate Using Code Table

Validate Using Code **T**able forces the user to enter one of the display values
or data values. If the user enters something else, he or she will get an error
message saying that what they entered for this column did not pass the validation test.

Drop-Down List Box

A *list box* is a box that has a list of choices. To make a choice in a list box,
simply click on that choice. PowerBuilder employs a drop-down list box. This
is a column whose list box doesn't appear until that column has focus. To
make a column a drop-down list box, right-click on the column, and choose
Edit Styles, DropDown**L**istBox, as seen in figure 9.3.

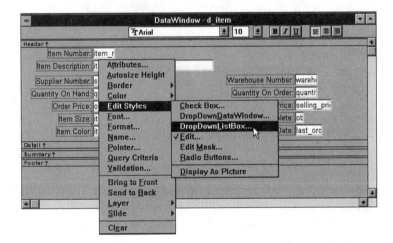

Fig. 9.3
To make a column
into a drop-down
list box, right-click
on that column,
and choose
Edit Styles,
DropDown**L**istBox.

The DropDownListBox Style dialog box appears, as shown in figure 9.4.

You'll notice that many of the options for the list box style are the same for
the edit style. The different attributes are as follows.

Sorted

Clicking on the **S**orted check box shows the Display Values in ascending
order.

Fig. 9.4
The
DropDownListBox
Style dialog box is
used to define a
drop-down list box.

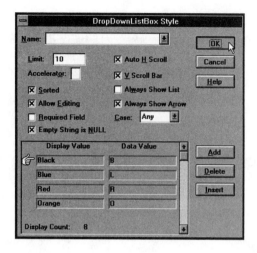

Allow Editing

Sometimes you'll want to give the user a set of choices, but other times you'll want the user to be able to type in his or her own choice. Clicking on the Allow **E**diting check box allows the user either to select a choice from the list box or to type in a new choice. If the Allow **E**diting check box is not selected, the user must fill the field by choosing from the list box.

Always Show List

Al**w**ays Show List converts the drop-down list box into a list box. By clicking on the Al**w**ays Show List check box, the list box is always displayed. If the Al**w**ays Show List check box is not selected, the column's list box then will drop down when the column has focus.

Tip
If you click on the Allow Editing check box, a gap is placed between the arrow and the field boxes. If the Allow Editing check box is not selected, the arrow box is flush against the field box.

Always Show Arrow

Always Show A**r**row shows the arrow that pulls down the list box at all times. If the Always Show A**r**row check box is not selected, the arrow is shown only when the field has focus.

Unlike the edit code table, the code table for the drop-down list box is used to display choices. Any choice made is then translated to the proper data value.

You can see in figure 9.5 what this does to your field. Since you added an arrow, an arrow appears in the DataWindow painter. Notice that the arrow is set off from the field. This is because this drop-down list box is editable as opposed to strictly multiple-choice.

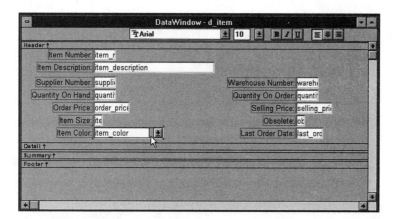

Fig. 9.5
Item Color shows
what a drop-down
list box looks like
in the
DataWindow
painter.

Figures 9.6 and 9.7 show how this drop-down list box looks while running. Notice that the user can quickly choose a common value but also can enter a not-so-common value if needed. Speeding data entry while allowing flexibility is a big benefit when using a drop-down list box.

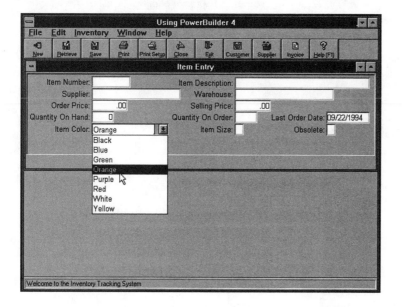

Fig. 9.6
Using a drop-down
list box, the user
can quickly choose
an option.

Fig. 9.7
Since this drop-down list box allows edits, the user is allowed the flexibility to enter a value not on the list.

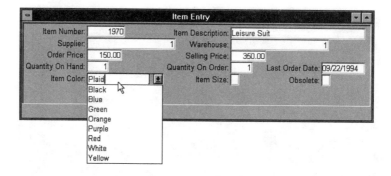

> **Note**
>
> You can either allow edits or not allow edits with a drop-down list box. Allowing edits adds to flexibility (as shown in figs. 9.6 and 9.7), yet keeps the advantage of the list of commonly used values for the column.
>
> However, sometimes such flexibility is not desired. By not allowing edits, you easily limit the valid values for the column without a lot of difficult coding to test for the proper values, displaying error messages, re-entering the column, and so on.
>
> For each column, you must decide whether you want to allow the user as much flexibility as possible, or if you want to limit the choices of a column to a select set of answers.

Radio Button

Radio buttons, like drop-down list boxes, are a multiple-choice of sorts for the user to quickly select the value for a column. To make a column into a radio button, choose **E**dit Styles, **R**adio Button.

The RadioButton Style dialog box appears, as shown in figure 9.8.

In the RadioButton Style dialog box, you define your radio button column with the following attributes.

Columns Across

The **C**olumns Across box controls the number of columns displayed across.

Left Text

The **L**eft Text check box tells PowerBuilder to put the text on the left side of the radio button. If this is not clicked, the text will be placed on the right side of the radio button.

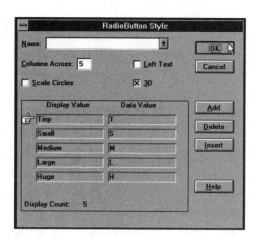

Fig. 9.8
The RadioButton
Style dialog box
enables you to
define your radio
button column.

Scale Circles

Scale Circles tells PowerBuilder to scale the radio buttons to the size of the field.

3D

3D gives radio buttons a lowered appearance. This usually is a good look for a radio button.

The code table used is similar to the drop-down list box. If you click on a display value, the data value is returned to the program. You can see how the radio button you defined in figure 9.8 looks when completed in figure 9.9.

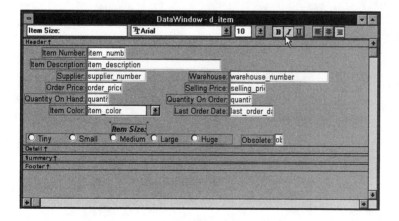

Fig. 9.9
Radio buttons
shown underneath
Item Size: are
quick ways of
entering a
multiple-choice
questions.

> **Note**
>
> Notice how the Item Size prompt has changed. Now, the Item Size is in bold and italics. You can select it by clicking on the Item Size prompt, and then clicking on B *and* I, as shown in figure 9.9.

In Version 3, PowerBuilder always marked at least one radio button during execution. If your column was initialized with an invalid value, the last radio button was marked but the invalid value stayed in the column. This could cause problems at run time for a user who thought one value was marked but internally an invalid value was stored.

In Version 4, PowerBuilder doesn't mark any button if an invalid value is in the field. This aids in run-time testing and execution.

> **Note**
>
> Radio buttons are very fast to enter. However, you should limit the number of radio buttons in a column before making the column a no-edit drop-down list box. Too many radio buttons clutter a screen and slow down data entry as the user hunts for the right button. (Anything over six radio buttons in one column typically becomes difficult to use, but it's a matter of preference.)

Check Box

Check boxes are yes-no boxes that are clicked on or off. To make a column into a check box, choose **E**dit Styles, **C**heck Box. The CheckBox Style dialog box appears, as shown in figure 9.10.

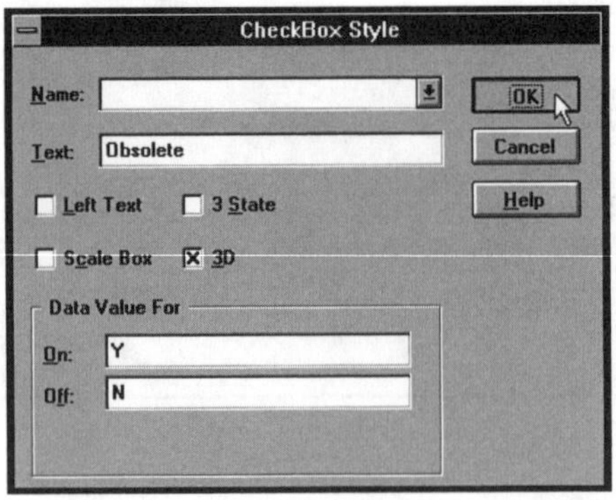

Fig. 9.10

The CheckBox Style dialog box defines your check box column.

In the CheckBox Style dialog box, you define the attributes of your check box. The following are attributes specific to check boxes only.

Text

Text is the prompt that is shown on one side of the check box.

Scale Box

Scale Box is similar to the Scale Circle used with radio buttons. Scale Box makes the square box as large as the defined field will allow.

3 State

Check boxes don't always have to be yes or no. Windows (and PowerBuilder) allow for a 3 State check box. This is usually checked, not checked, or grayed-in.

Data Value For

The Data Value For attribute allows you to define what values are returned for each state of the check box. Usually, this is just Y or N.

Returning to Your DataWindow with a Check Box

When you're finished defining your check box, click on OK, as shown in figure 9.10. Your DataWindow will now be formatted with a new check box, as seen in figure 9.11.

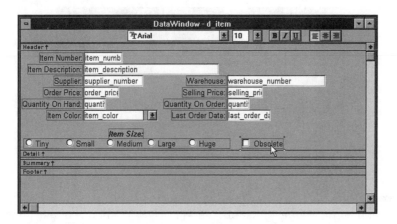

Tip
3 State check boxes can be confusing. Although it's a matter of preference, try using three radio buttons instead.

Fig. 9.11
This is how the Obsolete check box looks when implemented in the DataWindow painter.

III

Using DataWindows

Edit Masks

Edit masks are used for formatted input while the user is typing in a column. For instance, if you declared an edit mask of ###,### for a field, PowerBuilder would only allow numeric input. (# is numeric.) Also, using an edit mask inserts the appropriate markings (such as commas) during entry as opposed to after entry like the format box in the default edit style. To make a field an edit mask, select the column by right-clicking on that column, and choose **E**dit Styles, Edit **M**ask.

Tip
To avoid confusion, be sure to initialize all your check box and radio button variables. That way, what the user looks at will be what is represented in the program.

The Edit Mask dialog box appears, as shown in figure 9.12.

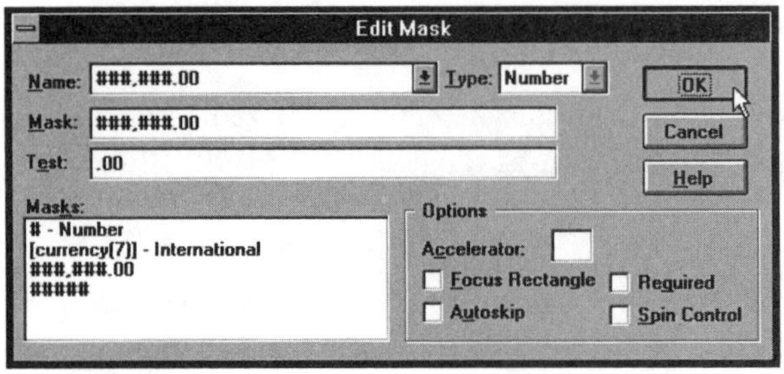

Fig. 9.12
The Edit Mask
dialog box is used
to define the
attributes for the
edit mask column.

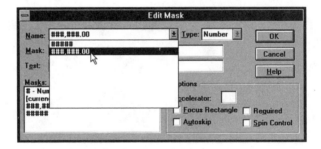

The edit mask dialog box enables you to define the attributes of the column by using the edit mask. Some of these attributes are the same as the ones used for the default edit style. New attributes used for edit mask are as follows.

Name

Name is used to choose a predefined edit mask. However, unlike other edit styles, PowerBuilder has predefined edit masks available, as shown in figure 9.13. User-defined edit masks will be discussed later in this chapter.

Fig. 9.13
Using **N**ame
allows you to
choose a pre-
defined edit mask
or any developer-
defined edit style.

Mask

Mask is the format you define for your field. For instance, a social security number might have the format of "###—##—####". A phone number might have the format of "(###) ###—####".

Test

After you define your Mask, T**e**st lets you type in the field to see how your Mask works.

Masks

The Mas**k**s box allows you to choose a predefined or user-defined mask.

Type

Usually the **T**ype box is set as Display Only. The only time you are allowed to change the type is if PowerBuilder cannot determine what type the field in question is. (For example, a computed field would allow you to choose the type.)

Autoskip

The A**u**toskip attribute skips over this field when you use Tab.

> ### Note
>
> Autoskip is not often turned on. In fact, if you were to use this attribute, you would probably do so with PowerScript during execution as opposed to setting Autoskip as the default. More than likely you would set the Tab Order to 0 to skip the field entirely.

Spin Control

Spin Control allows the user to use the mouse to increment or decrement the edit mask value by placing an up arrow button and a down arrow button within the edit mask box. By clicking on Spin Control, your Edit Mask dialog box doubles in size to include attributes used for Spin Control, as shown in figure 9.14. The mouse pointer in figure 9.14 is pointing to an example of what Spin Control on a field looks like in the Spin Increment box.

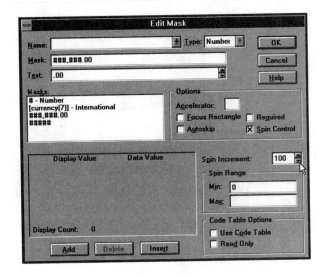

Fig. 9.14
Clicking on **S**pin Control allows you to designate Spin Control attributes. The mouse is pointing to **S**pin Increment, which is itself a Spin Control field.

III

Using DataWindows

The following are new attributes that are related to Spin Control.

Spin Increment. Spin Increment is the increment (or decrement) that you can click on to increase (or decrease) the current value in the edit mask box. Each time you click on the Spin Control arrows, the increment increases or decreases. For instance, if you have a spin increment of 100, and you have 0 in your edit mask box, clicking on the up arrow once will place 100 in the box, twice will place 200, and so on.

Spin Range. The Spin Range area allows you to specify a minimum and a maximum for your spin increment.

Code Table. This Code Table is defined exactly as the code tables you've seen before in the default edit style, the radio button style, and the drop-down list box. However, when an edit mask uses a Code Table, the Spin Control transverses through the code table values instead of incrementing and decrementing the value in the edit mask box.

Code Table Options. The Code Table Options area controls if the Spin Control transverses numbers as defined by the Spin Increment and the Spin Range, or if it transverses the values defined in the Code Table. Clicking on Use Code Table makes the Spin Control use the Code Table instead of the Spin Increment and Spin Range values. Clicking on Read Only forces the user to change the value in the edit mask box by using the Code Table and Spin Control only, and doesn't allow them to type in the Spin Control edit mask box (see fig. 9.15).

Fig. 9.15

You can see the use of Spin Control now present in the d_item DataWindow.

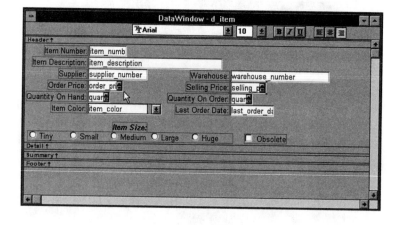

Note

It's very important to give some keyboard alternatives to the user who doesn't like to use a mouse. Conversely, Spin Control is nice for the user who doesn't like to let go of the mouse and hates the keyboard. In figure 9.15, Spin Control is placed on four columns.

Using Drop-Down DataWindows (DDDWs)

Often, you'll need to hook the entry in one DataWindow to an entry in another DataWindow. For example, figure 9.15 includes both the supplier and the warehouse in the d_item DataWindow. Although it's necessary for the users to enter these fields, it's unreasonable to assume that they know the numbers for all the warehouses and all the suppliers. More likely, they know the name of the suppliers and the description of the warehouses.

It's also unreasonable to force every user to type in the name of the supplier or the description of the warehouse exactly the same as every other user. Allowing the users to type in names instead of numbers also becomes a PowerScript editing nightmare.

These problems are answered by Drop-down DataWindows. Drop-down DataWindows are a type of drop-down list box. Instead of using constant display values that are translated into internal data values, a Drop-down DataWindow (or DDDW) uses two values from an existing DataWindow, making a DDDW a DataWindow-within-a-DataWindow.

To add a DDDW to an existing DataWindow, you must first create a new DataWindow to define what you want to display. Although any type of DataWindow will work, the most used for a DDDW is a tabular quick-select DataWindow.

Tip
Drop-down DataWindows (DDDWs) are sometimes called *child DataWindows*.

First you must add the field you want to display and the field you want to be translated to the program. In the supplier number's case, you probably want the user to choose the supplier name and return the supplier number, so these two fields should be added to your DataWindow, as shown in figure 9.16.

When you arrive at the DataWindow painter, delete all the headings and all the fields you do not want to display. Since you only want to display the supplier name, that should be the only field shown (see fig. 9.17).

III

Using DataWindows

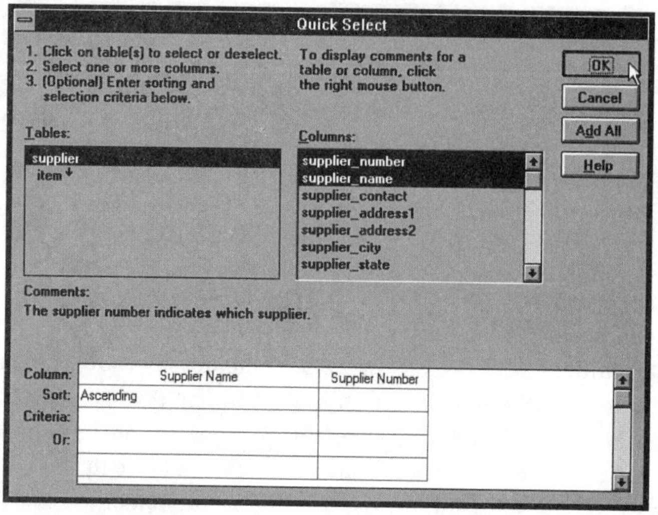

Fig. 9.16
To make a DDDW, start by defining a DataWindow with the field that you want to display and the field that you want to return.

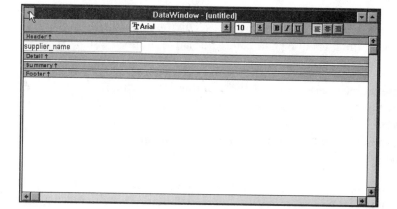

Fig. 9.17
Delete all non-display fields and all headings from the DataWindow painter when defining a DDDW.

Note

Even though you deleted a field out of the DataWindow painter, the field is no longer displayed but still remains and is internally processed.

Save this DataWindow. It's probably a good idea to include a DDDW somewhere in the name if this DataWindow is used only for DDDWs. (I called this DDDW d_supplier_dddw.) Now return to your DataWindow that you are adding your DDDW to (d_item). Select the column by right-clicking on it, and choose **E**dit Styles, DropDown**D**ataWindow.

Now you will see the DropDownDataWindow Edit Style dialog box. Choose the DataWindow that you want to associate with this column (see fig. 9.18). In this case, that would be d_supplier_dddw.

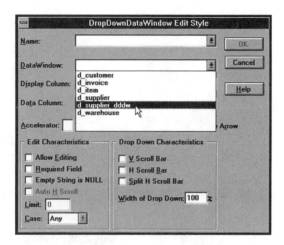

Fig. 9.18
To make a column a DDDW, you must choose the DataWindow you want associated with that column.

After you choose your DataWindow for the DDDW, click on the column from the DDDW that you want to display. Now also choose the Data Column from the DDDW. This is the value that is returned to the DataWindow when a display value is chosen.

Now fill in the rest of your DDDW attributes. These correspond to the list box attributes. (This probably isn't surprising to you, since a DDDW is a type of list box.) Click on OK. To run the DDDW, you need to enter data in the Supplier table. Figure 9.19 shows us using the database painter to enter data.

Now you're ready to run. Click on the Run icon and open your application. Since the Item window is pulled up first, you can see the supplier DDDW. Click on the down arrow to view and choose a supplier, as seen in figure 9.20.

The supplier number will be stored in the DataWindow column after you choose the supplier name.

III

Using DataWindows

Fig. 9.19
You can use the database painter to enter data into your table to test your DDDW.

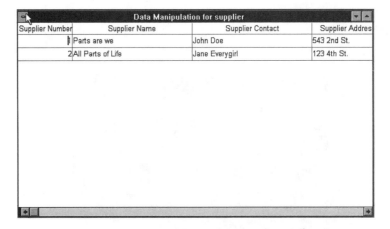

Fig. 9.20
Click on the displayed value in the DDDW, and a data value will be returned.

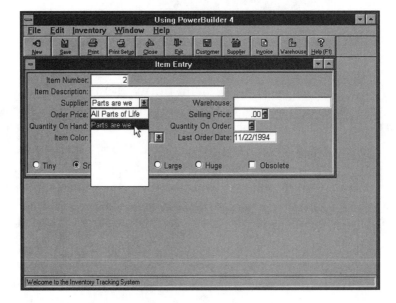

Using Conditional Attributes

In previous versions of PowerBuilder, the developer was required to use PowerScript and the dwModify statement to alter any DataWindow attributes (such as field color). In Version 4, the developer can use DataWindow conditional attribute definitions to change attributes based on a condition.

To define a conditional attributes for a column on your DataWindow, right-click on the column you want to define and click on **A**ttributes. This will pull up the Attribute Conditional Expressions dialog box. In this dialog box, you typically use an If( ) function to set the attribute. You can double-click on the definition area of the Attribute Conditional Expressions dialog box to pull up the Modify Expression dialog box.

I double-clicked on the color attribute. I then used the Modify Expression dialog box to return a red color if the Quantity On Hand field was less then 10. Otherwise, the black color is returned. You can see the color attribute now is set to be red if the Quantity On Hand is less than 10; otherwise the attribute is black.

Using Display Formats

Display formats are a lot like edit masks. The main difference is that display formats are applied to a field after entry, while edit masks are applied to a field during entry. To define a format for a field on your DataWindow, right-click on the field you want to define and click on Format, as seen in figure 9.21.

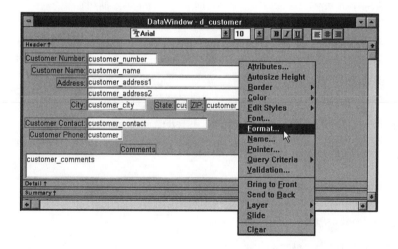

Fig. 9.21
To define a format for a column, right-click on the column and choose Format.

The Display String Formats dialog box opens, and all existing formats for this data type are displayed. From here, you can define the format for your field and test the result. In figure 9.22, the format for a ZIP code is defined.

III

Using DataWindows

Fig. 9.22

You can define
a format in the
Display String
Formats dialog
box.

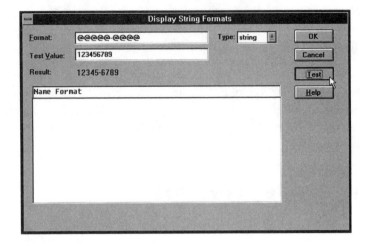

Troubleshooting

*I'm using '#' in my format string, but the numbers aren't printing. All that's showing is
the actual # sign.*

With a string, the at sign (@) is used to tell PowerBuilder to allow any character. In a
numeric column, the pound sign (#) is used to allow any number. However, you
cannot use '#' in a string format unless you want '#' to appear in your string column.

With a numeric format, you can define different formats for positive and
negative numbers by defining two formats separated by a semicolon. A format of

```
#,##0.00;[red]#,##0.00
```

will turn your number red if it is negative.

When you actually enter a format string, your type looks normal, as seen in
figure 9.23. However, as soon as the column you're typing in loses focus, the
format style is applied (see fig. 9.24).

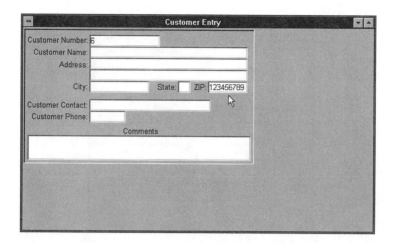

Fig. 9.23
Unlike edit masks, format styles are not applied to the column until after the column loses focus.

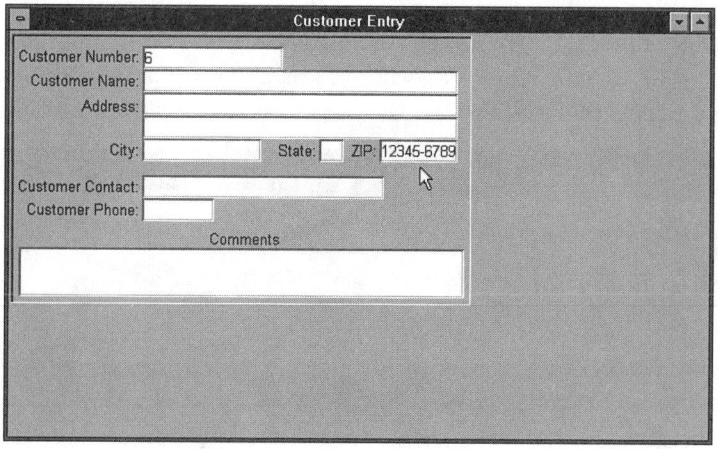

Fig. 9.24
As soon as a column loses focus, any format style is applied to the display.

Using Validation Rules

Validation rules don't allow your column to lose focus if the value entered does not meet the criteria you defined for that column. For example, the order price can't be negative. If the user enters a negative number, you want to stop right there and make him or her correct the entry.

To define a validation rule for a column, right-click on that column and choose **V**alidation. The Column Validation Definition dialog box opens, as shown in figure 9.25.

III

Using DataWindows

Fig. 9.25
The Column
Validation
Definition dialog
box is used to
define a validation
rule for a column.

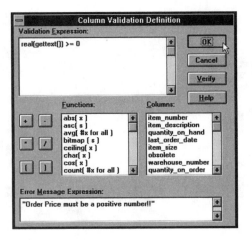

As seen in figure 9.25, you type in the rule you want to define using
PowerScript functions (like **abs( )**) and relativities (like < and >). Here, you
use GetText( ) to return the string value of the current column, convert it to
a real number, and make sure that the number is not negative.

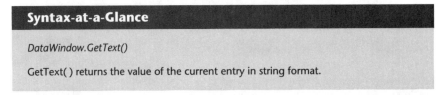

Syntax-at-a-Glance

DataWindow.GetText()

GetText( ) returns the value of the current entry in string format.

Syntax-at-a-Glance

Real(string)

Real converts a string into a real number. For instance, a string containing "49.95"
would be converted to 49.95.

As you can see in figure 9.26, an error message box appears when a validation
rule has been violated. Validation rules make coding for exceptions and invalid situations easier.

Fig. 9.26
An error message
is displayed if
what the user
entered violates
the validation rule
for that column.

Troubleshooting

I'm using a validation rule, but my column allows me to enter an invalid entry occasionally. Other times, I get an error message when the incorrect value has been fixed. What gives?

Validation rules are first checked before the entered value is stored in the column. If you use the column name in your validation rule, you may experience a "lagging effect," where the column is checked before the value in the column is changed. Try using the GetText() function as seen in figure 9.25 to get the current string shown in the column and convert it to a value you can test with.

Using the Database Painter to Define Different Column Attributes

You are able to define many column attributes that are often used in the database painter. For instance, if you use a Yes-No check box often, you may want to define a Yes-No check box. If you use phone numbers, you might want a phone number edit mask. If many of your strings need to be numeric, you might want to define a numeric validation rule.

Defining Your Own Edit Styles

To define your own edit styles, get into the database painter and choose **O**bjects, Edit **S**tyle Maintenance, as shown in figure 9.27. This pulls up the Edit Styles dialog box, shown in figure 9.28. As you can see, many edit styles (mostly for date and DateTime data types) have been defined for you. PowerBuilder also lets you define new drop-down list boxes and drop-down data window, check box, radio button, default edit, and edit mask edit styles. To create a new edit style, click on one of the new buttons that define the edit style type, as seen in figure 9.28.

Since you clicked on the Edit Mask button, the Edit Mask dialog box appears, as shown in figure 9.29. From here, you can define the edit mask just as you would for a DataWindow column. The only difference is that you need to name the edit mask so that many columns can use it.

III

Using DataWindows

Fig. 9.27
To define an
edit style, open
Objects in the
DataWindow
painter and choose
Edit **S**tyle Mainte-
nance.

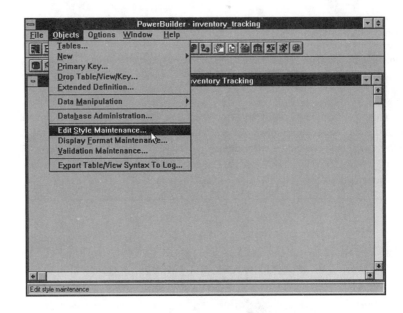

Fig. 9.28
The Edit Style
dialog box will let
you edit or create
edit styles used
with DataWindow
and database
columns.

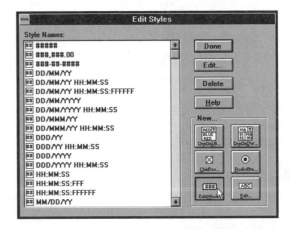

Fig. 9.29
The Edit Mask
dialog box in the
database painter is
identical to the
Edit Mask dialog
box in the
DataWindow
painter except you
can enter a name
in the database
painter.

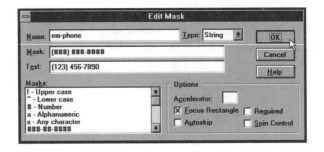

> **Note**
>
> Notice how the name of the edit mask definition began with em_ and the name of the check box definition began with cbx_. Naming prefixes will group all your defined edit masks together with those of the same type and will let other developers know that this is a user-defined edit mask. Similarly, you should prefix your other defined edit styles with the appropriate prefix (for example, use rb_ for radio button, cbx_ for check box, ddlb_ for drop-down list box, and ed_ for edit).

You can also define other edit style types. If you click the new radio button command button in figure 9.28, a CheckBox Style dialog box pops up allowing you to define a default check box, as seen in figure 9.30.

When you return to the Edit Styles dialog box, you can see the new edit styles you defined. These styles can be used in the name field of all the column edit style dialog boxes in the DataWindow painter.

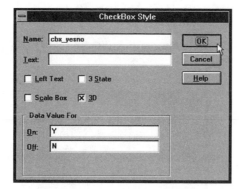

Fig. 9.30
You can define a default check box in the CheckBox Style dialog box.

Defining Your Own Display Formats

To define your own display formats, get into the database painter and choose **O**bjects Display **F**ormat Maintenance. The Display Formats dialog box appears, as shown in figure 9.31. As with edit styles, there are several display formats defined. However, these are all for numeric fields.

To define your own display format, click on **N**ew in the Display Formats dialog box. This pulls up the Display Format Definition dialog box (see fig. 9.32).

The Display Format Definition dialog box shown in figure 9.32 allows you to define a display format for use in the DataWindow and database painters. When you have defined your display format, it appears in the Display Formats dialog box.

III

Using DataWindows

Fig. 9.31
The Display
Formats dialog box
is used to edit or
create display
formats for use in
the database
painter and the
DataWindow
painter.

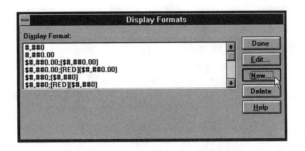

Fig. 9.32
The Display Format
Definition dialog
box is used to define
a format for use in
the database and
DataWindow
painters.

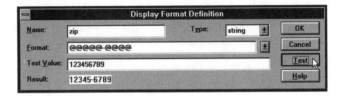

Defining Your Own Validation Rules

To define your own validation rules, get into the database painter and choose **O**bjects, **V**alidation Maintenance. The Validation Rules dialog box appears, as shown in figure 9.33.

Fig. 9.33
The Validation
Rules dialog box is
where you first
define and then
later define or edit
validation rules.

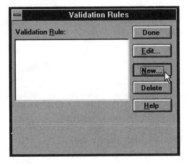

Unlike edit styles and display formats, there are no predefined validation rules. To define a validation rule, click on **N**ew in the Validation Rules dialog box (refer to fig. 9.33). The Input Validation dialog box appears, as seen in figure 9.34.

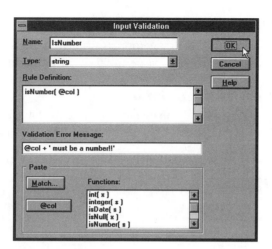

Fig. 9.34
The Input
Validation dialog
box lets you define
the name, rule,
and error message
of a validation
rule.

As with the Validation Rules dialog box used in the DataWindow painter
(refer to fig. 9.33), the Input Validation dialog box shown in figure 9.34
allows you to use PowerScript functions to define your edit rule. Unlike the
Validation Rules dialog box, the Input Validation dialog box forces you to use
the *@col* variable at least once in your validation rule. The *@col* variable is a
variable used in the Input Validation dialog box denoting the current column.

> **Note**
>
> You must refer to the current column at least once in a validation rule. This makes
> using GetText() impractical. Because of this, you could define your validation rules at
> the DataWindow level.

Once you're done defining your rule, click on OK. This will return you to the
Validation Rules dialog box, and your new rule will be listed there, as seen in
figure 9.35.

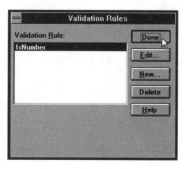

Fig. 9.35
After you define
a validation rule,
it's listed in the
Validation Rules
dialog box.

III

Using DataWindows

Setting Different Column Defaults

You can set default edit styles, display formats, validation rules, and values for your columns in either the database painter or the DataWindow painter.

Setting Defaults in the Database Painter

To set column defaults in the database painter, open the table whose columns you want to set and double-click on the table. The Alter Table dialog box opens, as shown in figure 9.36.

Fig. 9.36

You can assign an edit mask or display format to a field in the Alter Table dialog box.

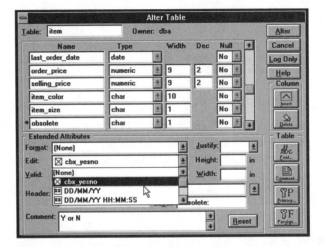

> ### Note
>
> The Create Table dialog box used for creating new tables and the Alter Table dialog box used for updating existing table definitions are almost identical. Information about setting defaults in the Alter Table dialog box also applies to the Create Table dialog box.

Assign the em_zip to be the format display for the customer_zip. In a similar way, you could also set the validation rule in the Alter Table dialog box by choosing a column and then choosing the appropriate validation rule.

You also can set a default (empty string) in the zip code column. Here you are allowed to set defaults for field values.

As seen in figure 9.37, you can also change default values in the database painter by right-clicking on a field displayed in a table.

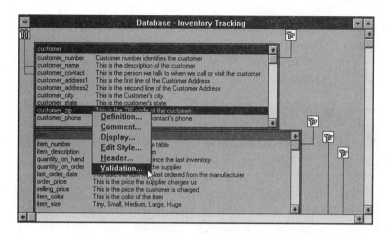

Fig. 9.37
Right-clicking on a column in the database painter allows you to define table and column defaults.

Right-clicking on a column in the database painter allows you to define default values, edit styles, display formats, or validations, and to change the column comments. You can also enter the Alter Table dialog box by clicking on **D**efinition, or change the table header.

By right-clicking on customer_zip and choosing **V**alidation, you can change the validation rule (or create a new rule) or change the initial (default) value (see fig. 9.38).

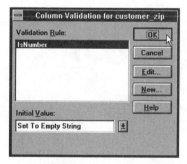

Fig. 9.38
By right-clicking on a column in the database painter and choosing **V**alidation, you can change the validation rule or the initial column value.

III

Using DataWindows

Caution

When you add default definitions to your database, they only apply to DataWindows you *will* create, not to DataWindows you already have created. For those DataWindows, you'll either need to redefine the fields in the DataWindow painter or delete the DataWindow and re-create it.

Setting Defaults Using the Rows Column Specifications

You can also set defaults for columns in your DataWindow by choosing **R**ows, **C**olumn Specifications, as seen in figure 9.39. The Column Specifications dialog box appears, as shown in figure 9.40.

Fig. 9.39

To define default values for your DataWindow columns, choose **R**ows, **C**olumn Specifications.

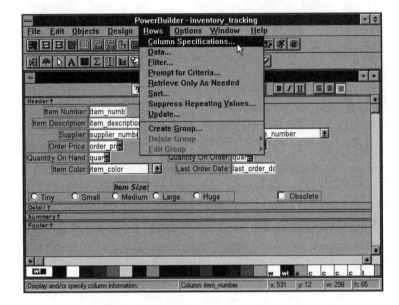

Fig. 9.40

You can set the defaults for your DataWindow columns in the Column Specifications dialog box.

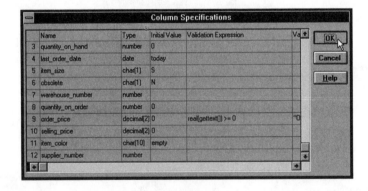

In the Column Specifications dialog box, you can set the initial value, validation expression, validation message, and database column relating to the DataWindow column. Using the Column Specifications dialog box is one of the easiest ways to manipulate your default values.

From Here...

This chapter teaches you how to make your DataWindows more useful to the end user. It also shows you ways to avoid long and lengthy editing scripts by using the tools that PowerSoft provides with PowerBuilder. More information can be found in the PowerBuilder User's Guide in Chapter 15, "Displaying and Validating Data."

Refer to these chapters in this book for additional information on DataWindows and databases:

- Chapter 2, "Understanding Analysis, Design, and Databases," gives a detailed description of the database painter and setting up tables in your database.

- Chapter 8, "Creating DataWindows," describes how to define your DataWindows.

- Chapter 10, "Manipulating Data Using DataWindows," shows how to use your DataWindow to access your database.

III

Using DataWindows

Chapter 10

Manipulating Data Using DataWindows

Now that you've seen how to format a DataWindow, you can start using it. This chapter doesn't discuss the format of the DataWindow, but rather how to manipulate data through your DataWindow. In this chapter, you'll learn how to:

- Suppress, filter, and sort your data

- Modify your data source

- Specify retrieval arguments and retrieve data from a database

- Retrieve from and update your database from your DataWindow

- Work with crosstabs

Filtering

Sometimes you'll want to limit the access your DataWindow has to your data either for security considerations or to make the DataWindow easier to use for the end user. You can achieve this by using a filter. To specify a filter in the DataWindow painter, open **R**ows and choose **F**ilter, as seen in figure 10.1.

Now you'll see the Specify Filter dialog box, where you enter the condition you want all rows to meet. PowerBuilder gives you a list of functions to choose from and a list of columns in the DataWindow. Figure 10.2 shows all the obsolete items eliminated from the DataWindow.

Fig. 10.1
To establish a filter for a DataWindow, open **R**ows and choose **F**ilter.

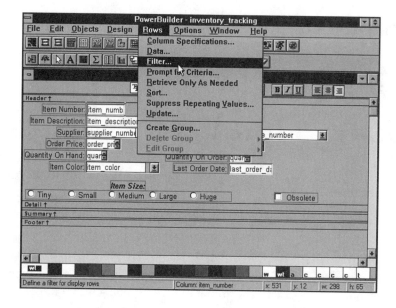

Fig. 10.2
In the Specify Filter dialog box, you enter the condition you want all rows to meet in the DataWindow.

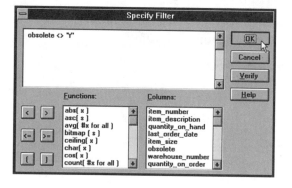

The filtered data is not deleted from the DataWindow entirely. (Indeed, deleted rows are not deleted off the DataWindow entirely.) PowerBuilder establishes buffers for primary data, filtered data, and deleted data. Ordinarily, your DataWindow automatically uses the primary buffer. However, several DataWindow functions allow you to access the other buffers or even change their state so that they return to the primary buffer (see fig. 10.3).

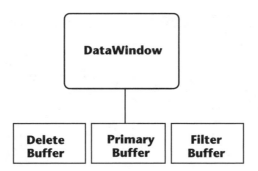

Fig. 10.3
Although the primary buffer is used to populate columns on the DataWindow, DataWindow functions have access to all filtered and deleted rows.

Sorting

You'll almost always want to establish a sort criteria for your DataWindow. This can be done two ways. The hard (but more efficient) way is to code an order by clause in the DataWindow SQL (covered later in this chapter in the "Using the SQL Toolbox" section). The other way is to establish a sort column in your DataWindow painter.

> **Note**
>
> Just because a table has a primary key does not necessarily put the table's rows in primary key order. If you want to view the table in any order, you'll have to either specify a sort criteria or add a sort/order by clause to your DataWindow's SQL.

To establish a sort through the DataWindow painter, perform the following steps:

1. Open **R**ows and choose **S**ort.

2. The Specify Sort Columns dialog box appears. Here, you select the column from the Source Data area and move it to the Columns area, as seen in figure 10.4.

> **Note**
>
> The Ascending check box is automatically selected. To have the field selected in descending order, unselect the check box.

Tip
If you notice that you are sorting the fields in the wrong order, simply click on the field you need to move and drag it to the new location.

◀ See "Creating Tables," p. 56

III

Using DataWindows

Fig. 10.4
The Specify Sort
Columns dialog
box allows you to
specify the sort
order by dragging
the columns you
want sorted from
the Source Data
area to the
Columns area.

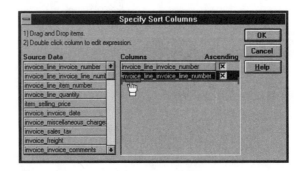

Modifying Your Data Source

The data source is where the data for the DataWindow comes from. By clicking on the SQL Select icon, you go into PowerBuilder's select painter, as seen in figure 10.5.

Fig. 10.5
Clicking on the
SQL Select icon
puts you into the
select painter.

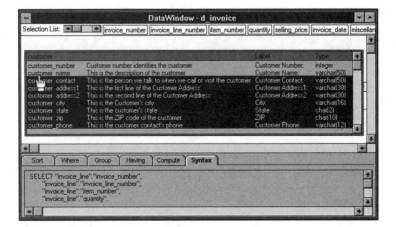

Customizing Your Data Source Viewing Area

The select painter has changed a lot in Version 4.0. Most of these changes—such as resizable database windows with more information and the SQL toolbox—are impressive but take up space in the painter. However, with the changes, PowerBuilder has also added several features to control the display of the select painter.

Using Show

Under O**p**tions, PowerBuilder adds **S**how, as shown in figure 10.6. Show allows you to customize your display by toggling on and off your data type display, labels display, comments display, and SQL toolbox.

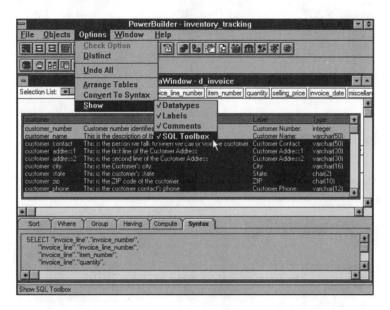

Fig. 10.6
You can toggle on or off what you want to display by opening O**p**tions and choosing **S**how.

Resizing, Arranging, and Dragging Your Database Windows

After choosing what you want to display, you can resize your database windows to an appropriate size. At any time during this process of showing only the options you want to see and resizing your database windows, you can also arrange your database windows much like you would arrange icons by opening O**p**tions and choosing **A**rrange Tables.

If you drag your table windows around and turn off all the table information displays, you can end up with the screen shown in figure 10.7. As you can see, this is similar to the older version's methods of displaying tables, and may be easier to follow. (However, on a quick select DataWindow, the full function display seems to work better.)

Displaying Columns vs. Displaying Joins

Columns are automatically joined by foreign keys, and you can define your own (as seen later in this chapter). To display the joined fields, open **O**bjects and choose **J**oins. This will highlight only the columns that are joined to other tables, as seen in figure 10.8. To re-highlight the columns selected for the DataWindow, choose **O**bjects, Display **C**olumns.

◀ See "Creating Tables," p. 56

III

Using DataWindows

Fig. 10.7
You can drag your table windows around for a better display.

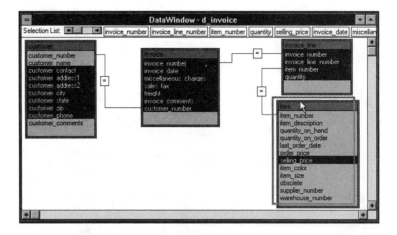

Fig. 10.8
Choosing **O**bjects, **J**oins will highlight only the columns that are joined to other tables.

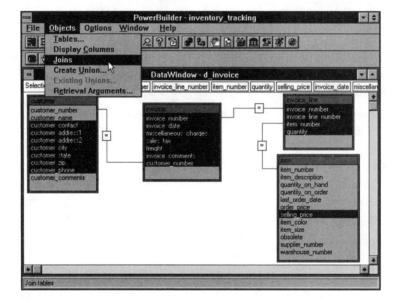

Converting to SQL Syntax or Graphics

You can also modify your SQL statements that are used to retrieve data into your DataWindow. This is done by choosing **O**ptions, Con**v**ert To Syntax.

If you were in the d_item Data Window, the painter now shows you the SQL syntax behind the d_item DataWindow, as shown in figure 10.9. To return to Graphics mode, choose **O**ptions, Con**v**ert To Graphics.

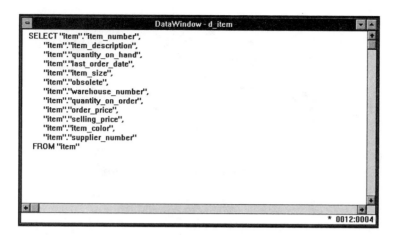

Fig. 10.9
When you convert to SQL, the select painter shows the SQL syntax that lies behind the DataWindow.

Changing Your Data Source

Often you will find that you need additional information on a DataWindow, or that you don't need all the tables and/or columns that you originally specified. In this case, you can change the data source that you originally specified.

> **Caution**
>
> Changing your data source will affect your DataWindow. You may see an additional field or some fields missing in your DataWindow painter after using the select painter.

Modifying Joins

Joins are how tables relate to each other. When you select the columns for your DataWindow, joins are automatically set up for all foreign-primary key matches. You can add new joins and delete or modify existing joins in the select painter.

To add a new join, click on the join table icon and then click on the two columns from the two different tables that you want to join. This will establish a join between the two tables when the two clicked columns are equal.

To modify an existing join, click on the join box. (The join box is on the line connecting two tables.) Usually the join box contains an equal sign (=).

When you click on the join box, the Join dialog box appears, as seen in figure 10.10.

III

Using DataWindows

Fig. 10.10
The Join dialog box is used to select join type or delete a join.

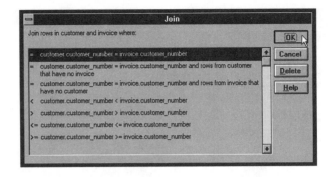

Tip
Make sure that you choose **O**bjects, Display **C**olumns from the menu if you were just experimenting with the table joins.

Here you can specify whether a table join is an exact match to another table's column, or if it's some other relationship.

Changing a DataWindow's Columns

When you open the select painter from the DataWindow painter, all the relevant tables are displayed. To add or remove a column, simply click on one of the columns. In figure 10.11, customer_address2 was clicked off. This removed it from the selection list at the top of the painter. Re-clicking on customer_address2 will put it back on the list.

Fig. 10.11
Clicking on a column in the select painter will toggle a column on and off the selection list.

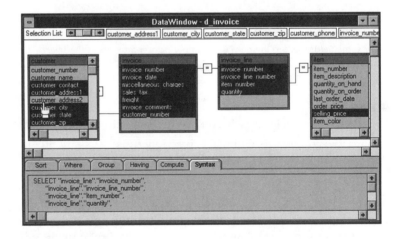

Changing a DataWindow's Tables

▶ See "Using Queries," p.577

Adding or removing a column from your DataWindow is relatively easy. Conversely, adding or removing an entire table is somewhat difficult. You also have the option of starting over with a new query for your tables, but this means you have to start your definition over and have a query defined.

Adding a Table. To add columns from another table to your DataWindow, you must first add that table to your DataWindow. This is done by clicking on the Tables icon and selecting the table you wish to add to your DataWindow. In figure 10.12, the warehouse table is added to the d_invoice DataWindow. After you add the table, you can choose columns that you want to manipulate in your DataWindow.

> **Caution**
>
> After selecting new columns to add to your DataWindow and clicking the design button, you may be tempted to click on the column icon to add your new columns. PowerBuilder has already added them for you at the top of the detailed section and to the right of the last field.

> **Note**
>
> To add new columns to your DataWindow, first select the new columns and then click on the **D**esign icon. The new icon will automatically be added to the right side of the Detail section of your DataWindow.

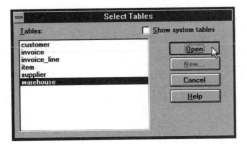

Fig. 10.12
The warehouse table is added to the d_invoice DataWindow.

Removing a Table. Removing a table is somewhat more difficult. In Version 4, you must follow a multi-step process:

1. Delete all your joins to the table. This is done by double-clicking on your join box and choosing **D**elete.

2. Choose **O**bjects, Display **C**olumns and then toggle off all columns on the table so that none of the table's columns are on the Selection List. When you're done, your display should have a completely separated table (see fig. 10.13).

III

Using DataWindows

Fig. 10.13
To delete a table from your DataWindow, first make sure it's totally disconnected from your other tables and no fields are on the Selection List.

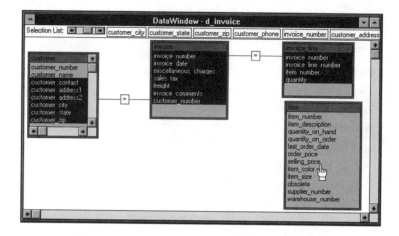

3. Choose Options, Convert To Syntax.

4. Delete the table reference (with applicable comma) from the SQL syntax. The syntax for this example is highlighted in figure 10.14.

Fig. 10.14
Delete the table reference from the SQL to remove a table from a DataWindow.

Tip

If you know SQL, you can delete a table by deleting all references to it in the SQL. The method discussed here makes use of the select painter and minimizes the non-graphical work.

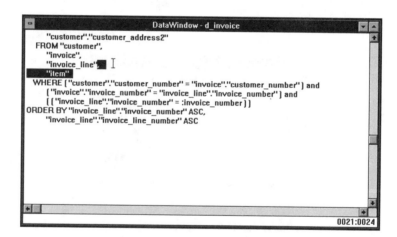

5. Choose Options, Convert To Graphics. This shows the select painter seen in figure 10.15 with the table missing.

TrackNote

Since I'm only illustrating a method to delete a table from your DataWindow, I really don't want to delete my item table from my invoice DataWindow. Hence, I'll close this window without saving after these modifications.

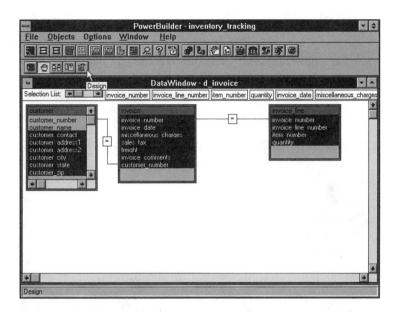

Fig. 10.15
The table is now missing from the select painter.

Using DISTINCT

A DISTINCT SELECT SQL statement eliminates all duplicate rows from the result of the SELECT statement. To place DISTINCT in the SQL statement, choose Options, **D**istinct. This will put a check mark beside Distinct to let future developers know that you have selected this option.

> **Note**
>
> DISTINCT can slow down an application, since every row retrieved is compared against existing rows selected. In the above case, DISTINCT was added to a SELECT that by its nature would never return a duplicate row since the primary key was part of the SELECT. Therefore, the DISTINCT option is turned off when you look at the application.
>
> DISTINCT also eliminates duplicate rows. If a row has similar columns but is not entirely the same as another row, it is not eliminated.

Using the SQL Toolbox

The SQL toolbox is new to Version 4.0. The toolbox, as shown in figure 10.16, is a handy way to review all facets of the SQL behind your DataWindow.

Sort

To establish an SQL sort, first click on the Sort tab, and then click and drag a column from the list of columns to the list of columns to be sorted, as seen in figure 10.16. This statement puts an ORDER BY clause in the SELECT statement. Therefore, this sort is different than the **R**ows, **S**ort selection in the DataWindow Painter.

Fig. 10.16

To establish an ORDER BY clause, drag a column from the column list to the sort list.

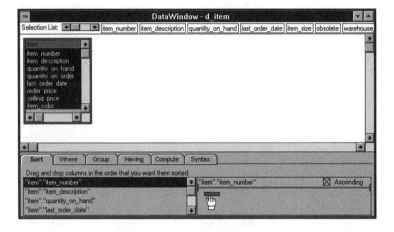

This sort should *always* be used instead of the **R**ows, **S**ort selection whenever possible. The limitation of this sort is that you can't sort on computed columns. Other than that, this sort is usually faster than the equivalent sort inside the DataWindow painter.

Caution

Never issue the same sort in the DataWindow painter as you have in the select painter. This has the effect of performing two of the same sorts on the same data. In other words, it will slow you down.

Where

The WHERE SQL clause joins tables together in SQL. WHERE can also be used to filter out unwanted records or to select only certain records based on a retrieval argument.

Establishing Retrieval Arguments. A *retrieval argument* (or arguments) forces the user to pass an argument (or arguments) in the Retrieve() PowerBuilder function. To establish a retrieval argument, choose **O**bjects, **R**etrieval Arguments.

The Specify Retrieval Arguments dialog box appears, as seen in figure 10.17. Here, type in the argument Name and choose the Type of the argument. If there is more than one argument, click on the Add button or the Insert button and add more arguments.

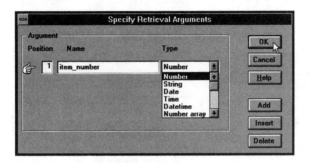

Fig. 10.17
In the Specify Retrieval Arguments dialog box, you choose the argument name and choose the type of your retrieval arguments.

Now every time you issue a Retrieve statement in a PowerScript statement for this DataWindow, you'll need to pass these arguments.

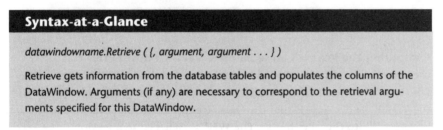

Syntax-at-a-Glance

datawindowname.Retrieve ({, argument, argument . . . })

Retrieve gets information from the database tables and populates the columns of the DataWindow. Arguments (if any) are necessary to correspond to the retrieval arguments specified for this DataWindow.

Using the Where Tab in the SQL Toolbox. By clicking on the Where tab in the SQL toolbox, you can use your retrieval argument to specify which row will be retrieved from the database into the DataWindow. You can also use Where to act as a type of filter, as seen in figure 10.18.

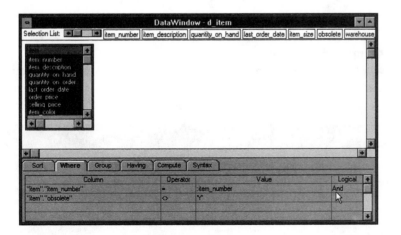

III

Fig. 10.18
You can use the retrieval argument and also add a filter (of sorts) to screen out any obsolete records.

Using DataWindows

TrackNote

Once you screen out obsolete records, you can no longer retrieve obsolete records. Hence, the row screening out obsolete records was for discussion purposes only and will not be saved in the Inventory Tracking system.

However, the retrieval argument (item_number) is necessary to use this DataWindow as a data entry as well as a data retrieval DataWindow. In fact, you should also create the following retrieval arguments:

DataWindow	Retrieval Argument
d_customer	customer_number
d_invoice	invoice_number
d_item	item_number
d_supplier	supplier_number
d_warehouse	warehouse_number

Comparing the Where Clause and the DataWindow Filter. You can use the WHERE SQL clause to filter out unwanted data much like the DataWindow filter. The major difference between the DataWindow filter and the WHERE SQL clause is that the DataWindow filter still pulls in the data and puts it into the filter buffer. The WHERE SQL clause does not.

Caution

Don't use the WHERE SQL clause as a filter and then repeat the same filter using a DataWindow filter. This performs the same task twice. If you don't need to access the Filter! buffer, a Where clause is more efficient.

Tip
Always rename your computed fields to something meaningful. If you have several computed fields, you could get lost determining which one you want.

SQL Computed Columns

Instead of establishing a computed field in the DataWindow painter, you could add a computed column with the SQL statement using the Compute tab (see fig. 10.19). This returns a computed field to your DataWindow.

TrackNote

The changes adding the profit column are not saved to the final system. The profit column was added for discussion only.

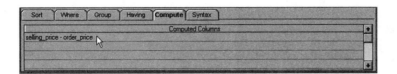

Fig. 10.19
Using the
Compute tab, you
can enter your
own computed
field.

Note

If you want your field on your DataWindow constantly changing based on what is entered in other columns, an SQL computed column will not work. An SQL computed column is evaluated based only on the data that was retrieved from the database. A DataWindow computed field bases its value on the current displayed columns in the DataWindow.

If your DataWindow is static (as in a report) or the fields used in the computation don't change, an SQL computed column edges out a DataWindow computed field in performance. However, the DataWindow computed field has more functionality that is quite useful at times.

Group

The Group tab establishes a GROUP BY SQL clause in your SELECT statement. To group by a column, move that column from the column list to the group by list.

Grouping your data allows aggregate SQL functions (like MIN and AVG) to affect a segment of related rows instead of the whole database. Unfortunately, when you GROUP BY a column or columns, you can only use those GROUP BY columns and aggregate SQL functions in your SELECT. Using aggregate functions forces many of your retrieved columns to be SQL computed fields, thereby not allowing their update.

TrackNote

The changes adding a GROUP BY are not saved to the final system. The GROUP BY was added for discussion only.

Having

The Having tab generates an SQL HAVING clause. The HAVING clause is a type of filter for GROUP BY clauses. As you see in figure 10.20, you can use an aggregate function to SELECT only those groups with an above average order price.

III

Using DataWindows

Note

▶ See "Creating a Grouped Report," p. 300

The DataWindow Painter also allows you to establish groups. However, these groups are radically different than the groups set up by a SQL GROUP BY statement.

The DataWindow groups allow you to display detailed information and then subtotal and total the information in different bands. Conversely, the SQL GROUP BY statement only returns summary information, and returns it into (mainly) computed columns.

For DataWindows, the use of a GROUP BY clause is limited. However, if you're only interested in summary information, use the SQL GROUP BY clause. If you're interested in seeing the detailed information that makes up the summary information, use the DataWindow Group. DataWindow groups are covered more in the next chapter on reports.

Fig. 10.20
A HAVING clause is generated by selecting only those groups with an above average order price.

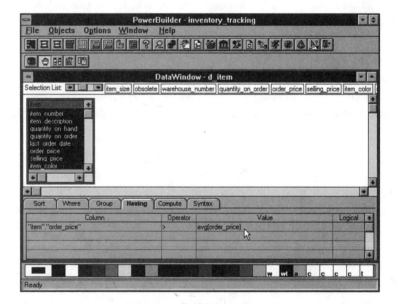

HAVING is only valid for use on SELECT statements that only retrieve aggregate functions or in SELECT statements with a GROUP BY clause. Since the use of aggregate functions and GROUP BY is limited, the use of HAVING is also limited.

SQL Syntax

Many developers like to see the effects of their actions on the SQL statement behind that DataWindow. This SQL statement can be modified only by choosing Options, Convert To Syntax, as discussed previously. However, you can view the SQL syntax as PowerBuilder sets it up by clicking on the Syntax tab, as shown in figure 10.21.

Fig. 10.21
By clicking on the Syntax tab, you can view the SQL syntax as PowerBuilder sets it up.

SQL Statements vs. DataWindow Setup

You have found out how to set up your DataWindow—through the DataWindow painter or through SQL in the select painter. The basic flow of data from the database to the DataWindow can be seen in figure 10.22.

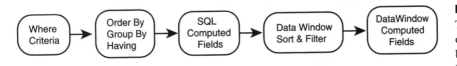

Fig. 10.22
The SQL statements can eliminate data before the DataWindow processes it.

The basic rule in PowerBuilder is the sooner you isolate the data you need, the faster your program will run. Also note that the DataWindow filter does not actually remove data from the DataWindow like a WHERE statement would, but rather moves it to the filter buffer.

DataWindow commands are much more versatile than SQL commands. However, if SQL commands can process the data for you, it's a good idea to let them. That way, your program will run faster, and you may save some development and maintenance work in the process.

Updating Your Database with Your DataWindow

Although you haven't used it yet, there is already enough code to update the database. It can be found on the File, Save not script in m_ancestor and in the user-defined save event in w_data_window.ancestor. Now, when you click or the Save toolbar item your changes will be saved. If you try to add new records or try to exit from the window or application without saving your changes, you'll be asked to do so.

III

Using DataWindows

Verifying Actions before Losing Data

It's probably a good idea to verify the user's actions often. Before any retrieval or insertion that wipes out existing data, you will want to see if the user would like to save or not. Also, when you exit, you'll want to check to see if the user wants to save. All of this is done with a window function in the w_datawindow_ancestor window. This function is called wf_asktosave, and is listed as follows:

```
// wf_AskToSave for w_datawindow_ancestor by Chuck Wood
// This function checks to see if any changes have been made to
➡dw_data.
// If changes were made, wf_AskToSave asks the user if he / she
➡wants to
// save before retrieving a row or creating a new row.
➡wf_AskToSave
// returns a TRUE if the user answers yes or no, and a FALSE if the
➡user
// cancels.
int answer
if ib_changes_made then
   if gb_ask_about_update then
      answer = Messagebox("You're about to lose your changes!", &
                "You have made unsaved changes.  " &
                + "Would you like to save now before proceeding?", &
                STOPSIGN!, YESNOCANCEL!, 1)
   ElseIf gb_automatic_update_or_not = TRUE then
      answer = 1
   else
      answer = 2
   End if
   if gb_set_update_without_asking then
      gb_ask_about_update = FALSE
      gb_set_update_without_asking = FALSE
      gb_automatic_update_or_not = FALSE
   end if
   Choose Case answer
      Case 1
         dw_data.Update()
         if gb_set_update_without_asking then
            gb_automatic_update_or_not = TRUE
         end if
      Case 3
         Return FALSE
   End Choose
End If
ib_changes_made = FALSE
Return TRUE
```

Now you can call this function whenever the users risk losing changes that have been made to your DataWindow. For instance, instead of a simple HALT

CLOSE coded for the File, Exit choice, you are forced to add the following code:

```
gb_set_update_without_asking = TRUE
If IsValid(w_customer) then
    close (w_customer)
end if
If IsValid(w_invoice) then
    close (w_invoice)
end if
If IsValid(w_item) then
    close (w_item)
end if
If IsValid(w_supplier) then
    close (w_supplier)
end if
If IsValid(w_warehouse) then
    close (w_warehouse)
end if
HALT CLOSE
```

Finally, you make wf.ask_to save() function calls in every close and close query event of every window. These precautions protect you from exiting without saving our data.

Retrieving Data from a DataWindow

Using the datawindowname.Retrieve() PowerBuilder function clears out your DataWindow of all existing rows and populates your DataWindow with information on your database tables.

Using a DDDW for Retrieval

To make life easy, you can add a primary key number field to each of the DataWindows. These fields will be drop-down DataWindows that are filled in automatically on an insert as well as used for retrieving existing clients.

Figure 10.23 shows how you can add a customer number DDDW to the d_customer DataWindow.

This DDDW is defined, as shown in figure 10.24. You'll notice that the display column and data column are displayed on the DDDW, but both are filled in with customer_number. The customer name is displayed. Since the customer name is larger than the customer number, you can change the width of the DDDW to 200 percent of the width of the customer number field.

III

Using DataWindows

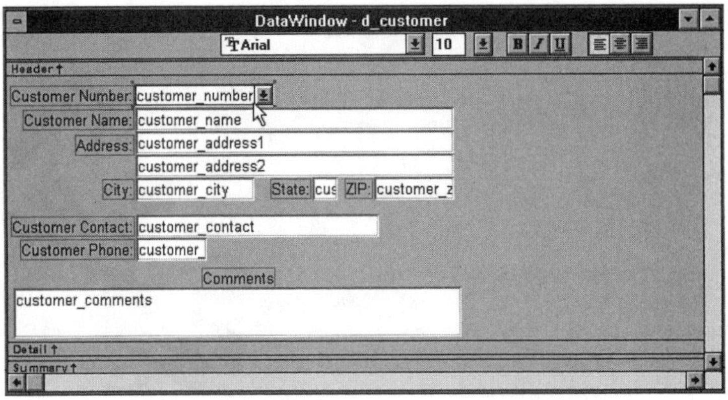

Fig. 10.23
A DDDW was added to retrieve existing customers on the d_customer DataWindow.

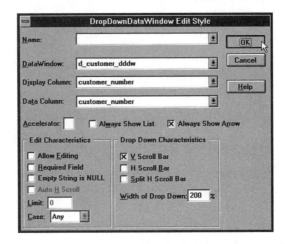

Fig. 10.24
You can use the same column for both the display and data columns, and end up updating a different column altogether.

To enable the DDDW to retrieve data for use, you have to code for the itemchange event on dw_data in w_datawindow_ancestor with the following PowerScript:

```
if GetColumnName() = is_retrieve_column then
   // Save out if necessary
   if wf_asktosave() = FALSE then
      SetActionCode(2)        // Make the itemchange event fail
      PostEvent("reset_key")
   else
      PostEvent("after_change")
   end if
else
   ib_changes_made = TRUE
end if
```

Note

The primary key string variable, *is_retrieve_column*, is set in the open event of each Window.

The itemchange event tests to see if the column retrieved is the key column set up in the open event of each window. If it's the key column, the itemchange event calls the wf_asktosave function. With a YES or NO response from wf_asktosave, the itemchange event posts an event to run after the itemchange event is complete. This posted event (after_change) is a user-defined event with the following line of code in it.

```
Retrieve(GetItemNumber(getrow(), is_retrieve_column))
```

If the Cancel button is pressed in wf_asktosave, the key column is reset in the user-defined reset_key event with the following PowerScript command:

```
settext(string(getitemnumber(getrow(), is_retrieve_column)))
```

In figure 10.25, you can see how the DDDW is now used to select an existing customer. When the selection is complete, the entire row is filled in (see fig. 10.26).

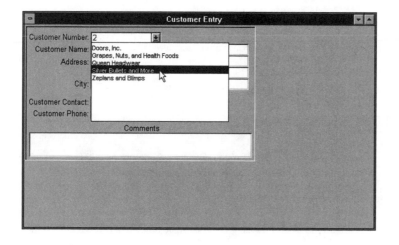

Fig. 10.25
Along with identifying the primary key number, the DDDW is also used for retrieving data.

Retrieving Data inside a DDDW

Normally, a DDDW does not require any special processing to function. However, if the DataWindow behind the DDDW contains a retrieval argument, you must retrieve the DDDW *with a valid retrieval argument* before retrieving the rest of your DataWindow. DDDW retrievals are usually done in the window open event before retrieving the rest of the DataWindow.

III

Using DataWindows

Fig. 10.26

As you can see, the name is converted into a number while the rest of the row is displayed.

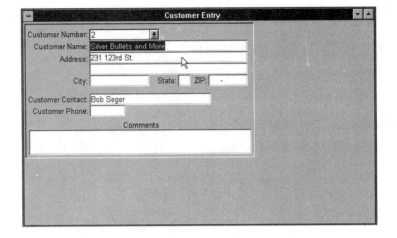

Assume you have a state field and a city field on your window. Your city field requires a state code as a retrieval argument, and the DDDW will list all the cities for that state. The following code could be used to retrieve your city DDDW before retrieving your parent DataWindow.

```
DataWindowChild dwc
// Assign the warehouse to a DataWindow child.
dw_data.dwGetChild("city",dwc)
dwc.SetTransObject(SQLCA)
dwc.Retrieve("IN") // IN is a valid state

// Now retrieve the parent data window
dw_data.retrieve

// If you want, you can now reset the city field list to be blank
dwc.retrieve(" ")
```

Caution

If you have a retrieval argument on your DDDW and do not fill it before you retrieve the rest of your DataWindow, PowerBuilder will prompt you for the missing argument.

Since this window is usually unplanned, a retrieval window can get messy in a run time executable, so be sure to fill in the code in advance of a DataWindow retrieve.

Now you'll need to code the itemchange event in your DataWindow to re-trieve a new city list every time a new state is entered:

```
// Assign the warehouse to a DataWindow child.
if GetColumnName() = "state" then
   DataWindowChild dwc
   string state
```

```
      state = GetText()
      dwGetChild("city",dwc)
      dwc.Retrieve(state)      // retrieve state
end if
```

Syntax-at-a-Glance

DataWindowChild

DataWindowChild is a data type used in PowerBuilder. The DataWindowChild data type is used for DataWindows within DataWindows, like DDDWs.

Syntax-at-a-Glance

datawindowname.GetColumnName()

GetColumnName() returns a string containing the column name that has focus in a DataWindow.

Syntax-at-a-Glance

datawindowname.GetText()

The itemchange event is executed just before an item changes value. To get the text of the current column that is being changed, use the GetText() function.

Syntax-at-a-Glance

datawindowname.dwGetChild(column name,dwc variable)

dwGetChild() associates a DataWindowChild variable with a DataWindow column.

Now every time you enter a new state in the state field, city will retrieve the valid cities for that state.

Inserting Rows and Clearing Your Window

Insert can take two forms. The insertrow user-defined event simply inserts a row into the DataWindow with the dw_data.InsertRow(0) function call. This method is used to insert an invoice line onto the invoice.

III

Using DataWindows

However, most of the DataWindows only display one row at a time. All of the
DataWindows allow the user to clear out all data and start over by clicking on
the **N**ew toolbar item, which accesses the new user-defined event. The new
event is coded as follows:

```
int rownum
// Save out if necessary
if wf_asktosave() = FALSE then
    return          // The user hit the CANCEL button, so return
end if
// Set the next key number
TriggerEvent("getnewkey")
if SQLCA.SQLCode < 0 then
    MessageBox("SQL Error " + string(SQLCA.SQLDBCode), &
        "Error in getnewkey event " + SQLCA.SQLErrText)
end if
// delete all active rows
rownum = dw_data.getrow()
do while dw_data.getrow() > 0
    dw_data.deleterow(0)
loop
// clear all connections with the database and the DataWindow
dw_data.reset()
// Insert a new row
dw_data.InsertRow(0)
if IsNull(il_newkey) or il_newkey = 0 then
    il_newkey = 1
end if
dw_data.SetItem(dw_data.getrow(), is_retrieve_column, il_newkey)
```

As you can see, before clearing out all data, Inventory Tracking makes a call
to wf_asksave to make sure this is okay. Then the new event triggers the
getnewkey event, which simply assigns an unused value to the primary key
with the following SQL syntax:

```
SELECT MAX(customer_number)
    into :il_newkey
    FROM customer;
il_newkey++
```

(This SELECT varies from table to table, the only difference being the primary
key that is SELECTED reflects the primary key of the other table.)

The new event then deletes all existing rows, resets the DataWindow and
frees it from all database calls, does an insert, and puts the new primary key
into the primary key field.

Deleting Rows and Clearing Your Window

It's important to verify before deleting a row. The delrow event (called by the **E**dit, **D**elete option) has been changed to add the following code:

```
if MessageBox("Delete Row", &
   "Are you sure you want to delete this row?", &
   STOPSIGN!, YESNO!, 2) = 1 then
      dw_data.deleterow(0)   // Deletes currently selected row
end if
if dw_data.getrow() = 0 then
   PostEvent("new")
end if
```

Not only can you verify before deleting, but also you can access the new event used for inserting a row if you delete all the rows.

Using Crosstabs

Crosstabs are a special type of display that take a lot of data and condense it down into a grid, spreadsheet, or chart format. To make a Crosstab DataWindow, click on Crosstab when creating your DataWindow, as seen in figure 10.27. Then you choose the tables you want to be referenced by the Crosstab, as seen in figure 10.28.

Fig. 10.27
To create a Crosstab, click on Crosstab when creating your DataWindow.

Fig. 10.28

As with any DataWindow, you need to select the tables you want referenced by your Crosstab.

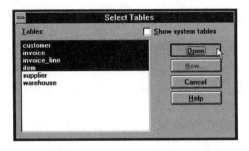

Choose the fields you want to include and click on the design button. After this is where crosstabs diverge from other DataWindows. After selecting the fields you want, the Crosstab Definition dialog box appears, and you are asked to take the source data you defined and divide it into one of three areas. The table column is either a row on the Crosstab, a column on the Crosstab, or a data value on the Crosstab. Notice how data values are automatically computed when moved in to the values box, as seen in figure 10.29.

Fig. 10.29

In the Crosstab Definition dialog box, you must move your source data to one of the three other categories.

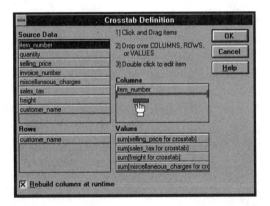

When you're done, click on OK, and the DataWindow painter appears with your Crosstab definition. From here, you can define the Crosstab like other DataWindows, as shown in figure 10.30.

Although there are no crosstabs in the Inventory Tracking system, Crosstabs are a good way to make sense of a lot of numbers. The User's Guide has a very comprehensive chapter on crosstabs. It may be useful to you or your organization someday.

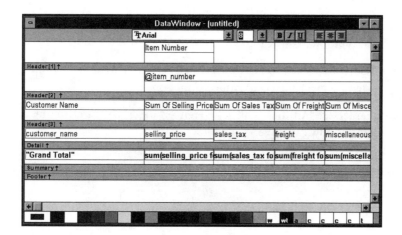

Fig. 10.30
Although it looks slightly different, the DataWindow painter can modify and enhance your Crosstab.

From Here...

DataWindows are the heart of PowerBuilder—they're what makes PowerBuilder so unique and easy to develop in. Using DataWindows, you can generate user-friendly, easy-to-develop windows to access and update the data on your database.

In this chapter, you learned how to choose the data you want to display and modify, how to join tables through the DataWindow painter, and how to use the SQL toolbox to customize your DataWindow.

If you want to read more about DataWindows, refer to the following chapters:

- Chapter 6, "Programming in PowerScript," shows how to write script that will be behind all DataWindow objects.

- Chapter 7, "Using SQL in PowerBuilder," can help you manipulate data that is beyond the scope of DataWindows.

- Chapter 8, "Creating DataWindows," shows how to choose and create the DataWindow you want.

- Chapter 9, "Enhancing DataWindows," describes how to define fields and validation rules, display formats, and edit styles.

III

Using DataWindows

■ Chapter 11, "Creating Reports," will show you even more uses for DataWindows as reports.

■ Chapter 21, "Function & Event Quick Reference," can be helpful when reviewing available DataWindow functions.

■ Chapter 23, "Attribute Quick Reference," describes the attributes a DataWindow can have.

Chapter 11

Creating Reports

by   Blaine Bickar

When you create an application, it's inevitable that you will be creating reports as well. In PowerBuilder, creating reports is very easy. In fact, you already know how! That's because reports are almost identical to DataWindows, and you already know how to create DataWindows.

In this chapter, you learn how to:

- Understand the differences between a report and a DataWindow
- Open the report painter in Run or Edit mode
- Create and modify a grouped report
- Add a graph to a report
- Create labels
- Include another report or DataWindow in your report

Understanding PowerBuilder Reports

A PowerBuilder report is the result of an SQL Select statement, formatted and organized in a particular way. The principle use of a report is to print them out on paper.

Similarities between Reports and DataWindows

Reports can be created using all the same presentation styles and all the same data sources as DataWindows.

To create a report, you go through the same steps you would to create a DataWindow: you start with the SQL Select area to define your data source, and then move into the design area to format the report however you want. The options available in the design area for a report are the same as for a DataWindow (for example, borders, colors, and fonts).

> **Note**
>
> Since reports have a lot in common with DataWindows, you may want to see some other chapters in this book: Chapter 8, "Creating DataWindows," and Chapter 9, "Enhancing DataWindows."

Differences between Reports and DataWindows

The major difference between DataWindows and reports is that reports are not able to be edited by the user, while DataWindows certainly can. Because of this, a report has no tab order (all columns have a zero tab order, actually), and therefore the user cannot get to an individual column to edit it. Since reports are not editable, there would be no need to allow them to update the database, nor would there be a need for any validation rules.

Using the Report Painter

When bringing up the report painter from PowerBuilder, you have two choices. You can bring up the report painter in Edit mode or in Run mode. The Edit mode of the report painter is where you create and modify reports. The Run mode of the report painter only allows you to bring up reports to preview them.

Adding the Report Painter Icons to the Toolbar

The easiest way to launch the report painter, either in Edit mode or Run mode, is from the PowerBar. By default, however, the report painter icons do not appear on the PowerBar. To add them, follow these steps:

◀ See "Using the Toolbars Dialog Box," p. 39

1. Right-click on the PowerBar and choose Customize from the pop-up menu (see fig. 11.1).

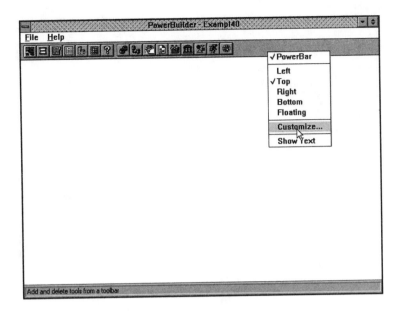

Fig. 11.1
By right-clicking while the pointer is on the toolbar, you will see a pop-up menu that allows you to make changes to the toolbar.

2. In the Customize dialog box, drag the Run Report Painter icon to the Current Toolbar area (see fig. 11.2). Place the icon wherever you want it to appear amid the existing icons.

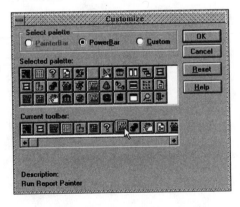

Fig. 11.2
The Customize window allows you to add, move, or remove icons from your PowerBar.

3. Repeat the preceding step to add the Report Painter (Run mode only) icon.

4. Click on OK. The Customize window closes, and your toolbar appears similar to the one shown in figure 11.3.

III

Using DataWindows

Fig. 11.3
If you forget
which Report
button is which
or if you have a
monochrome
monitor, the
PowerTips help
shows you the
name of each icon
when the mouse
comes over top of
the icon.

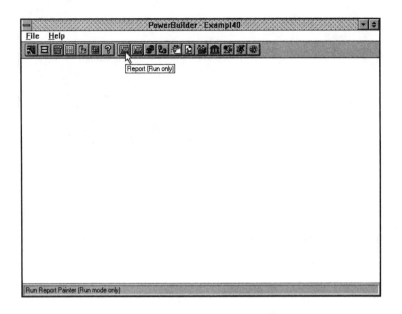

Launching the Report Painter in Run Mode

To open the report painter in Run mode, follow these steps:

1. Click the Report (Run only) icon on the PowerBar. The Select Report
dialog box appears (see fig. 11.4).

Fig. 11.4
Just as with the
other painters, the
first thing you do
when you start up
the report painter
is select an
existing report to
preview.

2. Select a library from the **A**pplication Libraries list, and then select the report you wish to preview. Both DataWindows (objects whose names start with d) and reports (objects whose names start with r) will appear in this list.

> **Note**
>
> If you open a DataWindow object inside the report painter, the DataWindow will act like a report. This is good because you do not have to create a report that does the same thing as an existing DataWindow, but rather you can simply use the DataWindow as a report.

Tip
The difference in figure 11.4 is that the **New** command button is disabled, because in Run mode you cannot create new reports.

3. When you have found the report you want, click on **P**review. The report automatically retrieves the data specified by the report's SQL Select statement and displays it in the preview window (see fig. 11.5).

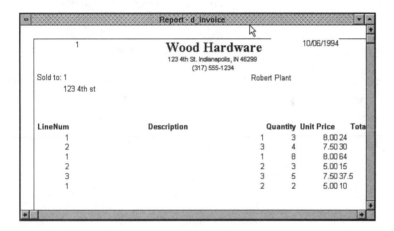

Fig. 11.5
This is the preview of the d_invoice DataWindow as a report.

This window looks a lot like the DataWindow preview window. All the things you can do from the DataWindow preview window can be done from here, with only a few small differences:

- Reports are not updateable; therefore, the icons that represent insert, delete, and update are not on this preview window.

- Because this is a report in Run Only mode, there is no menu choice for returning to the design area to modify the look of the report.

◄ See "Using the Data Manipulation Dialog Box," p. 69

III

Using DataWindows

■ The report preview shows a border around it, as if it were on a piece of paper. This makes sense, as most reports will ultimately end up in hard copy.

The report preview window is the only window available for the report painter in Run mode.

Launching the Report Painter in Edit Mode

To create a new report or to change an existing report, use the Edit mode.

Click the Report icon on the PainterBar. The Select Report dialog box appears. This dialog box is identical to the one that appears in Run mode, except that the **N**ew button now is available.

To create a new report, it isn't necessary to look through the lists of existing reports and libraries; just click on **N**ew. To edit an existing report, select the library you want and the report you want to work on, and then click on OK.

Creating a Grouped Report

In this section, you create a Customer Order History Report, which is a report of all invoice activity grouped together by the customer placing the order. The following steps show you how to create such a report:

◀ See "Under-
standing Data
Sources,"
p. 210

◀ See "Determin-
ing Presenta-
tion Style,"
p. 210

1. To create a new report from the Select Report dialog box, click on **N**ew. (If you are already in the report painter, select **F**ile, **N**ew.) The New Report dialog box appears, as shown in figure 11.6.

This dialog box is just like the New DataWindow dialog box, where you must select a data source and a presentation style. All the same data sources and presentation styles are available.

Fig. 11.6
You must select
one Data Source
and one Presenta-
tion Style from
this dialog box to
begin creating a
new report.

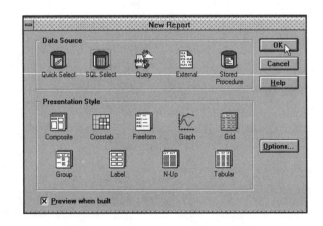

2. Since you are building a group report, select the Group presentation style. You must also select a data source. For this report, choose SQL Select as your data source, and then click on OK. The Select Tables dialog box appears (see fig. 11.7).

3. Just as with DataWindows, you must set up the SQL Select statement. First, decide which tables to use. For this example, use the Customer, Invoice, and Invoice_line tables. After you make your selections, click on **O**pen.

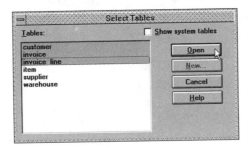

Fig. 11.7
The Select Tables dialog box displays the list of tables in the database. Select the tables you wish to use for this report by clicking on them once.

4. Next, decide which columns from these tables you want to use (see fig. 11.8). Since this report is for all the orders placed for a customer, you would want the customer_name and phone_number columns from the Customer table, as these fields help describe the customer for the report. You also want the invoice_comments column from the Invoice table and the item_number and quantity from the Invoice_line table.

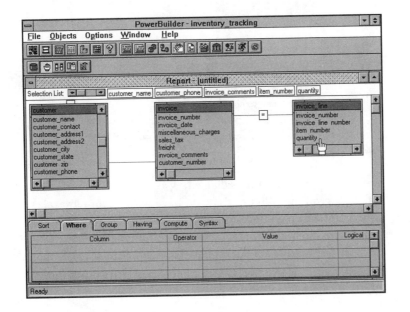

Fig. 11.8
The SQL Select window of the Report Painter is used for setting up the SQL Select statement. Click on the desired column once to select columns for the report.

III

Using DataWindows

For this example, you do not need to do anything else at the SQL Select level. You might decide to limit the amount of data this report produces by specifying some kind of where clause; however, the goal of this unit is not so much to discuss the possibilities of an SQL Select as it is to show you how to create a report. As you can see already, creating reports is similar to creating DataWindows.

You might be thinking, since you want this data grouped by customer, you need to add a Group By clause to the SQL Select statement. As you will soon see, for a group report (or a group DataWindow, for that matter), the grouping is not done in the SQL statement.

5. If you are done with the SQL Select level, it's time to move on to the design level. To do that, choose **F**ile, **D**esign.

6. The Specify Page Header dialog box asks you to supply a title for this report (see fig. 11.9). The default title is a concatenation of all the tables used by this report with the word Report thrown in at the end. Hence, the default name for this report is Customer Invoice Invoice Line Report. Usually this default title is not sufficient, so you have the opportunity to put in your own title. How about Customer Order History Report? After entering your own title, click on OK.

Fig. 11.9
The Specify Page Header dialog box allows you to modify the title for this report.

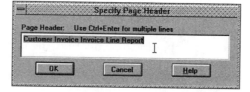

> **Note**
>
> Although you are asked to change the title of the report here, this is not your last chance to do so. You can change the title at any time during the design level, since the title is actually nothing more than a static text field.

7. The Specify Group Columns dialog box asks how you want to group the data. It lists all the columns that you have selected for retrieval. You must select which column(s) from this list that you want to group. You should group together all information for one customer. The customer_name column is a unique name for each customer; by using this field to group by you can be sure that you will not get more than one customer's data mixed together.

8. To select customer_name as the column to group by, drag it from the list on the left to the list on the right (see fig. 11.10).

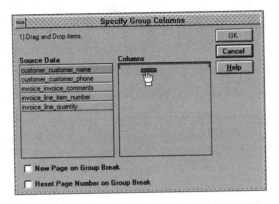

Fig. 11.10
The Specify Group Columns dialog box is the way to designate which column or columns should be used for grouping the resulting report.

> **Note**
>
> You can select more than one column to group by from the Specify Group Columns dialog box; simply repeat the steps to put the customer_name column in the list. For example, you might want to group by all orders for a date for a customer, instead of only by customer.

9. If you want to have your report perform a page break when a new group is encountered, click on New Page on Group Break to enable this feature.

10. If you want each new group to begin at page 1, click on the Reset Page Number on Group Break check box. This feature is useful if you are printing a report that groups information by department, and you must give a copy of the report to each department. You could use this feature and give each department only its portion of the report. The fact that each department's portion of the report would start on page 1 would minimize confusion for the recipient.

11. After you have selected the column to group by and decided upon your page breaks and page numbering, click on OK. Finally, you see the initial design of the report (see fig. 11.11).

Tip
This is a handy feature, since a fresh page for each customer makes it easier to read, and allows them to make a copy of the report for that customer without showing another customer's information.

III

Using DataWindows

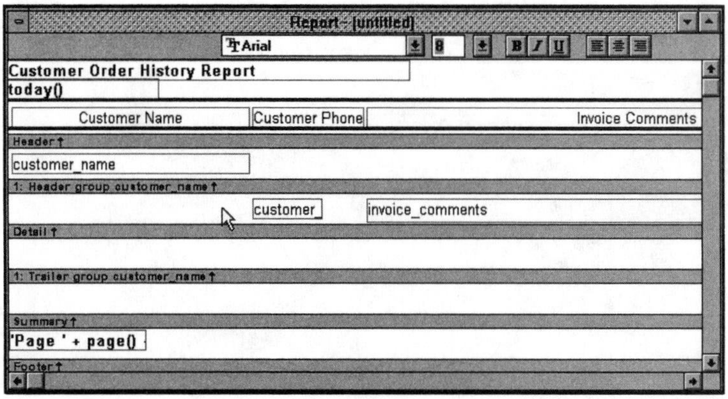

Fig. 11.11
The default design
of the group
report shows the
title you created
for the report, as
well as all the
columns chosen
for the report.

Again, this window looks almost exactly the same as the design window in
the DataWindow painter. The only differences are that there are no menu
choices for tab order or for update, since these do not apply for reports.

Understanding the Bands of a Group Report

In addition to the "normal" header, detail, footer, and summary bands, all
grouped reports (and grouped DataWindows as well) have two more bands to
them than tabular and freeform reports:

■ The *header group* band appears at the top of every group. This band is
typically used to display general information that applies to all the data
for that group. In the example, you see that the customer_name column is (by default) in the group header band, while the other columns
(those that are not used to group by) are in the detail band.

■ The *trailer group* band appears once at the end of every group. Since this
band prints at the end of the group, it is ideal for displaying subtotal
information for numeric data, such as the total for the quantity column
for a customer.

It is possible (and not uncommon) to have more than one group for a report,
that is, having a group inside another group. For example, you might want a
group by customers, and then for each customer, a group for each separate
invoice. You would then have a header and trailer band for each group. The
outermost group (in our example, the customer) would be called group 1, and
the innermost group (the invoice per customer) would be called group 2. You
can see this in figure 11.11, where the header and trailer bands for the
customer_name group start with 1:.

The next step in creating this report is to preview the report. Report preview works the same way that DataWindow preview does. It executes the underlying SQL Select statement, retrieving all rows that match the select statements' criteria.

▶ See "Adding Another Group," p. 314

> **Caution**
>
> You might be inclined to dive right into arranging the design of the report to suit your tastes, but that might not be smart. First, you should preview the report to make sure that it is using the correct data. Otherwise, you will be wasting your time making it look pretty.

To preview the report, select **D**esign, Pre**v**iew. A preview of the report you are working on appears in figure 11.12.

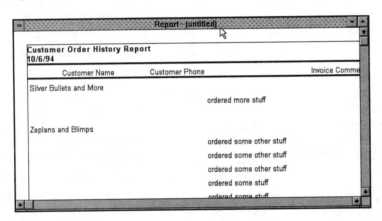

Fig. 11.12
Entering preview on this report shows the current design using actual data.

Generally, when creating a new report, the first thing to do when previewing is to determine if this is the correct data. Then and only then do you worry about what it looks like and how to arrange it. In this case, however, you will not be able to determine if the data is correct until you rearrange the design at least a little.

When PowerBuilder creates the report, it automatically puts a border around the entire report to represent the edges of a piece of paper. The way that this report is designed right now, all of the columns do not fit within this border. You must go back to design to fix it.

To return to design from preview, select **D**isplay, **D**esign. Just as in the DataWindow painter, you are free to change the look, color, border, and size of the columns on a report.

III

Using DataWindows

The problem with the Customer Order History Report is that it's too wide to fit on a page. To make it narrower, change the invoice_comments column from one long field to a field half as wide, but tall enough to display on two lines instead of one. You should also shorten the length of the corresponding label for this field in the header band (see fig. 11.13).

Fig. 11.13
Changing the size of the invoice_comments field involves selecting the field, and then making it both taller and narrower.

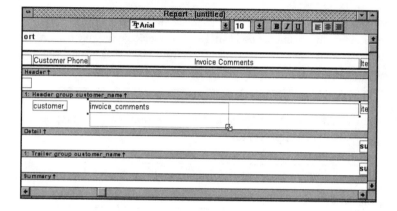

Tip
Be sure to make the detail band taller first, so that it can hold the taller invoice_comments field.

Now that you have shortened the comments field, you have a lot of space between that field and the next field. You could move the item number and the quantity fields to the left so that they are next to the comment field. In fact, you can move the columns, labels, and subtotals and grand total fields together as a unit. (The computed fields at the bottom of the screen are the subtotals and grand total fields, which are discussed later in more detail.) To select all eight of these fields together, click once on one of the fields, and while holding down the Ctrl key, click on the other seven fields. Now release the Ctrl key.

As you do this, you will notice that each one of the fields gets selected; you can tell this because their corners are highlighted. After selecting them, click on any one of those fields and drag to the desired position (see fig. 11.14).

> **Caution**
>
> If you accidentally click (without the Ctrl key depressed) somewhere else on the window, your previous selections will be lost, and you will have to repeat the process of selecting fields.

Now, the total of all the columns require a lot less width than they did at first.

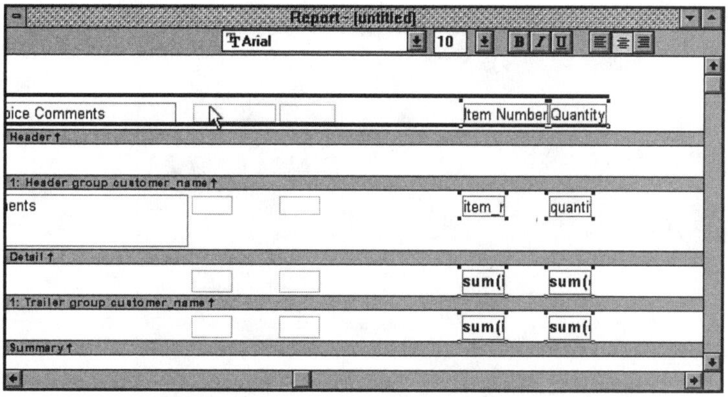

Fig. 11.14
After selecting
each field to be
moved, dragging
any one of them
will drag them all
to a new location,
closer to the
invoice_comments
field.

Before going back into preview to see the results of these changes, it would probably be a good idea to save what you have so far. To save the report, choose **F**ile, Save **A**s, and name the report **r_order_history**. Don't forget to put in a comment describing r_order_history. Save this report to your inventry.pbl library.

Note

To save the report, you must be in the Report Design window. The Save command is not available during preview nor while working with the SQL Select statement.

Next, go into preview again to see the results of the changes. The data now fits within the border that represents the piece of paper.

Note

Can you think of another way to solve the problem of fitting all the data within the paper's border? You could have shortened the width of the report in this example, but couldn't you have also just changed the size of the paper? Well, not exactly, but you could have changed the orientation of the paper. If this report were printed *landscape* (or sideways), it would be wider.

To change the page orientation, select **D**esign, **P**rint Specifications. In the Print Specifications dialog box that appears (see fig. 11.15), simply change **O**rientation to Landscape. The next time you preview the report, the page border is much wider.

III

Using DataWindows

Fig. 11.15
The Print Specifications dialog box allows you to designate how that report should print on hard copy.

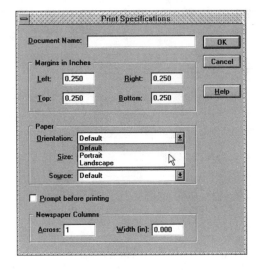

Working with Grand Totals and Subtotals

Grand totals and subtotals were mentioned earlier, and now it's time to examine them more closely. As you recall, subtotal and grand total are defined as the following:

- A *subtotal* is a summation for all occurrences within a group.

- A *grand total* is a summation for all occurrences for the entire report.

When you create a group report, PowerBuilder will, by default, create both a subtotal and a grand total for all columns whose data is numeric. Also, by default, subtotals appear in the group trailer band, which would display once for every group; therefore, each groups' subtotals display as the group is completed. Grand totals appear in the summary band, which would display once at the end of the report.

In the Customer Order History Report, there are two numeric fields: item number and quantity. PowerBuilder has created totals for both of these fields. It should be obvious to you, however, that a summation of the item numbers is not meaningful information. On the other hand, a summation of the quantity might very well be. This would not be obvious to PowerBuilder, however, because it sees that both fields are numeric.

You should remove the totals for item number from the report. To do this, you simply click once on the field, and then click on Delete; or you can press the Delete key on the keyboard.

Modifying Computed Fields

The total fields were created by PowerBuilder as computed fields. You can modify them just as you can any computed fields that you create yourself.

Although the fields are displaying the correct information (for example, correct subtotals and grand totals), how is the recipient of this report going to know what these numbers stand for? Like any other piece of information on report, it is not useful without some kind of label identifying the field.

Working with the Subtotal

To modify a computed field, you can double-click on the field or right-click on the field and select **E**xpression from the pop-up menu (see fig. 11.16). Select the subtotal field for the quantity column.

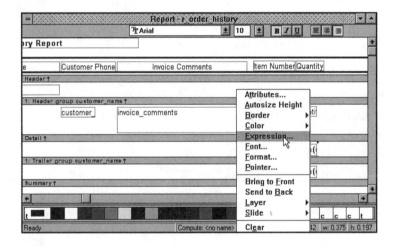

Fig. 11.16
Right-clicking on a field brings up a pop-up menu that allows you to modify the field selected (in this case, the subtotal for quantity). To change the computed expression, select **E**xpression.

The Computed Field Definition dialog box opens, as shown in figure 11.17. Notice that the existing formula for the calculation is sum(quantity for group 1). Totals would of course be summations, but what makes this a subtotal is the for group 1 clause. Remember that groups are numbered, the first (outermost) group being group 1. If a formula says for group x, then that formula would be applied to all rows from that group only. In the example, group 1 is a customer, so the summation is total quantity for one customer.

What this computed field needs is a label. You can accomplish this in one of two ways. You could create a static text field on the report saying "Total for customer" and place it right next to the computed field. This is a simple way of doing things, but it can be tiresome to line everything up and assure that the spacing between the static text and the computed fields is proper.

III

Using DataWindows

Fig. 11.17
The Computed
Field Definition
dialog box shows
you the current
expression and
allows you to
change it.

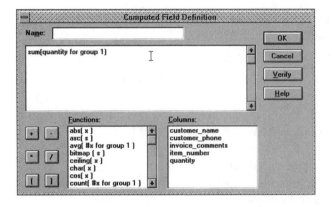

The other way of doing this is to add the static text right into the computed field. To do this, follow these steps:

1. Place your cursor at the beginning of the formula.

2. Type (including the quotation marks) **"Total for"** + .

3. While leaving the cursor right where it is, click on customer_name in the **C**olumns list box. This places the field customer_name right inside the computed field, too. Since the customer_name is a string, the + sign will be taken to mean string concatenation between the static text "total for" and the customer_name field from the database.

4. Your cursor should be right after customer_name and just before sum(). Add another + sign to add one more string concatenation in the actual total amount. At this point, your computed field should look like figure 11.18.

Fig. 11.18
This is how your
computed field for
the subtotal of
quantity should
look (be sure you
have the plus signs
and the quotes in
the appropriate
places).

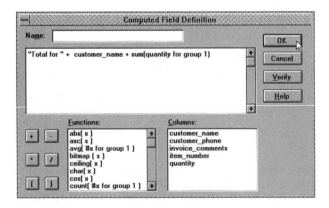

5. Before you click on OK, you must turn the total field into a string. (At this point you would be mixing data types, since you have a string + a string + a number.) To do this, type **string(** right after the second plus sign and before sum( ). Go to the end of this formula and add a close parenthesis **)** to balance out the parenthesis. The string() function that you just used converts a number into a string. It takes one argument inside the parenthesis—a number. Your computed field should now look like figure 11.19. When finished, click on OK.

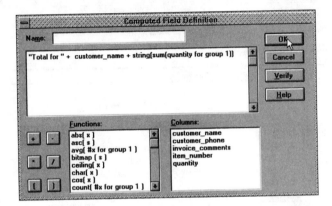

Fig. 11.19
The computed field is completed after using the string function, so that the entire expression is considered a string.

Troubleshooting

When I clicked on OK I got an error message, `Expression is not valid.`

When you click on OK, PowerBuilder tries to make sense out of the expression. If you have forgotten the plus signs or left out the quotation marks, PowerBuilder cannot understand the expression. Correct the problem, and click on OK again.

---

6. Before you go back to preview to check it out, you need to make the field a little wider to display all this information. In the Report Design window, stretch this field out to the left to make it wider.

Now, go back into preview and see the results of your changes (see fig. 11.20). As you can see, the field wasn't stretched quite wide enough—the left part of the expression is truncated.

III

Using DataWindows

Note

The reason why the left is truncated and not the right is that this field has been designated as right-justified.

Fig. 11.20
A preview of the order history report shows the subtotals with their labels.

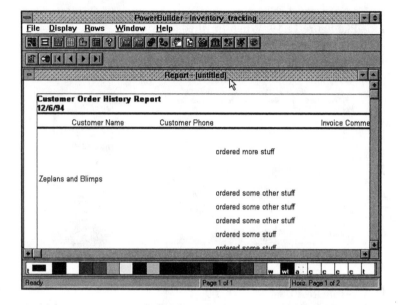

Also, there is no space in between the customer name and the quantity total. To fix these problems, go back to design, stretch the field out some more (although yours might already be stretched wide enough) and double-click on the computed field.

Tip
Preview often while making changes, because one seemingly small change can have a big impact on your report.

You should add one space (inside of quotes) and another plus sign after the customer_name column and before the total, as shown in figure 11.21.

Preview the report once again. It should look much better (see fig. 11.22).

You might have noticed a pattern as you work on reports. You change one or two things, then preview, change one or two things, and then preview.

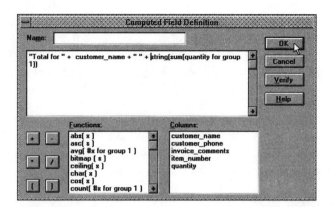

Fig. 11.21
To correct the fact that the label and the data are running together, place a blank (one space) in between the label and the data.

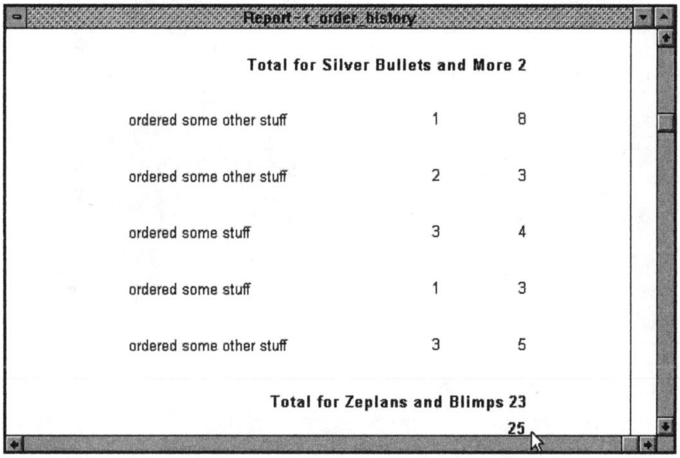

Fig. 11.22
Now that the subtotal field is wide enough and there's a space between the customer name and the subtotal, the report looks much better.

Working with the Grand Total

Notice in figure 11.22 the number 25 right next to the pointer. Do you know what that number is? Do you think the recipient of this report would know what that number is? It is the grand total quantity for all customers. In order for the readers to know that, this field needs a label similar to the label you just built for subtotals. The difference would be that you would not be including a customer name in this computed field, since this number applies to all customers.

III

Using DataWindows

To create the label, double-click on the grand total field (it's in the summary band). The Computed Field Definition dialog box appears again, this time for the grand total. Notice that the formula is the same (for example, sum), but that this time it says for all. The for all clause means all rows of data retrieved, which is exactly what a grand total is supposed to do.

For the grand total, the formula will be a little simpler than for subtotals since the customer_name field is not involved. It should read something like the text in figure 11.23. Do not forget the plus sign in between " and the string() around the summation. When you are done, click on OK.

Fig. 11.23
Here you add a label for the grand total of quantity, as well as a string function to make the entire expression a string.

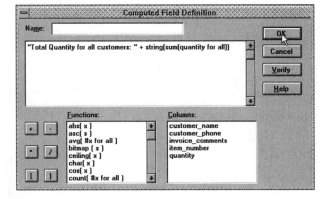

Your report should look a lot better than it did when you first started. There are many other things you can do to a report (and all of this applies for DataWindows as well). For instance, as mentioned earlier, you can have more than one group within a group report.

Adding Another Group

It is very common to want more than one group in a report. For example, you might want to group some information by state, and within state by county. In this example, state would be the outermost group (group 1) and county would be the innermost group (group 2).

In our Customer Order History Report, you will be grouping by invoice number within customer. Each invoice's information will be grouped together for that customer.

At this time, the report does not retrieve the invoice number. In order to group by the invoice number, however, it must be one of the columns retrieved from the database. Therefore, you must change your SQL Select statement to include the invoice number field.

To change the SQL Select statement, go back to the SQL Select dialog box. Include `invoice_number` from the invoice table by clicking on that column once, as shown in figure 11.24.

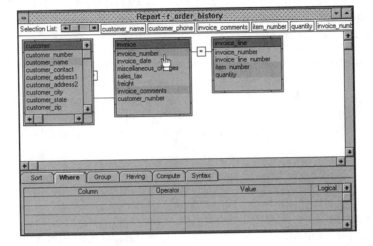

Fig. 11.24
From the SQL Select window, click on the field once to add another column to the report.

Now that you have done that, it's time to return to design. Click on the Design icon from the toolbar. When you return to design, PowerBuilder adds the new column to the report, but you cannot see this new field right away. You will find this new field in the detail band to the far right (you will probably have to scroll the screen to the right to see it). However, you should leave it alone for now.

Now that you have included this column, you can group your data by it. To create another group, select **R**ows, Create **G**roup. When you do, you will see the Specify Group Columns dialog box as you did for the first group you created. And, just like for the first group, you click on the column (or columns) you want to group by from the list on the left and drag them to the list on the right. When you have selected all the columns you want for this second group (which would be only the invoice_number column), click on OK.

When you return to the Report Design window, you can see that two new band areas have been created: a header band for group 2 and a trailer band for group 2. As mentioned earlier, all groups have their own header and trailer bands. These bands will print once for each new group 2 occurrence. In this case, you will see a group 2 header and trailer once for every invoice in the database.

III

Using DataWindows

Since there are now two groups, you might want to have two subtotals, a total quantity for each invoice, and a total quantity for the customer (which was already created by PowerBuilder), as well as the grand total quantity for all customers (which was also already done by PowerBuilder). It makes sense that you would want the total quantity for each invoice to display at the end of the invoice, which would be in the group 2 trailer.

There are two ways to create a summation field in PowerBuilder. There's the hard way and there's the easy way. The hard way is to pull down the group 2 trailer band to make room for a column, then click on the Compute icon on the toolbar, click on the report where you want to place the computed field, then type in **sum(quantity for group 2)**, and then click on OK.

Whew! That's a lot of work! Now, the easy way: click once on the Quantity column in the detail band to select it, and then click on the Summation icon on the toolbar.

That's all there is to it. Wasn't that a whole lot easier? PowerBuilder automatically makes room for it in the group 2 trailer band and places the exact same computed field just described in that band (see fig. 11.25).

Fig. 11.25
The Summation icon provides an easy way to get summary information into a trailer band.

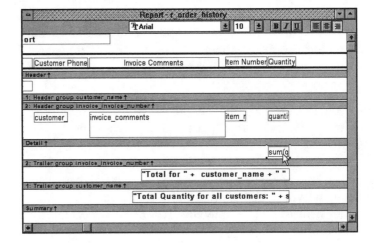

Now, just fix that subtotal to include a description of what is being totaled, as you did for the other subtotal and for the grand total.

Before previewing this report, there is something else that must be done in order for the second group to work correctly. You see, the data must be sorted in the same order as the grouping or you might get more groups than you thought.

If you have one row from invoice #4, followed by one row from invoice #7, followed by another row from invoice #4, and it is not sorted, that's three groups. You can see that it should be only two groups, since there are only two invoices represented. If, however, the data was sorted by invoice number, you would see only two groups, one for each invoice.

You might be saying to yourself, "I didn't have to do that with the first group, and it worked OK." That is because PowerBuilder does the first group for you automatically. With any other groups you create thereafter, you're on your own to sort them correctly.

Setting the Sort Order

To set up the report's sort order, select **R**ows, **S**ort. The Specify Sort Columns dialog box appears. As you can see from figure 11.26, the customer_name column is already in the sort order as the outermost sort column.

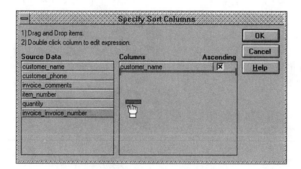

Fig. 11.26
The Specify Sort Columns dialog box allows you to modify the sort order for this report.

To add the invoice_number column to the sort order, drag the invoice_number column from the list to the right. If you wish to sort in ascending order, leave the ascending selected. If you wish to sort in descending order, click on the Ascending check box to deselect it. When you have done this, click on OK.

Troubleshooting

I forgot to set up my sort order before previewing the report.

You can go back at any time to change the sort order. Simply follow the steps outlined before while in the Report Design window.

III

Using DataWindows

Now, preview the report. The only thing left to do (besides maybe add some color, change a few borders, and other cosmetic things) would be to show the invoice number somewhere on the report. (The invoice number is on the report now; it is just too far to the right to be seen within the piece of paper's border.) You should move the invoice number to where it can be seen. In fact, you should put it in the group 2 header band instead of the detail band so that it appears only once for an invoice that has more than one item on it.

To do this, follow these steps:

1. Make room in the group 2 header band. From the Report Design window, move the mouse on top of the group 2 header band. You will see the pointer change to a double-arrow pointer. Click and drag the band down until there's enough room in between the group 1 header band and the group 2 header band.

2. Find the invoice number field; it should be to the far right. Drag it into the group 2 header band and to the left so that it appears in the same general area as the other fields.

3. Add a label for the field so that the reader would know what that number stands for.

To see how this looks, refer to figure 11.27.

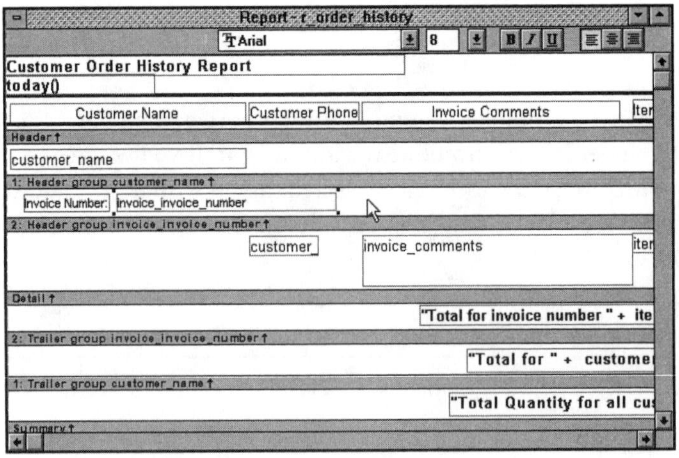

Fig. 11.27
The label and the invoice_number field have been placed in the group 2 header, so that they will appear once for every invoice.

Suppressing Duplicated Information

You might also want to move the invoice_comments column into the group 2 header band, since this comment is the same for each item in any given invoice (for example, there is only one comment for an invoice, and that's the comment you see repeatedly in the detail area of the report). While you are at it, the phone_number column should be moved to the group 1 header band, since this is the customers' phone number, which is the same for every invoice for a given customer.

This is one way to get rid of duplicated information—by moving the information into a band other than the detail band, it will not print each time there is a row retrieved from the database. However, moving things from one band to another also affects where that information is displayed on the report. All header bands are above the detail, and all trailer bands are below the detail. If you want to get rid of duplicated information from the detail line, but leave the data in the detail band, you can follow these steps:

1. Select Suppress Repeating Values from the Rows menu. The Specify Repeating Values Suppression List dialog box appears (see fig. 11.28).

Fig. 11.28
The Specify Repeating Value Suppression List dialog box allows you to designate a column or columns to display only once when the same information is repeated.

2. Select the columns that, when they repeat, you want to be suppressed. Drag and drop them to the list on the right side of this window. When you have selected all the columns you want, click on OK.

So there you have it—a group report with two groups! And of course, you could have as many groups as you'd like. Each group gets its own header and trailer band, whether you use them or not. Keep in mind that when you create a new group, you must set up the sort order in the same order you grouped by, in order for the grouping to be effective.

> **Note**
>
> Be sure to save your report again so that all the changes you made are not lost. In fact, it's a good idea to save all PowerBuilder objects frequently when modifying them.

The next thing to do is add a graph to the report. While you can create an entire report that is a graph itself (since graph is one of the presentation styles to select from when creating a new report), you can also inlay a graph on a report.

Creating Graphs

A *graph* is basically the same as any other report, except that instead of displaying data to users as raw numbers, the data is presented in a graphical format. To create graphs, there are some terms that must be understood. In a graph, you will have categories, values, and series.

- The *category* is the independent data. It can include things such as departments, months, quarters, years, and states.

- The *value* is the dependent data. This information will typically vary by category, such as number of employees (per department), total sales (per quarter), and number of counties (per state).

- The *series* is the set of data points for the graph.

When you create a graph, you must decide what your categories and values will be. The series will "fall out" of the graph based upon the categories and values. The categories will typically be a column in the SQL Select statement. The value might also be a column, but it is more likely that it will be data derived from a column—that is, a summation, a count, or an average of some column from the data.

With this information in mind, you can add a graph to this report.

For this example, you will graph the total quantity for each customer. This information is already available in the report, but sometimes it helps to see such information in graphical format, particularly when it comes to doing comparisons. This graph will make it easy to tell which customers are purchasing in heavy volumes.

To add a graph to an existing report, you simply click on the Graph icon on the Design toolbar, and then click on the report where you would like to place the graph. The Graph Data dialog box appears (see fig. 11.29).

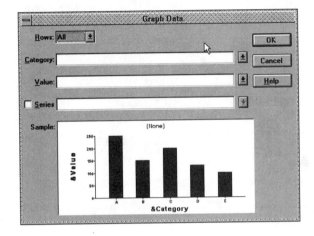

Fig. 11.29
The Graph Data dialog box allows you to designate the Category, Value and Series for the graph.

From the Graph Data dialog box, you select the **C**ategory and **V**alue. Each of these is a drop-down list box.

The list box for the category contains all the columns that are part of the SQL Select statement for this report. You should select customer_name as the category.

The Value list box for the value contains more possibilities than the Category list box. It lists all the columns from the SQL Select statement, such as the Category list box, but it also includes a count for all the non-numeric fields, such as customer_comments (to count the number of comments) and a summation for all the numeric fields, such as item_number (to add up the item numbers). You can pick from this list or you can create your own value. For instance, you might want to use the average for the quantity, and not the sum of the quantity. In this example, however, you should select sum (quantity for graph).

When you have selected both the category and value, click on OK.

PowerBuilder places a small graph on your report (see fig. 11.30). The default type for the graph is a 2D column graph. This graph also has, by default, a resizeable border. You might want to make the graph a little larger so that its information is legible when the report is created. Also, notice that the graph does not sit inside any bands. The graph is in the foreground of the report, which means that it does not belong to any band.

▶ See "Selecting a Different Kind of Graph," p. 325

III

Using DataWindows

A discussion of the different types of graphs that are available is found later in this chapter.

Fig. 11.30

The graph that is added to the existing report can be moved around and resized. This graph is not part of any layer; it's in the foreground of the report.

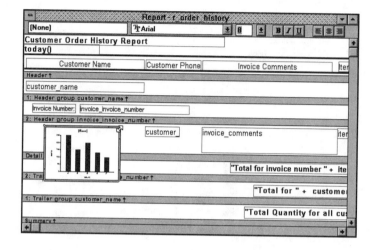

> ## Note
>
> Graphs are, by default, in the foreground layer, but can be placed into a band. As a matter of fact, any object on a report, including columns and static text, can be placed in the foreground, background, or the band layer. To change the layer of an object, right-click on the object and select **L**ayer from the pop-up menu, which gives you the choice of foreground, band, or background.

Before doing anything else, preview the report to see what the graph looks like. Notice that the initial size of the graph is probably too small to be useful. However, since this graph is in the foreground and is resizeable, the user can both move the graph and change its size at run time. In figure 11.31, the graph is larger and is moved a little so that the data in the graph becomes more legible.

Since this graph is in the foreground, it does block the data that it is on top of, so it is a good thing that the graph can be moved around on-screen. (Of course, once it is printed out on paper, it cannot be moved around!)

Remember that this is a graph of the quantity by customer. This graph needs some labels so that the user would know this, too. You need to go back to design (when you do, notice that the graph that was resized retains this new size back in design) and make some changes to the graph.

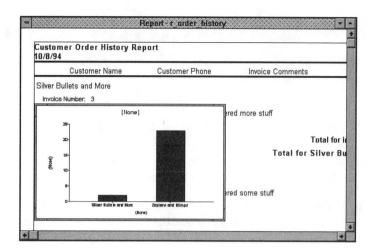

Fig. 11.31
The graph that
appears while
previewing is both
moveable and
resizeable.

Modifying a Graph

To change a graph, you can do one of two things: double-click anywhere on the graph or right-click on the graph, bringing up a pop-up list to choose from; or select **N**ame.

From this dialog box, you can modify a number of things. (In general, graphs have a great many options and attributes available to them, most of which will not be covered in the book.) The things to be concerned about are adding labels to the graph.

First, give this graph a title. In figure 11.32, you see a field labeled **T**itle. It defaults to saying (None). Type in a new title to read something like **Quantity by Customer**.

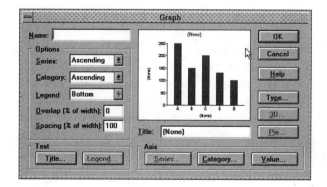

Fig. 11.32
The Graph
window allows
you to change
various informa-
tion about how
the graph should
be displayed,
including the **T**itle
of the graph.

III

Using DataWindows

Note

If you want to change other aspects of the title, such as the font or point size, click on the Title button in the Graph dialog box, shown in figure 11.32.

Next, label the categories and values axis. At this time they both are labeled with the default <none>. To do this, there are buttons labeled **C**ategory and **V**alue in the Axis section. Each of these buttons brings up another dialog box, called Category Axis and Value Axis, respectively.

Figure 11.33 shows the Category Axis dialog box. Both the Category Axis dialog box and the Values Axis dialog box have all the same information, each dealing with their respective axis. They each have a lot of information to them. This information deals with the tick marks, the major and minor divisions, and so on. For more information on these items, see the PowerBuilder on-line help or the PowerBuilder manuals.

Fig. 11.33
The Category Axis dialog box allows you to modify how the category data should be graphed.

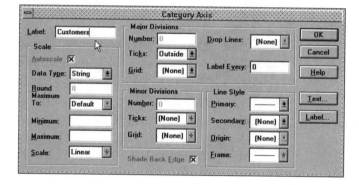

The item you are interested in is the **L**abel. You will find that on the left side of either dialog box. Change <none> to Customers for the category, and click on OK to close the Category Axis dialog box. Then pull up the Value Axis dialog box and change the default label <none> to Quantity Purchased, and then click on OK. This way, the user of this graph will know that they are looking at a graph of quantity purchased by customer.

Note

To change other aspects of the labels, such as the font and point size, click the **L**abel button on each of these windows.

You now return to the Graph dialog box. You can see the new labels reflected in the Graph window's mock-up of your graph. From the Graph dialog box, click on OK to clear that dialog box from the screen. Your changes will now be reflected in the report.

Selecting a Different Kind of Graph

The graph you are building—a comparison of each of the customers and the quantity they purchased—might be better served by using a pie chart. *Pie charts* are useful for comparisons of how much of the overall amount is attributed to each category. The column chart you are using now shows the total quantity for each customer. As discussed previously, this information is already available on your report. To show that information in a different way, you could use the pie chart.

To change the type of graph you are using, once again you would double-click on the graph, bringing up the Graph dialog box as seen in figure 11.32. To change the type, click on the Ty**p**e button. You will then see the Graph Type dialog box. Here you can see all the available graph types in PowerBuilder (see fig. 11.34). While this is not the most exhaustive list of graphs, it is pretty comprehensive, particularly for business graphing applications.

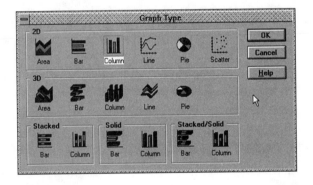

Fig. 11.34
The list of graph types for PowerBuilder allows you to take your existing data and graph it another way.

The 2D column graph type is currently highlighted since it's the default graph. Select the 3D Pie graph by clicking on it and click on OK. You then return to the Graph dialog box where you will see the mock-up change to reflect that you are now using a pie chart (see fig. 11.35). The Category and Value buttons are now disabled since they do not apply for pie charts. You might have also noticed that two more buttons are now enabled that were not before.

The Pie button allows you to change the Text for Pie Chart labels. The 3D button allows you to change the perspective, elevation, rotation, and depth of the graph.

Fig. 11.35
Now that the graph is a 3D Pie chart, the 3D and Pie buttons are enabled.

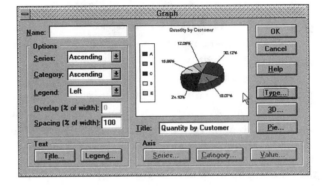

From the Graph dialog box, click on OK to return to the report window. You then will see that your graph has changed to a Pie chart. Preview the report at this time to see the difference that the Pie chart makes.

> **Note**
>
> Notice there was no change in the information that the graph uses, only the type of graph that it is. If you wanted to change the data, you would right-click on the graph, pulling up the pop-up menu for the graph, and select **D**ata from the menu.

You should save your report again at this point, so that the effort you have just put forth is not lost. Next, preview your report, observing the pie chart on your report. Notice that in the case of a pie chart, each customer is represented as a different colored slice of the pie, and that the percentage of the grand total that each customer is responsible for appears.

Creating Label Reports

A *label report* is a report that is designed to create labels, usually by using label paper. Label is one of the presentation styles that's available for a new report.

As an example, you can create a customer mailing label report. This label report will use only one table, the Customer table. The Customer table contains all the information about a customer that is necessary to mail something to that customer, such as an invoice.

To create the label report, click on the Report icon, and then choose **N**ew in the Select Report dialog box. You then see the New Report dialog box. Since the labels use only one table, select Quick Select as the data source and Label as the presentation style, and then click on OK.

The next thing you see is the Quick Select dialog box. Select customer as the table, and when the list of columns from the customer table appears, select the following fields: customer_name, customer_address1, customer_address2, customer_city, customer_state, and customer_zip (see fig. 11.36). When you have done this, you might also want to set up a sort order so that the labels are in some kind of order. When completed, click on OK.

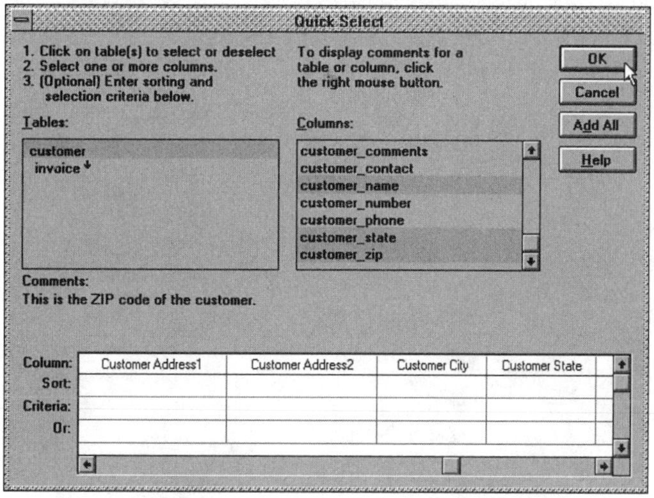

Quick Select

Fig. 11.36
Using a quick select for the customer table only, select the fields from the customer table that handle address information.

Since this is a label report, the next dialog box you see is the Specify Label Specifications dialog box. You use this dialog box to determine the dimensions of your labels, as well as how the labels are laid out on the label paper. After all, the principle reason for creating a label report is to print it on label paper and use the individual labels. If you have not laid out your labels correctly, when you print them on paper you will not get a one-to-one correspondence between your labels and each row of data.

III

Using DataWindows

> **Caution**
>
> You can select from the drop-down list box of predefined labels. In doing so, PowerBuilder will fill in all the information on this dialog box, based upon your selection. Each of these fields can be edited. However, you should exercise caution in making changes to these settings since you might be messing up something that is already laid out nicely.

In this dialog box, you must also decide whether the paper to be printed on is Continuous Feed or Sheet Feed, and whether the labels should print **L**eft-to-Right or **T**op-to-Bottom.

For this example (which won't be printed anyway), you can select whatever predefined labels you want. I have selected Laser Address 1 X 2.63, 3 labels across, 10 down, which will fit the customer information nicely (see fig. 11.37). After making your selection, click on OK.

> **Note**
>
> If you make a selection here that does not work out for you, you can always change these settings later by right-clicking on the label in the Report Design window and selecting **L**abel.

Fig. 11.37
The Specify Label Specifications dialog box allows you to designate the size and arrangement of your labels.

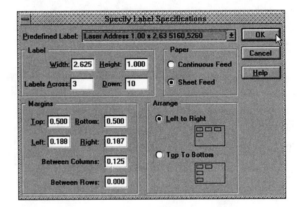

You then see the design window for your label report, with the outline of your label and the columns you selected during Quick Select within the label (see fig. 11.38). It almost seems as though the label height of one inch is not enough to display all the fields.

Making Adjustments

Before returning to the Label Specifications dialog box and changing the height of the label, take another look at figure 11.38. Although the last two fields do not fit vertically, do you really want them in that position anyway? Those last two fields are customer_state and customer_zip. They should be moved up next to the customer_city field. When you do that, everything fits inside the border of the label.

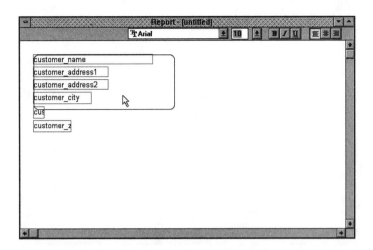

Fig. 11.38
The initial design of your labels shows all the fields you selected and an outline of the label size you specified.

Note

It is important that everything fit within the border of the label, so that when it is printed out on label paper, all the information needed for each label appears on the label.

Before you do anything else, you should save this report. Select Save As from the File menu. Name this report **r_customer_labels** and provide a description of the report in the Comments area.

Now, preview this report. Click on the Preview icon on the Report Painter toolbar. All of the customers from your customer table will have a label (see fig. 11.39). This looks pretty good so far, but there a couple of things you can do to improve this report.

First of all, the City, State, and Zip columns are lined up properly, but there is a big gap in between most of the data. The City field is pretty wide to allow for cities with many letters; therefore the State field cannot be any closer than it is. To solve this problem, you need to create a *computed field*.

Normally when you think of computed fields, you probably think of calculations to be performed. However, you can use a computed field simply to do string concatenation.

After getting back into Design mode, the first thing you must do is remove the City, State, and Zip fields from the report. Highlight each one of them and click on the Delete icon. Now, in their place you will create a computed field.

III

Using DataWindows

Fig. 11.39
Previewing the label report shows how the actual data fits within the borders of a label.

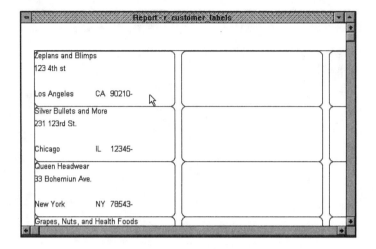

 To create the computed field, click on the Compute icon on the Report Painter toolbar, and then click on the report where you want this field to be placed. The Computed Field Definition dialog box appears. Figure 11.40 shows you what the expression should look like. To create this expression, click once on customer_city in the **C**olumns list box, and it will be pasted into the expression wherever your cursor is. Watching for the needed quotes, place a comma and a space between the City and State fields, and just a space between State and Zip. When you have completed this, click on OK, which takes you back to the Report Design window.

Fig. 11.40
The computed field, in this case, is nothing more than several string fields concat- enated together (don't forget the plus signs in between each string).

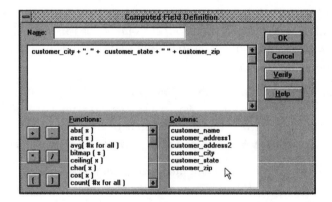

When you are back in the Report Design window, you see the computed field just created. It will probably need to be stretched out to make sure that it is wide enough to display all three fields. It might also need to be aligned and spaced properly to fit in with the other fields.

When you are finished, preview the report again. Notice how the City, State, and Zip are all nicely spaced! Be sure to test that the width of your field is adequate by including in your test data the city that has the most letters in it.

Sliding a Column

The report looks better but is still not complete. As you can tell, the customer_address2 column is not always used. You have to include it here in your labels in case it is used for some customers. It would be nice if you could leave room for it, but not have that gap when there is no data.

PowerBuilder has a feature called a *sliding column*. Each column in a report (and in a DataWindow) can be set up as a slider. What is meant by *sliding* is that if there is no data in the designated direction (either to the left or above), this column will slide in to fill the gap.

It's very easy to designate a column as a slider. You just right-click on top of the column (here, you want the computed column to be the slider) and select **S**lide. This shortcut menu has a cascading child menu (see fig. 11.41). In here you must decide to slide to the left or up. You want to select up. Since the column is above, you must decide between Up - **A**ll Above or Up - **D**irectly Above. The difference between these two is that with All Above, all the fields that make up the line above must be emptied before it can slide up; Directly Above means only the fields that are directly overhead must be blank. In this case, however, there is only one field overhead (customer_address1), so either choice will do.

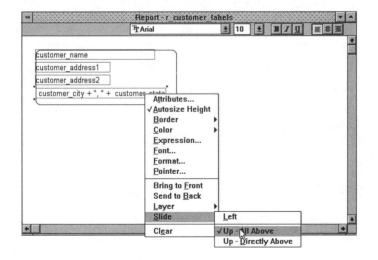

Fig. 11.41
Designating a column as a slider means that if there is no data in the designated direction, that data will slide to fill in the gap.

III

Using DataWindows

> **Note**
>
> The field to slide into (for example, customer_address2) must have no data in it for the other column to slide into its place. Anything in there, even one space, would not be considered blank.

There is one more thing you must do before this can work. You must make sure that the Autosize Height attribute is turned on for the column that might be blank (in this case, the customer_address2 column). Autosize Height assures that the column has a specific height that the sliding field can utilize for its repositioning.

You turn on Autosize Height for the customer_address2 field by right-clicking on that column and clicking on the **A**utosize Height attribute. (If it is already turned on, you will see a check mark next to Autosize Height.)

Now, preview the report again (see fig. 11.42). Notice that for any customer who did not have address2 field information, the City, State, and Zip fields moved up to appear directly below the address1 field.

Fig. 11.42
With the city-state-zip computed field designated as a slider, the computed field slides up to fill in the gap when there is no address2 information.

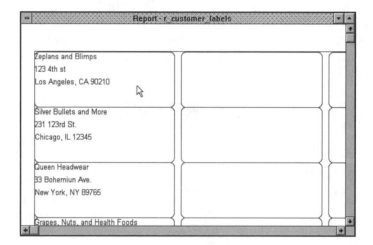

Creating Nested Reports

In PowerBuilder, you can put a report inside of another report. (This works for DataWindows, as well.) A report inside of another report is referred to as a *nested report*. Although the Inventory Tracking system you are creating here does not lend itself to nested reports very well, you could do something like change the Customer Order History Report created in this chapter to include the customer DataWindow (d_customer) created in an earlier chapter. If you were to do this, of course, you would probably delete the fields from the customer table that you included in the report initially (at least pull them off-screen, but you would still need the customer_name column to be retrieved because you grouped this report using that field).

To add a nested report in the Customer Order History Report, open r_order_history in the report painter. To do this, click on the report painter from the PowerBar and scroll through the list of reports until you find r_order_history. Click on it once, and then click on OK.

Delete (from the screen only) the customer_name and customer_phone columns. (To do this, click on each one once, and then click on the Delete icon on the Report Painter toolbar.)

Now, click on the Report icon on the Report Painter toolbar, and then click on the screen where you want the nested report to go. (You should click in the header for group 1 band, as this is where you were displaying the customer_name column.)

Next you see the Select Report dialog box (see fig. 11.43), where you see a list box of all the reports and DataWindows in your application. Select the one you want (d_customer) by clicking on it once, and then click on OK.

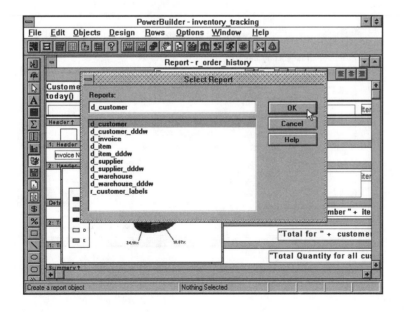

Fig. 11.43
The Select Report dialog box allows you to choose which report (or DataWindow) you wish to nest into your report.

III

Using DataWindows

You then see a rectangular object on your report that is labeled d_customer (see fig. 11.44). This represents the nested report. You cannot see any of the details for this report, such as the columns or their labels; all you ever see of d_customers from here is this rectangle. You must resize the rectangle so that all of the data from d_customer would fit within its border. This can only be accomplished by good ol' fashioned trial-and-error. Size it up and preview the report; if it doesn't quite fit, size it up and preview again, and so on (see fig. 11.45).

Fig. 11.44

The nested report shows up in your report as an empty rectangle during design. It must be sized up appropriately so that when the report is previewed, all the data from the nested report will fit.

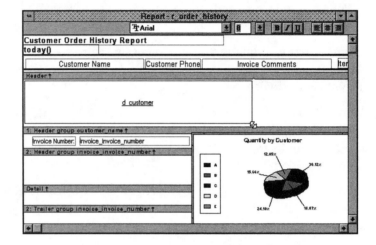

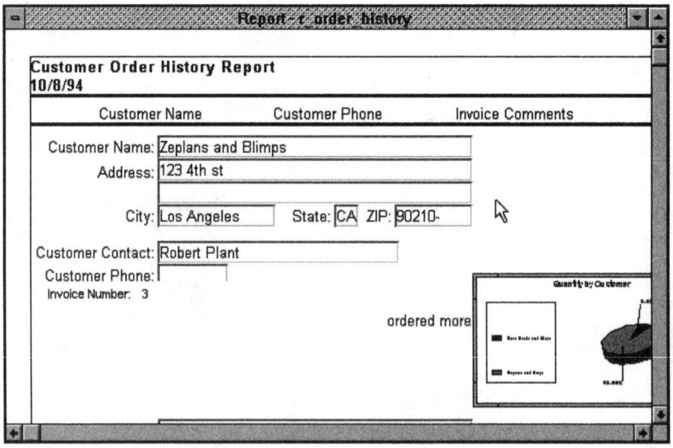

Fig. 11.45

The results of the nested report are shown here while previewing the report.

From Here...

In this chapter you learned how to create grouped reports, graphs, labels and reports within reports. Along the way, you used computed fields in innovative ways.

You saw that reports (and DataWindows) are a very powerful means of displaying data. For more on what DataWindows can do, refer to the following chapters:

- Chapter 8, "Creating DataWindows," describes several DataWindow development techniques. You learn how to create three DataWindows and hook your DataWindows to your application.

- Chapter 9, "Enhancing DataWindows," shows you how to modify, enhance, and use your DataWindow.

- Chapter 10, "Manipulating Data Using DataWindows," shows how SQL can be used to define a DataWindow. This chapter covers the SQL toolbox and the SQL syntax behind a DataWindow.

III

Using DataWindows

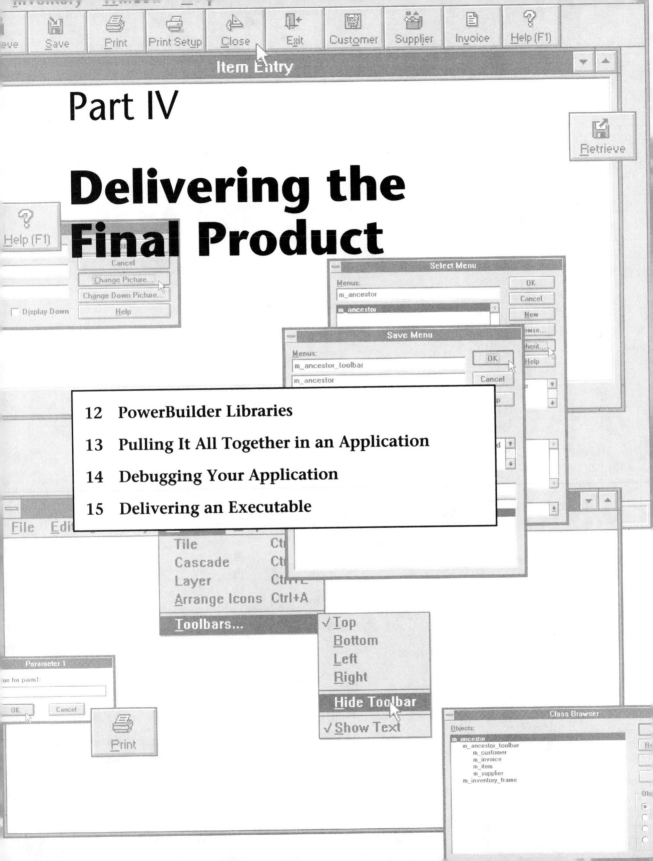

Part IV

Delivering the Final Product

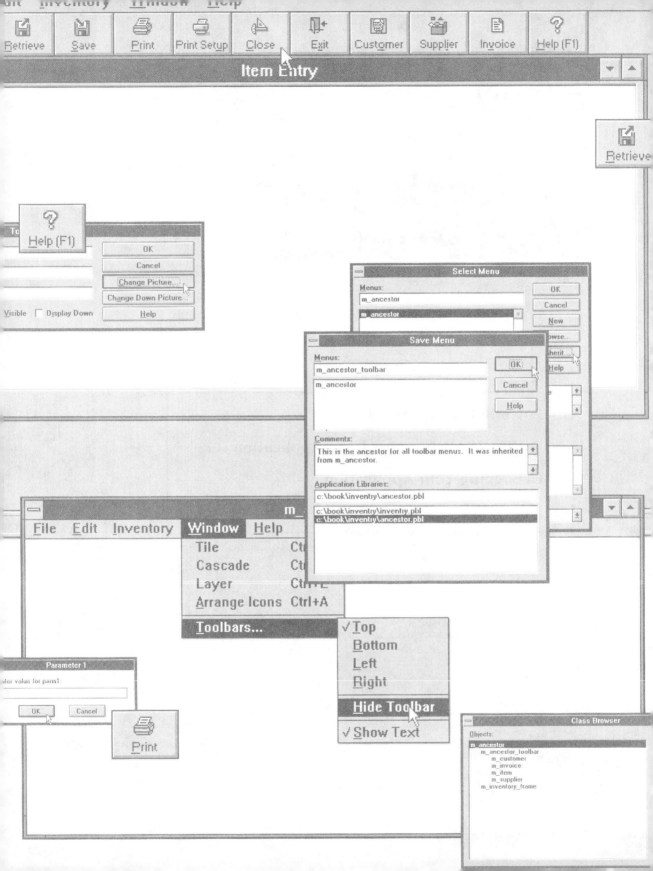

Chapter 12

PowerBuilder Libraries

PowerBuilder libraries are where PowerBuilder stores all of its objects. Most developers use the library painter method to navigate through their systems.

In this chapter, you learn how to:

- Use the library painter to pull up different painters

- Move, copy, and delete library entries

- Manage several entries at once

- Use the library painter to manage multi-developer projects

- Use system regeneration from the library

Using the Library Painter

The library painter is how most developers navigate through their system. To pull up the library painter, click on the Library icon. Along with pulling up the library painter, this shows you all the objects in the PBL containing the application you're working on. If you've been coding the Inventory Tracking system so far, your library should look something like what is shown in figure 12.1.

Fig. 12.1

The library painter as it first appears.

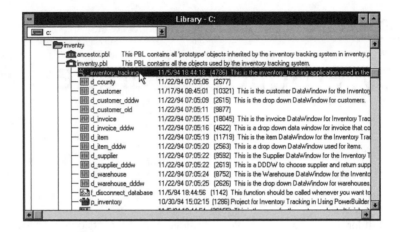

Jumping to a Painter

Tip

When you first bring up the library painter, it displays only the PBL that contains the application. You can display or stop displaying other directories by double-clicking them.

One of the library painter's best features is its capability to jump to a painter and pull up an entry for you. This saves you the time of going through the long process of selecting the painter, PBL, and then the module you want to update.

With the library painter, simply find the entry you want and double-click it. This automatically brings up the proper painter, with the module you clicked already open inside the painter.

Selecting Entries

Most library painter functions require you to select one or several PBL entries first. There are several different ways to select a single PBL entry or a set of PBL entries:

- To select a single PBL entry, click it with the mouse.

- To select every entry in a PBL, click that PBL, then click the Select All icon. All your entries are now selected, as seen in figure 12.2.

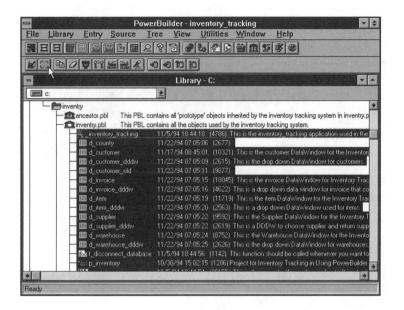

Fig. 12.2
To select all of your entries in a PBL, click that PBL and then click the Select All icon.

■ To select several entries—even across PBLs—make sure all entries you want to select are displayed and not hidden behind a PBL or directory. Select the first entry by clicking it. Use the scroll bar on the far right side of the window to scroll to the bottom of the entries to select. While holding down the Shift key, click the bottom entry. This selects contiguous entries across libraries, as seen in figure 12.3.

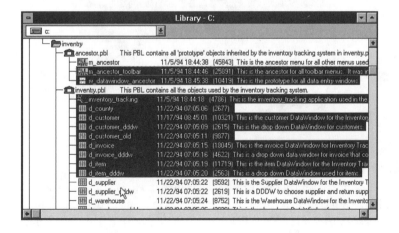

Fig. 12.3
By clicking a library entry and then holding down the Shift key while clicking another, you can select those entries and all entries in between.

Tip
Any current selections stay selected.

- To select additional non-contiguous entries after you already selected entries, hold down the Ctrl key while clicking your additional entry, as seen in figure 12.4.

Fig. 12.4
If you already have one or several items selected and you want to select more, but all the items aren't contiguous, hold down the Ctrl key and select your additional entry.

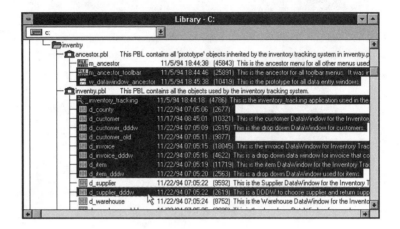

Copying Selected Entries

To copy a library entry or entries to another library, select the entry(ies) you want to copy and click the Copy icon. This opens the Copy Library Entries dialog box, seen in figure 12.5. Click the proper directory and the proper PBL, and then click OK. Your entry is copied to the new PBL.

Fig. 12.5
The Copy Library Entries dialog box allows you to copy entries from one PBL to another.

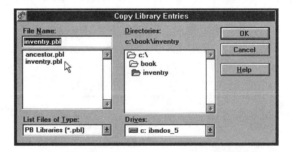

Deleting Selected Entries

To delete a library entry or entries, select the entry(ies) and click the Delete icon. PowerBuilder then asks if you are sure you want to delete this library entry, as seen in figure 12.6. Click **Y**es (if you're sure); the entry is deleted.

IV

Delivering the Final Product

Fig. 12.6
PowerBuilder
always verifies
before you delete
a library entry.

Moving Selected Entries

To move a library entry or entries to another library, select the entry(ies) you
want to move and click the Move icon. This opens the Move Library Entries
dialog box, seen in figure 12.7. Click the proper directory and the proper PBL,
and then click OK. Your entry is moved from its existing PBL to the new PBL.

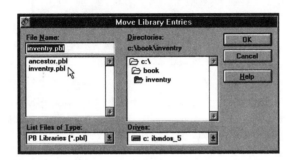

Fig. 12.7
The Move Library
Entries dialog box
allows you to
move entries
from one PBL
to another.

Understanding Regeneration

Regeneration is important during the development of your PowerBuilder
application. *Regeneration* realigns all your objects and internal object calls.
Often, your PowerBuilder application will halt for no apparent reason. This
happens if the internal calls no longer match the existing structure; it usually
can be solved by regeneration.

To regenerate, select the entries you want regenerated (usually all of them
in an application) and click the Regeneration icon. This regenerates all selected entries.

Browsing Library Entries

Often, you will want to find out where you declare or use a variable, or all occurrences of an object, and so on. To search through your entries:

1. Select the entries and then click the Browse icon. This opens the Browse Library Entries dialog box, seen in figure 12.8.

Fig. 12.8

The Browse Library Entries dialog box allows you to search through entries for the occurrence of a variable or text.

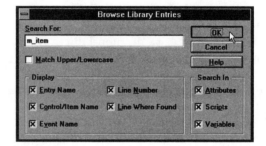

2. In this dialog box, type in what you want to search for. You can choose to match case and which entries to display. You can also choose where to search in the entries you've chosen.

3. When you've decided what to search for and the search criteria, click OK. All selected entries are searched, based on the criteria you've chosen. When the search is finished, the Matching Library Entries dialog box appears, as seen in figure 12.9. This displays the criteria you've selected in the Browse Library Entries dialog box.

4. From the Matching Library Entries dialog box, you can print the results of your search by clicking **P**rint, or copy the results of your search to a DOS file by clicking **C**opy To..., or you can immediately pull up the painter of the entry where the search string is located by clicking **G**o To Painter.

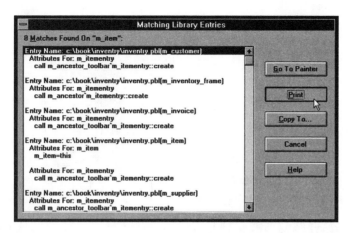

Fig. 12.9
The Matching
Library Entries
dialog box displays
the results of your
search described in
the Browse Library
Entries dialog box.

Browsing Class Hierarchies

An important feature of the library painter is the ability to browse class hierarchies. Often, as with the case of the menus in Inventory Tracking, you have several layers of inheritance. It is useful to see what inheritance is present in a system, especially when you modify someone else's work.

To view the inheritance in a system, follow these steps:

1. Choose **U**tilities, Browse Class **H**ierarchy. The Class Browser dialog box appears, as shown in figure 12.10.

2. Click the object type you want to view:

- **M**enu views inheritance in the menu structure.

- **S**ystem views the system structure put in place by PowerBuilder.

- **U**ser Object views any user objects you may have defined.

- **W**indow views inheritance in the window objects.

3. From here, you can print your hierarchy. You can also regenerate from here, since most errors that can be solved by regeneration come from the use of inheritance.

Fig. 12.10

The Class Browser dialog box shows inheritance in all your objects.

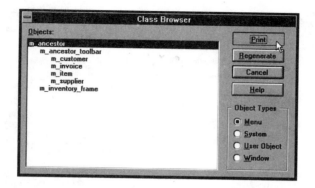

Managing Multi-Developer Projects

Several people may be working on a project at once. The PowerBuilder library painter has tools to help manage multi-developer projects.

Checking Out an Entry

PowerBuilder enables any developer to "check out" an entry from the library. If this is done, no other person can update or delete that entry until that entry is "checked in."

To check out an entry, click the Check Out icon. This opens the Set Current User ID dialog box, as seen in figure 12.11. The Set Current User ID dialog box lets you specify who you are. Be reasonably descriptive so that other developers really do know who checked out the entry.

After you enter your User ID, PowerBuilder asks you which PBL to copy your entry to, as seen in the Check Out Library Entries dialog box in figure 12.12. Choose your work PBL, and the entry is copied there.

Now that the entry is checked out, no one can modify the original copy until the entry is returned. If you try to open the entry, a warning message appears, as seen in figure 12.13. However, you can still open the checked out entry for viewing.

If you try to make changes and save them over the checked out entry, an error message appears telling you that the entry is checked out and cannot be overwritten, as shown in figure 12.14.

If another developer tries to check out your entry, PowerBuilder stops him or her with another error message stating that the entry is already checked out to someone else, as seen in figure 12.15.

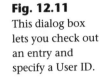

Fig. 12.11
This dialog box lets you check out an entry and specify a User ID.

Fig. 12.12
You specify which PBL to copy your entry to in the Check Out Library Entries dialog box.

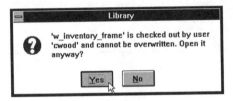

Fig. 12.13
A warning message appears if you try to open an entry that is checked out.

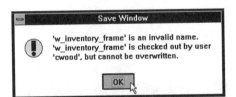

Fig. 12.14
You get an error message if you try to overwrite an entry that has been checked out.

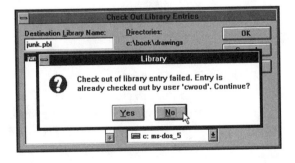

Fig. 12.15
Only one developer is allowed to check out an entry at a time.

IV

Delivering the Final Product

Listing the Status of an Entry

To list the status of an entry, click the entry, and then click the Check Status icon. The View Entries Check Out Status dialog box appears, showing the check out status of all selected entries, as seen in figure 12.16.

Fig. 12.16
The View Entries
Check Out Status
dialog box shows
the check out
status of all
selected entries.

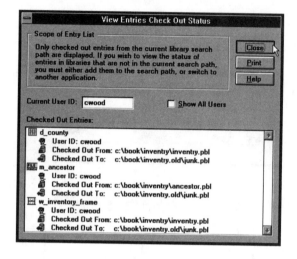

Checking In an Entry

After you're done with an entry, select it and click the Check In icon. The entry then automatically overwrites the older version.

If you try to check in an entry that wasn't checked out, you get an error message, as seen in figure 12.17.

Fig. 12.17
You can't check
in an entry that
hasn't been
checked out.

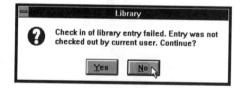

Clearing the Check Out Status

Finally, there are times when you need to clear the check out status of an entry. (Suppose there was a hard drive crash where the checked out version was, or the developer who checked the entry out left the company and took the hard drive.)

To clear the check out status of an entry, choose **S**ource, C**l**ear Check Out Status, as seen in figure 12.18. This allows you to update that entry.

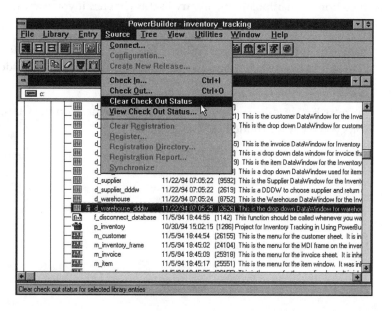

Fig. 12.18
To clear the check out status of an entry, choose **S**ource, C**l**ear Check Out Status.

Caution

Make sure you have a good reason for clearing the check out status. Otherwise, you'll have two developers overwriting each other's changes!

Working with PVCS

There are other third-party packages available (such as PVCS—available for PowerSoft) that allow version control. Version control saves old versions and can be very handy if you've overwritten or deleted something you need later.

Also, PVCS works seamlessly with Windows. You can learn more about PVCS in Appendix F, "Third-Party Products and Support (What's on the CD?)."

From Here...

You learned how to manipulate the library in this chapter. If you want to know more about what you can do with libraries, refer to the following:

■ Chapter 1, "Introducing PowerBuilder," introduces windows, menus, libraries, and painters. It's a must-read for the beginning PowerBuilder developer.

■ Appendix F, "Third-Party Products and Support (What's on the CD?)," shows you what is included on the CD-ROM.

Chapter 13

Pulling It All Together in an Application

The Inventory Tracking system is almost complete. There are only a couple of things you need to pull together before running through the system.

In this chapter, you learn the following:

- How to go about making and showing a help file

- How to override inheritance

- How to add the finishing touches to an application

- How to run the Inventory Tracking system

Adding Help for Inventory Tracking

Every Windows application should have some form of on-line help, especially when Windows does most of the work for you in a help file. Unfortunately, PowerBuilder and Windows have no method of generating a help file without additional third-party support.

To generate a help file, you need a help compiler. The Windows Software Developer's Kit comes with a help compiler, or you can write your own. Most developers, however, use a third-party help compiler because writing your own help compiler is very difficult and time-consuming.

Note

I used RoboHelp from Blue Sky Software for my on-line help file, INVENTRY.HLP.

You use the ShowHelp() command for displaying help files. In the Inventory Tracking system, the **H**elp menu item still needs to be coded for all options except **A**bout (which is covered in the next section). The following choices are coded as follows:

Menu Option	Command	Description
Table of Contents	ShowHelp ("INVENTRY.HLP", INDEX!)	Displays the table of contents of the help file.
Search	ShowHelp ("INVENTRY.HLP", KEYWORD!, "")	When you use a keyword, the Windows help system opens a search with those letters in it. An empty string opens a search at the beginning of the help file.
Introduction	ShowHelp ("INVENTRY.HLP", KEYWORD!, "Introduction")	Pulls up the introduction help topic.

Adding an About Window

You now need to make an About window. This About window is displayed whenever the user chooses **H**elp, **A**bout. The About window is also displayed while the Inventory Tracking system starts to execute.

The About window consists of static text, bit maps, and an OK command button. The script behind the OK command button is:

```
Close(Parent)
```

You can see the About window in figure 13.1.

To access the About window through PowerBuilder, choose **H**elp, **A**bout, as seen in figure 13.2. This opens the w_about window. Click on the OK command button to close your window.

The About window has other uses as well. It often takes quite a while to start a Windows application; however, the About window, while conveying information, gives the illusion of a faster start up to your application because the user is too busy reading the About window to notice the time he or she is waiting. On the application open event, code the following lines:

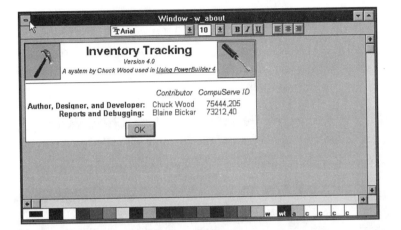

Fig. 13.1
The About window conveys information about the system to the end user.

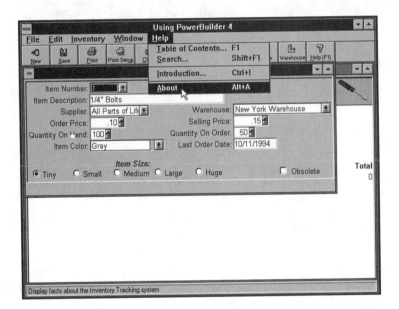

Fig. 13.2
To display the **A**bout window, click **H**elp, **A**bout.

```
Open(w_about)              // Open the w_about window
w_about.cb_OK.hide()       // Disable the button to close the window
   .
   .            // The body of the application open event goes here.
   .
     Close (w_about)
```

This opens and closes your w_about window in your application open event.

◀ See "Imple-
menting
Window
Inheritance,"
p. 96

◀ See "Imple-
menting Menu
Inheritance
and Toolbars,"
p. 109

Adding to Inheritance

Inheritance has become a big part of the Inventory Tracking system. However, sometimes you want to add on to or overwrite what the ancestor does
in order to customize your object.

Handling Ancestor Events from the Child Event

From any script, you can view what the ancestor has coded by choosing
Compile, Display **A**ncestor Script, as seen in figure 13.3.

Fig. 13.3

To view what an
ancestor has
written, choose
Compile, Display
Ancestor Script.

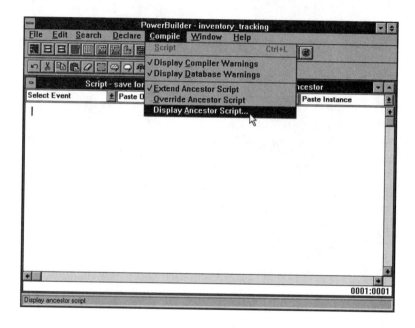

This displays the ancestor of your event, as seen in figure 13.4. Inheritance
can be more than level deep; therefore, if the Ancestor button is enabled, that
signifies there is yet another ancestor script. Although you can't modify the
ancestor script from the child script, you can copy the contents if you wish.
This may come in handy if you need to make only minor modifications to
the event.

When coding a script that already has an ancestor script coded, you have two
choices for handling the ancestor script. You can extend the ancestor script
(which is the default), thereby adding the child script to the end of the existing ancestor script. You also can override the ancestor script, thereby making
the child script ignore the ancestor script.

When you choose to extend or override the ancestor script, choose **C**ompile,
Extend Ancestor Script or **O**verride Ancestor Script.

Fig. 13.4
The Display Ancestor Script dialog box allows you to view the contents of the ancestor of the current event you are working on.

As you can see in figure 13.5, you have three different types of marks on your events. The first mark of a half-red, half-white Script icon next to your event name indicates that you have an ancestor script and have written a child script for your event. An all-red Script icon indicates that only an ancestor script exists for this event. An all-white Script icon indicates that only a child script exists for this event. The different shaded Script icons should tip you off to look at the code in the ancestor before adding and/or modifying any code in the current script.

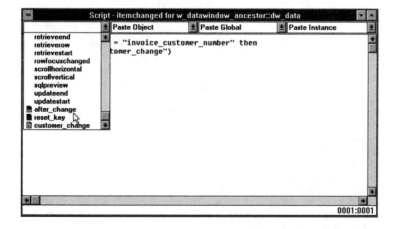

Fig. 13.5
The Script icon next to the event names indicates where code for the event is located.

Updating a Multiple-Table Window

The Invoice window is different than all other windows in the Inventory Tracking system, since you need to update multiple tables in your database when updating your window.

The best way to do this is with the following steps:

1. Choose **R**ows, **U**pdate in your DataWindow painter.

2. In the Specify Update Characteristics dialog box shown in figure 13.6, select the table to update and the unique key columns. In the **U**pdate-able Columns section, select all of the columns that are updated in the detail section of the DataWindow.

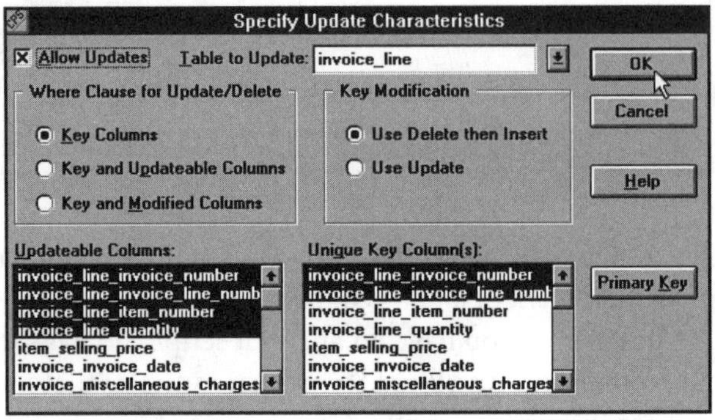

Fig. 13.6
The Specify Update Character-istics dialog box allows the user to specify what table and columns to update with a DataWindow.

3. Update the rest of the information by overriding the save and insert row events in your w_invoice window and the itemchanged event in the dw_data DataWindow control of your w_invoice window. Use SQL and PowerScript to update the non-detail columns.

Tip
Always check the update characteris-tics of your DataWindows before completing your project.

Override the save event of w_datawindow.ancestor using the technique described earlier in this chapter and code the following in the save event of w_invoice:

```
// Save for w_invoice

// We could not use the default save in w_datawindow_ancestor since
// we have to update multiple tables with this DataWindow.
int rownum
int invoice_number
date invoice_date
decimal miscellaneous_charges
decimal sales_tax
decimal freight
string invoice_comments
decimal customer_number
rownum = dw_data.getrow()
invoice_number = dw_data.getitemnumber(rownum,
➥"invoice_invoice_number")
invoice_date = dw_data.getitemdate(rownum, "invoice_invoice_date")
miscellaneous_charges = dw_data.getitemnumber(rownum,
➥"invoice_miscellaneous_charges")
sales_tax = dw_data.getitemnumber(rownum, "invoice_sales_tax")
freight = dw_data.getitemnumber(rownum, "invoice_freight")
invoice_comments = dw_data.getitemstring(rownum,
➥"invoice_invoice_comments")
```

◄ See "Specifying Update Charac-teristics," p.227

◄ See "Under-standing SQL Syntax," p. 190

IV

Delivering the Final Product

```
customer_number = dw_data.getitemnumber(rownum,
➡"customer_customer_number")

INSERT INTO invoice (invoice_number,
                     invoice_date,
                     miscellaneous_charges,
                     sales_tax,
                     freight,
                     invoice_comments,
                     customer_number )
    VALUES ( :invoice_number,
             :invoice_date,
             :miscellaneous_charges,
             :sales_tax,
             :freight,
             :invoice_comments,
             :customer_number );
if sqlca.sqlcode <> 0 then
    UPDATE invoice SET   invoice_date = :invoice_date,
                         miscellaneous_charges =
                         ➡:miscellaneous_charges,
                         sales_tax = :sales_tax,
                         freight = :freight,
                         invoice_comments = :invoice_comments,
                         customer_number = :customer_number
        WHERE invoice_number = :invoice_number;
end if
if sqlca.sqlcode <> 0 then
    messagebox("SQL Error", &
               "SQL error "+ string(sqlca.sqldbcode) &
               + " in save for w_invoice~r~n"+sqlca.SQLerrtext)
end if
dw_data.update()
```

As you can see by the previous code, you need to update the Inventory table before updating the Inventory_line table because the Inventory_line table has a foreign key to the Inventory table. You can try to insert a record, and then update the record if the insert failed. (You also could have coded a Select statement and then UPDATEd or INSERTed based on the results, but this method has one less SQL call to code.) After it's over, you then can issue the dw_data.update().

The insertrow event of w_invoice needs more attention than the insertrow event of other windows to ensure that the invoice_line_invoice_number field is filled with the proper invoice_number. To do this, you need to override the insertrow event in w_invoice with the following script:

```
int rownum

rownum = dw_data.getrow()
if rownum = 0 then
    triggerevent("getnewkey")
```

```
            if IsNull(il_newkey) or il_newkey = 0 then
                il_newkey = 1
            end if
        end if
        dw_data.insertrow(0)
        dw_data.SetItem(dw_data.getrow(), "invoice_line_invoice_number",
        ➥il_newkey)
```

You need to make sure that you have an invoice number—assign that number to invoice_line_invoice number. This ensures that all of the rows match the number on the invoice.

In the itemchanged event in the dw_data DataWindow control, you need to check for a customer number change and react appropriately. You *extend* (not override) the itemchanged event in w_datawindow_ancestor, and add the following code:

```
        if GetColumnName() = "invoice_customer_number" then
            postevent ("customer_change")
        end if
```

◀ See "Implementing User-Defined Events," p. 126

This entails adding a customer_change user-defined event to the dw_data DataWindow control with the following code:

```
        int rownum
        int customer_number
        string customer_address1
        string customer_address2
        string customer_city
        string customer_state
        string customer_zip
        string customer_phone

        rownum = getrow()
        customer_number = getitemnumber(rownum, "invoice_customer_number")
        SELECT   customer_address1,
                 customer_address2,
                 customer_city,
                 customer_state,
                 customer_zip,
                 customer_phone
            INTO :customer_address1,
                 :customer_address2,
                 :customer_city,
                 :customer_state,
                 :customer_zip,
                 :customer_phone
            FROM customer
            WHERE customer_number = :customer_number;
        if sqlca.sqlcode <> 0 then
            messagebox("SQL Error", &
                        "SQL error "+ string(sqlca.sqldbcode) &
                        + " in customer_change of dw_dat in w_invoice~r~n" &
                        +sqlca.SQLerrtext)
```

```
else
   SetItem(rownum, "customer_customer_address1",customer_address1)
   SetItem(rownum, "customer_customer_address2",customer_address2)
   SetItem(rownum, "customer_customer_city",customer_city)
   SetItem(rownum, "customer_customer_state",customer_state)
   SetItem(rownum, "customer_customer_zip",customer_zip)
   SetItem(rownum, "customer_customer_phone",customer_phone)
end if
```

The above code fills in the customer information if the customer number has been changed.

> **Note**
>
> Interestingly enough, the user never sees what customer number he or she is updating. As far as the user is concerned, only the customer name is chosen. Internally, that will convert to the customer number for this invoice.

Last-Minute Cleanup of Your System

When you think you're finished with your system (until testing, of course), there are *always* two steps you should take. First, go into every DataWindow and choose **R**ows, **U**pdate as before. This opens a dialog box similar to the one seen in figure 13.6.

Here, make sure the update characteristics of your tables and fields are defined as you like them. Throughout development, you add fields and tables. These new fields and tables may not have the update characteristics you want, and it's a good idea to check them. If you add a field to a DataWindow, it will not be automatically selected as an updateable field.

Also, check and set the tab order on all your fields and windows. Again, since you've added columns and objects to your windows and DataWindows, you'll need to make sure the tab order is what you want. There's nothing more annoying than trying to tab to the next field and losing your cursor to a field at the bottom of the screen.

Running through the Inventory Tracking System

Thanks to inheritance from w_datawindow_ancestor, the Inventory Tracking system requires only five lines of code for every window except the w_invoice window. This is a pretty amazing feat for a development language.

A quick run-through of the Inventory Tracking system can show you what you've created. When the system first comes up, you see the Item Entry dialog box displayed, as seen in figure 13.7. Here you add and modify items.

Fig. 13.7

The Item Entry dialog box is the first dialog box displayed in the Inventory Tracking system.

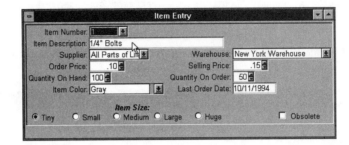

Clicking on the Customer toolbar item opens the Customer Entry dialog box. Here, you can add and modify customers, as seen in figure 13.8.

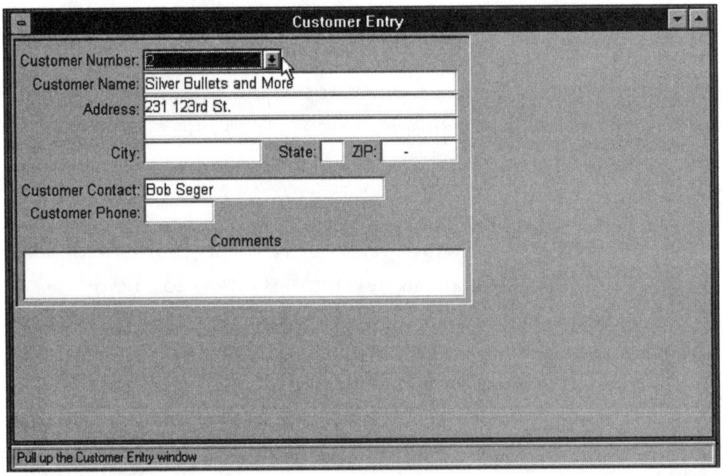

Fig. 13.8

The Customer Entry dialog box is where you add and modify customers.

Clicking on the Supplier toolbar item opens the Supplier Entry dialog box. Here, you enter and change supplier information, as seen in figure 13.9.

Clicking on the Warehouse icon opens the Warehouse Entry dialog box, seen in figure 13.10. Here, you add and modify warehouses.

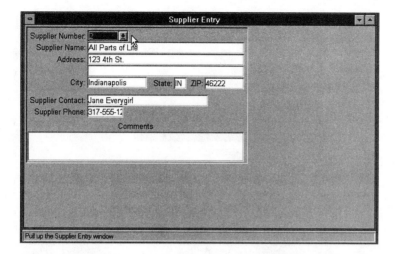

Fig. 13.9
The Supplier Entry dialog box is where you add and modify suppliers.

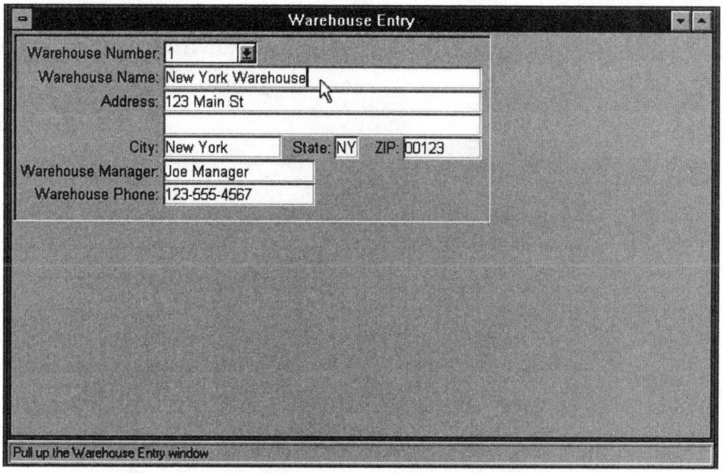

Fig. 13.10
The Warehouse Entry dialog box is where you add and update warehouses.

The Invoice Entry dialog box is where you can edit the invoice information (see fig. 13.11). This window allows you to add and modify invoices and invoice lines. It also can be printed to give to the customer.

Fig. 13.11

The Invoice Entry dialog box allows you to update invoices and invoice lines.

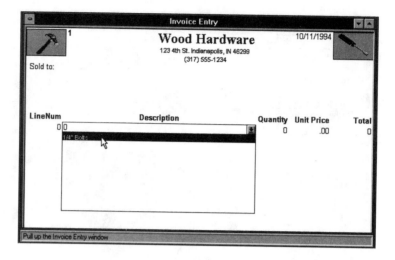

To allow the user to enter the invoice header information, an invoice header window was added that was inherited from w_datawindow_ancestor, as seen in figure 13.12.

Fig. 13.12

The Invoice Header dialog box allows you to update invoices and invoice lines.

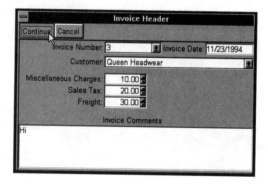

This window is has been changed to a response window, with the following script added to the Continue button:

```
int rownum
int invoice_number

dw_data.AcceptText()
dw_data.update()
rownum = dw_data.getrow()
invoice_number = dw_data.GetItemnumber(rownum, "invoice_number")
if isvalid (w_invoice) then
    close(w_invoice)
end if
```

IV

Delivering the Final Product

```
opensheetwithparm(w_invoice, invoice_number, w_inventory_frame, 4,
➥layered!)
w_invoice.ii_invoice_number = invoice_number
w_invoice.id_invoice_date = dw_data.GetItemDate(rownum,
➥"invoice_date")
w_invoice.ii_customer_number = dw_data.GetItemnumber(rownum,
➥"customer_number")
w_invoice.idbl_miscellaneous_charges = &
          dw_data.GetItemnumber(rownum, "miscellaneous_charges")
w_invoice.idbl_sales_tax = dw_data.GetItemnumber(rownum,
➥"sales_tax")
w_invoice.idbl_freight = dw_data.GetItemnumber(rownum, "freight")
w_invoice.is_invoice_comments = dw_data.GetItemstring(rownum,
➥"invoice_comments")
w_invoice.triggerevent("new")
cb_cancel.triggerevent(clicked!)
```

The following instance variables were added to the w_invoice window:

```
int ii_invoice_number
date id_invoice_date
int ii_customer_number
double idbl_miscellaneous_charges
double idbl_sales_tax
double idbl_freight
string is_invoice_comments
```

Now simply do a retrieve based on header information passed to w_invoice from w_invoice_header.

From Here...

Now you need to debug your application and deliver the executable version of your program. To do this, refer to the following chapters:

- Chapter 14, "Debugging Your Application," is where PowerBuilder guru Blaine Bickar shows you how to debug an application.

- Chapter 15, "Delivering an Executable," describes how to compile the application you developed and how to distribute the compiled application.

Chapter 14

Debugging Your Application

by Blaine Bickar

If your application acts strangely or displays some kind of unexpected behavior, odds are that you inadvertently introduced a bug during the development process. If so, you may want to run your application under the Debugger to see what exactly is happening. PowerBuilder's Debugger is very powerful, but at the same time also easy to use. If used correctly, it should meet most of your debugging needs.

By the end of this chapter you should be able to:

- Invoke the Debugger

- Set break points or stops in your application

- View and modify variables while debugging your application

- Step through your code

- Know what not to do during debugging

The Debugger enables you to suspend execution of the application and examine the application while it is running. You can step through your scripts one line at a time, watching the values of variables and attributes as the code executes. You also can modify the values of variables and attributes while the Debugger is running.

> **Note**
>
> What you cannot do with the Debugger is modify the scripts in any way while the Debugger is running. Once a programming error has been discovered using the Debugger, you would have to return to the PowerBuilder development environment to correct the mistake.

Running the Debugger

You can access the Debugger at any time while using PowerBuilder, except under the following situations:

- When you have the script painter open

- When a response window is opened, such as the Select Window dialog box

To run your application through the Debugger, click on the Debug icon on the Window or Menu toolbar.

> **Note**
>
> You must save all objects before beginning a debug session. If you have made changes to any objects without saving, PowerBuilder first asks if you want to save your changes. If you choose No, the Debugger won't start.
>
> PowerBuilder provides this protection for good reason. It is possible that, while using the Debugger, you might experience a General Protection Fault (GPF) or other "fatal" error. If so, you will likely be forced to reboot your PC and lose any unsaved changes.

The Debugger will start in one of two places:

- If you have no debugging stops set up yet, which might very well be the case if you have never used the Debugger before, you will start with the Select Script dialog box (see fig. 14.1).

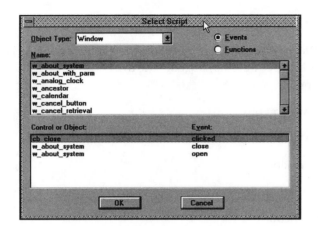

Fig. 14.1
The Select Script dialog box allows you to find the scripts that exist in the various objects in your application.

■ If you already have stops set up, the Edit Stops dialog box appears (see fig. 14.2).

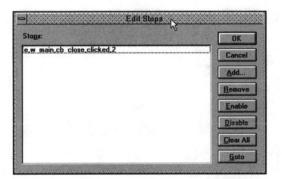

Fig. 14.2
The Edit Stops dialog box displays a list of existing stop points.

Note

If you already have some stops set up and are not starting in the Select Script dialog box, skip ahead to "Step 2: Setting Additional Stops."

Step 1: Setting the First Stop

The PowerBuilder Debugger works by placing a stop on a specific line of code in a script. As that line of code is preparing to execute, the Debugger will be invoked and the program execution is suspended.

Use the Select Script dialog box to find the scripts you wish to stop on. To find the right place for a stop, you need to know the answers to five important questions:

1. What type of object is it?

   The **O**bject Type drop-down list box at the top of the Select Script dialog box (see fig. 14.3) includes the five types of PowerBuilder objects that contain code:

   ■ Applications

   ■ Menus

   ■ Windows

   ■ User objects

   ■ Functions

   Choose the appropriate object type. For the purposes of this example, choose Window.

Fig. 14.3

Select the type of object from the drop-down list box to view all objects in your application of that type.

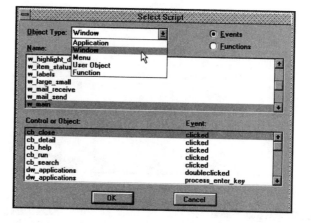

◀ See "Implementing User-Defined Functions," p. 171

2. Is the code in an event or a function?

   Choose either the **E**vents or the **F**unctions option button. You are most familiar with events such as the open event for a window or the Clicked event of a menu item. All five of the object types available here have events available to them. But remember that some objects, such as windows, can also have functions inside them, called *object-level functions*. These functions are just like events, insofar as they both have PowerScript code in them. Choose whichever type is appropriate.

3. In which object is the code to stop on?

   Depending upon what type of object was selected from the drop-down list box, the **N**ame list box contains a list of all the objects of that type in your application in alphabetical order by their names. Select the object that has the code you want.

4. Which event has the code to stop on?

The Function list box directly below the **N**ame list box contains a list of either all the object-level functions for the object (if you selected **F**unctions, as shown in fig. 14.4), or a list of all the controls and events where script has been coded.

Now, select the object and event (or function) from this list box where you want to place a stop by either clicking on the object name once and choosing OK, or by double-clicking on the object name.

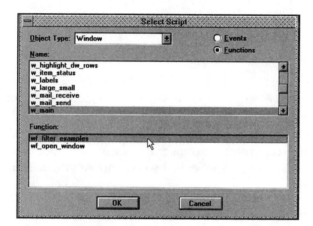

Fig. 14.4

Selecting the event or function you wish to place a stop on is the last step for the Select Script dialog box.

Note

If you have coded at least one line of code—even just a comment—for an event for an object, it will show up in this list.

If you have coded for more than one event for the same object (such as some code for both the clicked and double-clicked events for a DataWindow control), each event shows up in the list as a separate entry.

---

5. What line (or lines) of code do you stop on?

After you select the script, the Debug window opens. The Debug window contains up to three separate areas, as shown in figure 14.5: the code area, in which you can see the current script; the Watch section; and the Variables section. (Your Debugger might or might not be displaying the Watch and Variables sections—you will find out what determines if these other sections appear later in this chapter.)

Fig. 14.5

The Debug window displays the script that was selected using the Select Script dialog box.

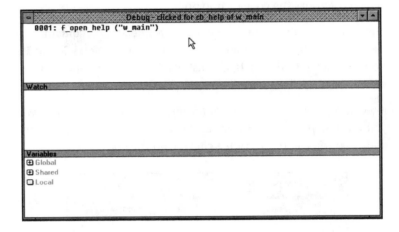

At this time, you are only concerned with the area that displays your script. As you can see, this area shows us the code for the script that was selected from the Select Script dialog box. The code here looks a lot like it does to you from inside the script painter, except that a line number appears to the left of each line of code. (Also remember that you cannot edit the code in this window.)

What you need to do now is to decide which line (or lines) of code you want to stop at. Select the line by double-clicking anywhere on it. When you do this, PowerBuilder places a small Stop Sign icon to the left of the line number of that line, as shown in figure 14.6.

Fig. 14.6

After double-clicking on the first line of code, a stop sign icon displays, indicating that a stop has been placed on this line.

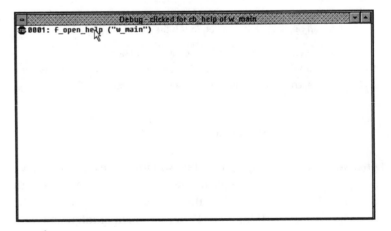

IV

Troubleshooting

When I double-clicked on a blank line of code, nothing happened.

You can only place stops on lines of code that are executable. A line in your script that is left blank is not executable. Other examples of lines of script that are not executable would include comment lines and ones that declare variables.

You can place as many stops in one script as you need. It's more likely, however, that you will place a stop somewhere near the beginning of the script only, so that when this script is triggered at run time, the Debugger will be invoked right away. You can add stops at that time or just step through the script until you reach another place where you care to stop.

Step 2: Setting Additional Stops

Before you set stops in other scripts, you might first want to pull up a list of stops that are already set. This way you can make sure that you are not getting ready to set up a stop in a place where you already have one.

To bring up the Edit Stops dialog box, choose **D**ebug, Edit **S**tops, or click on the Edit Stop icon.

The Edit Stops dialog box (see fig. 14.7) shows you a list of existing stops. Each existing stop is preceded by the letter e or d (which designate the stop's enabled status), then the name of the object (a window name or a menu name for example), and then the name of the control (such as the name of a button if the object is a window), the name of the event, and the line number where the stop is.

Fig. 14.7
The Edit Stops dialog box displays a list of all existing stops for the application.

If you add or delete lines from a script after stops have been placed, the stops may not be where you placed them, because they are still at their old line number, which may now be at a completely different place in the code.

Enabling and Disabling Stops

Why would you want to disable a stop? Suppose you wanted to set multiple stops for multiple bugs. You would then disable all the stops that deal with a particular bug, while leaving the other stops enabled. After you corrected one bug, you can disable the stops for that bug and enable those for the other bug.

The e at the beginning of the stop description stands for enabled. If a stop is *enabled*, the Debugger will be activated when that line of code is executed. The d at the beginning of the stop description stands for disabled. A *disabled* stop means that the Debugger will ignore the stop when that line of code is executed.

To enable a stop, follow these steps:

Tip

You can select more than one entry at a time by clicking once on each entry in the stop list. To deselect an entry, just click it again.

1. Select the entry by clicking on it.

2. Click on the **E**nable button. The first part of the description changes to an e.

To disable the stop, highlight it and click on **D**isable. The first part of the description changes to a d. You can enable and disable stops as many times as you like.

Removing Stops

To remove a stop from the list altogether (not just disable it temporarily), highlight the entry (or entries) and click on **R**emove.

> **Note**
>
> A stop may also be removed while a debugging session is in progress. When you are in a script that has a stop, double-click on the stop sign next to the line of code that you don't want to stop on anymore and it will disappear. This will also remove it from the Edit Stop list.

To remove all the stops from the stop list, click on **C**lear All. All stops, regardless of whether they were highlighted or not, will be removed from the list.

> **Caution**
>
> You won't be prompted to confirm that you want to remove these stops. However, if you want to undo the removal, you can choose Cancel. The Edit Stops dialog box closes, leaving the removed stops in place.

IV

Go To

To take another look at the code where you set a stop (you might want to do this if you are not sure if you put the stop where you wanted to), click on the entry from the list and choose **G**oTo. This takes you to the Debug window in which you placed the stop. From here, you can do all the things you can normally do from this window, such as adding another stop, removing the existing stop (or stops), and so on.

Add

To place another stop in a different script from any that have already been set, click on **A**dd. The Select Script dialog box opens. From here, you follow the same process for setting a stop as described above.

When you are finished editing the stops, choose OK.

Step 3: Launching the Debugger

To start the debugging session, click on the Start icon from the Debug window. When you start the application under the Debugger, the application executes just as if you had clicked on the Run icon. The difference is that when a line of code that has been set up to be a stop point is about to execute, the Debugger opens.

When the Debugger appears, you will see the same Debug window used earlier to set the stops (see fig. 14.8). This time, however, you are not setting stops; you are looking to "watch" your code execute and hopefully discover what is wrong with it.

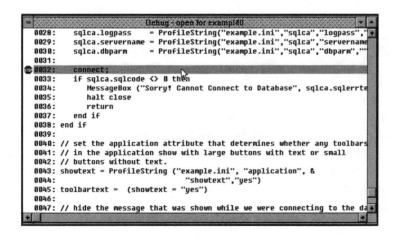

Fig. 14.8
The Debug Window will appear at run time when it is time to execute a line of code with a stop on it.

```
0028:    sqlca.logpass     = ProfileString("example.ini","sqlca","logpass",
0029:    sqlca.servername  = ProfileString("example.ini","sqlca","servername
0030:    sqlca.dbparm      = ProfileString("example.ini","sqlca","dbparm",""
0031:
0032:    connect;
0033:    if sqlca.sqlcode <> 0 then
0034:        MessageBox ("Sorry! Cannot Connect to Database", sqlca.sqlerrte
0035:        halt close
0036:        return
0037:    end if
0038: end if
0039:
0040: // set the application attribute that determines whether any toolbars
0041: // in the application show with large buttons with text or small
0042: // buttons without text.
0043: showtext = ProfileString ("example.ini", "application", &
0044:                              "showtext","yes")
0045: toolbartext =  (showtext = "yes")
0046:
0047: // hide the message that was shown while we were connecting to the da
```

Debug - open for exampl40

Notice that when the Debugger first comes up, the line of code that has the stop on it is highlighted. The highlighted line is the line that is about to be executed.

Using the Variables List

When it comes time to debug a problem with your application, examining the values of certain variables defined in your application is usually involved. Before you can see any variables, however, you must first show the Variables list. In fact, the Variables list can be shown or hidden at any time during a debug session.

To toggle the Variables list on or off, click on the Show Var icon on the Debug toolbar.

The Variables list appears at the bottom of the Debug window. The amount of space used by the Variables list can be changed by simply pointing to the title bar of the Variables list and dragging the list up or down (see fig. 14.9).

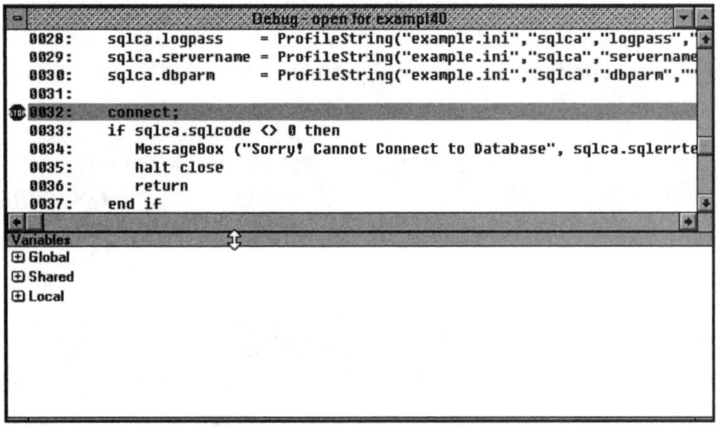

Fig. 14.9

The Variables List is used to display the value of variables in your application.

The Variables list categorizes all variables by their scope. The Global, Shared, and Local variables are each represented by a listing in the Variables list. If any variables in each of these categories exists, you will see a plus sign next to the variable category, as shown in figure 14.10. If there are no variables of that category (for example, if the script you put the stop on does not have any local variables defined for it), you will not see the plus sign for that category.

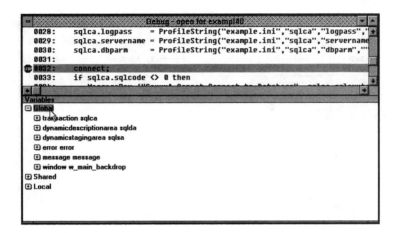

Fig. 14.10
The Variables List is categorized by scope, shown here with the Global variables expanded.

IV

Delivering the Final Product

To expand the Variables list for that category, double-click on the name of the category. The plus sign changes to a minus sign. To contract the Variables list for that category, you would double-click again on the name of the category.

Generally, one level into the list of variables is all that there is. However, in the case of Global variables, there are often more levels than the first one. For example, the first variables listed under the Global variables are always *transaction sqlca*, and this Global variable has its own plus sign, indicating there is yet another level to go down. The reason for this, in the case of sqlca, is that the transaction object has a series of attributes.

The Debugger not only lets you look at the value of the more traditional variable (that is, a local String variable called lastname), but also at the values of attributes of PowerBuilder objects. For sqlca, double-clicking on it in the Variables list would expand out the transaction objects attributes, so that you can see the value for each attribute of the object.

The Variables list shows you the values of any variables declared, as well as the values of attributes of existing objects, like sqlca. In fact, if you have any windows opened in your application (and you are bound to), you can see the values of their attributes too (such as the title, background color, and so on). For example, figure 14.11 lists a window from the PowerBuilder 4 sample application called w_main_backdrop, as well as its attributes.

Fig. 14.11

Expanding out the Global variable called w_main_backdrop allows you to view the values for its attributes.

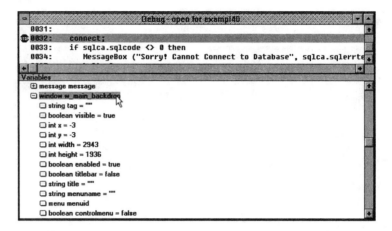

This is a good thing because it is possible that the problem with your application might not be with the variables, but with the objects themselves. Being able to view the attributes of the object allows you to essentially see the object itself.

> **Note**
>
> You might have noticed that only Global, Shared, and Local variables are listed under the Debugger. Does this mean that you cannot view the value of Instance variables in the Debugger? Of course you can—you just have to dig a little deeper! An Instance variable is actually considered an attribute of the window it was declared for; thus, Instance variables are listed as part of the attributes for a window in the Debugger. Most Instance variables in Windows will be found near the bottom of the Global Variable list.

So now you know how to view variables in the PowerBuilder Debugger. But, as you can see, the list of variables (because it includes attributes) can get pretty long—too long, much of the time. In fact, out of all the variables and attributes available from the Debugger, you are likely to only be interested in a handful for any one problem you are trying to solve. To get through the clutter and to get to what you need, you have the Watch list.

Using the Watch List

The Watch list is a way to show only selected variables and attributes, ignoring all the others that you are not concerned with at the time.

Like the Variables list, the user decides whether or not to display the Watch list. To toggle viewing or hiding the Watch list, click on the Show Watch icon on the Debug toolbar. Also, like the Variables list, the user can decide how much of the Debug window the Watch list shall use.

Adding to the Watch List

Because the purpose of the Watch list is to selectively view attributes and variables, you must have a way to indicate which variables (or attributes) to include in the Watch list. To add something in the Watch list, you must first select the variable or attribute from the Variables list (see fig. 14.12), and then click on the Add Watch icon from the Debug menu bar.

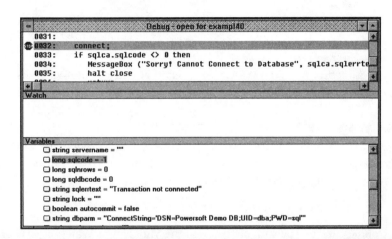

Fig. 14.12
Adding to the watch list is easy. Just select the variable or attribute you want, and click on the Add Watch icon.

Note

In order to add to the Watch list, the Variables list must be showing, but the Watch list might not be. If the Watch list is hidden when you click on the Add Watch icon, the Watch list will automatically appear.

When you do this, you see a copy of that variable or attribute appear in the Watch list (see fig. 14.13). Notice that the variable or attribute is still in the original Variables list. Anything that is placed in the Watch list is always still in the Variables list.

Tip
Another way to quickly and easily add entries to the Watch list is to Shift-click on the entry in the Variables list.

IV

Delivering the Final Product

Fig. 14.13
The attribute
selected is now
part of the Watch
list, as well as the
Variables list.

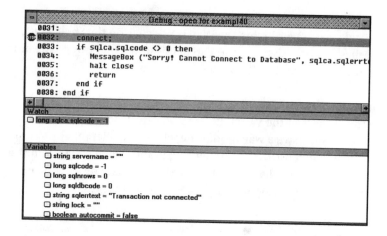

Removing Entries from the Watch List

To remove an entry from the Watch list, select that entry in the Watch list,
and then click on the Remove Watch icon from the Debug toolbar.

Modifying the Value of a Variable

So far, you've used the Variables list and the Watch list to observe the values
of variables and attributes. In addition to simply observing their values, however, you can change their values, as well.

To modify a variable's value, complete the following steps:

1. Double-click on the variable name in the Variables or Watch list. When
   you do, you see the Modify Variable dialog box (see fig. 14.14).

   The Modify Variable dialog box shows you the name of the variable, its
   data type (in fig. 14.14, the variable is `sqlca.sqlcode`, which is a long),
   and its current value.

Fig. 14.14
The Modify
Variable dialog
box allows you to
change the value
of a variable or
attribute.

2. To make the value of a variable go to null, you must click on the **N**ull
   check box in the Modify Variable dialog box.

3. In the New **V**alue edit box, you can overwrite the current value, putting
   a new value in its place.

4. When you finish modifying the value, click on OK.

Note

The Modify Variable dialog box will not respond to the OK button if you have changed the value to an invalid value, such as entering an **x** for the value of sqlca.sqlcode (which is a numeric long).

Note

Not all variables values can be changed during debugging. In particular, attributes whose values are not numeric or string are usually not able to be changed.

Troubleshooting

I have a String variable that can have a lot a characters in it. While using the debugger, I do not see all the characters; instead, I see some of them and then (more).

The Variables list and Watch list can only display the first 128 characters of String variables. If their variables value is more than 128 characters, the first part of the string is displayed, followed by (more). To see the entire value, double-click as you would to modify the value. You will then be able to scroll through to see the entire string. Of course, you can modify the value from this dialog box as well.

Note

If you do have a long value like this, after you've double-clicked on it, copy it to the Clipboard by pressing Ctrl+C, switching to Notepad (or use PowerBuilder's text editor—Shift+F6), pasting in the value by pressing Ctrl+V, and selecting **E**dit, **W**ordwrap. Now you will be able to see the whole variable all at the same time.

Printing Variables

In addition to being able to view and modify variables from the Debugger, you can also print them out on paper. This can be very handy—the list of variables and attributes can get long. By being able to print them out, you then would be able to send that information to PowerSoft Technical Support or to another PowerBuilder developer at your company, so that they might be able to help you determine the cause of the bug.

To print the variables, choose **D**ebug, Pri**n**t Variables (see fig. 14.15).

Fig. 14.15
Print Variables will
produce a hard-
copy listing of all
the variables
expanded out in
your Variables list.

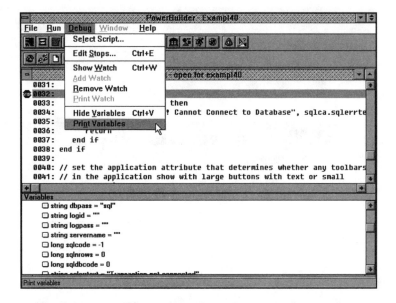

> **Note**
>
> The list of variables that prints on paper basically looks exactly like the Variables list
> you have set up at the time of printing. Therefore, whatever objects you have ex-
> panded will print as expanded; for collapsed objects, you only see the name of the
> object (with the plus sign next to it, of course).

Stepping Through the Code

When the Debugger is invoked, it always highlights a line of PowerScript
code. Note that the line of code that is highlighted is the line of code that is
about to be executed. So, in figure 14.16, for example, the line of code that
reads CONNECT; is about to be executed.

If you look at the values of any variables at this point, you are seeing their
values before the connection happens. So, in figure 14.16, you can see that
the value of sqlca.sqlcode is -1, and the value of sqlca.sqlerrtext is Transaction
not connected.

To see if the connection works, you would want the line of code that reads
CONNECT; to execute, then look at the values for sqlca.sqlcode and
sqlca.sqlerrtext. To do this, you must instruct the application to take a step.

IV

Delivering the Final Product

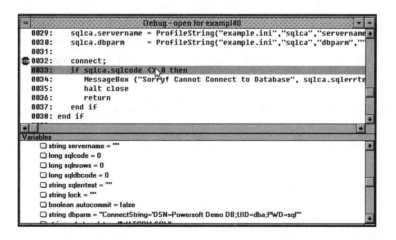

Fig. 14.16
At this point (just before the line of code that attempts to connect to the database is executed), the value of sqlca.sqlcode is -1.

To step through the code one executable line at a time, click on the Step icon on the Debug toolbar.

After clicking on the icon, the application executes the CONNECT; command to connect the application to the database. When the connection is completed (this might take a few seconds), you see that the values of both sqlca.sqlcode and sqlca.sqlerrtext have changed, and the highlighted line has moved down to the next executable line of code, as shown in figure 14.17.

Fig. 14.17
After taking one step, the highlighting moves to the next line of code to be executed, and some values in sqlca have changed.

Note

On code that covers multiple lines (such as SELECT, UPDATE, or INSERT statements), the last—not the first—line of the statement will be highlighted when the statement is about to be executed.

Continue to step through your code, one line at a time as you have done here, all the way to the end of this script. When the last line of the script has executed, the Debugger will disappear, and the application will resume normal processing until another stop is encountered, if any.

Continuing Script Execution

There are times when you will not be interested in watching the value of your variables as each line of code executes, but only at some point in your script (probably at or near the point in your script that you placed a stop). After having seen what you needed to see, you would just as soon the application proceed to continue executing as though the debugger were not running.

 Instead of repeatedly clicking on Step, click on the Continue button or choose **D**ebug, Continue. The Continue button informs the application to resume normal processing.

Learning What Not to Do during Debugging

So far, you hopefully have learned how and when to use the Debugger. However, you have not seen when not to use the Debugger. A good rule of thumb is to avoid debugging focus-related events. Examples of such events would include getfocus, losefocus, and datawindow events that simulate focus events (such as itemsfocuschanged). The reason being that focus-related events can cause PowerBuilder's Debugger to engage in an infinite loop. Even worse, events can begin to recurse on each other, each event spawning others, until a Windows General Protection Fault (GPF) occurs. Although the Debugger is powerful, it does have this known limitation.

Caution
Never try to quit the Debugger while you are in the middle of a stopped script. If you do, you get a warning message saying that PowerBuilder can become unstable (see fig. 14.18). This means that if you do quit in the middle, PowerBuilder may GPF.

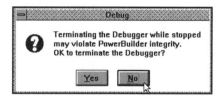

Fig. 14.18
Attempting to quit
the Debugger
while it is running
results in a dialog
box warning you
that this may be a
bad idea.

IV

Delivering the Final Product

From Here...

In this chapter you learned how to work with PowerBuilders Debugging facility; from setting up stop points to walking through a running application.

You learned how to set up the Watch list to narrow down all the variables and attributes available to the ones you care about, as well as how to modify the values of some variables during execution. For more on PowerBuilder applications, refer to the following chapters:

- Chapter 13, "Pulling It All Together in an Application," shows you how to finalize your application before you compile.

- Chapter 15, "Delivering an Executable," describes how to compile the application you developed and how to distribute the compiled application.

Chapter 15

Delivering an Executable

Now that you've wrapped up development, you need to deliver your executable. This involves building your executable (EXE) file and distributing it with the right DLLs. By the time this chapter is complete, you should be able to do the following:

- Assign an icon to your program

- Compile your program with the Application Painter into an EXE

- Compile your program with the Application Painter into a DLL

- Use the Project Painter

- Discuss PowerBuilder Dynamic Libraries and PowerBuilder Resource Files

- Learn various techniques for debugging at run time

Understanding What To Do before Compiling

Before you begin a compile, you need to optimize your system. This first involves regenerating your entire application. To begin, follow these steps:

1. Get into the library painter, open all PBLs, and then select all PBL members. Click on the Regen icon, as shown in figure 15.1.

Fig. 15.1
Regeneration of all your PBLs should be the first step in building an executable.

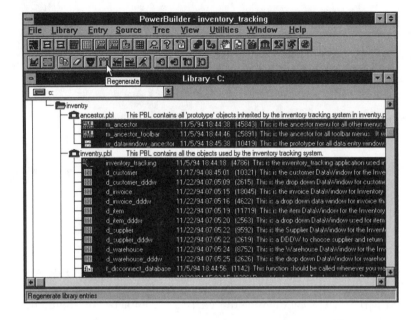

2. Next, you need to optimize your libraries. This is done by opening **Li-**brary and choosing **O**ptimize. The Optimize Library dialog box appears, as seen in figure 15.2.

Fig. 15.2
Use the Optimize Library dialog box to optimize every PBL in your application before creating your executable.

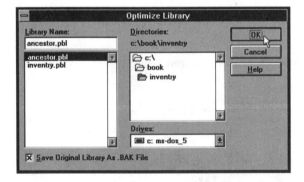

3. Make sure that the **S**ave Original Library As .BAK File check box is selected. This backs up your original PBL in case something goes wrong with your computer or your optimization during this process.

4. Repeat this procedure for every PBL in your application.

5. Finally, go into the Application Painter and click on the Icon icon. The Select Icon dialog box appears and allows you to assign an icon to your application (see fig. 15.3). Simply pick the icon you want to assign.

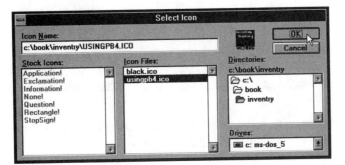

Fig. 15.3
The Select Icon dialog box allows you to associate an icon with your application.

> **Note**
>
> You can't create an icon file within PowerBuilder. You can, however, use the Watcom Image Editor to create an icon. Also, many third-party icon makers are available.

Compiling an EXE

There are two ways to compile a PowerBuilder application into a Windows Executable application. The first is to use the Application Painter to generate the EXE. The second way (new with PowerBuilder 4) is to use the Project Painter.

Compiling an EXE with the Application Painter

To compile an executable using the application painter, follow these steps:

1. Click on the Create EXE icon on the PainterBar. The Select Executable File dialog box appears, as illustrated in figure 15.4.

> **Caution**
>
> There is a similar icon on the PowerBar called the Project Painter. Don't confuse it with the Create EXE icon on the PainterBar. You'll learn more about the Project Painter later in this chapter.

Fig. 15.4

The Select
Executable File
dialog box allows
you to choose the
drive, path, and
name of the
executable.

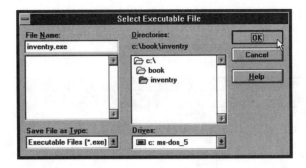

2. In the Select Executable File dialog box, choose the drive, path, and
   name of the executable, and then choose OK.

3. After you have chosen the name of your executable, the Create Executable dialog box opens (see fig. 15.5). Here you can simply click on OK,
   and the executable is created with your specified icon in your specified
   path.

Fig. 15.5

The Create
Executable dialog
box is where the
EXE file is created.

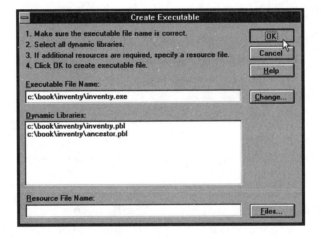

Now, switch to the Windows Program Manager and open File and choose
New. Click on Item and type in the path and description of your application.
Notice how the icon automatically attaches itself to your program, as shown
in figure 15.6.

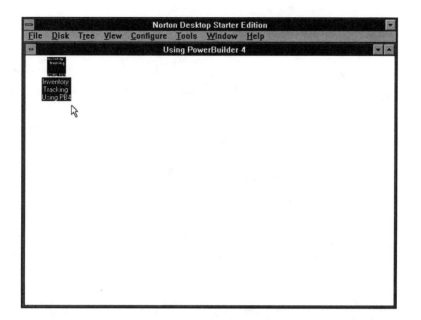

Fig. 15.6
An executable
must be run
through Windows.

IV

Delivering the Final Product

Using PowerBuilder Dynamic Libraries (PBDs)

As an application increases in size, it may become difficult to distribute and may take a long time to load. These problems can be resolved by using PowerBuilder Dynamic Libraries, or PBDs.

PBDs are a lot like Dynamic Link Libraries (DLLs) in that they aren't bound to the executable until run time. (However, PBDs aren't DLLs and can't be interchanged with them.) By using PBDs, you decrease the size of your application to a shell and then make calls to your PBDs. Also, if one PBD changes, you can redistribute those changes in a PBD without releasing the entire application.

To create a PBD, follow these steps:

1. Open the library painter and choose **U**tilities, Build **D**ynamic Library. This opens the Build Dynamic Runtime Library dialog box (see fig. 15.7).

Fig. 15.7
The Build
Dynamic Runtime
Library dialog box
lets you specify
the drive, path,
and PBL that you
want to compile
into a PBD.

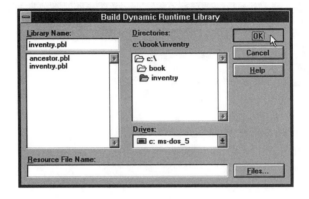

2. From here you specify the drive, path, and PBL that you want to compile into a PBD. Choose your library and click on OK.

3. Do this for all PBLs you want to convert to PBDs.

> **Note**
>
> Converting a PBL into a PBD does nothing to the original PBL. When you are done converting, you'll have your original PBL and a new PBD file.

4. In the Create Executable dialog box, highlight the PBLs you want to use as dynamic PBDs, as you saw in figure 15.5.

5. Start the compile by clicking on OK. You'll find your compile runs faster, and you end up with a smaller executable.

> **Caution**
>
> You must create your PBDs in the library painter before specifying them in the application painter. PowerBuilder assumes that you've already created them. If you specify dynamic libraries that don't exist, you will get a run time error.

Tip
Remove all objects
that aren't used
from your PBL
before creating a
PBD or executable.
These unused
objects take up
space and slow
down the load of
your executable
or the search
through your PBD.

Using Resources and PowerBuilder Resource Files (PBRs)

Often, you'll want to include other resources in your executable. A *resource* is any icon (ICO file), picture (BMP and RLE files), pointer (CUR files), or DataWindow object that you use in your program. For example, you may use a specific icon when a window is minimized, a bit map picture on a DataWindow, or a special mouse pointer for an object. You also may want to switch DataWindow objects of a DataWindow control during run time.

All of these take resources not found in your PBLs. You can have PowerBuilder search the path of the application to try to find them, or you can specify them in a PowerBuilder resource file (PBR).

To avoid forcing the user to have these resources in a path, you can make a PowerBuilder resource file. A *PBR* is an ASCII text file that provides the locations of your resources. For instance, on the d_invoice DataWindow, use bit maps are declared. These bit maps must be present on every computer that runs the Inventory Tracking system. To avoid putting bit maps everywhere, you could just make a resource file before compiling called INVENTRY.PBR. Inside INVENTRY.PBR are the following lines:

```
\PB4\FLATHEAD.BMP
\PB4\HAMMER.BMP
```

Now reference the resource file either when you compile your INVENTRY.PBD or when you compile your application.

> **Note**
>
> The two bit maps used were taken from PowerBuilder Version 3. PowerBuilder Version 4 no longer has these bit maps, although several other bit maps are included.

You can include resource files in PBDs as well as executables. To include a PBR, type the name of the PBR in the **R**esource File Name field in the Build Dynamic Runtime Library dialog box (refer to fig. 15.7) or the Create Executable dialog box (refer to fig. 15.5). If you want to browse for the name of your PBR, click on **F**iles next to the Resource File Name field. This opens the Select Resource File dialog box, as illustrated in figure 15.8.

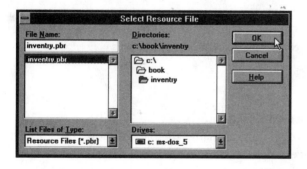

Fig. 15.8
The Select Resource File dialog box is used to choose the resource for your EXE or PBD.

Choose the file you want for your resource file and click on OK. This puts the file you chose into the **R**esource File Name field (see fig. 15.9). When you compile, your application will then contain the resources it needs.

Fig. 15.9

The resource file name is now placed in the **R**esource File Name field and ready for compiling.

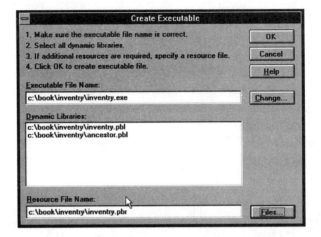

Note

You may wonder how to decide whether or not to include your resource file in a PBD or in the application. If you include it in the application, the resource is compiled with the application. If you include it in the PBD, the resource is not loaded into memory until it is needed.

If you seldom use the objects that access the resource, then you can compile your resource with the object's PBD. This saves time because the resource is loaded into memory when it's needed.

However, if you use the objects that compile the resource throughout your application, you should compile the resource file with the application. This saves time because the resource only needs to be loaded into memory once and not every time a new PBD is accessed.

Adding DataWindow Resources

Sometimes you'll want to change the DataWindow object of a DataWindow control. For example, if you sold hardware and food, you would want different information about the inventory of each type of product.

To change a DataWindow object during run time, you simply assign the DataObject of the DataWindow control to the new DataWindow Object with the following command:

```
datawindow.DataObject = 'new name'
```

So, if you had a new DataWindow object called "d_item_food" to assign in the place of d_item in the w_item window, you would use the following command:

```
w_item.dw_data.ObjectName = "d_item_food"
```

You would then have to add d_item_food to the resource file with the following line:

```
c:\book\inventry\inventry.pbl(d_item_food)
```

Using Project Objects

Project objects are new to Version 4. *Project Objects* are an easier way to manage and compile a project, especially if you are responsible for multiple projects. To use the project painter, do the following steps:

1. Click on the Project Painter icon. This opens the Select Project dialog box (see fig. 15.10).

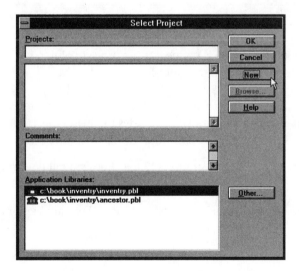

Fig. 15.10
You can edit a new project or create a new project from the Select Project dialog box.

2. Click on New to pull up the project painter.

3. Immediately you will be asked for the executable name in the Select Executable File. Choose the executable drive, path, and file name, and click on OK.

4. Now you will be able to enter information in the project painter, as shown in figure 15.11. Here you can enter resource names and libraries. You also can specify whether or not to regenerate, and whether or not to convert each PBL into a PBD.

Fig. 15.11
Define your
project in the
project painter.

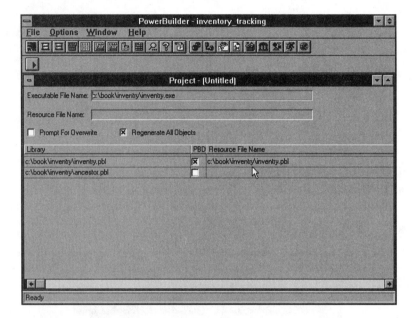

5. After your executable is defined in the project painter, click on the Build icon. This will create your EXE file.

After you're finished, every time you use the Project Painter to recompile, the Project Painter regenerates, converts libraries to PBDs, pulls in all desired resources, and compiles your application into a Windows EXE.

You can then save your project into a PBL. When you tell PowerBuilder to save your project, the Save Project dialog box appears (see fig. 15.12).

Projects are a big time saver, and they prevent bad executables or mismatch executables and libraries from being delivered.

IV

Fig. 15.12
To save your project, enter the name, comments, and PBL of your new project and click on OK in the Save Project dialog box.

Delivering the Final Product

Delivering the Right DLLs Using the Development and Deployment Kit

PowerBuilder offers a Development and Deployment kit. This allows the developer to distribute his or her new executable. To deliver your executable, include the following:

- The EXE

- All PBDs and DLLs that are used with your EXE

- All resources that are not in an included resource file

- All DLLs that PowerBuilder includes in its Development and Deployment kit

---

Troubleshooting

I distributed my executable, but I still can't connect to my database. Why not?

This is always a tricky problem. Here are a few solutions:

1. You did not install the run time version of Watcom SQL or your current database when you installed your program.

2. You installed Watcom SQL, but did not change the DBSTARTW to RTSTARTW (or DB32W to RT32W, and so on) for your startup program on your database. Because you are using the run time version, you'll need to do this.

(continues)

(continued)

3. You installed your database, but do not have a path set to it in the AUTOEXEC.BAT file.

4. You do have the proper path set to the programs in the AUTOEXEC.BAT file, but you haven't rebooted since installing your database to make that path change take effect.

This is always tricky at first. Play around with the database and make sure that it's pointing to files in their right location, using the right driver, and so on.

Debugging at Run Time

▶ See "Comparing the Run Time Version and the Developer's Version," p. 568

By the time you release your product, it should be flawless. Unfortunately, sometimes bugs creep into a delivered executable. If you included a string of a column on a DataWindow that doesn't exist, or tried to access a window after it was closed, you will receive a system error describing where the error took place. (This is especially true if you coded the system error application event.)

Note

There is a list of PowerBuilder system messages in Chapter 24, "Message Quick Reference."

Sometimes, however, the error bypasses the system error event and causes a Windows error. In this case, you may try running your program with a "/pbdebug" flag. This action traces your application by telling you which lines are executed and lets you know exactly where the error occurred. All of your PowerBuilder calls are also placed in a DBG file with the same name as your program.

> **Caution**
>
> Use the debug trace as a last resort. Turning on the trace with /pbdebug, entering the Inventory Tracking system, and immediately exiting can generate 504 lines of debug code. Even a simple event with a simple script causes a lot of debug trace statements. If you were to run through an entire program, the result could be more than you're equipped to handle!
>
> Still, there are some errors that debug finds. However, if you can solve your problems without resulting to debug, you'll be happy you did.

From Here...

This chapter provided information about delivering your executable. You can also consult your PowerBuilder User's Guide on delivering an executable. For related information, consult the following chapters:

- Chapter 13, "Pulling It All Together in an Application," shows you how to finalize your application before you compile.

- Chapter 14, "Debugging Your Application," demonstrates the debugging process, as explained by expert Blaine Bickar. You'll need to debug your application before compiling.

- Appendix B, "Using Watcom Database and Watcom SQL," discusses the differences between the run time and developers' versions of Watcom SQL. If you're distributing with a Watcom database, you really should review this chapter carefully.

Part V

Techniques from the Pros

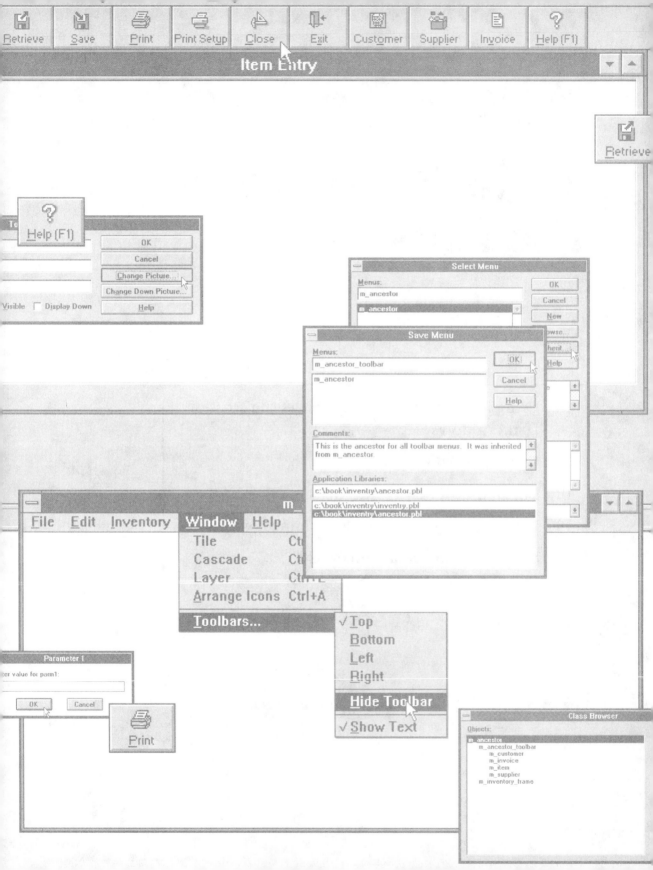

| Retrieve | Save | Print | Print Setup | Close | Exit | Customer | Supplier | Invoice | Help (F1) |

Item Entry

Retrieve

Help (F1)

| To |
| OK |
| Cancel |
| Change Picture... |
| Change Down Picture... |
Visible ☐ Display Down | Help |

Select Menu

Menus:
m_ancestor

m_ancestor

OK
Cancel
New
...owse...
...herit
Help

Save Menu

Menus:
m_ancestor_toolbar

m_ancestor

OK
Cancel
Help

Comments:
This is the ancestor for all toolbar menus. It was inherited
from m_ancestor.

Application Libraries:
c:\book\inventry\ancestor.pbl

c:\book\inventry\inventry.pbl
c:\book\inventry\ancestor.pbl

m_

| File | Edit | Inventory | Window | Help |

Tile   Ctr
Cascade   Ctr
Layer   Ctrl+L
Arrange Icons   Ctrl+A

Toolbars...

√Top
Bottom
Left
Right
Hide Toolbar
√Show Text

Parameter 1

ter value for parm1:

OK   Cancel

Print

Class Browser

Objects:
m_ancestor
  m_ancestor_toolbar
    m_customer
    m_invoice
    m_item
    m_supplier
m_inventory_frame

Chapter 16

Using Modify and Describe to Get the Most of DataWindows

by Dave Fish

The DataWindow in PowerBuilder is often described as the most powerful feature of the tool. DataWindows provide you with the ability to create a powerful, yet easy-to-use interface between the user and the database.

PowerBuilder has several functions to manipulate a DataWindow control (the DataWindow control appears on the window). To manipulate the data object (which resides inside the DataWindow control and which you create using the DataWindow painter), you use the Modify and Describe functions.

Many developers think that Describe and Modify are the most difficult PowerBuilder functions to use. I'm not sure that's true, but I agree that it can sometimes be hard to get the syntax right. Sometimes debugging Describe and Modify statements has made me wish I had gone to law school instead of pursuing a career in computer science. I've learned from my mistakes, and in this chapter I give you a few tips and tricks to make using these functions a whole lot easier.

In this chapter you learn:

- Why you should use the Describe and Modify functions with your DataWindows

- How to update more than one database table from a single DataWindow

- How to conditionally alter your DataWindow at run time

- How to improve the performance of your DataWindow

- How to handle tricky syntax problems, such as embedded quotes, in your Modify statements

- How to use Help Bookmarks to allow quick reference to provide information about DataWindow attributes

- How to use the DataWindow syntax editor distributed with PowerBuilder

> **Note**
>
> In Version 3, most DataWindow functions contained the prefix dw (dwModify, dwDescribe). This prefix has been dropped in Version 4. The dw prefix will still work with Version 4, but I recommend that you use the new convention for all future development (that is, Modify instead of dwModify).

If DataWindows are so powerful, why do I need these functions?

As a software developer, you know that to be successful you need to customize your applications to suit your users' needs. While you can certainly do a lot with DataWindows without ever using these functions, using Modify and Describe will give you the ability to develop applications that exactly meet your users' requirements. Properly utilized, these functions can reduce the amount of code you need to write, improve performance, and make your application easier to maintain.

For example, let's say you developed a DataWindow to display employee information such as employee ID, first name, last name, social security number, date of birth, and salary (see fig. 16.1). Your boss has been using this

DataWindow for a while, but now she wants to delegate the maintenance of the data to her assistant. She asks you to set it up so that the assistant can view and update all of the data except the salary column. How do you accomplish this?

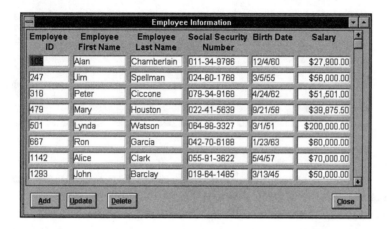

One way would be to create another DataWindow with the same data, except you would omit the salary column. This seems like a lot of work, and now you have doubled your maintenance requirements. If you need to add more columns in the future, you will have to add them to both DataWindows.

A better solution would be to use the Modify function and display or hide the salary column based on the user id. With a few lines of code, you save yourself from having to create another DataWindow, and you still have only the one DataWindow to maintain.

Place this code in the open event for the window:

```
if sqlca.logid <> 'manager' then
  dw_1.Modify("salary.visible=0")
  dw_1.Modify("salary_t.visible=0")
end if
dw_1.SetTransObject(sqlca)
dw_1.Retrieve()
```

Your non-manager users now see the same DataWindow, except the salary column is not visible when they run the application (see fig. 16.2).

Fig. 16.2

Non-manager's
view of the
DataWindow with
salary column
hidden.

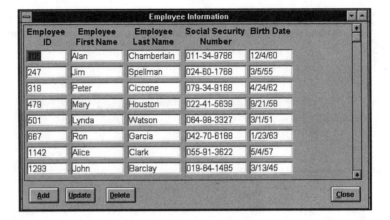

That's a neat trick. What else can I change on my DataWindow using Modify?

You can change just about anything! Using Modify, you can add, delete, and move columns, rename a header, change the column tab sequence, background color, and so on.

Look at the Modify function and its syntax:

```
DataWindowname.Modify ( modstring )
```

Parameter	Description
DataWindowname	The name of the DataWindow control or child DataWindow you are modifying.
modstring	A string containing the specifications for the modification.

You can use three types of statements in *modstring* to modify a DataWindow object:

Statement type	How it's used
CREATE *object*	Add objects like columns, drawing objects, text, bit maps, and computed fields to the DataWindow object.
DESTROY *object*	Remove objects from the DataWindow object.
Attribute *assignments*	Dynamically set attributes such as background color, font size, and tab sequence.

All PowerBuilder functions return a value. Modify returns an empty string if it's successful, otherwise it returns an error message. For simplicity, the examples here do not always check the return value, but it's important that you check the return value after each Modify function call and act accordingly.

[Q] What is the purpose of the Describe function?

You can use Describe to get information about the DataWindow. You might want to modify the where clause of your SQL Select statement. To do this, you would use Describe to get the select statement and use Modify to change it. You might want to know the first visible row on your DataWindow. Again, you use the Describe function to return the first row on page attribute.

Take a look at the Describe function and its syntax:

```
DataWindowname.dwDescribe ( syntax )
```

Parameter	Description
DataWindowname	The name of the DataWindow control or child DataWindow.
syntax	A string containing a blank-separated list of attributes.

Describe returns a string value that can be one of three things:

- A description of the object and attributes requested.

- An exclamation point (!) if an illegal item is found.

- A question mark (?) if there's no value for the attribute.

[Q] I have a DataWindow with columns from more than one table. I need to be able to update all of the columns, but the DataWindow Painter will only allow me to specify one table for update. Can I get around this?

Yes, but it can be a little tricky. The SQL standard only allows you to update one table at a time. PowerBuilder enables you to create a DataWindow from joined tables, but the DataWindow will only allow you to update one of those tables automatically. To get around this, use the Modify function.

Here's an example of updating two tables from one DataWindow:

```
integer l_i_rc //Return code from Update function
l_i_rc = dw_1.Update(TRUE,FALSE) // Do A GetText(), don't reset
➥flags in DW if successful update
// If the update against customer is successful, modify the update
// characteristics of the DataWindow object to point to the next
➥table.
IF l_i_rc = 1 THEN
  //Turn off update for customer columns
  dw_1.dwModify("customer_custnum.Update = No")
  dw_1.dwModify("customer_name.Update = No")
  dw_1.dwModify("customer_address.Update = No")
  dw_1.dwModify("customer_custnum.Key = No")
  //Make cust_order table updateable.
  dw_1.dwModify("DataWindow.Table.UpdateTable = ~"cust_order~"")
  //Turn on update for desired cust_order columns.
  dw_1.dwModify("cust_order_custnum.Update = Yes")
  dw_1.dwModify("cust_order_ordnum.Update = Yes")
  dw_1.dwModify("cust_order_duedate.Update = Yes")
  dw_1.dwModify("cust_order_balance.Update = Yes")
  dw_1.dwModify("cust_order_custnum.Key = Yes")
  //Update the cust_order table.
  l_i_rc = dw_1.Update()
  IF l_i_rc = 1 THEN
   dw.1.ResetUpdate
   COMMIT USING SQLCA;
  ELSE
    MessageBox("Status","Update of cust_order table failed. "+ &
              +"Rolling back changes customer and cust_order.")
    ROLLBACK USING SQLCA;
  END IF
ELSE
  MessageBox("Status","Update of customer table failed. " + &
            +"Rolling back changes to customer.")
  ROLLBACK USING SQLCA;
END IF
```

Make sure you reset your customer columns so that they can be updated:

```
//Turn off update for cust_order table.
dw_1.dwModify("cust_order_custnum.Update = No")
dw_1.dwModify("cust_order_ordnum.Update = No")
dw_1.dwModify("cust_order_duedate.Update = No")
dw_1.dwModify("cust_order_balance.Update = No")
dw_1.dwModify("customer_custnum.Update = Yes")
dw_1.dwModify("customer_name.Update = Yes")
dw_1.dwModify("customer_address.Update = Yes")
dw_1.dwModify("customer_custnum.Key = Yes")
//Make customer table updateable .
dw_1.dwModify("DataWindow.Table.UpdateTable = ~"customer~"")
```

Q Can I temporarily delete columns from a DataWindow? I don't want to remove them permanently, and I don't want to hide them.

Using Modify, you can destroy a column. The syntax is:

```
<DW Control Name>.Modify(&
"destroy <optionally specify the keyword 'column'> <Columnname>")
```

Here's another example:

```
dw_1.Modify("destroy column salary")
```

Or, you can try this:

```
dw_1.Modify("destroy salary")
```

The advantage of using Destroy over Hide is that the Destroy command will remove the column from the DataWindow rather than merely make the column invisible. If you use the keyword "column", the column is removed from the DataWindow and the result set retrieved from the database. Without the keyword "column", the column is removed from the DataWindow, but the data remains in the result set.

Q What about the reverse? Let's say I want to add a column to a DataWindow at run time. Can I do that as well?

Of course! Again, the Modify function lets you create the column and a heading or label for it.

This is not for the faint of heart! Here's an example of the attributes you can set using the Modify function to create a column.

```
<DW Control Name>.Modify(&
"create column(band=detail id=1 alignment='1' tabsequence=10
➥border='5'" + &
"color='0' x='412' y='24' height='65' width='165'
➥format='[general]'" + &
"name=id edit.limit=0 edit.case=any edit.focusrectangle=no
➥edit.autoselect=yes" + &
"edit.autohscroll=yes  font.face='Arial' font.height='-10'
➥font.weight='400'" + &
"font.family='2' font.pitch='2' font.charset='0'
➥background.mode='1'" + &
"background.color='536870912')")
```

You won't have to set all these attributes, but you could! This should give you an idea of the power and flexibility available in DataWindows.

Q You mentioned earlier about changing the SQL select statement. I see a need for that. How do I do that?

You can set the Table.Select attribute using Modify:

```
<DW Control Name>.Modify("DataWindow.Table.Select='<string contain
➥ing the SQL select source of the DW>'")
```

If you want to dynamically add a WHERE clause for the salary example so that only employees making less than $25,000 a year are selected, do the following:

```
string l_s_rc, l_s_orig_sql, l_s_ mod_sql, l_s_where_clause
➥//Declare local variables
dw_1.SetTransObject(sqlca)
l_s_orig_sql = dw_1.Describe("DataWindow.Table.Select")
l_s_where_clause = "Where employee.Salary < 25000"
l_s_mod_sql = "DataWindow.Table.Select~"" + l_s_orig_sql +
➥l_s_where_clause + "~""
l_s_rc = dw_1.Modify(_s_mod_sq)
IF l_s_rc = "" THEN
  dw_emp.Retrieve( )
ELSE
  MessageBox("Status","dwModify Failed" + l_s_rc)
END IF
```

Q I'm using a column with a code table and I need to find out the display value. All I seem to get is the data value. Is there a way to do this?

This requires the use of the Describe, Evaluate, and LookupDisplay functions. The following example retrieves the name of the state from the code table based on the state id selected.

```
string l_s_data_value, l_s_row
l_s_row = string(dw_1.GetRow())
l_s_data_value = dw_1.Describe &
➥("evaluate('lookupdisplay(state_id)',"+l_s_row+")")
```

Q I like the way the data manipulation grid in the Database Painter shows me the range of rows visible in the DataWindow and how many rows were retrieved. How can I incorporate that feature into my DataWindows?

Many developers want to incorporate this feature into their applications. You can accomplish this by using the Describe and RowCount functions. Basically, you use the attributes DataWindow.FirstRowOnPage and DataWindow.LastRowOnPage to display the range of rows visible on the page, and use the RowCount function to display the total number of rows retrieved, as shown in figure 16.3.

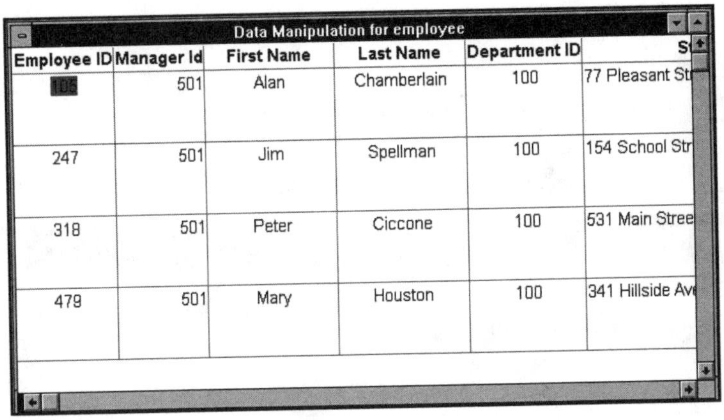

Fig. 16.3

Rows visible and total rows retrieved.

```
long  l_l_first_row, l_l_last_row, l_l_row_count
string l_s_rows_information
l_l_first_row =  dw_1.Describe("DataWindow.FirstRowOnPage")
l_l_last_row =  dw_1.dwDescribe("DataWindow.LastRowOnPage")
l_l_row_count = dw_1.RowCount()
l_s_rows_information = "Rows " + string(l_l_first_row) + " to " +
➥string(l_l_last_row) + &
" of  " + string (l_l_row_count)
mdi_frame.SetMicroHelp(l_s_rows_information)
```

For efficiency, create a custom user event for this code on your DataWindow control, and trigger it from the RetrieveEnd and RowFocusChanged events.

```
TriggerEvent("ue_row_count")
```

Q If you have a lot of Modify statements in your script, won't that impact performance?

Yes, if you have a DataWindow with a lot of columns from multiple tables and you want to update them as you did previously, you might notice a decrease in performance. There's a way around this. You can concatenate your Modify statements into one Modify function call. This will result in a significant performance increase. A word of warning, however—concatenate your Modify statements only after you have debugged them. It's hard enough trying to debug a Modify function call with a single Modify statement. When you combine several Modify statements, the task becomes nearly impossible!

You can combine multiple Modify statements into one Modify function using embedded tab characters. Use the tilde (~) and the letter *t* to accomplish this (~t).

V

Techniques from the Pros

So from our previous example, this:

```
dw_1.dwModify("customer_custnum.Update = No")
dw_1.dwModify("customer_name.Update = No")
dw_1.dwModify("customer_address.Update = No")
dw_1.dwModify("customer_custnum.Key = No")
```

would look like this:

```
dw_1.dwModify("customer_custnum.Update = No~t &
              customer_name.Update = No~t &
              customer_address.Update = No~t &
              customer_custnum.Key = No")
```

Note

You removed the quotes around each update statement, so now you have only two quotes, one to start the Modify string and one to end it.

It's easy to understand how calling a function once instead of four times will result in performance improvements.

Q All these quotes and tildes are confusing. What are the rules to using them in Modify and Describe?

Many developers have trouble with this when they first start using Modify and Describe. You can avoid this trouble if you remember a couple of rules:

- To embed a string within a string, single quotes are recognized as separate from double quotes.

- A single quote represents a ~ "

There's a string parser in PowerBuilder used to evaluate your string. The tilde is used to tell the parser that the following character should be taken as a literal.

You have already read about embedding tabs with ~t. You also can embed a carriage return and new line by using ~r~n.

```
Modify("subtitle.Text='The quick brown fox~r~njumped over the lazy dog's back.'")
```

Q These functions sound great if I know what I want to Modify or Describe when I'm writing my code. What if I want to conditionally change things at run time? Can I do that?

Yes. You can use expressions in most Modify and Describe statements.

For example, say you wanted to highlight a column if the value was higher than an amount specified by the user. Since you don't know what that amount will be when you are creating your application, you will need to do something like this:

```
string l_s_mod_string, l_error
l_s_mod_string = "salary.color= '0~tif (salary >" +&
 sle_amount.Text + ",255,0)'"
l_error = dw_1.dwModify(l_s_mod_string)
```

In the above example, you are taking the value entered by the user in sle_amount.Text and embedding it in your modification string.

▣ I've used (dw)Modify and (dw)Describe in Version 3 of PowerBuilder. Are there any new attributes in Version 4?

Some new DataWindow attributes have been added for Version 4. These attributes mainly support features in the new Print dialog box available with PowerBuilder 4.0. They can also be used with the Modify and Describe functions:

Attribute	Type and Description
DataWindow.printer	Type string. Contains the name of the current printer device.
DataWindow.print.*filename*	Type string. Contains the name of a file to receive the printed report. If the string is empty, the report is sent to the printer.
DataWindow.print.*page.range*	Type string. Contains the numbers of the pages to be printed. If the string is empty, all pages are printed.
DataWindow.print.*page.rangeinclude*	Type integer. Indicates the range of pages to print. 0 will print all, 1 prints all even pages, and 2 prints all odd pages.
DataWindow.print.*collate*	Value equals Yes or No. Choosing Collate will slow printing as the print job is repeated to produce collated sets.
column.protect	Type integer. 1 is protected; 0 is not protected. When a column is protected, it cannot be modified. This can be used instead of modifying the tab sequence.
font.escapement	Type long. Specifies the rotation of text in tenths of a degree.

V

Techniques from the Pros

Q How do you keep track of all the DataWindow attributes? There must be hundreds of them.

You will really want to take advantage of the on-line help available in PowerBuilder. You can set up bookmarks in Help to allow you to quickly reference help information about DataWindow attributes.

■ Valid Attributes for Describe and Modify (see fig. 16.4).

■ Attributes of a DataWindow control (see fig. 16.5).

Fig. 16.4

Help Bookmark Set showing the valid attributes for Describe and Modify.

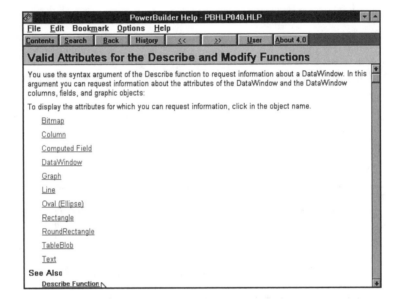

Fig. 16.5

Help Bookmark Set showing attributes of a DataWindow control.

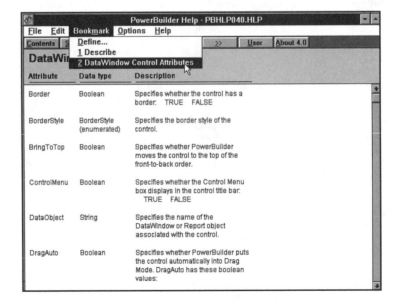

These will be a great help as you begin using the Modify and Describe functions. The bookmarks will still be a useful reference even after you become a pro at using Modify and Describe.

Ⓠ Writing Modify and Describe statements can be tricky. Is there a syntax editor to help me do the job?

Yes, there is. There's a tool called dwsyn40. You can download it from the PowerSoft Bulletin Board, or from the PowerSoft forum on CompuServe. It lets you paint Describe and Modify statements very quickly and easily. It also comes with an RGB calculator that's handy for getting the RGB values of colors. You can customize your PowerBar so you can call dwsyn directly from PowerBuilder.

Figure 16.6 is an example of the Modify Syntax painter in dwsyn40.

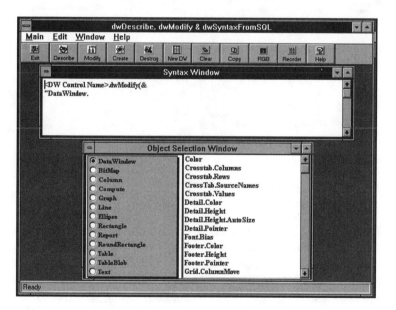

Fig. 16.6
Using the
dwSyn40 Modify
Syntax painter.

Clicking on the Describe icon will present you with the Describe Syntax painter, shown in figure 16.7.

Fig. 16.7
Using the
dwSyn40 Describe
Syntax painter.

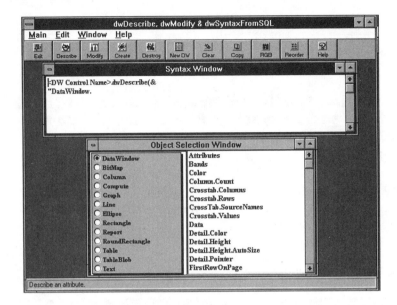

Once you have painted your Modify or Describe syntax, you can copy and paste it into the PowerScript painter. Then all you have to do is replace the generic object names with the appropriate object names for your DataWindow.

```
<DW Control Name>.Modify(&
"<Columnname>.Edit.CodeTable=<Yes or No>")
```

becomes:

```
dw_1.Modify("Gender.Edit.CodeTable=Yes")
```

Any final tips about using Modify and Describe?

Practice, practice, practice! Another thing, you don't want to start out with something too complicated because you will only wind up frustrated. Add complexity as you go along. When it comes to customizing your DataWindows, you are limited only by your own imagination.

Chapter 17

Using the Data Pipeline

Data pipelines are new to PowerBuilder 4. Using data pipelines, you can transfer large amounts of data from one database to another. These databases don't even have to use the same driver. For example, you could transfer data from a Watcom SQL 4.0 database to an Oracle 7.1 database.

Although the idea of transferring data is appealing, especially if you are switching from one database to another, the pipeline can be used for other functions, including a distributed data network.

In this chapter, you will:

- Learn how to create and use a data pipeline

- Understand the concept of a data warehouse

- Understand how to implement a pipeline inside an application using a user object

- Become familiar with pipeline user object attributes, events, and functions

Creating and Using a Data Pipeline in PowerBuilder

To create a data pipeline, click on the Pipeline icon. This will open the Select Data Pipeline dialog box seen in figure 17.1. Click on **New**.

Fig. 17.1
Use the Select
Data Pipeline
dialog box to edit
or create a data
pipeline.

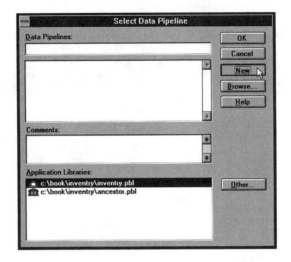

When you are creating a data pipeline, you must choose both a source connection and a destination connection. The source connection is where the data and table definitions currently reside. The destination connection is where the data and table definitions will be transferred. The source and destination connections are chosen in the Choose Database Profiles dialog box, as seen in figure 17.2. This dialog box automatically opens when you're creating a new data pipeline.

Fig. 17.2
The Choose
Database Profiles
dialog box is used
to define your
source and
destination
connections in a
data pipeline.

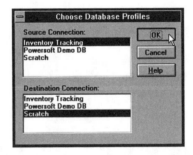

The Select Tables dialog box opens inside the select painter, as seen in figure 17.3. (You've seen the select painter before when you defined DataWindows.) Choose the table or tables you want to process and click on OK.

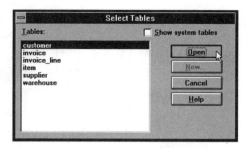

Fig. 17.3
Use the Select
Tables dialog box
to choose the
tables you want to
transfer over the
data pipeline.

As with DataWindows, you can use the select painter to choose which columns you want to transfer. You can also control what data you transfer by
using the Where tab, as seen in figure 17.4. By allowing you to choose the
columns and order of the columns that are transferred as well as allowing you
to filter data with a Where SQL statement, the data pipeline is more efficient
than a simple export/import combination.

◄ See "Using the
SQL Toolbox,"
p. 277

V

Techniques from the Pros

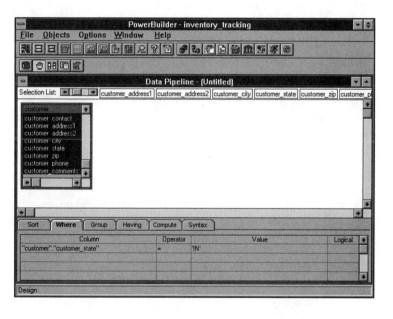

Fig. 17.4
The select painter
lets you choose
what columns to
transfer as well as
what data.

When you've defined the tables, columns, and Where criteria to be used in
the data pipeline transfer, click on the Design icon. This opens the data pipeline painter, as seen in figure 17.5.

Fig. 17.5

The data pipeline painter lets you define how the data will be received by the destination database.

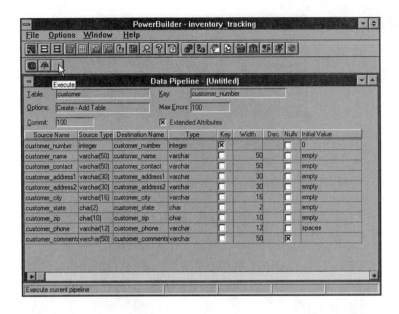

The data pipeline painter contains many fields which must be filled in before the transfer takes place:

- **T**able allows you to name the table you are creating with the data pipeline. Usually, this will be the same table name as the source database's table.

- **K**ey allows you to name your primary key of the destination table. Usually, this is the same key which is used in the source database's table.

- **O**ptions allow you to describe how you want the data transfer to take place. Valid options from which you can choose using the drop down list box are:

  - Create - Add Table allows you to create a new table. The data pipe line will fail if this table already exists on the destination database.

  - Replace - Drop/Add Table drops the table from the destination data base if that table exists, and then creates a new table with the source database's information.

  - Refresh - Delete/Insert Rows keeps the destination database in place, but makes all the rows match the source database by using SQL Deletes and Inserts.

- Append - Insert Rows allows you to insert rows that do not exist on the destination database. Any duplicate keys will not be appended and will receive an error.

- Update- Update/Insert Rows inserts rows that do not exist on the destination database, as well as update those rows that do exist with new information from the source database.

■ Max Errors lets you determine how many errors your transfer can receive (for example, duplicate key) before halting. Valid values are No Limit, 1, 10, 100, 200, 300, and so on, up to 1,000.

Note

When setting Max Errors, you should determine how error prone you can be. For instance, if you are using the Replace - Drop/Add Table option, you should not receive any errors, and should mark Max Errors to reflect this.

If, on the other hand, you're using the Append - Insert Rows option and expect a lot of duplicate rows, you should mark this at a high setting so that your data transfer goes through.

■ Commit allows you to choose how many SQL statements get executed before committing. Commits usually take a lot of time. When doing bulk transactions (as is done with the data pipeline), it may be better if the database were committed at the end of the pipeline processing.

However, you may try to commit as many as possible, especially with a low Max Error count, before rolling back your transaction.

■ Destination Name lets you change the name of the column on the destination table.

■ Type allows you to change the data type (for example, from an integer to a float) of the column on the destination table.

■ Key lets you indicate which fields will be part of the primary key on the destination database.

■ Width lets you resize the field on the destination database.

■ The Dec column allows you to enter the number of decimals for a field.

■ The Nulls column indicates which fields are allowed to be NULL.

Tip
You cannot change the Source Name or Source Type columns in the data pipeline painter.

V

Techniques from the Pros

■ Initial Value sets the default value on the new database if the end user tries to update a column with a NULL value. You cannot have an Initial Value if you allow a column to contain NULL.

When you're finished defining your pipeline, click on the Pipeline Profile icon to make sure the destination profile setup is correct. This will pull up the Select Destination Profile dialog box seen in figure 17.6.

Fig. 17.6
The Select Destination Profile dialog box allows the user to redirect the output of a pipeline to another data source.

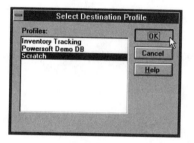

The Select icon will return you to the select painter with the SQL toolbox. The select painter and the Select Destination Profile dialog box are useful if you want to use the same pipeline to populate different databases using different Where criteria.

Finally, save the data pipeline using the Save Data Pipeline dialog box, as shown in figure 17.7, by choosing **File**, **Save**.

Fig. 17.7
The Save Data Pipeline dialog box is used to save the data pipeline into a PBL.

Click on OK and then click on the Execute icon to start the transfer.

Using a Data Pipeline in an Application

You can execute a data pipeline in the PowerBuilder environment, but you could also put a pipeline into an application using User Objects.

First, declare a user object by clicking on the User Object icon. This opens the New User Object dialog box. Choose the standard class type of user object, as seen in figure 17.8.

Fig. 17.8
Data pipelines must be used as standard class user objects.

PowerBuilder then opens the Select Standard Class Type dialog box to ask you what type of user object you want to declare. Click on `pipeline`, as seen in figure 17.9.

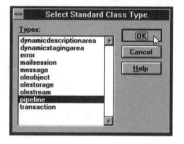

Fig. 17.9
Click on `pipeline` in the Select Standard Class Type dialog box.

Now code the following script in the constructor event of your user object:

```
DataObject = "l_inventry_to_scratch"

// Define database transactions
transaction Source
transaction Destination
// Define datawindow for process
DataWindow customer
```

V

Techniques from the Pros

```
// --- Define the parameters necessary to connect to the database.
Source.DBMS            = "ODBC"
Source.Database        = "INVENTRY"
Source.UserID          = "dba"
Source.DBPass          = "sql"
Source.DBParm          = "Connectstring='DSN=INVENTRY;UID=DBA;PWD=SQL'"

// --- Define the parameters necessary to connect to the database.
Destination.DBMS       = "ODBC"
Destination.Database   = "SCRATCH"
Destination.UserID     = "dba"
Destination.DBPass     = "sql"
Destination.DBParm     = "Connectstring='DSN=SCRATCH;UID=DBA;PWD=SQL'"

start ( Source, Destination, customer )
```

Save your user object. (The user object in the example is named u_inventry_to_scratch.) Finally, start your pipeline with the following user object declaration. Put this line of code behind a command button or in your application open event:

```
u_inventry_to_scratch start_this          // start the pipeline
```

The pipeline attributes are listed in table 17.1.

Table 17.1 Pipeline Attributes		
Attribute	**Data Type**	**Description**
RowsInError	Long	The number of rows the pipeline found in error (for example, rows containing a duplicate key).
RowsRead	Long	The number of rows read by the pipeline.
RowsWritten	Long	The number of rows written by the pipeline.
DataObject	String	The name of the pipeline object (the object created in the data pipeline painter).
Syntax	String	The syntax used to create the pipeline object (the object created in the data pipeline painter).

Pipeline events are listed in table 17.2.

Table 17.2	Pipeline Events
Event	**Occurs**
Constructor	When the user object is created.
Destructor	When the user object is destroyed.
PipeEnd	When Start or Repair is completed.
PipeMeter	After each block of rows is read or written. The Commit factor specified for the pipeline determines the size of each block.
PipeStart	When a Start or Repair is started.

Pipeline functions are listed in table 17.3.

Table 17.3	Pipeline Functions	
Function	**Returned Data Type**	**Description**
Cancel()	Long	Stops execution of a pipeline.
ClassName()	String	Returns the name assigned to the user object.
PostEvent(event_name)	Boolean	Runs the event after the function or event currently running is finished.
Repair(transaction)	Integer	Updates the transaction database with corrections that have been made in the pipeline user object's Error DataWindow.
Start(src, dest, dw)	Integer	Executes a pipeline.
TriggerEvent(ename)	Boolean	Runs the event immediately.
TypeOf()	Object	Returns the type of the user object.

Understanding Data Warehouses

Data pipelines can be used to administer a data warehouse. A *data warehouse* is a read-only storage area. This storage area can be periodically updated from remote areas where the data is maintained.

For example, say you were running a company. Your company has offices all over the country, and each remote office is responsible for maintaining its own data. You would like a copy of the data at the home office to run reports, process information, and complete other tasks.

Each remote office could process the data relevant to them (say, by region or state) and on a daily basis, use the data pipeline to transmit data to you over the wide area network (WAN) data warehouse.

What is described here is a type of distributive database, where one central store of data can be populated by remote sites without too much "traffic" over the WAN.

The pros of using a data pipeline to implement a distributive database are as follows:

- Not much line traffic is involved, so your WAN or LAN (local area network) won't be overloaded.

- Any WAN line traffic can be controlled, so large data transfers can occur at light periods of WAN or LAN use.

- Remote sights are responsible for their own data, so the burden of data control is taken off the home office.

- The home office still can access the data warehouse for reports or to copy the data.

The cons of using a data pipeline to implement a distributive database are as follows:

- Remote sites are responsible for their own data, so the burden of data control as well as database management is added to their tasks.

- The data in the data warehouse must be read-only, or else there's a chance that some updates to the data will be overwritten. This limits the processing available.

- Huge bulk data transfers are necessary periodically. During these transfers, the LAN or WAN access will slow down.

If needed, the home office can pipeline data "the other way" to populate read-only data on the remote sites, or to update remote sites after processing. This must be used judiciously to avoid overwriting changes at the remote sites. You could use this technique to send back a compilation of data from all sites so that each individual site could see how they compare.

If the pros of this situation appeal to you and the cons don't concern you too much, you could implement a distributed data network using data warehouses and remote sites with the data pipeline.

V

Techniques from the Pros

Chapter 18

DataWindows Tips and Tricks

*by   Victor Rasputnis and Anatole Tartakovsky
with David O'Hearn*

When moving from one project to another, you often find yourself doing the same thing over and over. This is especially true with DataWindow related coding. You select rows, code search dialog boxes, create print option dialog boxes, and put DataWindows in a query mode again and again. Of course, every application brings some specifics, but still, isn't it beneficial to have a generic DataWindow where most of the functionality is built in?

This chapter introduces a generic DataWindow object with built-in functionality designed to reduce much of the repetitive DataWindow coding. This object is called u_DataWindow. It is based on the simplified version of the corresponding object from CTI PowerBase Class Library. You'll learn about some of the features of u_DataWindow. You can get more familiar with it by running the CTI PowerBase Class Library Demo from the CD-ROM.

CD-ROM

In this chapter, you learn how to:

- Work with basic features of the u_DataWindow object

- Attach a generic print window to u_DataWindow

- Create a print preview window

- Build a universal search engine

- Create DataWindow groups dynamically

Understanding Basic Features

The main concept behind u_DataWindow is to provide you with the same standard features in any DataWindow you use. Access to these features is provided through a pop-up menu, available when the right mouse button is clicked on the DataWindow. This simple add-on feature gives the user all the functionality needed to customize reports or forms.

The standard features provided through the u_DataWindow object are:

- Filtering and sorting

- Search capabilities

- Data regrouping defined by a user at run time

- Printer and page setup

- Print preview, rulers, and zoom

- Selective printing of the needed pages or highlighted rows

- Enhanced Query mode

With its comprehensive array of features, the u_DataWindow can be used in many applications just as it is. If you need to expand or suppress any of the features on the menu, you can inherit a new DataWindow object from u_DataWindow and supply it with a modified or inherited menu like the one shown in figure 18.1.

Fig. 18.1

A pop-up menu for u_DataWindow edit control can be accessed by right-clicking on the control.

Some additional features that you might want to add include the following:

- Multiple selection of rows—Program Manager style

- Automatic scrolling, resizing, and focusing synchronization

- Enhanced handling, reporting, and logging of DataWindow errors

- Drag-and-drop capabilities

- Clipboard support

Several of the specific reporting facilities of u_DataWindow (filtering, sorting, grouping, querying, and searching) are not restricted to the use of the more cryptic database column names, but can instead use names more meaningful to the user.

Using Selective Printing

Windows standards require every application to have some standard facilities, such as selective printing or Clipboard support. It is almost impossible to do all these standard facilities in the window (report or form) level. One of the advantages of the u_DataWindow object is that it comes with most of the functionality built-in and readily accessible. These functions can also be invoked programmatically through user events or object functions.

◀ See "Creating a Quick Select/ Free Form DataWindow," p. 211

To add printing functionality to u_DataWindow, you must first create the w_DataWindow_print window (see fig. 18.2).

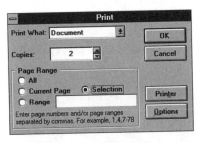

Fig. 18.2
A Print function dialog box is used as a basic print functionality for the generic DataWindow.

V

Techniques from the Pros

> **Note**
>
> Some other features introduced in PowerBuilder 4 (such as printer name, collate copy, print to file options, and so on) can be added to the Print dialog box to enhance functionality. Developers upgrading to PowerBuilder 4 should consider problems that can arise with support compatibility to previous releases of PowerBuilder.

In addition to the visible controls in figure 18.2, the invisible dw_print DataWindow control is placed on this dialog box. All print functions and events are then placed on this control to isolate the print functionality. As a result, your u_DataWindow object does not have any additional scripts and does not have to go through any modifications.

Whenever the user selects **P**rint from the pop-up menu, the menu item's clicked event will open the w_DataWindow_print window, passing the u_DataWindow control as a parameter to w_DataWindow_print. As shown in the following code segment, the open event of w_DataWindow_print assigns the parameter containing u_DataWindow (Message.PowerObjectParm) to idwSource. idwSource is an instance variable of w_DataWindow_print and has a data type of DataWindow. The other events and functions of the w_DataWindow_print window can then access the data and format of u_DataWindow from idwSource.

The rb_current_page radio button is tested next. If you select it, printing begins from the page associated with the current row of u_DataWindow. This is accomplished by setting isPrintSelection (instance variable of w_DataWindow_print of type string) to the result string from the dwDescribe function listed below.

Finally, you should set the print range for dw_print with the dwModify function. If no range was selected, isSelectPrint will be an empty string, causing dw_print to default to printing all the rows. The dw_print DataWindow is then printed using the *DataWindow*.Print function. The dwShareDataOff function turns off sharing between the two DataWindows (u_DataWindow and dw_print).

The following is the open event code for w_DataWindow_print:

```
idwSource= Message.PowerObjectParm
...
em_copies.Text = idwSource.dwDescribe("DataWindow.Print.Copies")
IF (trim(em_copies.Text = "")) THEN em_copies.Text = "1"
.....
```

For the OK button the following script has to be entered for the `clicked event for cb_OK`:

```
dw_print.dwCreate(idwSource.dwDescribe("DataWindow.syntax")) //
... // Additional code to eliminate unwanted bands, place comments,
etc.
isPrintSelection = ""
IF rb_selection.Checked THEN
  /Only selected rows have to be moved to different dw
  //Copy rows with v4 RowsCopy or ImportString from SelectedData
  for v3
  idwSource.uf_Copy_Selected_Rows( wPrint.dw_print )
  dw_print.Print()
ELSE
```

```
        idwSource.dwShareData(dw_print)
        dw_print.dwModify("DataWindow.print.preview=yes")
        IF rb_current_page.Checked THEN
            long lRow
            string sRowNumber
            lRow = idwSource.GetRow()
            sRowNumber = string( lRow )
            isPrintSelection =
              dw_print.dwDescribe( "evaluate('Page()',"+ sRowNumber + ")" )
        ELSEIF rb_range.Checked THEN
            isPrintSelection = sle_selection.text
        ELSEIF rb_page_range_all.Checked THEN
            // Standard DataWindow Print will do it
            // all parameters are already set
        END IF
        dw_printdwModify("DataWindow.print.page.range='"
                +isPrintSelection+"'")//PB4
        dw_print.Print()
        dw_print.dwShareDataOff()
    END IF
    close(Parent)
```

For PowerBuilder 3 you have to place these two scripts on "dw_print" control.

Using Print Preview

Another usable object you may want to connect to all of your DataWindows is the Preview Options dialog box. The purpose of this dialog box is to switch u_DataWindow from the normal screen mode to Print Preview mode. This allows you to view how the DataWindow will appear on paper. It also controls the percentage of reduction or enlargement of the text (Zoom), and the display of the Print Preview rulers. To include this dialog box as part of your u_DataWindow features, you must first build the w_print_preview dialog box (see fig. 18.3) and connect it to the Print Preview menu item's clicked event on u_DataWindow's pop-up menu (refer to fig. 18.1).

Once the w_print_preview window is coded and connected to u_DataWindow's pop-up menu, several events will have to be coded to make this window functional.

V

Techniques from the Pros

Fig. 18.3
The
w_print_preview
dialog box
(Preview Options)
allows the user to
control the print
preview display of
u_DataWindow.

1. First, you must code an open event for w_print_preview (see the following code segment). Just like the open event for w_DataWindow_print, u_DataWindow is passed as a parameter, and it is assigned to the instance variable idwSource.

2. The edit controls on w_print_preview (em_zoom, rb_rulers_on, rb_rulers_off, rb_preview_on and rb_preview_off) are then set to their corresponding values found in idwSource. Using the dwDescribe function, idwSource is queried for each needed piece of information, and the result is used to set the initial values of each edit control.

3. Along with the open event, each window control needs to have an event coded that will change the print preview values in the DataWindow as the corresponding controls are changed.

> ### Note
>
> As an example, the checked event for the rb_preview_on control is listed in the following code segment. When the mouse is clicked on this radio button, the script in the clicked event will test the value of rb_preview_on.checked. If it is set to TRUE, the dwModify function will set the PrintPreview=Yes. If not, the PrintPreview value will be set to =No. The other edit controls will need similarly coded events. The clicked event for the cb_OK command button will also need a statement to close the w_print_preview window.

The following is the **open event code for w_print_preview:**

```
idwSource = Message.PowerObjectParm
em_zoom_level.Text =
    idwSource.dwDescribe("DataWindow.Print.Preview.Zoom")
IF (Trim(em_zoom_level.Text)="") THEN em_zoom_level.Text = "100"
IF idwSource.dwDescribe("DataWindow.Print.Preview.Rulers") = "yes"
THEN
    rb_rulers_on.Checked=TRUE
ELSE
    rb_rulers_off.Checked=TRUE
```

```
    END IF
    IF idwSource.dwDescribe("DataWindow.Print.Preview") = "yes" THEN
        rb_preview_on.Checked=TRUE
    ELSE
        rb_preview_off.Checked=TRUE
    END IF
```

The following is the **clicked event for rb_preview_on:**

```
        idwSource.dwModify("DataWindow.Print.Preview=yes")
```

Sorting and Filtering

Sorting and filtering are some of the most frequently used functions. The simplest way to provide these capabilities is to use the SetFilter() and SetSort() functions. However, those functions do not have data-dictionary support capability. The Expression painter is difficult to use and can be substituted with a more friendly interface. A dialog box like the one in figure 18.4 is both easier to use and does not have column name limitations.

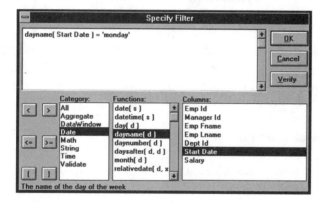

Fig. 18.4
A Specify Filter dialog box can be used as a more user-friendly replacement for the default filter window.

Building a Search Engine

Many PowerBuilder applications provide search capabilities within the DataWindow. In most cases, application-specific search facilities are created from scratch. The following section discusses approaches for building a universal search engine and the coding problems behind it.

Understanding the Issues

In designing a generic search engine, the first issue you must address is, what is the subject of the user's search?

What Are You Looking for?

The purpose of doing a search is that the user is looking for a specific record where columns match some values. But what is a *column* from the search perspective? At first glance, any DataWindow column deserves to be a search subject. Thus, the simplest approach is to let the user make a selection from the generic list of columns in a DataWindow, similar to the DataWindow Painter's Sort or Filter. But a few concerns arise:

- What if a DataWindow column (where the user can look for a specific value) is not visible? Or what if that column is not a part of any band in a DataWindow (when you delete columns from the DataWindow canvas they still exist, don't they)? In either case, the user cannot visually check that the found record indeed contains the specific value.

- What if the DataWindow column is a computed column and is not specifically named? It has an Expression attribute, but it is doubtful that the user feels comfortable using it.

As you can see, a plain column list does not work for two reasons: it violates the WYSIWYG principle (What You See Is What You Get) by allowing the user to search on columns that are not displayed on the DataWindow, and it may meet basic implementation problems. Now look at an alternative solution. If you confine a search to the visible set of columns in the detail band, the user may *point* to the column(s) to search in. So, there is no need to display the list of column names.

What Type of Search is Involved?

The next issue you have to determine is, are you providing a search on a column-by-column basis (one column at a time), or on complex criteria (a combination of columns)?

Theoretically, everything that you can find via the dwFind( ) function can also be found by using SetFilter( ) and Filter( ). When the data is sorted in the order of the search criteria, searching the data using the filtering functions achieve the same result as using the dwFind( ) function. However, when the data is not sorted in the order of the search criteria, dwFind( ) allows the user to see the search record surrounded by its neighboring records—an essential advantage over filtering.

How Should the Process Work?

From a design perspective, it is important to consider which search processes are most effective for the user. Should the user be forced to compose search expressions every time he or she wishes to search data? Or would a visual approach, allowing the user to easily choose the search criteria, be more effective?

Considering all of this, it would be best to develop a more visual point-and-click driven search engine, allowing the user to search one column at a time. This intuitive approach eliminates the problems associated with a column list method and allows the user to view the matching rows with the neighboring rows. Complex, multi-column searches do not have to be incorporated into the search engine, since those searches can still be processed using the filter function.

Developing the Engine

Once you have decided that you are implementing a search on a column-by-column basis and that the user has a way to point to a search column, you must now develop your search engine to support the following:

- The ability to search on any column regardless of datatype

- An interactive access to any column for the search

- The ability to search by display or code value

Remember that some DataWindow columns may contain "hidden" lookups, depending on the edit style. Edit code tables, drop-downDataWindows, and list boxes can all use lookups to change the displayed data. Naturally, the user prefers (at least initially) to search the data the same way it appears.

Figure 18.5 shows a simple search engine from the PowerBase Class Library. The search is implemented as one of the functions of the pop-up menu.

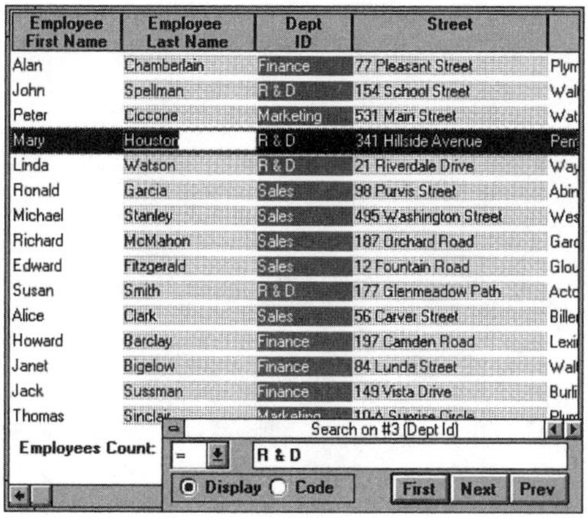

Fig. 18.5
The search window displayed at the bottom of the window allows the user to search the DataWindow. The highlighted column is the current search column.

The following is a brief description of functions provided by the Search dialog box:

- By clicking on the arrow buttons, the user can select which column is the focus of the search engine (Dept ID in this example).

- Using the Display and Code radio buttons, the user can switch between Code and Display values of the DataWindow columns.

- The drop-down list contains conditions such as = and < to be used in a search expression.

- The First, Next, and Previous command buttons let the user move between the matching rows for the search.

Two functions play a key role in the implementation of the search engine. The first function is uf_prepare_dwFind(). Its purpose is to prepare the search string for the next function. When the uf_prepare_dwFind() function is called, it is passed the column number to be searched (piCol) and the search string (psItem). The column's datatype is then retrieved from the DataWindow syntax using the dwDescribe() function, and assigned to the string sColumnType. By testing sColumnType in several IF statements, psItem is used to build the proper syntax depending on the search column's datatype.

The second function, wf_search(), is the primary search function. This function builds the search syntax for the dwFind() function and then processes it. The start and end rows are passed to this function from the Search dialog box (refer to fig. 18.5). The other search data entered and selected by the user is retrieved from the controls on the dialog box and DataWindow. After verifying that valid data exists, the search string is then assembled into the sModel string variable. The dwFind() function is then used to search the DataWindow.

```
uf_prepare_dwFind (string psItemText, int piCol)
        // Part of U_DataWindow
string sColumnType, sModel
sModel = ""
sColumnType = dwDescribe("#" + String(piColumn) + ".ColType")
IF (sColumnType<>"!") AND (sColumnType<>"?") THEN
    IF Pos(sColumnType, "char") <> 0 THEN
        sModel = "'" + psItemText + "'"
    ELSE
            IF Pos(sColumnType, "decimal") <> 0 THEN
                sModel = "Dec('" + psItemText+ "')"
        ELSE
            CHOOSE CASE sColumnType
```

```
                CASE "date"
                    sModel = "Date('" + psItemText + "')"
               CASE "time"
                    sModel = "Time('" + psItemText + "')"
               CASE "datetime"
                    sModel = "Datetime('" + psItemText + "')"
               CASE "number"
                    sModel = psItemText
                    END CHOOSE
        END IF
    END IF
END IF
return sModel
wf_search (long plstartrow, long plendrow)
          //Actual search
long        lFoundRow
long        lRowCount
string      sColumnName,      sColumnType ,     sModel,      sSearchKey
pointer     poOldPointer
poOldPointer = SetPointer(HourGlass!)
IF iiSearchColumnID  <>0 THEN
    lRowCount =  idwSearch.RowCount()
      // We'll check for possible absence of data at all
    IF lRowCount > 0   THEN
        sSearchKey = sle_search_value.text
        sColumnType = idwSearch.uf_Get_Column_Type(iiSearchColumnID)
        // Check if current search column has "Code Table"
        // Translate Code/Display value to appropriate value
        sSearchKey =
    idwSearch.uf_Convert_To_Code_Text(sSearchKey,iiSearchColumnID)
        sModel = idwSearch.uf_Prepare_dwFind(sSearchKey,
iiSearchColumnID)
        sModel = "#" + String( iiSearchColumnID) +
    ddlb_operator.Text + sModel
        lFoundRow = idwSearch.dwFind(sModel, plStartRow, plEndRow)
        IF lFoundRow > 0 THEN
            ilCurrentRow = lFoundRow
            idwSearch.ScrolltoRow(ilCurrentRow)
            idwSearch.SetRow(ilCurrentRow)
        ELSE
            Beep(1)
        END IF
    END IF
END IF
SetPointer(poOldPointer)
```

Exploring Dynamic Grouping

Dynamic grouping is the most advanced feature of a u_DataWindow object.
One of the biggest limitations of a DataWindow object is that it does not
allow modification of existing groupings. Grouping expressions are not available through dwDescribe or dwModify statements.

Also, you cannot create a new group dynamically. In most cases, this means that developers have to pre-design the same DataWindow with different groupings and let the user choose among them. This approach leads to complicated maintenance of additional DataWindows and limited functionality.

The only way to change the grouping is to re-create the DataWindow with a modified syntax. However, when you change the grouping you must consider some complications:

- Group headers have to be changed to reflect new grouping titles.

- Total and aggregate functions must be placed in the trailer band for each group.

- The sort order needs to reflect the new grouping.

- Page control (page breaks, numbering, and so on) might need changes.

u_DataWindow provides the user with the ability to specify grouping at run time. Such user-defined groups can maintain standard headers, provide replication of summary fields at the group level, and automatically update the sorting order in accordance with the group definition. All of these options are available via the Grouping editor (see fig 18.6).

Fig. 18.6

The Grouping Editor dialog box allows the user to add or change grouping controls on the DataWindow at run time.

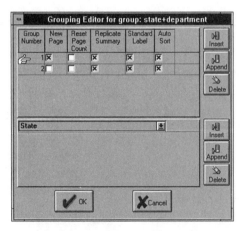

> **Note**
>
> u_DataWindow provides the ability to attach and detach the data in the DataWindow so that you can reconnect your data after you re-create your DataWindow. This is important when using the Grouping editor, because the editor must destroy and re-create the DataWindow when changing group controls.

Using the Grouping Editor

For the Grouping editor to achieve the correct result, it must complete several processing steps in the correct order:

1. Destroy previous groups or bands.

2. Define new groups or bands.

3. Replace the original DataWindow with a new one from new syntax.

4. Create new headers for each group.

5. Replicate the summary band through all group trailers.

Some of the code used by the Grouping Editor dialog box to dynamically change group information is contained in a nonvisual user object called the u_group_description_scanner. The following code segment contains the syntax that PowerBuilder uses to create this user object. Several functions are displayed, along with the constructor event.

The first of these functions is uf_get_group_count( ). It is a simple function that returns the upper bound (the highest numbered index in the array) of an instance string array, isGroupByList.

The second function, uf_get_group_expression(), returns the string isGroupExpression based on the piGroupID integer passed to it. If this integer is valid, it is used as an index to look up the correct Group Expression from the isGroupExpressionList array. The uf_get_group_by() function is very similar to the uf_get_group_expression() function. It returns a string from isGroupByList array based on the index of the passed integer, piGroupID.

The rest of the code segment displays the constructor event for the u_group_description_scanner user object. It is executed just after the user object is created. It retrieves the syntax for the DataWindow that was passed to it via the Message.PowerObjectParm, and then proceeds to search and extract the group control information from the DataWindow syntax. As each group level is found, the control data is stored in instance arrays using the group level as the index. These arrays are then used to populate the Grouping Editor dialog box.

```
$PBExportHeader$u_group_description_scanner.sru
global type u_group_description_scanner from nonvisualobject
end type
global u_group_description_scanner u_group_description_scanner
type variables
string isGroupBYList[]
string isGroupExpressionList[]
```

V

Techniques from the Pros

```
end variables
public function integer uf_get_group_count()
   return UpperBound(isGroupBYList)
end function
public function string uf_get_group_expression (integer piGroupID)
string sExpression
   sExpression = ""
   IF NOT (piGroupID > uf_Get_Group_Count() or piGroupID <=0) THEN
     sExpression = isGroupExpressionList[piGroupID]
   END IF
   return sExpression
end function
public function string uf_get_group_by (integer piGroupID)
string sGroupBY
   sGroupBY = ""
   IF NOT (piGroupID > uf_Get_Group_Count() or piGroupID <=0) THEN
     sGroupBY = isGroupBYList[piGroupID]
   END IF
   return sGroupBY
end function
on constructor
string sdwSyntax
long iGroupCnt, iPosCntlong, iPosCnt1
DataWindow pdwSource
   pdw_source = Message.PowerObjectParm
   sdwSyntax = pdwSource.dwDescribe("DataWindow.syntax")
   iPosCnt = 1
   DO
      iPosCnt = Pos( sdwSyntax , "group(", iPosCnt+1)
      IF iPosCnt <> 0 THEN
         iPosCnt = Pos( sdwSyntax , "by=(",      iPosCnt ) + 4
         iPosCnt1 = Pos( sdwSyntax , ")",      iPosCnt )
         iGroupCnt++
         isGroupBYList[iGroupCnt]  &
   =Mid(sdwSyntax,iPosCnt,iPosCnt1-iPosCnt)
      END IF
   LOOP WHILE iPosCnt <> 0

string sCurrentColumn, sNormalHeader, sSummaryField, sFormat
int ij , ii

FOR ii = 1 TO iGroupCnt
   ij = 1
   sNormalHeader = ""
   DO WHILE ij > 0
      ij = f_get_token( isGroupBYList[ii], " ", ij, sCurrentColumn
)
      if Mid(isGroupBYList[ii], ij, 1) = " " and ij > 0 THEN ij++
      sCurrentColumn = Trim(sCurrentColumn)
      IF sCurrentColumn > "" THEN
// Create Standard Header
         IF    sNormalHeader<>"" THEN   &
   sNormalHeader=sNormalHeader+"+~" ~+"
         IF pdw_source.dwDescribe(sCurrentColumn+".coltype") = "!"
         ➥OR &
```

```
                pdw_source.dwDescribe(sCurrentColumn+".coltype") = "?"
            ➥THEN
                    MessageBox("Unknown Datatype",
    "Column:"+sCurrentColumn+ ":"+&
                        pdw_source.dwDescribe(sCurrentColumn+".coltype"))
            END IF
            IF Pos(pdw_source.dwDescribe(sCurColumn+
        .coltype"),"char")>0 THEN
                sNormalHeader = sNormalHeader + sCurrentColumn
            ELSE
                sFormat =
    pdw_source.dwDescribe(sCurrentColumn+".format")
                IF sFormat ="?" OR sFormat ="!" OR sFormat="[general]"
            ➥THEN
                    sNormalHeader=sNormalHeader+
    "string("+sCurrentColumn+')'
                ELSE
                 sNormalHeader=sNormalHeader+"string("+sCurrentColumn+&
                        ",~~~""+sFormat+"~~~")"
                END IF
            END IF
        END IF
    LOOP
    isGroupExpressionList[ii] = sNormalHeader
NEXT
end on
```

Exploring the Outliner Demo Window

The Outliner Demo window in figure 18.7 shows how powerful dynamic
groupings can be. This window contains a user object inherited from the
Microsoft OUTLINER.VBX object and an extended DataWindow. Any information provided in the DataWindow is reflected in the outliner, such as the
File Manager directory tree. The purpose of this window is to create a group
expression that can be placed in the outliner object to identify each group
break. In turn, the value from the outliner can be used to filter all the records
that belong to this group. When the DataWindow is populated with data, the
outliner is also populated. When you click on a particular item in the
outliner, the automatic filter is created and applied to the DataWindow.

Listed in the code segment below is the user event, ue_create_tree, and the
function, wf_sync_views(). This code is taken from the Outliner Demo window. The ue_create_tree event is triggered when the outliner DataWindow is
displayed. It leads you step-by-step through the data in the DataWindow and
builds the group hierarchy tree from it. The wf_sync_views() functions keeps
the levels of group information on the outliner DataWindow in sync.

V

Techniques from the Pros

Fig. 18.7

The left side of the
Outliner Demo
window shows the
structure of the
group bands on
the right.

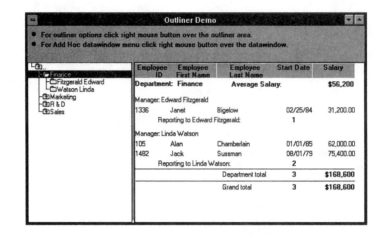

```
on ue_create_tree
string sBand, sExpression
string sTag
long lGroupBreak, l, lGroupStart, lCurrentInOutliner
int j, k, m
dw_data.SetFilter("")
dw_data.Filter()
s_Group_Start_Stop strGroupStartStop[]
lCurrentInOutliner = 1
FOR j = 1 To dw_data.uo_group.uf_Get_Group_Count()
   strGroupStartStop[j].lStartRow = 1
   strGroupStartStop[j].lEndRow = 0
NEXT
uo_tree.DeleteItem(1)
lCurrentInOutliner = 1
uo_tree.Indent[ lCurrentInOutliner ] = 1
uo_tree.List[ lCurrentInOutliner ] = ".."
FOR l=1 TO dw_data.RowCount()
   FOR j = 1 TO dw_data.uo_group.uf_Get_Group_Count()
      IF l > strGroupStartStop[j].lEndRow THEN
         lCurrentInOutliner ++
         uo_tree.Indent[ lCurrentInOutliner ] = j + 1
      uo_tree.List[lCurrentInOutliner]=dw_data.dwDescribe("evaluate('"+&
dw_data.uo_group.uf_get_group_expression(j)+&
      "',"+string(l)+")")
         IF j = dw_data.uo_group.uf_Get_Group_Count() THEN
            uo_tree.PictureType[ lCurrentInOutliner ] = 2
         ELSE
            uo_tree.PictureType[ lCurrentInOutliner ] = 0
         END IF
         strGroupStartStop[j].lStartRow = l
         strGroupStartStop[j].lEndRow =
dw_data.uf_FindGroupChange(l,j)
         IF strGroupStartStop[j].lEndRow < 0 THEN
            strGroupStartStop[j].lEndRow = dw_data.RowCount()
         END IF
```

```
      NEXT
   NEXT
   uo_tree.ListIndex = 1       // Start at the root
   uo_tree.Expand[1] = 1    // and expand it
   end on
   public function int wf_sync_views (long plindex)
   string sFilter
   int j
   IF plIndex >=1 THEN
      sFilter = "~".. \~""
      FOR j = 2 TO uo_tree.Indent[plIndex]
         sFilter=sFilter+"+"+ &
      dw_data.uo_group.uf_get_group_expression(j-1)+"+~"\~""
      NEXT
      sFilter = sFilter + "='" + uo_tree.FullPath[plIndex] + "\'"
      dw_data.SetFilter( sFilter )
      dw_data.Filter()
   ELSE
      dw_data.SetFilter( "" )
      dw_data.Filter()
   END IF
   return 1
   end function
```

V

Techniques from the Pros

Chapter 19

Exploiting the Power of Inheritance

by   Ron Cox

Perhaps the greatest promise of object-oriented software development tools is that of productivity gains through code reusability. Code reusability has been an elusive goal of developers for decades. Whether it's copy books, run time linking, or simply copying and pasting code, none of the previous methods that developers have used matches the enormous potential for reusability that inheritance has.

With inheritance, you can develop a new object class by building on a previously developed object class. The new object class, the descendant, "inherits" the attributes and functionality of the ancestor object class. You can then add to the new object class whatever is specific about it, building on the more generic aspects of the ancestor.

One of the many good things about PowerBuilder is that you're not forced to use any of the object-oriented features it has. You can write full production-quality applications without giving a single thought to object-oriented programming (OOP). But if you're looking for productivity gains through code reuse, you owe it to yourself to take a serious look at inheritance.

In this chapter, you'll look at:

- The benefits of inheritance
- Which PowerBuilder objects can be inherited
- Object class design
- A case study

Understanding the Benefits of Inheritance

Exploiting the power of inheritance can help you obtain several of the following benefits:

- Reuse

- Productivity

- Standardization/Consistency

- Maintenance Ease

The number of objects in a real-world PowerBuilder application can grow to be quite large. It's not unusual for a production application to contain over 100 windows, each with a menu and many command buttons, DataWindows, and other controls on the window. With a procedural software development tool, you'd likely end up with more repetitive code than you'd care to admit.

For example, every window with an updatable DataWindow control on it is going to require functionality to have that DataWindow update the database. Common aspects of that functionality might include data validation, error handling, database updating, and committing or rolling back the transaction. So, if your application has 20 windows with updatable DataWindows, you need the update functionality just described to be available on all 20 of those windows.

Of course, any experienced software developer would decompose that update functionality and produce functions that could be called by those 20 windows. Thus the amount of repetitive code would be reduced, but certainly not eliminated. Every one of those 20 windows needs the code for the function calls.

Any way you look at it, that's a lot of repetitive code. And how would you develop it? Maybe you could develop one window, get it working exactly the way you want, and then copy it. That method is certainly a widely used one. When working with development tools lacking in OOP features, that may be the only method available. But that method has obvious weaknesses to it.

Developing that first window just right the first time is a big task, and generally an impossible one. So, a change to the update functionality later means changing that first window and all of the windows copied from it. Not as productive as you'd like it to be, is it?

And don't forget maintenance. At some point, either you, the developer, or someone else is going to have to maintain that application. A change to the update functionality in one window may mean modifying all 20 of those windows, and testing all 20 modifications.

You need to add one more aspect into this picture. Suppose the application is being developed by a team. If those 20 different updatable windows are being developed by multiple members of the team, what level of standardization do you suppose you'd get?

Now imagine that you could write and test that code once, and every window that needed it would have it. And the functionality would be consistent across all those windows, no matter how many different developers were working on the project. And when it came time to modify the code, you only had to modify it once. These are the benefits of inheritance.

Identifying Inheritable Objects

In PowerBuilder, you can use inheritance to build three types of objects:

- Windows

- Menus

- User objects

> **Note**
>
> At first glance, having only three types of inheritable objects may seem to be a little restrictive. Just three types of objects? What about all the rest of the objects you use in PowerBuilder? Keep in mind that the user object is a very flexible tool. A standard user object can be made from any of the controls that can be placed on a window. A custom user object can be made from groups of those controls. In PowerBuilder, the User Object Painter is your method of creating custom controls. And you can use inheritance to use those custom controls over and over again.

Inheritance with Windows

Without a doubt, windows will be the objects you use inheritance with most often. Because PowerBuilder applications are generally on-line, interactive applications, they center around windows. A well-developed library of window object classes will enable you to realize significant productivity gains through reusability.

◀ See "Implementing Window Inheritance," p. 96

Inheritance with Menus

◄ See "Imple-
menting Menu
Inheritance
and Toolbars,"
p. 109

How useful you find inheritance with menus depends on how heavily you
use menus in your application. My own design philosophy is that nearly
every window has a menu. For that reason, I use inheritance with menus
almost as frequently as I use it with windows. Almost every window object
class I build has a corresponding menu object class.

Inheritance with User Objects

◄ See "Examining
DataWindow
Controls,"
p. 224

Inheritance with user objects is a very powerful tool. Remember our example
of 20 windows with updatable DataWindows? Those DataWindow controls
could all be inherited from a common ancestor, eliminating the need for that
repetitive code you're trying to do without. You could build a DataWindow
control object class that has all of the database update functionality required,
and then inherit from it to place the required DataWindow controls on each
of those 20 windows.

Employing Object Class Design

The benefits of using inheritance are plentiful—build an object class and then
inherit from it over and over again. What could be easier? The inheriting part
of it *is* easy. Building the object class, on the other hand, can be challenging.

Building an object, a window for example, by inheriting from an ancestor is
like having a foundation to build on. The base functionality and attributes
you need for that window are already there; they were inherited from the
ancestor. All you need to do with the new window is add whatever functionality is specific to it.

Designing an object class that you intend to inherit from can be a complicated process. It takes a lot of thought to look at the big picture and visualize
what windows in your project can be built on a common foundation. What
generic functionality and attributes will the descendants need? It's also important to look ahead to future projects. Designing generic object classes
now—classes that can be used over and over again in future projects—will
provide you with untold productivity gains. Object class design is a skill in its
own right. Good design of your class library is absolutely essential in order for
you to get any real benefits from inheritance.

Different windows need different functionality and attributes, right? The
same is true for menus and user objects. Is it possible to design an object class
that is all things to all descendants? It depends on your particular project and
what the descendants need to inherit from the ancestor. The answer is almost
assuredly, "No." In this case, what you need is an object class hierarchy.

Note

While it's not possible to delete controls on an object that were inherited from the ancestor, it is possible to make them invisible. Similarly, functionality in the ancestor that you don't want in the descendant can be overridden or simply ignored, depending on how it's implemented. But if you find yourself continually performing this kind of "negative inheritance," inheriting from an ancestor object and then taking away the inherited features you don't want, then the ancestor object probably wasn't designed quite right. In this case, it's best to reevaluate the design of the object class.

An object class hierarchy is like a tree. You start with a base ancestor, and then branch out from there. As shown in figure 19.1, when designing a class hierarchy it's best to start with very generic functionality and attributes in the base ancestor and then develop more specific ones in the descendants. It's common to get several levels deep before you have an object class that you will inherit from to build a production object class. In such a case, the first couple of levels of ancestors serve as foundations for their descendants, which in turn are the foundations for their own descendants.

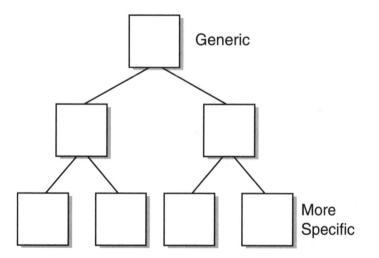

Fig. 19.1
Class Hierarchy design begins with generic features in the base ancestor. Descendants have more specific features.

Tip
An object class you inherit from, but never directly use, is sometimes called a *virtual class*. A class you use directly, such as a window that you open in an application, is known as a *production class*.

Caution

While there are no defined limits to how many levels a class hierarchy can have, there are practical limits to it. If you go beyond six levels, you may begin to encounter a performance degradation.

V

Techniques from the Pros

Analyzing the Case Study

To illustrate the value of inheritance and the process of designing an object class hierarchy, the rest of this section will focus on a case study. Though fictitious, the case study is representative of the kind of real-world issues PowerBuilder developers encounter on every project.

The Premise

Suppose that your consulting firm has just been hired to build a new system for the customer service division of a small firm, Sample, Inc. The new system will be used by the customer service representatives who answer questions from both customers and company employees.

Project Requirements

After the analysis and design phases, the project team has come up with a project plan that includes building a front-end to the database tables, shown in figure 19.2.

Fig. 19.2
These database tables are used for the fictitious project at Sample, Inc.

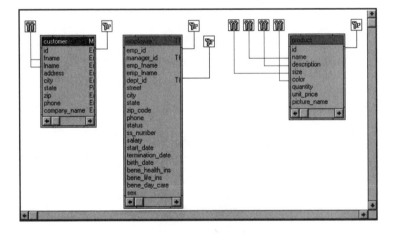

◀ See "Designing a System with the Power-Builder Data-base Painter," p. 52

The team has also come up with a basic design philosophy for development of the new system. The new system is to be developed with a focus on what the team has termed *business objects*. Business objects are what the users visualize when they think about the customer service business function.

Based on a study of how the users work and the database design, the project team has identified three business objects:

- Customer

- Product

- Employee

Because the customer service representatives need easy access to information in order to answer questions, each business object needs to be developed to have at least two types of functionality: *search functionality* and *detail functionality*. The search functionality is to be developed in such a way that it gives users everything they need to query the database and locate the record(s) they need. The search functionality must display enough information for the user to determine when they've found the record(s) they're looking for. The detail functionality must display the detail of the information the user found.

Already, you can see the potential for using inheritance during the project. There are only two basic categories of windows: search and detail. Fantastic. Two object classes and you're all set, right? Well, almost. The team has identified different functionality required for the windows for the different objects as described in table 19.1.

Table 19.1 Required Window Functionality	
Window	**Description**
Customer Search	Multiple record display
Customer Detail	Single record display
Product Search	Multiple record display
Product Detail	Single record display
Employee Search	Multiple record display plus a display of the detail of the currently highlighted record

In addition to the requirements listed in table 19.1, it has been decided that each window will have the company name (Sample, Inc.) in a *window label*, a text box placed across the top of the window. In addition, each window will have a micro help text box across the bottom of the window.

Of course you could develop these five windows individually and be done with it. But if you put a little effort into constructing an object class hierarchy, you can reap the benefits inheritance has to offer.

Tip
Adopt an object naming convention at the beginning of your project to ensure a consistent look and feel to the application, even though many developers may be working on it. It will make maintenance much easier.

▶ See "Naming Objects," p. 551

First of all, you have a situation where all windows have two things in common: the window label text box and the micro help text box. This leads you to develop your first object class from which all the other windows will be inherited, called *w_ma_base*.

w_ma_base

The w_ma_base object class is exactly what the name implies. It's the base for all other windows in the project. In this object class, you define a window with static text controls for the window label and micro help. Code the PowerScript in the window resize event required to resize the window label and micro help text boxes. Next, write a window function to place text in the micro help text box. In addition to functionality, set attributes that you want to carry forward to all descendants, such as a gray window background to facilitate implementation of the 3-D look.

Interestingly enough, w_ma_base is not only your first object class, but also your first opportunity to use your design skills to ensure that you're taking advantage of the chance to build a generic object class to use on other projects. When developing object classes, it's always in your best interest to attempt to design them in such a way that they're *portable*—not specific to the current project. Of course, with some object classes, that may not be possible. But it's possible with w_ma_base.

A static text box was placed on the window for the company name. The text attribute was set equal to the company name. All it takes to make this window object class generic is to program the functionality to set the text attribute of the window label text box dynamically at run time. But how does the window know what the text is supposed to be? There are several ways of handling this. In this example, pass a string parameter to the window. You can make the parameter a structure so you can add other elements to it later on if you need to. The completed w_ma_base object class is shown in figure 19.3.

The initial evaluation of required object classes holds true to some extent. There are definitely two basic categories of windows for this application: search and detail. In looking at the project requirements, it's probably safe to assume that all search windows will share some basic features. This leads you to develop the w_ma_search object class.

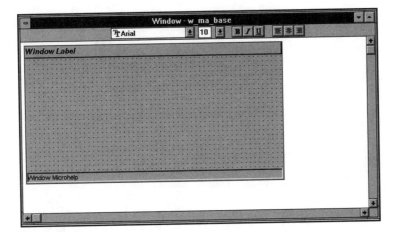

Fig. 19.3
The w_ma_base
window object
class.

w_ma_search

You can develop the w_ma_search object class by first inheriting it from the w_ma_base object class. The new window class inherits the functionality for the window label and the window micro help. You can then add what you need for a generic search window. Additions include a DataWindow control, static text control to display the record count, and command buttons for search, query, and opening a detail window. Query-by-example functionality is programmed, as is some basic DataWindow behavior. You can extend the script in the window resize event to size the DataWindow control to the maximum width of the window and the maximum height allowed, without changing its Y coordinate or overlaying the window's micro help text box.

◄ See "Using OpenSheet Commands," p. 183

Of course, a DataWindow control needs a transaction object if you're going to do any database access with it. Should you set the transaction object in this class? Not if you want it to be generic. If this is a virtual class and you intend to inherit from it not only during this project but in future projects as well, you can't guarantee that all descendants will use the same transaction object (SQLCA, for example). You could modify the u_str_open_window structure and add to it a transaction. Then a descendant of this class could use whatever transaction is passed to it. How's that? Pretty good. But, you can't guarantee every descendant will use a transaction that exists when the window is opened. Some search windows may create their own transaction (maybe they connect to different databases). The best thing for you to do is allow the descendant to deal with setting the DataWindow's transaction object. The finished w_ma_search window object class is shown in figure 19.4.

V

Techniques from the Pros

Fig. 19.4

The w_ma_search window object class.

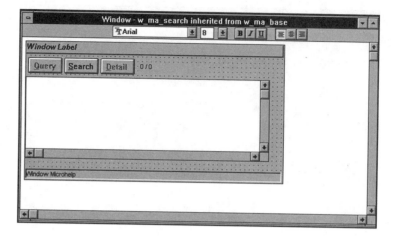

w_m_customer_search: Our First Production Class!

The requirements for the Customer Search window are fairly straightforward and can be satisfied with the features you've put into the w_ma_search object class. First, develop the DataWindow object needed for the Customer Search window. Then develop the Customer Search window by inheriting from w_ma_search. You can change the title of the window to "Customer Search." Next, associate the DataWindow object you just developed with the DataWindow control on the window. There's only one more thing to do—set the transaction object for the DataWindow. The w_m_customer_search window object class is shown in action in figure 19.5.

Fig. 19.5

w_m_customer_search window object class in action.

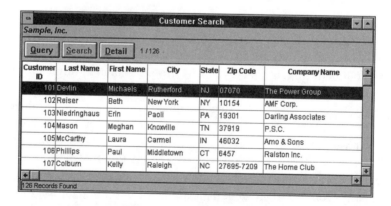

> **Note**
>
> Detailed coverage of creating a DataWindow object and associating it with a DataWindow control is given in Chapter 8, "Creating DataWindows."

w_m_product_search

That last window was easy to develop, so another search window won't be difficult. The Product Search window has the same basic requirements as the Customer Search window; you can develop it through exactly the same process:

◄ See "Associating DataWindow Controls with a DataWindow Object," p. 231

1. Develop the DataWindow object.

2. Develop the window by inheriting from w_ma_search.

3. Change the window title to "Product Search."

4. Associate the DataWindow object with the DataWindow control.

5. Set the transaction object for the DataWindow.

That's all there is to it! Inheritance gives the capability to develop a production window object class like this in five easy steps. The w_m_product_search window object class is shown in action in figure 19.6.

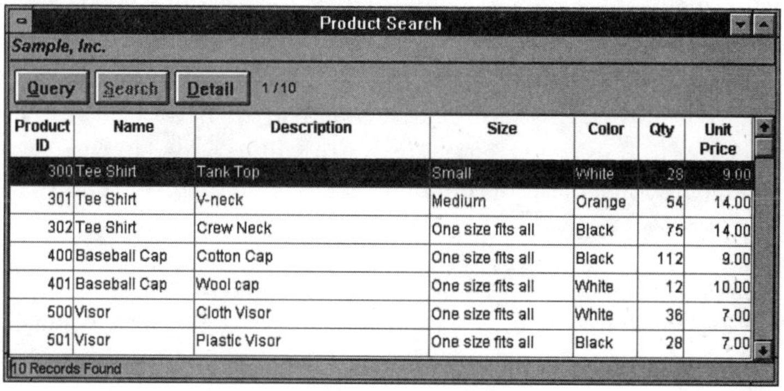

Fig. 19.6
w_m_product_search window object class in action.

You just developed two search windows with a minimal effort by taking advantage of the power of inheritance. The only real work you had to do was developing the DataWindow objects. Imagine the productivity gain if you had 20 of these windows to develop!

w_m_employee_search

The requirements for the Employee Search window are a little more demanding. In addition to the search capability you've already developed, this window requires an additional DataWindow control that displays the detail of the record currently highlighted in the original search DataWindow. The Employee Search window is the only window in the project that requires this kind of Search/Detail display. Fortunately, it still needs the same search functionality that is provided by w_ma_search. Inheritance will provide you with an excellent starting point.

▶ See "Understanding dwShareData Functions," p. 461

You can develop this new object class by inheriting from w_ma_search. Then develop another DataWindow object for the detail. Next, add another DataWindow control to the window for the detail. Extend the window's open event by adding the dwShareData function required to share data between the search DataWindow and the detail DataWindow. You then can extend the search DataWindow's rowfocuschanged event to keep the detail DataWindow in synch with it. Now you only have one task left: modify the window's resize event to handle resizing the two DataWindows.

You've had PowerScript in the window resize event since you first developed w_ma_base. That script was extended in w_ma_search. Can you extend it here to make the modifications you need? Unfortunately, you cannot. The technique you're using to resize the first DataWindow control—the search DataWindow—is inappropriate for this new window object class. You could override the ancestor's resize script, but there's other resizing code in there that you still need (for the window label and the micro help). So the best option is to modify the w_ma_base object class to give you a "hook" for resizing the DataWindow controls in the descendants. The new event won't have any PowerScript in it in w_ma_base. The script will be added in the descendants. That gives you a path for different search window object classes to do whatever resizing they need.

You can accomplish this by creating a custom user event named "ue_resize_dw" in w_ma_base. You then add the PowerScript to w_ma_base's resize event to trigger the ue_resize_dw event. Next, open the w_ma_search object class and move the DataWindow resizing script from the window's resize event to the new ue_resize_dw event. In the final step required to finish development of the new w_m_employee_search object class, you need to override the "ue_resize_dw" event's ancestor script with the new script to resize the two DataWindow controls in a way appropriate for this window class. The finished w_m_employee_search window object class is shown in figure 19.7.

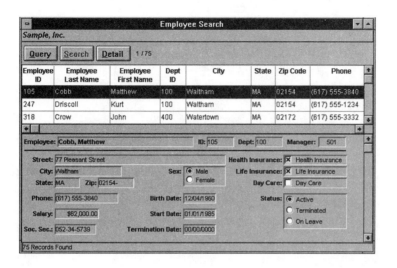

Fig. 19.7
w_m_employee_search
window object
class in action.

w_ma_detail

You've already figured out this project needs two basic categories of windows object classes: search and detail. You've developed the search window object classes. Now it's time to develop the detail window object classes.

◀ See "Triggering Windows Events," p. 180

You need two detail windows: one for Product and one for Customer. (The Employee business object doesn't require one because the detail is shown on the Employee Search window.) The good news is the two detail windows appear to have exactly the same requirements, so you'll be able to develop one detail window object class and then inherit from it to develop the two production detail windows.

You can develop the w_ma_detail window object class by inheriting from w_ma_base. You then add what is specific to this object class. Add a DataWindow control, which will hold the detail DataWindow objects in the descendants. Next, add the script to the ue_resize_dw event to size the DataWindow to use the maximum amount of window space available.

You have one final task. In this case, you will want the detail windows to display only the record the user selected. That means your detail DataWindow objects will have a retrieval argument. But how will the detail window know which record to retrieve? To meet this requirement, change your u_str_open_window structure to include two retrieval arguments: one that's a long data type, and one that's a string. You need both since you don't know what the descendant detail windows will need. When the detail window is opened (by the corresponding search window), you'll pass to the detail window the value it needs to retrieve the right record from the database. No

V

Techniques from the Pros

modification of the w_ma_base open event is needed to capture the retrieval arguments, as it captures the entire structure passed to it.

That's all there is to developing the detail ancestor object class, which is shown in figure 19.8. Now you can develop your two detail windows by inheriting from this class.

Fig. 19.8
The w_ma_detail window object class.

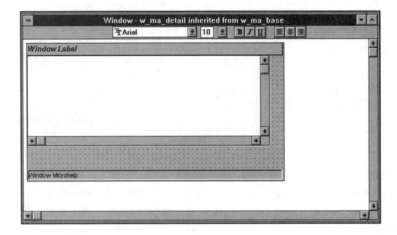

w_m_product_detail

◄ See "Specifying Retrieval Arguments," p. 285

The requirements for the Product detail window are very straightforward. Simply display a detail of the record selected in the corresponding search window. First you develop the Product detail DataWindow object. This DataWindow object needs a retrieve argument so you can retrieve only the record you want. Since the unique key for the product table is the product ID, you make a retrieval argument of type number.

You can develop the w_m_product_detail object class by inheriting from w_ma_detail. Then you associate the new DataWindow object with the window's DataWindow control. You can add script to the ue_addl_open event to make the DataWindow read-only and to set the transaction object. Next, you add script to the ue_post_open event to retrieve the record from the database by using the retrieve_arg_long element in the u_str_open_window structure passed to the window upon opening.

To implement the w_m_product_detail object class, you modify the ue_detail event in the w_m_product_search class to open an instance of the detail window, passing it the product ID of the selected record to be used as the retrieve argument for the detail data window. You now have a detail window for Product as shown in figure 19.9.

> **Note**
>
> The w_ma_base object class has an event named "ue_post_open" which is fired from the window's open event using the PostEvent function. The significance of this is that the event is placed at the end of the event queue, because it is posted rather than triggered. Therefore, the window finishes painting before the ue_post_open event fires. By placing the DataWindow retrieve function in this event, you can realize a gain in what is often termed *perceived performance*. The user sees the window before the record is retrieved, rather than after.

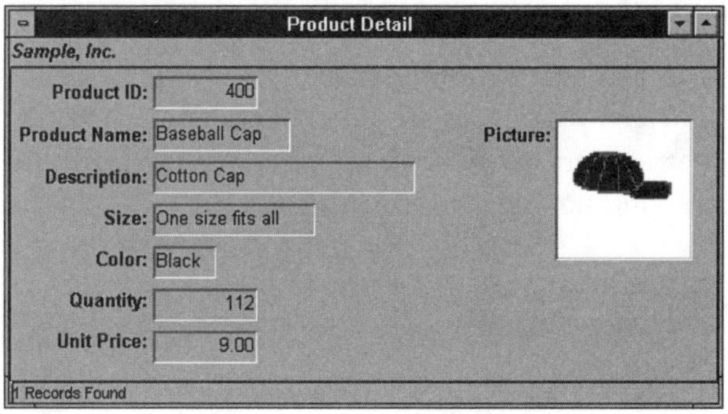

Fig. 19.9
w_m_product_detail window object class in action.

V

Techniques from the Pros

w_m_customer_detail

The requirements for the Customer detail window are exactly the same as those of the Product detail window. You need to follow the same steps to develop it:

1. Develop the detail DataWindow object.

2. Develop the new window object class by inheriting from w_ma_detail.

3. Associate the DataWindow object with the DataWindow control.

4. Add the required powerscript to w_m_customer_detail and w_m_customer_search.

The resulting w_m_customer_detail is shown in action in figure 19.10.

Fig. 19.10

w_m_customer_detail window object class in action.

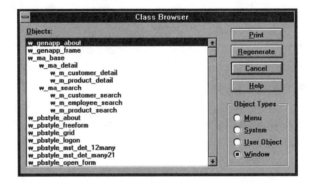

Examining the Results

◄ See "Browsing Class Hierarchies," p. 345

And you're done! As figure 19.11 illustrates, you now have a fully developed window class hierarchy that contains both virtual and production object classes. Because you were careful to develop the virtual classes, they're not specific to the application you were working on. They're fully reusable on other projects.

Fig. 19.11

The window class hierarchy for our case study project, showing the hierarchy we just built.

Do you see opportunities for more reusability? Perhaps the search/detail window class developed for w_m_employee_search has the potential to be a made into a virtual class of its own named w_ma_search_detail. The w_m_employee_search window would then be inherited from it, as would other windows requiring the same kind of functionality.

Inheritance is a powerful tool in the set of object-oriented features in PowerBuilder. The productivity gain you'll get from building reusable object classes will far outweigh the effort required to build them.

Chapter 20

Using dwShareData Functions

by   David J. O'Hearn

Fast development! Fast development! Fast development! This is arguably the most important reason for using PowerBuilder to create Windows applications. PowerBuilder has so many features and techniques that help speed up development that it's easy to miss some of the lesser known ones. The dwShareData function is one of these lesser known functions, but it is definitely worth the time to learn to use it.

In this chapter, you will learn to:

- Share two or more windows using the dwShareData function

- Share drop-down child DataWindows

- Share DataWindows with different formats and displaying different fields

- Allow multiple DataWindows to share current and selected rows

- Switch shared DataWindows

- Share summary and detail DataWindows, and report DataWindows

Understanding dwShareData Functions

There are actually two dwSharedata functions: dwShareData, which allows DataWindow control objects to share the same data; and dwShareDataOff, which causes the DataWindow control objects to stop sharing data. When sharing DataWindow controls, the primary DataWindow shares its data buffers (primary, delete, and filter) with the secondary DataWindow. Any function calls on the secondary DataWindow that change the data (for example, Retrieve, SetItem) will affect the primary DataWindow's data buffers and will appear in both DataWindows. If initial field values, a sort order, or filter statements are set in the DataWindow painter for the secondary DataWindow, they are ignored. Both DataWindows must have result sets from their data source. This means that the same number of fields must be selected in each data source and each field in the select list must have the same field type and length. For example, Emp_ID could be selected in one DataWindow and SSN in another. These DataWindows could share if both Emp_ID and SSN are defined as Numeric(9), but if Emp_ID was Numeric(10) and SSN was Numeric(9) they could not share. Other features, such as Where clauses in SQL and retrieval arguments, can also be different.

Syntax-at-a-Glance

```
dwprimary.dwShareData( dwsecondary )
DataWindowName.dwShareDataOff(  )
```

dwShareData function is used in PowerBuilder scripts to share data between two or more DataWindows. dwprimary and dwsecondary must be DataWindows, and their data source result sets must match. dwsecondary has no data buffers, but points to dwprimary's data buffers.

dwShareDataOff function causes the DataWindow DataWindowName to stop sharing. DataWindowName can be the dwprimary or dwsecondary DataWindow.

Understanding the Benefits of Using dwShareData

The benefit of sharing DataWindows is that they can have completely different formats. This allows the same data to be displayed and/or edited in many different ways. Data can be shared between tabular and freeform formats, summary and detail DataWindows, display and printed reports, and even grids and graphs. The DataWindows also can appear on the same window or different windows (as long as both windows exist). Costly retrieves or tedious coding to move data from one DataWindow to another can be avoided.

Examining Some Working Examples

To illustrate the benefits of the dwShareData functions, some examples from a sample application will be explained. Even with these simple examples, it is apparent that the dwShareData functions can be a useful and innovative tool to PowerBuilder developers and can help create more efficient and effective applications.

Example #1: Sharing Like DataWindows

Figure 20.1 is an example of the same DataWindow object being displayed in two DataWindow controls on the same main window. The upper DataWindow control (dw_data) is the primary, and the lower DataWindow control (dw_alternate) is the secondary. Because both controls use the same DataWindow object, they meet the criteria for having the same result set. Both DataWindows share the same data, so all the data displayed is the same (except for the Department field, which will be explained later in this chapter).

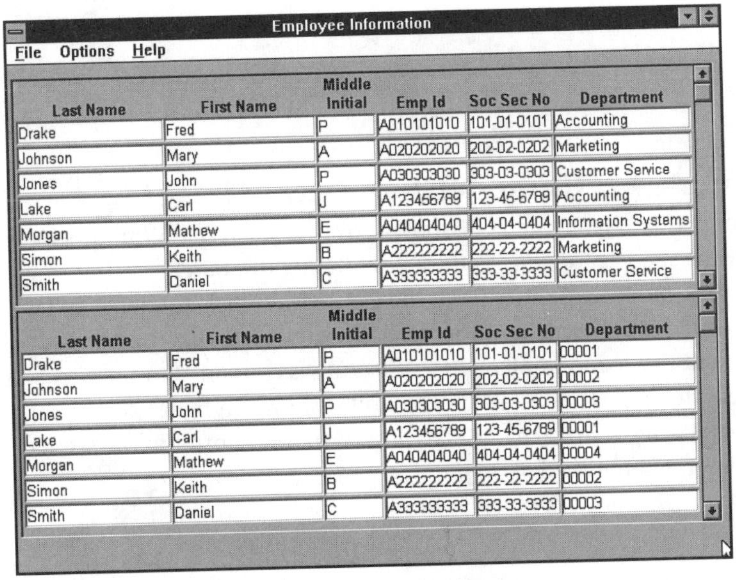

Fig. 20.1
Two DataWindow controls sharing the same data buffers display the same data. The Department field doesn't match because the drop-down child DataWindow that populates this field has not been shared from the primary DataWindow to the secondary.

The code to populate this window is contained in the open event of the main window (w_employee), and displayed in figure 20.2. First the transaction object is set for the primary DataWindow (dw_data), and then the dwShareData function is used to share the secondary DataWindow (dw_alternate) with the primary. When the retrieve function executes for the primary, both DataWindows are populated.

> **Note**
>
> In figure 20.2, the dwShareData function could also be coded after the retrieve function without changing the results. Only a slight timing difference might be noticeable when first displaying the DataWindows.

Fig. 20.2

The open event for w_employee shows how DataWindow dw_alternate is populated by sharing data with dw_data.

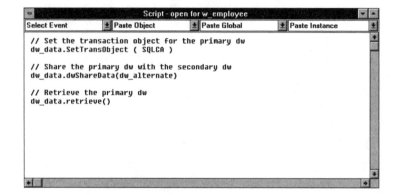

```
// Set the transaction object for the primary dw
dw_data.SetTransObject ( SQLCA )

// Share the primary dw with the secondary dw
dw_data.dwShareData(dw_alternate)

// Retrieve the primary dw
dw_data.retrieve()
```

Example #2: Using dwShareDataOff

The next example, figure 20.3, shows how the same DataWindows looks when the sharing function is turned off. Using dwShareDataOff is often unnecessary, because the sharing of the DataWindows is usually ended when the Window that contains either DataWindow is closed. The one coding statement needed to implement this feature is contained in the clicked event of menu item m_TurnDataShareOff, and is shown in figure 20.4. Changing the DataWindow from the primary DataWindow control to the secondary achieves the same results.

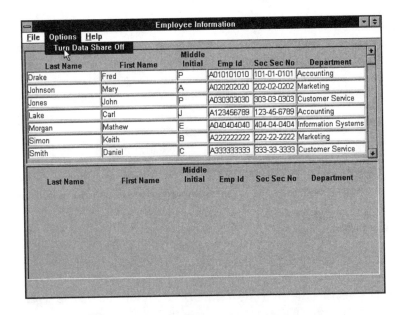

Fig. 20.3
This is what
you see when
DataWindow
sharing is turned
off.

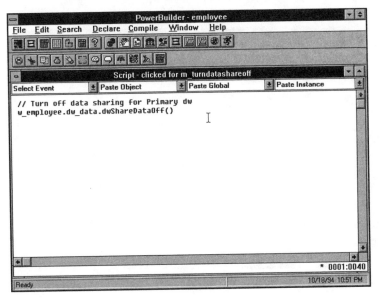

Fig. 20.4
The dwShareData
function is coded
in the clicked
event of the
m_TurnDataShareOff
menu item.

V

Techniques from the Pros

Example #3: Sharing Drop-Down Child DataWindows

As mentioned earlier, the department field does not appear to match in the two shared DataWindows in figure 20.1. This occurs because the department field is defined as a drop-down child DataWindow. When the primary DataWindow is retrieved, the drop-down child DataWindow is automatically retrieved from another table, and the department code is replaced with the department name. Unfortunately, when the DataWindows are shared, the drop-down child DataWindows are not shared automatically.

To remedy this, you add more code to the open event of the w_employee window to share the drop-down child DataWindows as seen in figure 20.5. First, two temporary variables of type DataWindowChild must be created, one for the drop-down child DataWindow in each DataWindow. The next two new statements assign the DataWindowChild handles to the temporary variables, using the GetDataWindowChild function. The last new statement is a dwShareData function that shares the child DataWindows. Figure 20.6 shows how sharing the drop-down child DataWindows makes the department fields for both DataWindows contain the department name.

Fig. 20.5

The open event of w_employee has been modified to share the drop-down child DataWindows.

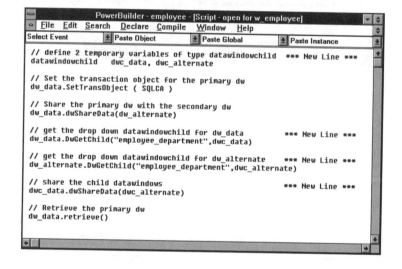

```
PowerBuilder - employee - [Script - open for w_employee]
 File  Edit  Search  Declare  Compile  Window  Help

Select Event        ± Paste Object     ± Paste Global    ± Paste Instance ±

// define 2 temporary variables of type datawindowchild  *** New Line ***
datawindowchild   dwc_data, dwc_alternate

// Set the transaction object for the primary dw
dw_data.SetTransObject ( SQLCA )

// Share the primary dw with the secondary dw
dw_data.dwShareData(dw_alternate)

// get the drop down datawindowchild for dw_data      *** New Line ***
dw_data.DwGetChild("employee_department",dwc_data)

// get the drop down datawindowchild for dw_alternate  *** New Line ***
dw_alternate.DwGetChild("employee_department",dwc_alternate)

// share the child datawindows                        *** New Line ***
dwc_data.dwShareData(dwc_alternate)

// Retrieve the primary dw
dw_data.retrieve()
```

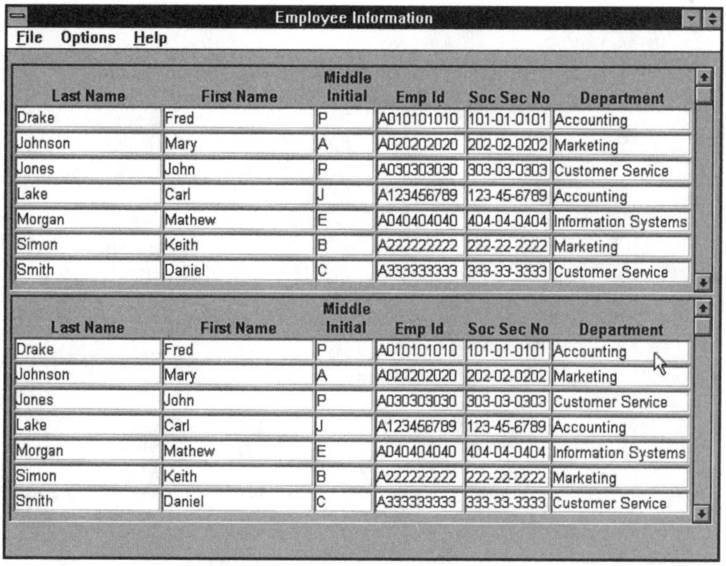

Fig. 20.6
The department field on both DataWindows contains the department name.

Example #4: Sharing DataWindows with Different Fields

In the next example, the sample application is changed by using different DataWindows in the shared DataWindow control objects. In figure 20.7, dw_alternate now displays a new DataWindow (d_employee_alternate), which has some different fields than the original DataWindow (d_employee_basic). Even though these two DataWindows display different data, they can still share the same data buffers because they use identical data source SQL. All the fields from both DataWindows are added to the data source SQL, and then only the desired fields are displayed. Figure 20.8 shows the SQL statement used by both DataWindows.

Note

To create a DataWindow that uses only part of the fields selected in the data source, simply delete those fields that should not be displayed. In the DataWindow painter, right-click on the field to display the pop-up menu and then choose **D**elete.

Fig. 20.7
Shared
DataWindows can
display like data in
different formats.

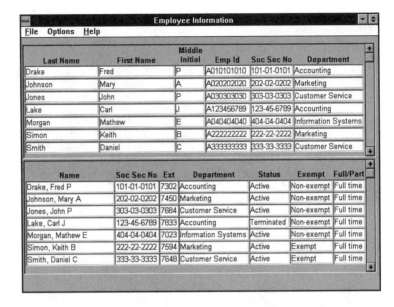

Fig. 20.8
This is the
SQL source
used by both
DataWindows. All
fields needed on
both are selected.

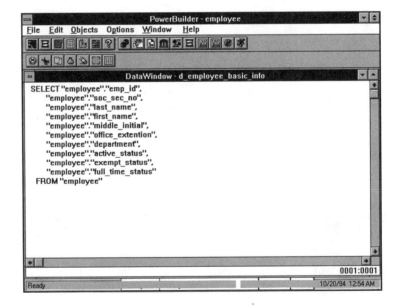

Note

When sharing many DataWindows, it is often necessary to make the same changes to the data source SQL on several DataWindows. One way to speed up this job is to make the modifications to one data source SQL, and then convert to SQL syntax using the menu option Convert to Syntax. Once converted, it can then be copied to the Clipboard and pasted in the other DataWindows data source SQL painters. The other data source SQL painters must also be converted to SQL syntax before pasting the new SQL. If desired, it can then be converted back to graphic mode.

Example #5: Sharing Row Settings

Shared DataWindows can have different current row and selected row settings, and can scroll separately. These independent actions may be desirable in some cases, but there will also be instances when row settings should be shared. One method to accomplish this is to change the current row settings for each DataWindow in the other DataWindow's RowFocusChanged event. This allows either DataWindow to shadow row changes from the other.

Caution

Use care when coding RowFocusChanged events that call each other; a looping effect can occur between these events.

One way to code this is to use a window function like wf_share_row, shown in figure 20.9. This function is called from both DataWindows RowFocusChanged events. The current row is passed from the RowFocusChanged event into the parameter variable (passed_row). The current row and selected row (highlighted) from both DataWindows are compared to the value of passed_row, and then changed if they do not match. This causes DataWindow row changes to shadow each other, giving the appearance of sharing row settings.

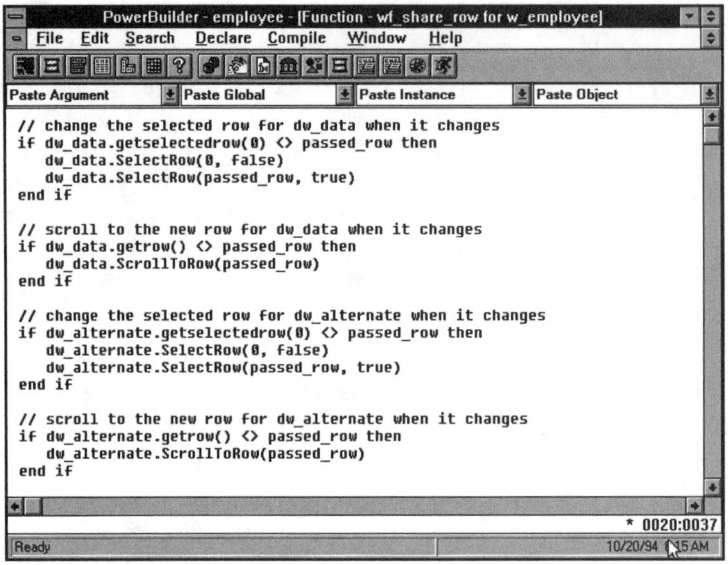

Fig. 20.9

wf_share_row is a window function of w_employee that keeps dw_data and dw_alternate on the same row.

```
┌─────────────────────────────────────────────────────────────────────┐
│ ▭       PowerBuilder - employee - [Function - wf_share_row for w_employee]  ▼ ▲│
│ ▭  File  Edit  Search  Declare  Compile  Window  Help                     ▲│
│ ┌──────────────────────────────────────────────────────────────────┐    │
│ │▐▌▐▌▐▌▐▌▐▌▐▌ ?│ ▐▌▐▌▐▌▐▌▐▌▐▌▐▌▐▌▐▌▐▌                              │    │
│ ├──────────────────┬──────────────┬────────────────┬──────────────┐│    │
│ │Paste Argument    ±│Paste Global  ±│Paste Instance  ±│Paste Object  ±││  ±│
│ ├──────────────────┴──────────────┴────────────────┴──────────────┤│  ▲│
│ │ // change the selected row for dw_data when it changes            ││   │
│ │ if dw_data.getselectedrow(0) <> passed_row then                   ││   │
│ │    dw_data.SelectRow(0, false)                                    ││   │
│ │    dw_data.SelectRow(passed_row, true)                            ││   │
│ │ end if                                                            ││   │
│ │                                                                   ││   │
│ │ // scroll to the new row for dw_data when it changes              ││   │
│ │ if dw_data.getrow() <> passed_row then                            ││   │
│ │    dw_data.ScrollToRow(passed_row)                                ││   │
│ │ end if                                                            ││   │
│ │                                                                   ││   │
│ │ // change the selected row for dw_alternate when it changes       ││   │
│ │ if dw_alternate.getselectedrow(0) <> passed_row then              ││   │
│ │    dw_alternate.SelectRow(0, false)                               ││   │
│ │    dw_alternate.SelectRow(passed_row, true)                       ││   │
│ │ end if                                                            ││   │
│ │                                                                   ││   │
│ │ // scroll to the new row for dw_alternate when it changes         ││   │
│ │ if dw_alternate.getrow() <> passed_row then                       ││   │
│ │    dw_alternate.ScrollToRow(passed_row)                           ││   │
│ │ end if                                                            ││  ▼│
│ ├──────────────────────────────────────────────────────────────────┤│   │
│ │←│                                                               │→││   │
│ │                                                    *  0020:0037    │    │
│ ├───────────────────────────────────────────────┬──────────────────┤    │
│ │Ready                                           │  10/20/94  ⏰5 AM │    │
│ └───────────────────────────────────────────────┴──────────────────┘    │
└─────────────────────────────────────────────────────────────────────┘
```

Example #6: Switching Shared DataWindows

The next change to the sample application is to show only one DataWindow at a time, and to enable switching between them. The lower DataWindow control is moved under the upper, and menu items are added to control the switching. Figures 20.10 and 20.11 demonstrate how the switching of the DataWindows is done. Figure 20.12 displays the code in the clicked event of the m_SwitchToAlternate menu item that makes the switch. The m_SwitchToBasic menu item has similar code that switches back. By expanding on this idea, many shared DataWindows with varying formats and fields could share the same window space as well as the same buffer space.

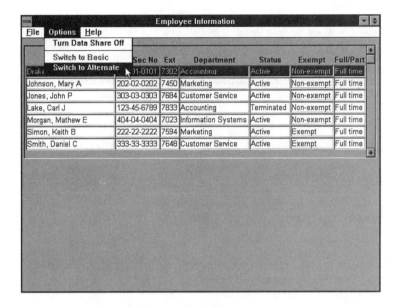

Fig. 20.10
By choosing
Options, Switch
to Alternate, the
DataWindow
d_employee_alternate
is displayed.

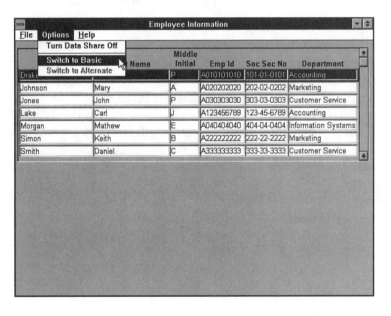

Fig. 20.11
By choosing
Options, Switch
to Basic, the
DataWindow
d_employee_basic
returns.

V

Techniques from the Pros

Fig. 20.12
The DataWindow
function
SetPosition causes
the control
dw_alternate to be
displayed over
dw_data. The
enable attributes
are set to make it
more user friendly.

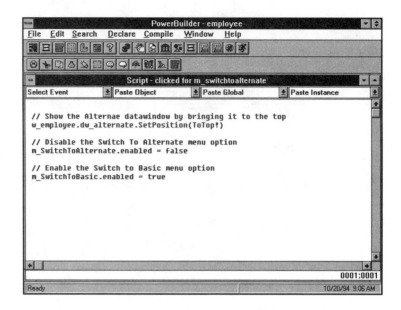

Example #7: Sharing Summary and Detail DataWindows

The next example shows how a summary window with multiple rows can be
shared with a detail window that displays only one row. In figure 20.13, a
new DataWindow control object (dw_detail) is added to the w_employee
window and is shared with dw_data in the open event. The DataWindow
attached to dw_detail (d_employee_detail) is designed so that only one row of
data can fit in the DataWindow control at a time. Headers, footers, and vertical scroll bars are omitted. More code is added to the wf_share_row function
so that clicking on a different row in dw_data will cause dw_detail to display
the detail data for that row. Figure 20.14 shows the new code added to the
wf_share_row function.

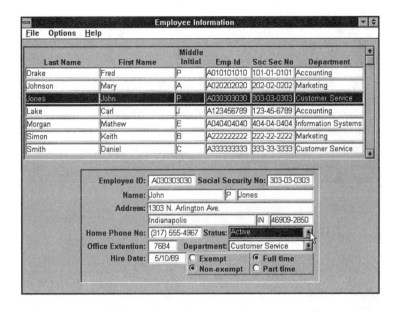

Fig. 20.13
DataWindow
d_employee_detail
displays the detail
for the selected
row in the
summary
DataWindow.

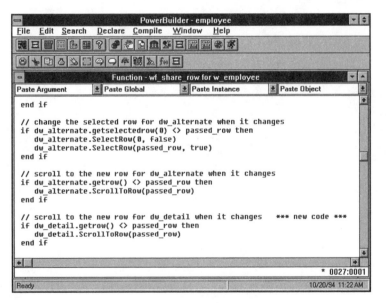

Fig. 20.14
New statements
are added to
wf_share_row to
keep dw_detail on
the same row as
dw_data and
dw_alternate.

V

Techniques from the Pros

Example #8: Sharing Report DataWindows

The last example, sharing a displayed DataWindow with a DataWindow used to print a report, might be the most frequently used method of the dwShareData function. This method is very useful when a report needs different formats for the displayed and printed copies. It is also useful when several different reports are created from basically the same data. An invisible DataWindow control (dw_print) has been added to the w_employee window. The m_PrintReport menu item has also been added, and the clicked event for it contains the code to share the dw_print DataWindow control with the dw_data DataWindow control. The report is then printed, and a dwShareDataOff function is used to turn off the sharing. Figure 20.15 shows a display of the dw_print DataWindow in report format, and figure 20.16 contains the code from the clicked event of the m_PrintReport menu item.

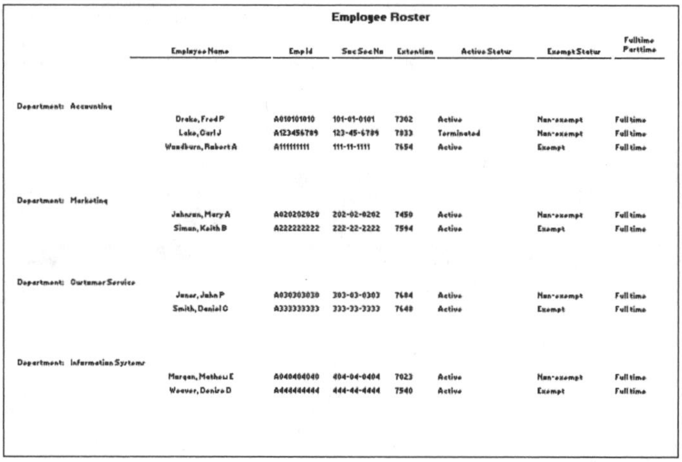

Fig. 20.15

This print preview of DataWindow d_employee_report is an example of a shared report DataWindow.

							Fulltime
	Employee Name	Emp Id	Soc Soc No	Extension	Active Status	Exempt Status	Parttime
Department: Accounting							
	Drake, Fred P	A010101010	101-01-0101	7362	Active	Non-exempt	Full time
	Lake, Carl J	A123456789	123-45-6789	7833	Terminated	Non-exempt	Full time
	Woodburn, Robert A	A111111111	111-11-1111	7654	Active	Exempt	Full time
Department: Marketing							
	Johnson, Mary A	A020202020	202-02-0202	7459	Active	Non-exempt	Full time
	Simon, Keith B	A222222222	222-22-2222	7594	Active	Exempt	Full time
Department: Customer Service							
	Jones, John P	A030303030	303-03-0303	7684	Active	Non-exempt	Full time
	Smith, Daniel G	A333333333	333-33-3333	7649	Active	Exempt	Full time
Department: Information Systems							
	Morgan, Mathew E	A040404040	404-04-0404	7623	Active	Non-exempt	Full time
	Weaver, Denise D	A444444444	444-44-4444	7540	Active	Exempt	Full time

Employee Roster

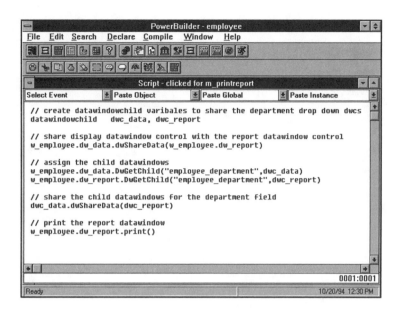

Fig. 20.16

The clicked event of menu item m_PrintReport shares and prints the d_employee_report DataWindow.

Part VI

References

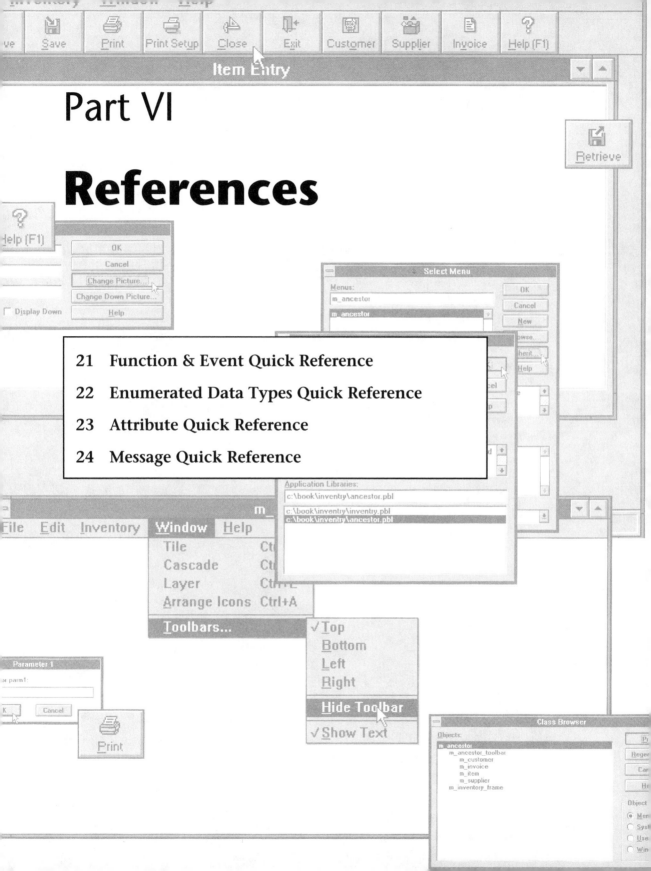

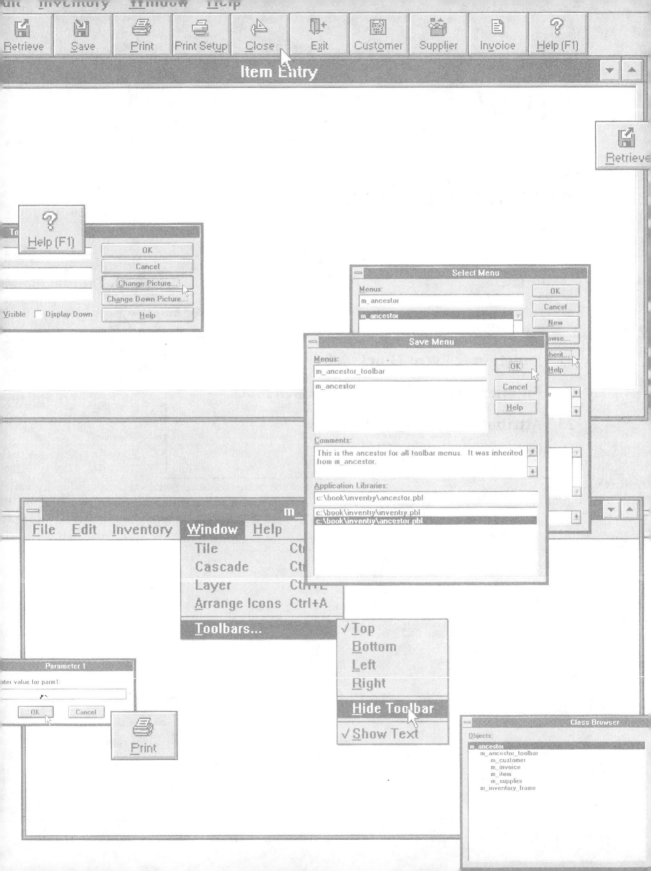

Chapter 21

Function & Event Quick Reference

PowerBuilder functions make coding your PowerScript easier. If you need to complete some task in your application, chances are that a PowerBuilder function exists that can complete your task for you.

This chapter deals with all the functions used inside PowerBuilder, starting with stand-alone functions that can be used in any PowerScript, and moving on to functions specific to an object or control.

> **Note**
>
> This reference chapter doesn't provide examples. If you need an example of a function after looking at the description, refer to the on-line help provided with PowerBuilder.

Stand-alone Functions

Stand-alone functions are listed alphabetically in the Function Reference manual that comes with PowerBuilder. For this quick reference, they are listed by function. Either will be helpful if you know the name of the function you want. If you browse through the functions by type and don't know the name of the function you want to use, this quick reference will be useful.

Date Functions

Dates can be difficult to process in many computer languages. PowerBuilder has added many date functions to help out. Date functions are used to set and retrieve dates and date information.

VI

References

Tip
If you can't find the function you need listed in its category, try looking in the datatype conversion functions.

> **Note**
>
> Some date functions are listed in the data type conversion function group later in this chapter.

Day(date)	Returns the day of the month
DayName(date)	Returns the name of the day of the week
DayNumber(date)	Returns a number representing the day of the week (for example, Sunday is 1 and Wednesday is 4)
DaysAfter(date1, date2)	Returns the number of days one date occurs after another
Month(date)	Returns the month (an integer between 1 and 12)
RelativeDate(date, n)	Returns the date that occurs a specified number of days after a date
Today( )	Returns the current system date
Year(date)	Returns the year

Dynamic Data Exchange (DDE) Functions

DDE (Dynamic Data Exchange) is a Windows convention that lets Windows programs "talk" or send data back and forth. DDE Server functions allow your program to be supplied with data from another program. DDE Client functions allow your program to supply another program with data.

DDE Client Functions

CloseChannel(handle, windowhandle)	Closes a channel to a DDE server application that was opened by the OpenChannel function.
ExecRemote(command, applname, topicname) ExecRemote(command, handle, windowhandle)	Asks a server application to execute a command. This function has two formats.
GetDataDDE(string)	Obtains the new data from the hot-linked server application.
GetDataDDEOrigin(appl, topic, item)	Determines the origin of data that has arrived from a hot-linked server application.
GetRemote(location, target, applname, topicname) GetRemote(location, target, handle, windowhandle)	Asks a server application for data. This function has two formats.

DDE Client Functions

OpenChannel(appl, topic, windowhandle)	Opens a channel to a DDE server application.
RespondRemote(Boolean)	Indicates to the server whether the command or data was acceptable to the client.
SetRemote(location, value, applname, topicname) SetRemote(location, value, handle, windowhandle)	Asks a server application to set an item to a specific value. This function has two formats.
StartHotLink(location, appl, topic)	Initiates a hot link to a server application so PowerBuilder is notified immediately of specified data changes in the server application.
StopHotLink(location, appl, topic)	Ends the hot link with a server application.

DDE Server Functions

GetCommandDDE(string)	Obtains the command the client application has sent.
GetCommandDDEOrigin(appl)	Determines what client application sent the command.
GetDataDDE(string)	Obtains data the client application has sent.
GetDataDDEOrigin(appl, topic,item)	Determines which client application sent the data.
RespondRemote(Boolean)	Indicates to the client whether the command or data was acceptable to the server.
SetDataDDE(string, appl, topic, item)	Sends data to the client application.
StartServerDDE(windowname, appl, topic, item)	Causes PowerBuilder to begin acting as a server.
StopServerDDE(windowname, appl, topic)	Causes PowerBuilder to stop acting as a server.

Numeric (Mathematical) Functions

Numeric functions perform complex mathematical equations. In addition to using these functions in PowerScript, the DataWindow painter uses the following functions in computed fields, filters, and validation rules.

Abs(number)	Obtains the absolute value of a number.
Ceiling(num)	Obtains the smallest whole number that is greater than or equal to a specified number.
Cos(num)	Obtains the cosine of an angle. The angle is measured in radians.
Exp(num)	Obtains e raised to the power of x.
Fact(num)	Obtains the factorial of x.
Int(num)	Obtains the largest whole number that is less than or equal to a specified number.
Log(num)	Obtains the natural logarithm (base e) of a number.
LogTen(num)	Obtains the decimal logarithm (base 10) of a number.
*Max(num1, num2)	Obtains the larger of two numbers.
*Min(num1, num2)	Obtains the smaller of two numbers.
Mod(num)	Obtains the modulus of two numbers (the remainder after dividing the first number into the other number).
Pi( )	Obtains pi (3.14...) times a number.
Rand( )	Obtains a random whole number (between 1 and a specified number).
Randomize( )	Initializes the random number generator.
Round(num)	Obtains a number rounded to a number of decimal places.
Sign(num)	Obtains a number (-1, 0, or 1) indicating the sign of a number.
Sin(num)	Obtains the sine of an angle. The angle is measured in radians.
*Sqrt(num)	Obtains the square root of a number.
Tan(num)	Obtains the tangent of an angle. The angle is measured in radians.
Truncate(num)	Obtains a number truncated to a specified number of decimal places.

Min, Max, and Sqrt are not valid in the DataWindow painter for computed fields, filters, and validation rules.

Print Functions

Many objects and controls provide their own print functions. However, sometimes you may want to send the printer some information developed in PowerScript. Print functions set up print jobs to handle such tasks.

Print(printjobnumber, string) Print(printjobnumber, string, tab) Print(printjobnumber, tab, string) Print(printjobnumber, tab, string, tab)	Prints a string in the current font. In all but one form of this function, you can control the spacing in the print area.
PrintBitmap(printjobnumber, bitmap, x, y, width, height)	Prints a specified bitmap image at a specified location in the print area.
PrintCancel(jobnum)	Cancels printing.
PrintClose(jobnum)	Closes the print job and sends the page to the printer.
PrintDefineFont(printjobnumber, fontnumber, facename, height, weight, fontpitch, fontfamily, italic, underline)	Defines a font for the print job. PowerBuilder supports eight fonts for each print job.
PrintLine(printjobnumber, x1, y1, x2, y2, thickness)	Prints a line of a specified thickness at a specified location.
PrintOpen(jobname)	Starts the print job and assigns it a print job number.
PrintOval(printjobnumber, x, y, width, height, thickness)	Prints an oval (or circle) with a specified line thickness at a specified location.
PrintPage(jobnum)	Sends the current page to the printer and sets up a new blank page.
PrintRect(printjobnumber, x, y, width, height, thickness)	Prints a rectangle with a specified line thickness at a specified location.
PrintRoundRect(printjobnumber, x, y, width, height, xradius, yradius, thickness)	Prints a round rectangle with a specified line thickness at a specified location.
PrintSend(jobnum, string, zerochar)	Sends a specified string directly to the printer.
PrintSetFont(jobnum, fontnumber)	Sets the current print job font to one of the defined fonts.
PrintSetSpacing(jobnum, factor)	Sets the spacing factor that will be used to determine the space between lines.
PrintSetup( )	Calls up the Printer Setup dialog box for the printer driver.

(continues)

VI

References

PrintText(jobnum, string, x, y, fontnumber)	Prints specified text at a specified location.
PrintWidth(jobnum, string)	Returns the width (in 1/1000 inches) of the specified string in the current font.
PrintX(jobnum)	Returns the X coordinate of the cursor.
PrintY(jobnum)	Returns the Y coordinate of the cursor.

Miscellaneous Functions

The following functions don't fit into a specific grouping, but can be useful nonetheless.

Beep(num)	Causes the computer to beep a specified number of times.
Clipboard(string)	Obtains the contents of the Microsoft Windows 3.x Clipboard.
CommandParm( )	Retrieves the parameter string, if any, that was specified when the application was run.
Cpu( )	Obtains the number of seconds of CPU time the current application has used.
DBHandle(transobj)	Returns the DBMS specific interface handle.
Idle(num)	Sends an Idle event if no user activity (for example, a keystroke or mouse movement) has occurred for a specified period of time.
IsDate(string)	Determines whether the specified string contains a valid date.
IsNull(variable)	Determines whether the argument is NULL.
IsNumber(string)	Determines whether the specified string contains a number.
IsTime(string)	Determines whether the specified string contains a valid time.
KeyDown(keycode)	Determines whether the specified key is pressed.
LowerBound(array,n)	Determines the lower bound of a dimension of an array.
Match(string, pattern)	Compares a string to a text pattern and determines whether or not they match.

MessageBox(title, text, icon, button, default)	Displays a box containing a message.
ProfileInt(filename, section, key, default)	Obtains an integer from a specified profile file.
ProfileString(filename, section, key, default)	Obtains a string from a specified profile file.
Restart( )	Stops the execution of all scripts, closes all windows, commits and disconnects from the database, and restarts the application.
RGB(red, green, blue)	Determines the long value that represents a specified color.
Run(string, windowstate)	Executes (runs) a specified program.
SetNull(variable)	Sets a specified variable to NULL.
SetPointer(type)	Sets the pointer to a specified type (Arrow, Cross, Beam, HourGlass, SizeNESW, SizeNS, SizeNWSE, SizeWE, or UpArrow).
SetProfileString(filename, section, key, value)	Writes a value to a specified profile file.
ShowHelp(helpfile, helpcommand, typeid)	Provides access to the Microsoft Windows 3.x based help system that you created for your PowerBuilder application.
SignalError( )	Causes a SystemError event at the application level.
Timer(num, windowname)	Sends a timer event to the active window.
UpperBound(array, n)	Determines the upper bound of a dimension of an array.

String Functions

PowerBuilder excels in string handling with its string functions. In the DataWindow painter, use the following string functions in computed fields, filters, and validation rules:

Asc(string)	The ASCII value of the first character of a string.
Char(num)	The character that corresponds to an ASCII value.
Fill(string, num)	A string of a specified length filled with occurrences of a specified string.
Left(string, num)	A specified number of characters from a string, starting with the first character.

(continues)

VI

References

Len(string)	The length of a string.
Lower(string)	A copy of a specified string with all uppercase letters converted to lowercase.
Left(string, num)	A specified number of characters from the start of a specified string.
LeftTrim(string)	A copy of a specified string with leading blanks deleted.
Mid(string, start, length)	A string containing a specified number of characters copied (starting at a specified position) from a specified string.
Pos(string1, string2, start)	The starting position of a string within a specified string.
Replace(string1, start, len, string2)	A copy of a specified string in which a specified number of characters, starting with a specified character, have been replaced with characters from another specified string.
Right(string, num)	A specified number of characters from the end of a specified string.
RightTrim(string)	A copy of a specified string with trailing blanks deleted.
Space(num)	A string of a specified length filled with spaces.
Trim(string)	A string with leading and trailing blanks deleted.
Upper(string)	A copy of a specified string with all lowercase letters converted to uppercase.

File Functions

File functions access any type of file on your system.

FileClose(filenum)	Closes a file.
FileDelete(filename)	Deletes a file.
FileExists(filename)	Determines whether a file exists.
FileLength(filename)	Obtains the length of a file.
FileOpen(filename, filemode, fileaccess, filelock, writemode)	Opens a file and returns a file number.
FileRead(filenum, buffer)	Reads a file into buffer.
FileSeek(file#, position, origin)	Seeks to a position in a file.
FileWrite(filenum, buffer)	Writes to a file.

Time Functions

Time functions return times and time information.

> **Note**
>
> Some time functions are listed in the data type conversion function group later in this chapter.

Hour(time)	The hour (an integer between 0 and 23).
Minute(time)	The minutes (an integer between 0 and 59).
Now( )	The current system time.
RelativeTime(time1, numsecs)	The time that occurs a specified number of seconds after a specified time.
Second(time)	The seconds of a specified time (an integer between 0 and 59).
SecondsAfter(time1, time2)	The number of seconds one time is after another.

Data Type Conversion Functions

Data type conversion functions convert from one data type to another.

> **Note**
>
> Numeric to numeric conversions are listed in the numeric functions. Data type conversion functions convert the entire meaning of one data type to another. Functions like int(number) truncate the value of the original number.

Char(variable)	A blob, integer, or string as a char.
*Date(datetime)	The date portion of a DateTime value retrieved from the database.
*Date(string)	A valid date if the string argument is a valid date.
*Date(year, month, day)	A date based on the integer values for year, month, and day.
Dec(string)	The contents of a string as a decimal.
Double(string)	The contents of a string as a double.

(continues)

VI

References

Integer(string)	The contents of a string as an integer.
Long(string)	The contents of a string as a long.
Real(string)	The contents of a string as a real.
String(date, format) String(datetime, format) String(number, format) String(string, textpattern) String(time, format)	A string containing the specified number formatted according to the argument or a string containing a date, time, or object name depending on the argument you enter in the function. The format or textpattern are optional variables that control the format of the new string.
Time(datetime)	The time portion of a DateTime value retrieved from the database.
Time(string)	Returns a valid time if the string argument is a valid time.
Time(hour, minute, second)	Returns a time based on the integer values for hour, minute, and second.

In the DataWindow painter, you can use the date conversion functions in computed fields, filters, and validation rules.

Object Functions

In addition to global functions that can be accessed by any PowerScript, PowerBuilder also includes object functions. These functions are accessed by listing the object name followed by a period and function name:

```
objectname.function(parameter)
```

Functions are specific to a particular object.

Functions Common to All Objects

All objects can access the following functions. Drawing objects, like Line and Oval, can't access the functions marked with an asterisk (*).

control.ClassName( )	Returns the name of the object or control.
*control.Drag(dragmode)	Starts or stops the dragging of an object. Dragmode is an enumerated data type of Begin!, End!, or Cancel!.
control.Hide( )	Hides an object if that object is showing.
control.Move(x, y)	Moves an object to new position relative to the parent window.

*control.PointerX( )	Moves an object to the left edge of a window in which an object is placed.
*control.PointerY( )	Returns the number of units from the top edge of a window in which an object is placed.
*control.PostEvent(event)	Triggers an event after the current function or event is complete. Event is either an enumerated data type or string.
control.Resize(width, height)	Adjusts an object to a new size and redraws the object.
*control.SetFocus( )	Sets focus to the object.
*control.SetPosition (position, preceding)	Sets the position in front to back order of an object in relation to other objects in a window. Position is an enumerated data type of Behind!, NotTopMost!, ToTop! ToBottom! and TopMost!. Preceding is an optional parameter listing the name of the object if Behind! is used for the position parameter.
*control.SetRedraw(boolean)	Sets the redraw status of redrawing every attribute change or not. The boolean variable is TRUE or FALSE.
control.Show( )	Shows an object if that object is hidden.
*control.TriggerEvent(event)	Triggers an event immediately. Event is either an enumerated data type or string.
control.TypeOf( )	Returns the type of object or control.

Drawing objects like Line, Oval, Rectangle, and RoundRectangle only can use the ClassName, Hide, Move, Resize, Show, and TypeOf functions.

Edit Functions

Edit functions are found in single line edits (SLE), multiline edits (MLE), drop-down list boxes (DDLB), edit masks (EM), and DataWindow (DW) controls. This table checks which control allows the use of each function.

> **Note**
>
> Some DDLB functions are also listed in the list box function section of this chapter.

Function Name	SLE	MLE	DDLB	EM	DW	Description
edit_name.CanUndo()	✓	✓		✓	✓	Returns a boolean TRUE or FALSE if the last edit can be undone.

(continues)

VI

References

Function Name	SLE	MLE	DDLB	EM	DW	Description
edit_name.Clear( )	✓	✓	✓	✓	✓	Deletes the selected text.
edit_name.Copy( )	✓	✓	✓	✓	✓	Puts the selected text in the Clipboard but does not delete (clear) it.
edit_name.Cut( )	✓	✓	✓	✓	✓	Deletes the selected text and places the text in the Clipboard.
edit_name.LineCount( )		✓		✓	✓	Returns the number of text lines.
edit_name.LineLength( )		✓		✓		Returns the length of the cursor line.
edit_name.Paste( )	✓	✓	✓	✓	✓	Puts the contents of the Clipboard at the cursor location.
edit_name.Position( )	✓	✓	✓	✓	✓	Returns the position of the cursor in the edit field.
edit_name.ReplaceText(string)	✓	✓	✓	✓	✓	Replaces the selected text with a string.
edit_name.Scroll(int)		✓		✓		Scrolls down (or up for negative numbers) a given number of lines.
edit_name.SelectedLength( )	✓	✓	✓	✓	✓	Returns the length of the selected string.
edit_name.SelectedLine( )		✓		✓	✓	Returns the line number where the selection is made.
edit_name.SelectedStart( )	✓	✓	✓	✓	✓	Returns the starting position of the selection.
edit_name.SelectedText( )	✓	✓	✓	✓	✓	Returns a string containing the selected text.
edit_name.SelectText (start, length)	✓	✓	✓	✓	✓	Selects text at a starting point for a given length.

Function Name	SLE	MLE	DDLB	EM	DW	Description
edit_name.TextLine( )	✓	✓	✓	✓	✓	Returns a string containing the line of text where the cursor currently is placed.
edit_name.Undo( )	✓	✓		✓	✓	Reverses the last edit.

List Box and Drop-Down List Box (DDLB) Functions

listbox.AddItem(string)	Adds the string to the bottom of a list box or DDLB.
listbox.DeleteItem(index)	Deletes the item referenced by index out of a list box or DDLB.
listbox.DirList(filespec, filetype, statictext)	Populates your list box or DDLB with a directory of files that match the filespec (for example *.pbl, *.ini, and so on) and filetype (0–Read/write files, 1–Read-only files, 2–Hidden files, 4–System files, 16–Subdirectories, 32–Archive (modified) files, 16384–Drives, 32768– Exclude read-write files from the list. Add the numbers together to combine file types. For instance, listing Read/write, Read-only, and System files would take a filetype of 3 (0+1+2 = 3)). Statictext is an optional parameter containing the name of the static text field where the directory will be displayed.
listbox.DirSelect(filename)	Retrieves the current selection of a list box or DDLB populated with DirList and places it in filename.
listbox.FindItem(string, index)	Returns the number of the string item. FindItem starts the search at a given index.
listbox.InsertItem(string, index)	Inserts an item string in your listbox before a given index.
listbox.Reset( )	Deletes all items from a listbox or a DDLB.
listbox.SelectItem(index) listbox.SelectItem(string, index)	Allows you to select an item in a list box indicated by either an index or a string and a starting search index.
*listbox.SelectedIndex( )	Returns the number of the selected item of a list box.
*listbox.SelectedItem( )	Returns a string containing the selected item of a list box.
*listbox.SetState(index, boolean)	Sets the state of a listbox item corresponding to an index. Requires a boolean variable of TRUE (high-lighted) or FALSE (unhighlighted).

VI

References

(continues)

*listbox.SetTop(index)	Places the item corresponding to an index at the top of a listbox.
*listbox.State(index)	Returns a boolean (TRUE or FALSE) indicating the state (highlighted or not highlighted) of the item in a list box that corresponds to the index.
listbox.Text(index)	Returns the text of an item in a list box or DDLB that corresponds to the index.
*listbox.Top( )	This returns the index (number) of the item at the top of a listbox. This item could be the first item or it could be a later item if the user scrolled down.
listbox.TotalItems( )	Returns the total number of items in a listbox or DDLB.
*listbox.TotalSelected( )	Returns the total number of items selected in a listbox.

Available only as a list box function and not as a drop-down list box function.

Graph Functions

Graph functions are used for graph objects. Some are also used for DataWindow graphs.

graph.grAddCategory(string)	Adds a category (denoted by a string) to a graph.
graph.grAddData(series, datavalue, categorylabel) scattergraph.grAddData (series, xvalue , yvalue)	Adds data to a series. Scattergraphs take the series number, an X coordinate, and a Y coordinate as parameters. Graphs that aren't scatter graphs take a series and a data value as parameters. In addition, you can pass an optional category label as a parameter to a non-scatter graph if you want a tick mark on the graph corresponding to the new data.
graph.grAddSeries(string)	Adds a series to the graph. The string parameter is the series name.
graph.grCategoryCount( ) *datawindow.grCategoryCount (control_name)	Counts the categories in a graph. If the graph is a datawindow control, the control name also must be passed.
graph.grCategoryName (category_number) *datawindow.grCategoryName (control_name, category_number)	Returns the category name of a category number. If grCategoryName is used on a DataWindow, the control name also must be passed.
graph.grClipboard() *datawindow.grClipboard (control_name)	Copies the graph control image to the Clipboard. If grClipboard is used on a DataWindow graph, the control name must also be passed.

graph.grDataCount(seriesname) *datawindow.grDataCount (control_name, seriesname)	Returns the number of data elements in a series. If grDataCount is used on a DataWindow graph, the control name must also be passed.
graph.grDataStyle	grDataStyle returns information about the color and pattern of a datapoint. If grDataStyle is used on a DataWindow graph, the control name must also be passed. Seriesnumber is the number of the series. Datapointnumber is the number of the data point.

Format 1

graph.grDataStyle(seriesnumber, datapointnumber, colortype, colorvariable) *datawindow.grDataStyle (control_name, seriesnumber, datapointnumber, colortype, colorvariable)	Colortype is an enumerated data type specifying the color type for which you want to obtain the color: • Background!—The background color • Foreground!—Text (fill color) • LineColor!—The color of the line • Shade!—Shade (shade applies only to graphics that are three-dimensional or have three-dimensional objects). The color is then stored in a long colorvariable.

Format 2

graph.grDataStyle(seriesnumber, datapointnumber, fillpatternvariable) *datawindow.grDataStyle (control_name, seriesnumber, datapointnumber, fillpatternvariable)	The fill pattern is stored in an enumerated fill pattern variable.

Format 3

graph.grDataStyle(seriesnumber, datapointnumber, linestyle) *datawindow.grDataStyle (control_name,seriesnumber, datapointnumber, linestyle)	The line style is stored in an enumerated line style variable.

Format 4

graph.grDataStyle(seriesnumber, datapointnumber, symbol) *datawindow.grDataStyle (control_name, seriesnumber, datapointnumber, symbol)	The symbol is stored in an enumerated variable of grSymbolType.
graph.grDeleteCategory(string)	Deletes the category name denoted from the string parameter from a graph.

(continues)

VI

References

graph.grDeleteData(seriesnumber, datapointnumber)	Deletes a datapoint from a series in a graph.
graph.grDeleteSeries(seriesname)	Deletes an entire series from a graph denoted by a passed series name.
graph.grFindCategory(categoryname) *datawindow.grFindCategory (control_name, categoryname)	Returns the number of the category name. If grFindCategory is used on a DataWindow graph, the control name must also be passed.
graph.grFindSeries(seriesname) *datawindow.grFindSeries (control_name, seriesname)	Returns the number of the series name. If grFindSeries is used on a DataWindow graph, the control name must also be passed.
graph.grGetData(seriesnumber, datapoint, datatype) *datawindow.grGetData (control_name, seriesnumber, datapoint, datatype)	Returns the data from the graph referenced by seriesnumber and datapoint. Datatype is an optional parameter used if the graph is a scattergraph. Use a grDataType enumerated variable to get the X or Y coordinate of the graph. If grGetData is used on a DataWindow graph, the control name must also be passed.
graph.grImportClipboard(startrow, endrow, startcolumn, endcolumn) *datawindow.grImportClipboard (startrow, endrow, startcolumn, endcolumn, dwstartcolumn)	Copies the contents of the Clipboard, beginning with startrow and startcolumn and ending with endrow and endcolumn, to datawindowname starting in column dwstartcolumn if grImportClipboard is used on a DataWindow Graph(s). No parameters are needed, and the default is assumed to be the whole Clipboard and dwStartColumn 1.
graph.grImportFile(filename, startrow,endrow, startcolumn)	Imports a file in TXT (tab separated) or DBF (dBase II or III) format into a graph. Startrow, endrow, and startcolumn are defaulted to be the entire file.
graph.grImportString (filename,startrow,endrow, startcolumn)	Imports a TAB delimited string into a graph. Startrow, endrow, and startcolumn are defaulted to be the entire file.
graph.grInsertCategory (categoryname, categorynumber)	Inserts a new category name before the given category number.
graph.grInsertData (seriesnumber, datapoint, datavalue, categorylabel)	Inserts a new datavalue before the given datapoint in a given series. If category label is specified, a tickmark is placed on the graph for this new data.
graph.grInsertSeries (seriesname, seriesnumber)	Inserts a new series name before the given series number.

graph.grModifyData (seriesnumber, datapoint, datavalue, categorylabel) scattergraph.grModifyData (seriesnumber, datapoint, xvalue, yvalue)	Changes a datavalue at the given datapoint in a given series in a non-scattergraph. If category label is specified, a tickmark is placed on the graph for this new data. In a scattergraph, you pass the series number, the datapoint, the new xvalue, and the new yvalue of the datapoint in your graph.
graph.grObjectAtPointer (seriesnumber, datapoint) *datawindow.grObjectAtPointer (control_name, seriesnumber, datapoint)	If the mouse pointer is pointing at the graph, grObjectAtPointer can tell where by returning the seriesnumber and the datapoint. If grObjectAtPointer is used on a DataWindow graph, the control name must also be passed.
graph.grReset(Graphresettype)	Deletes information from your graph. The grResetType enumerated data type specifying whether you want to delete only data values or all series and all data values: <ul><li>All!—Deletes all series, categories, and data</li><li>Category!—Deletes all categories and data</li><li>Data!—Deletes all data</li><li>Series!—Deletes all series and data</li></ul>
graph.grResetDataColors (seriesnumber, datapointnumber) *datawindow.grResetDataColors (control_name, seriesnumber, datapointnumber)	Resets the colors of a datapoint to the default color for a series set in grSetSeriesStyle. If grResetDataColors is used on a DataWindow graph, the control name must also be passed.
graph.grSaveAs(filename, saveastype, colheading) *datawindow.grSaveAs(control_name, filename, saveastype, colheading)	Saves the contents of a graph in a given type. Filename is a string containing the name of the file in which you want to save the contents. If you omit filename, PowerBuilder prompts the user for a file name. Saveastype is the format in which you want to save the graph data. The following enumerated data types are valid: <ul><li>CSV!—Comma separated values</li><li>Clipboard!—saves to the Clipboard</li><li>dBASE2!—dBASE-II format</li><li>dBASE3!—dBASE-III format</li><li>DIF!—Data Interchange format</li><li>Excel!—Microsoft Excel format</li><li>SQLInsert!—SQL syntax</li><li>SYLK!—Microsoft Multiplan format</li><li>Text!—(Default) Tab separated columns with a return at the end of each row</li><li>WKS!—Lotus 1-2-3 format</li><li>WK1!—Lotus 1-2-3 format</li></ul> Colheading is a boolean variable stating if the column heading will be saved. This is not valid for all data types. If grSaveAs is used on a DataWindow graph, the control name must also be passed.

VI

References

(continues)

graph.grSeriesCount( ) *datawindow.grSeriesCount (control_name)	Returns the number of series. If grSeriesCount is used on a DataWindow graph, the control name must also be passed.
graph.grSeriesName (seriesnumber) *datawindow.grSeriesName (control_name, seriesnumber)	Returns the name of a series. If grSeriesName is used on a DataWindow graph, the control name must also be passed.
graph.grSeries Style	grSeriesStyle returns information about the color and pattern of a series. If grSeriesStyle is used on a DataWindow graph, the control name must also be passed. Seriesname is the name of the series.

Format 1

graph.grSeriesStyle(seriesname, colortype, colorvariable) *datawindow.grSeriesStyle (control_name, seriesname, colortype, colorvariable)	Colortype is an enumerated data type specifying the color type for which you want to obtain the color: • Background!—The background color • Foreground!—Text (fill color) • LineColor!—The color of the line • Shade!—Shade (shade applies only to graphics that are three-dimensional or have three-dimensional objects) The color is then stored in a long colorvariable.

Format 2

graph.grSeriesStyle(seriesname, fillpatternvariable) *datawindow.grSeriesStyle (control_name, seriesname, fillpatternvariable)	The fill pattern is stored in an enumerated fill pattern variable.

Format 3

graph.grSeriesStyle(seriesname, linestyle) *datawindow.grSeriesStyle (control_name, seriesname, linestyle)	The line style is stored in an enumerated line style variable.

Format 4

graph.grSeriesStyle(seriesname, symbol) *datawindow.grSeriesStyle (control_name, seriesname, symbol)	The symbol is stored in an enumerated variable of grSymbolType.

Format 5

graph.grSeriesStyle(seriesname, overlay) *datawindow.grSeriesStyle (control_name, seriesname, overlay)	Overlay is a boolean set to TRUE if overlays are allowed and FALSE if they are not.

graph.grSetDataStyle

grSetDataStyle sets the color and pattern of a datapoint. If grSetDataStyle is used on a DataWindow graph, the control name must also be passed. Seriesnumber is the number of the series. Datapointnumber is the number of the data point.

Format 1
graph.grSetDataStyle(seriesnumber, datapointnumber, colortype, colorvariable)
*datawindow.grSetDataStyle (control_name, seriesnumber, datapointnumber,colortype, colorvariable)

Colortype is an enumerated data type specifying the color type for which you want to set:
- Background!—The background color
- Foreground!—Text (fill color)
- LineColor!—The color of the line
- Shade!—Shade (shade applies only to graphics that are three-dimensional or have three-dimensional objects)

The color is a long colorvariable.

Format 2
graph.grSetDataStyle(seriesnumber, datapointnumber, fillpatternvariable)
*datawindow.grSetDataStyle (control_name, seriesnumber, datapointnumber, fillpatternvariable)

The fill pattern is an enumerated fill pattern variable.

Format 3
graph.grSetDataStyle(seriesnumber, datapointnumber, linestyle)
*datawindow.grSetDataStyle (control_name,seriesnumber, datapointnumber, linestyle)

The line style is an enumerated line style variable.

Format 4
graph.grSetDataStyle(seriesnumber, datapointnumber, symbol)
*datawindow.grSetDataStyle (control_name, seriesnumber, datapointnumber, symbol)

The symbol is an enumerated variable of grSymbolType.

(continues)

VI

References

Graph.grSet Series Style	grSetSeriesStyle sets information about the color and pattern of a series. If grSetSeriesStyle is used on a DataWindow graph, the control name must also be passed. Seriesname is the name of the series.

Format 1 graph.grSetSeriesStyle(seriesname, colortype, colorvariable) *datawindow.grSetSeriesStyle (control_name, seriesname, colortype, colorvariable)	Colortype is an enumerated data type specifying the color type you want to set: • Background!—The background color • Foreground!—Text (fill color) • LineColor!—The color of the line • Shade!—Shade (shade applies only to graphics that are three-dimensional or have three-dimensional objects) The color is a long colorvariable.
Format 2 graph.grSetSeriesStyle(seriesname, fillpatternvariable) *datawindow.grSetSeriesStyle (control_name, seriesname, fillpatternvariable)	The fill pattern is an enumerated fill pattern variable.
Format 3 graph.grSetSeriesStyle(seriesname, linestyle) *datawindow.grSetSeriesStyle (control_name, seriesname, linestyle)	The line style is an enumerated line style variable.
Format 4 graph.grSetSeriesStyle(seriesname, symbol) *datawindow.grSetSeriesStyle (control_name, seriesname, symbol)	The symbol is an enumerated variable of grSymbolType.
Format 5 graph.grSetSeriesStyle(seriesname, overlay) *datawindow.grSetSeriesStyle (control_name, seriesname, overlay)	Overlay is a boolean set to TRUE if you allow overlays and FALSE if you do not.

These functions are used as DataWindow object functions.

MenuItem Functions

menuitem.Check( )	Places a checkmark next to menuitem.
menuitem.Disable( )	Disables the menuitem.
menuitem.Enable( )	Enables the menuitem.
menuitem.PopMenu(x, y)	Displays a pop-up menu at coordinates x and y.
menuitem.Uncheck( )	Removes the checkmark from menuitem.

DataWindow Functions

There are many types of DataWindow functions. Like all window controls, DataWindow controls can be manipulated using DataWindow functions. DataWindow object aggregate functions, like SUM and AVG, are used inside DataWindows and reports for processing groups of data. Finally, DataWindow painter funtions are functions that can be used inside DataWindow validation rules expressions, like the IF function.

DataWindow Control Functions

datawindow.AcceptText( )	Forces all text on the DataWindow to be accepted, especially the text on the current field when Tab or Enter has not been pressed.
datawindow.ClearValues (column)	Deletes all the values of the code table (if one exists) in the specified column.
datawindow.DBCancel( )	Cancels a current database retrieval.
datawindow.DBErrorCode( )	Returns the database specific error number.
datawindow.DBErrorMessage( )	Returns the database specific error message.
datawindow.DeletedCount( )	Returns the number of rows that have been deleted from the data window since the last retrieval or update.
datawindow.DeleteRow(rownum)	Deletes a row from the DataWindow. If rownum is 0, the current row is deleted.
datawindow.dwCreate (syntax, errorbuffer)	Creates a new DataWindow based on the passed syntax. Any errors are placed in errorbuffer.
datawindow.dwDescribe(string)	Returns the current description of a dynamic DataWindow.
datawindow.dwFind(condition, rowstart, rowend)	Searches for a row that meets a condition starting at rowstart and ending at rowend.
datawindow.dwFindGroupChange (rownum, level)	Searches for the first break in the DataWindow for the group identified by level after rownum.
datawindow.dwGetBandAtPointer( )	Returns a string containing the band in which the mouse pointer is currently located.
datawindow.dwGetChild (columnname, dwc)	Sets the DataWindowChild variable (dwc) with the contents of the child DataWindow (the DDDW). Use this to perform functions on the child DataWindow.

(continues)

VI

References

datawindow.dwGetItemStatus (rownum, column, dwbuffer)	Returns a dwItemStatus enumerated data type indicating the item status of the item at rownum and column in dwbuffer.
datawindow.dwGetNextModified (rownum, dwbuffer)	Returns the next row number that was modified after rownum.
datawindow.dwGetObjectAtPointer()	Returns the DataWindow object under the mouse pointer.
datawindow.dwGetSQLPreview()	Returns the current SQL statement.
datawindow.dwGetUpdateStatus (row, dwbuffer)	Determines what caused the DataWindow to submit SQL to the database server.
datawindow.dwGroupCalc()	Recalculates breaks in the grouping levels.
datawindow.dwModify(string)	Applies the string to modify the DataWindow.
datawindow.dwOLEActivate (row, column, OLEverb)	Activates OLE for a given column.
datawindow.dwResetUpdate()	Clears the update flags for a DataWindow.
datawindow.dwSetItemStatus (rownum, column, dwbuffer, status)	Sets the status of an item at rownum, column, in buffer dwbuffer.
datawindow.dwSetSQLPreview (string)	Modifies the SQL syntax for the DataWindow.
datawindow.dwShareData(dw2)	Shares data with DataWindow dw2.
datawindow.dwShareDataOff(dw)	Turns off all sharing on the DataWindow.
datawindow.Filter( )	Displays rows that pass the current filter definition.
datawindow.FilteredCount( )	Returns the number of rows not displayed because of the filter.
datawindow.GetBorderStyle (column)	Returns a Border enumerated data type describing the type of border at a column.
datawindow.GetClickedColumn( )	Returns the column number that was clicked.
datawindow.GetClickedRow( )	Returns the row number that was clicked.
datawindow.GetColumn( )	Returns the current column number.
datawindow.GetColumnName( )	Returns the current column name.
datawindow.GetFormat(column)	Returns a string containing the column format.

datawindow.GetItemDate (rownum, column)	Returns the date in a date column in the DataWindow.
datawindow.GetItemDateTime (rownum, column)	Returns the datetime in a datetime column in the DataWindow.
datawindow.GetItemDecimal (rownum, column)	Returns the decimal number in a decimal column in the DataWindow.
datawindow.GetItemNumber (rownum, column)	Returns the number in a numeric column in the DataWindow.
datawindow.GetItemString (rownum, column)	Returns the string in a string column in the DataWindow.
datawindow.GetItemTime (rownum, column)	Returns the time in a time column in the DataWindow.
datawindow.GetRow( )	Returns the current row.
datawindow.GetSelectedRow (rownum)	Returns the next selected row after the passed rownum.
datawindow.GetSQLSelect( )	Returns a string containing the SQL Select syntax of the DataWindow.
datawindow.GetText( )	Returns a string containing the text of the current field on the DataWindow.
datawindow.GetTrans (transaction)	Returns the transaction of a DataWindow and places it into the passed transaction variable.
datawindow.GetValidate (column)	Returns a string containing the validation rule of a column.
datawindow.GetValue (column, index)	Returns the display value of the code table of a column when passed the index.
datawindow.ImportClipboard (startrow, endrow, startcolumn, endcolumn, dwcolumn)	Imports tab-delimited Clipboard contents starting at startrow and startcolumn and going to endrow and endcolumn of the file. Places the result in the DataWindow starting at dwcolumn.
datawindow.ImportFile (filename, startrow, endrow, startcolumn, endcolumn, dwcolumn)	Imports a tab-delimited file starting at startrow and startcolumn and going to endrow and endcolumn of the file. Places the result in the DataWindow starting at dwcolumn.
datawindow.ImportString (string, startrow, endrow, startcolumn, endcolumn, dwcolumn)	Imports a tab-delimited string starting at startrow and startcolumn and going to endrow and endcolumn of the string. Places the result in the DataWindow starting at dwcolumn.

VI

References

(continues)

datawindow.InsertRow(rownum)	Inserts a row before the passed row number. If rownum is 0, this inserts a row before the current row.
datawindow.IsSelected(rownum)	Returns TRUE or FALSE indicating whether or not the row is selected.
datawindow.ModifiedCount( )	Returns the number of changed rows since the last retrieve or update.
datawindow.Print( )	Prints the contents of the DataWindow.
datawindow.PrintCancel( )	Cancels the current DataWindow print.
datawindow.ReselectRow (rownum)	Accesses the database to retrieve all changed columns in a row.
datawindow.Reset( )	Completely clears the contents of the DataWindow.
datawindow.ResetTransObject( )	Stops a DataWindow from using programmer-specific transaction objects.
datawindow.Retrieve (retrieveargument)	Retrieves data from the database and places it in a DataWindow. If the retrieval argument is passed, retrieve applies that retrieval argument to the DataWindow.
datawindow.RowCount( )	Returns the number of rows in a DataWindow.
datawindow.SaveAs(filename, saveas, columnheading)	Saves the contents of the DataWindow in a new format. SaveAs is an enumerated data type describing the new format. Column-heading is a boolean TRUE or FALSE decribing whether or not you want column headings on your output.
datawindow.ScrollNextPage( )	Scrolls forward one page and makes the row one page forward active.
datawindow.ScrollNextRow( )	Scrolls to the next row in a DataWindow and makes that row active.
datawindow.ScrollPriorPage( )	Scrolls backward one page and makes the row one page back active.
datawindow.ScrollPriorRow( )	Scrolls to the previous row in a DataWindow and makes that row active.
datawindow.ScrollToRow (rownum)	Scrolls to a row and makes that row active.
datawindow.SelectRow (rownum, boolean)	Makes a current row selected if boolean is set to TRUE or deselected if boolean is set to FALSE.

datawindow.SetActionCode( )	Sets the action code in a script. It should be the last line in the script.
datawindow.SetBorderStyle (column, borderstyle)	Changes the column's border to a new border based on a BorderStyle enumerated data type.
datawindow.SetColumn(column)	Sets a column number or column string to be the current column.
datawindow.SetFilter(string)	Sets the filter based on the string.
datawindow.SetFormat (column, formatstring)	Sets the display format for a column based on the format string.
datawindow.SetItem (row, column, value)	Sets the item to a new value at the specified row and column. The value's data type must match the column.
datawindow.SetRow(rownum)	Sets rownum to be the current row.
datawindow.SetRowFocus Indicator(FocusIndicator, X, Y)	Sets the mouse pointer to change to the focus indicator if the row receives focus. X and Y correspond to coordinates offsetting the corner of the row for the new pointer's display to take effect.
datawindow.SetSort(string)	Sets new sort criteria based on the value of the string.
datawindow.SetSQLSelect (SQLsyntax)	Replaces the current Select statement with a new Select statement for the DataWindow. (Often, you'll want to use dwModify instead.)
datawindow.SetTabOrder (column, tabnumber)	Sets the tab order inside the DataWindow for a given column.
datawindow.SetText(string)	Sets the text in the current cursor location in the DataWindow.
datawindow.SetTrans( )	Sets the transaction for the DataWindow.
datawindow.SetTransObject( )	Sets the transaction for the entire DataWindow and all child DataWindows.
datawindow.SetValidate (column, rule)	Sets the validation rule of a column to a new rule contained in a string parameter.
datawindow.SetValue (column, index, value)	Sets the column number or name's code table index to a new value.
datawindow.Sort( )	Sorts the rows of the database based on the sort criteria established in the DataWindow painter or using the SetSort function.
datawindow.Update( )	Updates the database with the DataWindow.

VI

References

DataWindow Object Aggregate Functions

In the DataWindow painter, you can use the following aggregate functions in computed fields, filters, and validation rules. You aren't allowed to use these functions inside PowerScript. Most aggregate functions allow the following parameters:

(column, {for range { DISTINCT {expression1 {, expression2 {, ...}}}}})	column is the column for which you want to apply the function. column can be the name of the column or the number of the column preceded by a pound sign (#). for range is optional. Values for range are: • All—(Default) Apply the function to all rows in column in the report. • Crosstab—(Crosstabs only) Apply the function to all rows in column in the crosstab. • Graph—(Graphs only) Apply the function to all rows in column for the graph. This value for range has effect only when you specify Page in the Rows option on the Graph DataWindow. • GroupNbr—Apply the function to all rows in column in the specified group. To specify a group, enter group and then the group number. For example: for group 1. • Page—Apply the function to the rows in column on a page. DISTINCT is used like the SQL SELECT DISTINCT. It eliminates duplicates from the expression.
expression*n*(optional)	One or more expressions that you want to evaluate. expression can be the name of a column, a function, or an expression.

The aggregate DataWindow functions are as follows:

Avg(column {for range { DISTINCT {expression1 {, expression2 {, ...}}}}})	Takes the averages of a column.
Count(column {for range { DISTINCT {expression1 {, expression2 {, ...}}}}})	Returns the number of columns.
CumulativePercent(column {for range { DISTINCT {expression1 {, expression2 {, ...}}}}})	Takes the cumulative percent of the total for a column. Usually this is in the detail section of the report.

CumulativeSum(column {for range { DISTINCT {expression1 {, expression2 {, ...}}}})	Returns the cumulative sum of the total for a column. Usually, this is in the detail section of the report.
Describe(string)	Returns the values described in the syntax of the string.
First(column {for range { DISTINCT {expression1 {, expression2 {, ...}}}})	Returns the first value in a column.
Last(column {for range { DISTINCT {expression1 {, expression2 {, ...}}}})	Returns the last value in a column.
LookUpDisplay(column)	Returns a string value of the corresponding column value in a code table.
Max(column {for range { DISTINCT {expression1 {, expression2 {, ...}}}})	Returns the maximum value of a column.
Min(column {for range { DISTINCT {expression1 {, expression2 {, ...}}}})	Returns the minimum value of a column.
Percent(column {for range { DISTINCT {expression1 {, expression2 {, ...}}}})	Converts the number as a percent of total for a column. Usually, this is in the detail section of the report.
StDev(column {for range { DISTINCT {expression1 {, expression2 {, ...}}}})	Returns the sample standard deviation of a column.
StDevP(column {for range { DISTINCT {expression1 {, expression2 {, ...}}}})	Returns the standard deviation of a column.

(continues)

Sum (column {for range { DISTINCT {expression1 {, expression2 {, ...}}}}})	Returns the sum of a column.
Var(column {for range { DISTINCT {expression1 {, expression2 {, ...}}}}})	Returns the sample variance of a column.
VarP(column {for range { DISTINCT {expression1 {, expression2 {, ...}}}}})	Returns the variance of a column.
WordCap(string)	Capitalizes the first letter in every word of the string.

Note

Do not confuse the Max and Min aggregate functions with the PowerScript Max and Min functions that compare two numbers and return the maximum or minimum number. Also, you can't nest aggregate functions. (*Nested functions* refer to the fact that you cannot call one aggregate function within another aggregate function.)

DataWindow Painter Functions

In the DataWindow painter, you also can use the following DataWindow object functions in computed fields, filters, and validation rules. These functions are not allowed in PowerScript, but only in the DataWindow Painter.

Bitmap(filename) Bitmap(columnname) Bitmap(columnnumber)	Places a bitmap in a computed field. The bitmap can either be a filename, a column name, or a column number. If a column is referenced, that column must contain a bitmap file name.
If(condition, TRUE string, FALSE string)	Tests a condition in a computed field, filter, or validation rule and either sets the column to a TRUE string or a FALSE string. (Also available in SetSort or dwModify statements.)
Number(string)	Converts the value of a string to a numeric data type.
Page( )	Returns the current page of a DataWindow or Report.
PageCount( )	Returns the PageCount of a DataWindow or Report.

Window Functions

window.ArrangeSheets (ArrangeType)	Arranges sheets in an MDI application. ArrangeType is an enumerated variable of either Cascade!, Tile!, or Layer!. Icons! is also available for arranging minimized sheets in an MDI application.
window.ChangeMenu (menuname, position)	Selects a new menu for a window. If the window is an MDI frame, position can be passed to determine which menu bar item lists the open sheets.
window.GetActiveSheet( )	Returns a window data type of the active sheet in an MDI application.
window.ParentWindow( )	Returns a window data type of the parent window. Usually, used with a child window.
window.SetMicroHelp(string)	Sets MicroHelp in an MDI application to display a string.
window.WorkSpaceHeight( )	Returns the height of a window.
window.WorkSpaceWidth( )	Returns the width of a window.
window.WorkSpaceX( )	Returns the X coordinate of the upper left corner of a window.
window.WorkSpaceY( )	Returns the Y coordinate of the upper left corner of a window.

User Object Functions

EventParmDouble(parameter, parmvariable)	For use with visual basic controls. Returns the double parmvariable denoted by the parameter number in a vbx control.
EventParmString(parameter, parmvariable)	For use with visual basic controls. Returns the string parmvariable denoted by the parameter number in a vbx control.

Chapter 22

Enumerated Data Types Quick Reference

Enumerated data types are constants defined by PowerBuilder that are used to set the value of many object attributes. Since you are using a descriptive enumerated data type name as opposed to a constant, enumerated data types make developing and future maintenance a little easier. Enumerated data types also ensure data integrity for the PowerBuilder application.

◀ See "Using the Object Browser," p. 164

PowerBuilder includes many enumerated data types. Most (but not all) of the enumerated data types can be found through the object browser, shown in figure 22.1.

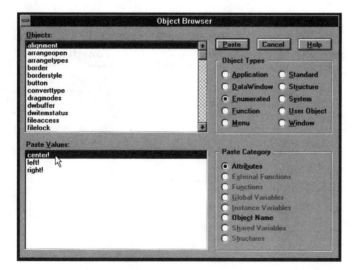

Fig. 22.1
You can find most enumerated data types through the object browser.

VI

References

An example of an enumerated data type is as follows:

```
sle_numsold.alignment = Right!
```

Many of the enumerated data types are listed in on-line help. Table 22.1 lists all of PowerBuilder's enumerated data types.

Note

Any time the enumerated name is listed as an attribute of an object or control, you should use the enumerated data type to test and set that attribute.

Troubleshooting

I'm trying to use an enumerated data type, but the script I'm using it in will not compile, and I keep getting errors. Why?

When you use enumerated data types, be sure to include a '!' at the end. PowerBuilder will not recognize them without the exclamation point.

Often, PowerBuilder allows you to either use an enumerated data type or a string. If you put an enumerated data type in quotes, PowerBuilder converts it to a string and does not process it as an enumerated data type. This causes a run time error; therefore, be sure not to put your enumerated data type within quotes.

Table 22.1 Enumerated Data Types

Category	Values	Comments
ArrangeOpen	Cascaded! Layered! Original!	How MDI sheets are arranged when opened.
ArrangeType	Cascade! Icons! Layer! Tile! Tile Horizontal!	How open MDI sheets are arranged.
Border	Box! Lowered! NoBorder! Raised! ResizeBorder! ShadowBox! Underline!	The type of the border.

Category	Values	Comments
BorderStyle	StyleBox! StyleLowered! StyleRaised! StyleShadowBox!	The style of the border.
Button	OK! OKCancel! RetryCancel! YesNo! YesNoCancel!	Message Box Button.
ConvertType	XPixelsToUnits! XUnitsToPixels! YPixelsToUnits! YUnitsToPixels!	How you want to convert units or pixels in the PixelsToUnits and Units ToPixels functions.
DragModes	Begin! Cancel! End!	The Drag mode for an object.
dwBuffer	Delete! Filter! Primary!	The DataWindow buffer.
dwItemStatus	DataModified! New! NewModified! NotModified!	The status of a DataWindow item.
FileAccess	Read! Write!	The file access allowed.
FileLock	LockRead! LockReadWrite! LockWrite! Shared!	The file lock for other users.
FileMode	LineMode! StreamMode!	The File mode for reading or writing.
FillPattern	BDiagonal! Diamond! FDiagonal! Horizontal! Solid! Square! Vertical!	The hatch pattern used to fill a drawing or graph object.
FontCharSet	ANSI! ChineseBig5! DefaultCharSet! HangEul!Shiftjis! OEM! Symbol!	The font character set.

(continues)

VI

References

Table 22.1 Continued

Category	Values	Comments
FontFamily	AnyFont! Decorative! Modern! Roman! Script! Swiss!	The font family.
FontPitch	Default! Fixed! Variable!	The font pitch.
grColorType	Background! Foreground! LineColor! Shade!	A color type in a graph.
grDataType	xvalue! yvalue!	The value of a data point in a graph.
grGraphType	Area3d! AreaGraph! Bar3dGraph! Bar3dObjGraph! BarGraph! BarStack3dObjGraph! BarStackGraph! Col3dGraph! Col3dObjGraph! ColGraph! ColStack3dObjGraph! ColStackGraph! Line3d! LineGraph! Pie3d! PieGraph! ScatterGraph!	The type of graph.
grLegendType	AtBottom! AtLeft! AtRight! AtTop! NoLegend!	The location of the graph legend.
grObjectType	TypeCategory! TypeCategoryAxis! TypeCategoryLabel! TypeData! TypeGraph! TypeLegend! TypeSeries! TypeSeriesAxis! TypeSeriesLabel! TypeTitle! TypeValueAxis! TypeValueLabel!	The type of graph object.

Category	Values	Comments
grResetType	All! Category! Data! Series!	The data you want to reset in a graph.
grScaleType	Linear! Log10! LogE!	The type of scale in a graph.
grScaleValue	Actual! Cumulative! CumulativePercent! Percentage!	The value of scale in a graph.
grSymbolType	NoSymbol! SymbolHollowBox! SymbolHollowCircle! SymbolHollowDiamond! SymbolHollowDownArrow! SymbolHollowUpArrow! SymbolPlus! SymbolSolidBox! SymbolSolidCircle! SymbolSolidDiamond! SymbolSolidDownArrow! SymbolSolidUpArrow! SymbolStar! SymbolX!	The symbol you want to use for a series in a graph.
grTicType	Inside! NoTic! Outside! Straddle!	The type of tick marks in the scale in a graph.
HelpCommand	Index! Keyword! Topic!	The type of command in the ShowHelp function.
Icon	Exclamation! Information! None! Question! StopSign!	The Message Box icon.
KeyCode	key0! key1! key2! key3! key4! key5! key6! key7! key8! key9! keyA!	The keycode argument in the KeyDown function.

(continues)

VI

References

Table 22.1 Continued		
Category	**Values**	**Comments**
	keyAdd!	+ on the numeric keypad
	keyAlt!	
	keyB!	
	keyBack!	Backspace key
	keyBackQuote!	´ and ~ keys
	keyBackSlash!	\ and	keys
	keyC!	
	keyCapsLock!	
	keyComma!	, and < keys
	keyControl!	
	keyD!	
	keyDash!	- and _ keys
	keyDecimal!	. on the numeric keypad when NumLock is on
	keyDelete!	
	keyDivide!	/ on the numeric keypad
	keyDownArrow!	
	keyE!	
	keyEnd!	
	keyEnter!	
	keyEqual!	= and + keys
	keyEscape!	
	keyF!	
	keyF1!	
	keyF10!	
	keyF11!	
	keyF12!	
	keyF2!	
	keyF3!	
	keyF4!	
	keyF5!	
	keyF6!	
	keyF7!	
	keyF8!	
	keyF9!	
	keyG!	
	keyH!	
	keyHome!	
	keyI!	
	keyInsert!	
	keyJ!	
	keyK!	
	keyL!	
	keyLeftArrow!	
	keyLeftBracket!	[and { keys
	keyM!	
	keyMultiply!	* on the numeric keypad
	keyN!	
	keyNumLock!	
	keyNumpad0!	
	keyNumpad1!	
	keyNumpad2!	
	keyNumpad3!	
	keyNumpad4!	
	keyNumpad5!	

Category	Values	Comments
	keyNumpad6!	
	keyNumpad7!	
	keyNumpad8!	
	keyNumpad9!	
	keyO!	
	keyP!	
	keyPageDown!	
	keyPageUp!	
	keyPause!	
	keyPeriod!	. and > keys
	keyPrintScreen!	
	keyQ!	
	keyQuote!	Single-quote and double-quote key
	keyR!	
	keyRightArrow!	
	keyRightBracket!	] and } keys
	keyS!	
	keyScrollLock!	
	keySemiColon!	; and : keys
	keyShift!	
	keySlash!	/ and ? keys
	keySpaceBar!	
	KeySubtract!	- on the numeric keypad
	keyT!	
	keyTab!	
	keyU!	
	keyUpArrow!	
	keyV!	
	keyW!	
	keyX!	
	keyY!	
	keyZ!	
LibDirType	DirAll!	The type of objects to be
	DirApplication!	included in the directory
	DirDataWindow!	list.
	DirFunction!	
	DirMenu!	
	DirStructure!	
	DirUserObject!	
	DirWindow!	
LibExportType	ExportApplication!	The type of object to be
	ExportDataWindow!	exported.
	ExportFunction!	
	ExportMenu!	
	ExportStructure!	
	ExportUserObject!	
	ExportWindow!	
LibImportType	ImportDataWindow!	The type of object to be
		imported.

(continues)

VI

References

Table 22.1 Continued		
Category	**Values**	**Comments**
LineStyle	Continuous! Dash! DashDot! DashDotDot! Dot! Transparent!	The style of the line.
mailFileType	mailAttach! mailOLE! mailOLEStatic!	Mail file types.
mailLogonOption	mailDownLoad! mailNewSession! mailNewSessionWithDownLoad! mailReadOption! mailBodyAsFile! mailEntireMessage! mailEnvelopeOnly! mailSuppressAttach!	Mail logon options. Mail read options.
mailRecipientType	mailBCC! mailCC! mailOriginator! mailTo!	Mail recipient types.
mailReturnCode	mailReturnAccessDenied! mailReturnAttachmentNotFound! mailReturnAttachmentOpenFailure! mailReturnAttachmentWriteFailure! mailReturnDiskFull! mailReturnFailure! mailReturnInsufficientMemory! mailReturnLoginFailure! mailReturnMessageInUse! mailReturnNoMessages! mailReturnSuccess! mailReturnTextTooLarge! mailReturnTooManyFiles! mailReturnTooManyRecipients! mailReturnTooManySessions! mailReturnUserAbort!	Mail function return codes.
MaskDataType	DateMask! DateTimeMask! DecimalMask! NumericMask! StringMask! TimeMask!	The EditMask data type.
MajorTic	Inside! NoTic! Outside! Straddle!	The type of major tick marks in the graph scale.

Category	Values	Comments
MinorTic	Inside! NoTic! Outside! Straddle!	The type of minor tick marks in the graph scale.
Object	checkbox! commandbutton! datawindow! dropdownlistbox! editmask! graph! groupbox! hscrollbar! line! listbox! mdiclient! menu! multilineedit! nonvisualobject! oval! picture! picturebutton! radiobutton! rectangle! roundrectangle! singlelineedit! statictext! userobject! vscrollbar! window!	The object type.
ParmType	TypeBoolean! TypeDate! TypeDateTime! TypeDecimal! TypeDouble! TypeInteger! TypeLong! TypeReal! TypeString! TypeTime! TypeUInt! TypeULong! Unknown!	The parameter data type.
Pointer	Arrow! Beam! Cross! HourGlass! SizeNESW! SizeNS! SizeNWSE! SizeWE! UpArrow!	The shape of the pointer for the SetPointer function.

(continues)

VI

References

Table 22.1 Continued

Category	Values	Comments
RowFocusInd	FocusRect! Hand! Off!	The method that will be used to indicate that a DataWindow row has focus.
SaveAsType	Csv! Clipboard dBase2! dBase3! Dif! Excel! SQLInsert! Sylk! Text! Wk1! Wks!	The type of file to create when saving the rows of a DataWindow.
SeekType	FromBeginning! FromCurrent! FromEnd!	The position at which you want to begin a seek in FileSeek.
SetPosType	Behind! NoTopMost! ToBottom! TopMost! ToTop!	Set the order of display in a window control.
TextCase	AnyCase! Lower! Upper!	The text case.
ToolbarAlignment	AllignAtBottom! AlignAtLeft! AlignAtRight! AlignAtTop! Floating!	The toolbar alignment.
TrigEvent	Activate! Clicked! Close! CloseQuery! DBError! Deactivate! DoubleClicked! DragDrop! DragEnter! DragLeave! DragWithin! EditChanged! GetFocus! Hide! HotLinkAlarm! Idle! ItemChanged!	The type of event to be triggered by the TriggerEvent function.

Category	Values	Comments
	ItemError!	
	ItemFocusChanged!	
	Key!	
	LineDown!	
	LineLeft!	
	LineRight!	
	LineUp!	
	LoseFocus!	
	Modified!	
	MouseDown!	
	MouseMove!	
	MouseUp!	
	Moved!	
	Open!	
	Other!	
	PageDown!	
	PageLeft!	
	PageRight!	
	PageUp!	
	PrintEnd!	
	PrintPage!	
	PrintStart!	
	RemoteExec!	
	RemoteHotLinkStart!	
	RemoteHotLinkStop!	
	RemoteRequest!	
	RemoteSend!	
	Resize!	
	RetrieveEnd!	
	RetrieveRow!	
	RetrieveStart!	
	RowFocusChanged!	
	ScrollHorizontal!	
	ScrollVertical!	
	Selected!	
	SelectionChanged!	
	Show!	
	SQLPreview!	
	SystemError!	
	Timer!	
	UpdateEnd!	
	UpdateStart!	
VTextAlign	Bottom! MultiLine! Top! VCenter!	The alignment of text.
UserObjects	CustomVisual! ExternalVisual!	The type of user object.
WindowState	Maximized! Minimized! Normal!	The state in which the window or program will run.

VI

References

(continues)

Table 22.1 Continued		
Category	**Values**	**Comments**
WindowType	Child! Main! MDI! MDIHelp! Popup! Response!	Type of window.
WriteMode	Append! Replace!	The mode for the FileOpen function.

From Here...

Enumerated data types allow the developer to code PowerScript without constantly looking up accepted values. They also aid in the maintenance of a system. For a list of functions that require enumerated data types, refer to the following chapters:

- Chapter 5, "Using Events, Functions, and the PowerScript Language," describes the basic PowerScript programming language. It's a must for the beginner.

- Chapter 21, "Function & Event Quick Reference," shows all the functions used inside PowerBuilder starting with stand-alone functions and moving on to functions specific to an object or control.

You could also check out the on-line help system for help on the enumerated data types or the Function reference provided with PowerBuilder to list how functions use enumerated data types.

Chapter 23

Attribute Quick Reference

Every object and control has attributes. All objects and most controls have events. Attributes determine the state of the object or control, whereas events implement the functionality of the object or control.

> **Note**
>
> Many window controls (like command button and list box) have similar or identical attributes and events. (However, the drawing objects, like rectangle and line, have no events.) Because of the similarity between window controls, the attributes and events for the window controls have been merged into a Window Control Attribute section and a Window Control Event section.

◀ See "Using Variables," p. 129

◀ See "Using the PowerBuilder Script Painter," p. 157

◀ See "Programming for Specific Events," p. 179

Application Attributes

AppName	String	A string containing the application name.
DDETimeOut	Integer	An integer specifying the time-out interval in seconds for a DDE conversation.
dwMessageTitle	String	A string containing the title of the DataWindow message boxes displayed during execution.
MicroHelpDefault	String	A string containing the default text for MicroHelp.
ToolbarText	Boolean	A TRUE or FALSE indicating whether or not to display the toolbar text. This attribute has effect only in an MDI frame window.

(continues)

Application Attributes   Continued

ToolbarFrameTitle	String	A string indicating the title of the frame toolbar when it is a floating toolbar. This attribute has effect only in an MDI frame window.
ToolbarSheetTitle	String	A string indicating the title of the sheet toolbar when it is a floating toolbar. This attribute has effect only in an MDI frame window.

Application Events

Close	Executed upon the close of the application.
Idle	Executed when the specified number of seconds have elapsed during the application with no activity.
Open	Executed upon the opening of the application.
SystemError	Executed during a system error anywhere in the application.

Window Attributes

BackColor	Long	An indicator of the background color.
Border	Boolean	A TRUE or FALSE indicating whether or not the window has a border.
BringToTop	Boolean	A TRUE or FALSE indicating if the window is supposed to be on top.
ColumnsPerPage	Integer	An integer indicating the number of units to scroll when the scroll over bar has been clicked on.
Control[ ]	Object array	An array listing the controls. You cannot change the values in this variable.
ControlMenu	Boolean	TRUE or FALSE indicating the presence of the control box and control box menu.
Enabled	Boolean	TRUE allows the window to send and receive messages.
Height	Integer	Indicates the height of the window.
HScrollBar	Boolean	TRUE or FALSE indicating the presence of a horizontal scroll bar.

Window Attributes

Icon	String	The icon associated with the window when the window is minimized.
LinesPerPage	Integer	An integer indicating the number of units to scroll when the scroll down bar has been clicked on.
MaxBox	Boolean	A TRUE or FALSE indicating the presence of a maximize box on the window title bar.
MenuID	String	The menu item associated with the window.
MenuName	String	The menu name associated with the menu ID.
MinBox	Boolean	A TRUE or FALSE indicating the presence of a minimize box on the window title bar.
Pointer	String	A string containing the name of the file containing the pointer used for the object or control.
Resizable	Boolean	A TRUE or FALSE indicating if the window is resizable or not.
Tag	String	A string containing the tag value of the window.
Title	String	A string containing the title of the window.
TitleBar	Boolean	TRUE or FALSE indicating the presence of a title bar on your window. Modifying this attribute in a script will cause an error during execution.
ToolbarAlignment	Enumerated	Controls whether a toolbar is on the top, bottom, left, right, or floating. This attribute has effect only in MDI frames and sheets.
ToolbarHeight	Integer	Sets the toolbar height. This attribute has effect only in MDI frames and sheets.
ToolbarVisible	Boolean	This makes the toolbar visible and invisible (TRUE or FALSE). This attribute has effect only in MDI frames and sheets.
ToolbarWidth	Integer	Specifies the width of a floating toolbar. This attribute has effect only in MDI frames and sheets.
ToolbarX	Integer	The X coordinate of a floating toolbar. This attribute has effect only in MDI frames and sheets.

VI

References

(continues)

Window Attributes	**Continued**	
ToolbarY	Integer	The Y coordinate of a floating toolbar. This attribute has effect only in MDI frames and sheets.
UnitsPerColumn	Integer	Indicates the number of PowerBuilder units a user scrolls when clicking on the scroll left or right.
UnitsPerLine	Integer	Indicates the number of PowerBuilder units a user scrolls when clicking on the scroll up or down.
Visible	Boolean	Makes the window visible or invisible.
VScrollBar	Boolean	TRUE or FALSE indicating the presence of a vertical scroll bar.
Width	Integer	Indicates the width of the window.
WindowState	Enumerated	Indicates what state (maximized, minimized, or normal) in which that window is currently displayed.
WindowType	Enumerated	Indicates the type of window (main, pop-up, MDI Frame, and so on).
X	Integer	Indicates the X coordinate of the upper left corner of the window.
Y	Integer	Indicates the Y coordinate of the upper left corner of the window.

Window Events	
Activate	The window has received focus.
Clicked	The user clicked on the window.
Close	The window is closing.
CloseQuery	The window is closing via the control box.
Deactivate	The window is losing focus.
DoubleClicked	The user double-clicked on the window.
DragDrop	A dragged object was dropped on the window.
DragEnter	A dragged object entered the window.
DragLeave	A dragged object has left the window.

Window Events

DragWithin	An object is being dragged within the window.
Hide	The window becomes hidden.
HotLinkAlarm	A server application has sent new (changed) data through the DDE.
Key	A key has been pressed (except Alt).
MouseDown	A mouse button is pressed in an empty area on the window.
MouseMove	The mouse is moving.
MouseUp	The mouse button is released in an empty area on the window.
Open	The window opens.
Other	A Windows 3.x event has occurred that has not been defined by PowerBuilder.
RButtonDown	The user is holding the right mouse button down on the window.
RemoteExec	A client application has sent a request through the DDE.
RemoteHotLinkStart	A client application wants to start a hotlink through the DDE.
RemoteHotLinkStop	A client application wants to end a hotlink through the DDE.
RemoteRequest	A client application has requested data through the DDE.
RemoteSend	A client application has sent data through the DDE.
Resize	The user is resizing the window.
Show	The window was hidden and is now being shown.
SystemKey	The Alt or Alt+ another key has been pressed.
Timer	The event has been triggered by the Timer function at some timed interval.

MenuItem Attributes

Checked	Boolean	TRUE or FALSE indicating if the menu item is checked.

(continues)

VI

References

MenuItem Attributes   Continued

Enabled	Boolean	TRUE or FALSE indicating if the menu item is able to send and receive messages.
Item[ ]	Menu array	A list of menu items.
MicroHelp	String	The MicroHelp associated with this menu.
Shortcut	Integer	An integer indicating the shortcut key used with this menu item.
ParentWindow	Window	The window containing the menu.
Tag	String	A string containing the tag value of the menu item.
Text	String	The text associated with this menu item.
ToolbarItemDown	Boolean	TRUE or FALSE indicating if the toolbar item defaults to down.
ToolbarItemDownName	String	The name of the picture displayed when a toolbar item is clicked on.
ToolbarItemName	String	The name of the picture displayed on the corresponding toolbar item.
ToolbarItemOrder	Integer	An integer specifying the order of the toolbar items.
ToolbarItemSpace	Integer	The size of the space before a toolbar item when ToolbarText is not displayed.
ToolbarItemText	String	The text displayed with the toolbar item.
ToolbarItemVisible	Boolean	TRUE or FALSE indicating if the Toolbar item is visible or not.
Visible	Boolean	TRUE or FALSE indicating if the menu item is visible or not.

MenuItem Events

Clicked	The menu item has been clicked on by the mouse.
Selected	The menu item has been selected (but not clicked on yet) by the user.

Window Control Attributes

Accelerator	Integer	An integer containing the ASCII value indicating the key you want to assign as the accelerator for a control.
Alignment	Enumerated	Enumerated data type specifying the alignment of text in a MultiLineEdit, StaticText, or PictureButton control. Valid values are Center!, Left!, or Right!.
AutoHScroll	Boolean	TRUE or FALSE indicating whether you want a field to automatically scroll horizontally.
AutoSkip	Boolean	An Edit mask attribute indicating whether or not you want to automatically skip this field and go to the next field in the tab order.
AutoVScroll	Boolean	TRUE or FALSE indicating whether you want a field to automatically scroll vertically.
AllowEdit	Boolean	TRUE or FALSE allowing the entry of a value not in the code table in a DropDownListBox.
Automatic	Boolean	TRUE or FALSE indicating whether to automatically check or uncheck the Checkbox or RadioButton with a mouse click.
BackColor	Long	A feature that uses the RGB function to set to background color of a window control. For example, to set the background color of a multiline edit to purple, you would type **mle_field.backcolor = RGB(255,0,255)**.
BeginX	Integer	The beginning X point of a line control in a window in relation to the upper left corner.
BeginY	Integer	The beginning Y point of a line control in a window in relation to the upper left corner.
Border	Boolean	TRUE or FALSE indicating whether or not the window control has a border.
BorderStyle	Enumerated	An enumerated variable describing the border style.
BringToTop	Boolean	TRUE or FALSE indicating whether or not to bring the window control to the top of the other controls.
Cancel	Boolean	TRUE or FALSE denoting whether or not to use this commandButton or pictureButton as a cancel button.

(continues)

VI

References

Window Control Attributes	Continued	
Category	grAxis object	Sets the attributes of the category axis in a graph control.
Checked	Boolean	TRUE or FALSE indicating if a Checkbox or RadioButton is filled in (radio button) or selected with an x (check box).
ClassName	String	A string containing the name of the window control.
ColumnsPerPage	Integer	An integer indicating the number of units to scroll when the scroll over bar has been clicked on.
Control[ ]	WindowObject	An array listing the array controls. You cannot change the values in this variable.
ControlMenu	Boolean	TRUE or FALSE describing whether or not a control box and control box menu are on the window control.
CornerHeight	Integer	The height of the rounded corner in a RoundRectangle.
CornerWidth	Integer	The width of the rounded corner in a RoundRectangle.
DataObject	String	A string indicating the DataWindow Object associated with the DataWindow control.
Default	Boolean	TRUE or FALSE denoting whether or not to use this commandButton or pictureButton as a default button.
Depth	Integer	An integer indicating the percentage the depth is of the width of the graph. For example, if the depth is 75, the depth of the graph is 75 percent of its width.
DisabledName	String	The name of the picture to be displayed when a PictureButton is disabled.
DisplayData	String	A string containing the data that initially appears in an EditMask.
DisplayOnly	Boolean	TRUE or FALSE indicating whether or not this field is updatable by the user.
DragAuto	Boolean	TRUE or FALSE indicating whether a click puts the window control automatically in Drag mode. (When DragAuto is TRUE, clicking on the control triggers a DragDrop event, not a Clicked event.)

Window Control Attributes

DragIcon	String	The icon appears when the user drags the window control.
Elevation	Integer	An integer specifying the angle of front-to-back elevation in a graph.
Enabled	Boolean	TRUE or FALSE indicating whether or not the window control can send and receive messages.
EndX	Integer	The ending X point of a line control in a window in relation to the upper left corner.
EndY	Integer	The ending Y point of a line control in a window in relation to the upper left corner.
FaceName	String	A string containing the name of the typeface (for example, Ariel) for the text in a window control.
FillColor	Long	The color to fill in an oval, rectangle, or roundrectangle control.
FillPattern	Enumerated	The pattern to fill in a static text, oval, rectangle, or roundrectangle control.
FocusRectangle	Boolean	TRUE or FALSE indicating whether or not to display a rectangle around the control when that control receives focus.
FontCharSet	Enumerated (CharSet!)	Specifies the font character set. Valid values are: ANSI!, ChineseBig5!, DefaultCharSet!, HangEul!, Shiftjis!, OEM!, and Symbol!.
FontFamily	Enumerated (Family!)	Specifies a group of typefaces with similar characteristics for text. Valid values are AnyFont!, Decorative!, Modern!, Roman!, Script!, and Swiss!.
FontPitch	Enumerated (Pitch!)	Specifies the horizontal spacing (pitch) of text. Valid values are: Default!—use standard pitch for the font (fixed or variable); Fixed!—use fixed pitch; Variable!—use variable pitch.
GraphType	Enumerated	An enumerated data type grGraphType specifying the type of a graph.
Height	Integer	A number indicating the height of the window control.
HScrollBar	Boolean	TRUE or FALSE indicating whether or not the window control has a horizontal scroll bar.

VI

References

(continues)

Window Control Attributes Continued

HSplitScroll	Boolean	TRUE or FALSE indicating whether or not the window control allows split scrolling.
HTextAlign	Enumerated	A feature that specifies the alignment of text in a PictureButton control. Valid Values are Center!, Left!, and Right!.
Icon	String	A string indicating the icon (.ICO file) displayed if the window control is minimized.
Increment	Double	A feature that specifies the increment used in a numeric Edit mask with spin control.
Invert	Boolean	TRUE or FALSE indicating whether or not a picture control is inverted.
Italic	Boolean	TRUE or FALSE specifying whether or not the text in a control is in italics.
Item[ ]	String Array	An array of display strings in a ListBox or DropDownListBox code table.
LeftText	Boolean	TRUE or FALSE indicating whether to display the text on the left side (TRUE) or right side (FALSE) of a check box or radio button.
Limit	Integer	An integer containing the maximum number of characters (0–32,767) the user can enter in a control. 0 indicates an unlimited number of characters.
Legend	Enumerated (grLegendType)	A number indicating the location of the legend of a graph. Valid values are: 0–None, 1–Left, 2–Right, 3–Top, 4–Bottom.
LegendDispAttr	grDispAttr object Graph	Defines how you want the legend to appear.
LibraryName	String	The name of the dynamic-link library (DLL) that contains a custom user object class.
LineColor	Integer	The color to draw lines in a Line, Oval, Rectangle, or RoundRectangle control.
LinesPerPage	Integer	An integer indicating the number of units to scroll when the scroll down bar has been clicked on.
LineStyle	Enumerated (Style!)	A Style! enumerated data type specifying the line style in a Line, Oval, Rectangle, or RoundRectangle control.

Window Control Attributes

LineThickness	Integer	An integer determining the line thickness in a Line, Oval, Rectangle, or RoundRectangle control.
LiveScroll	Boolean	TRUE or FALSE indicating if the clicking on the scroll bars allows scrolling of the DataWindow.
Mask	String	A string containing the format in an Edit mask control.
MaskDataType	Enumerated	An enumerated variable assigning a predefined format to an Edit mask control.
MaxBox	Boolean	TRUE or FALSE indicating the presence of a maximize box on the DataWindow.
MaxPosition	Integer	An integer containing the value of the position attribute when a horizontal scroll bar is at the far right or a vertical scroll bar is at the bottom. For use in HScrollBar and VScrollBar controls only.
MicroHelpHeight	Integer	An integer in the MDI Client (MDI_1) control determining the MicroHelp height.
MinBox	Boolean	TRUE or FALSE indicating the presence of a minimize box on the DataWindow.
MinPosition	Integer	An integer containing the value of the position attribute when a horizontal scroll bar is at the far left or a vertical scroll bar is at the top. For use in HScrollBar and VScrollBar controls only.
MinMax	String	A string containing the minimum and maximum values for a spin control in an Edit mask. The minimum and maximum values are separated with a tab (for example, em_field.minmax = "1000 5000").
MultiSelect	Boolean	TRUE or FALSE indicating whether or not the user can select multiple values in a ListBox.
ObjectType	Enumerated	An enumerated data type specifying the type of user object.
OriginalSize	Boolean	TRUE or FALSE indicating whether or not to override Height and Width attributes in Picture or PictureButton control and display the picture associated with the control at the original size.

(continues)

VI

References

Window Control Attributes   Continued

OverlapPercent	Integer	An integer specifying the percentage of the width of the data markers (for example, bars or columns) in different series overlap in a graph.
Password	Boolean	TRUE or FALSE indicating whether or not to make a Single Line Edit as password field.
Perspective	Integer	An integer (1 to 100) indicating the distance the graph is from the front of the window. The larger the number, the greater the distance and the smaller the graph appears.
PictureName	String	A string containing the name of the bit map in a Picture or PictureButton control.
Pointer	String	A string containing the mouse pointer for this object.
Position	Integer	The current position of a scroll bar. For use in the HScrollBar and VScrollBar attributes only.
Resizable	Boolean	TRUE or FALSE indicating whether or not the DataWindow is resizable.
Rotation	Integer	An integer indicating how much you want to rotate a graph from left to right.
Series	grAxis object	Sets the attributes of the series axis in a graph control.
ShadeColor	Integer	An integer determining the shading color of a graph.
ShowList	Boolean	TRUE or FALSE indicating whether or not to always show the list in a DropDownListBox.
Sorted	Boolean	TRUE or FALSE indicating whether or not to sort the elements in a ListBox or DropDownListBox by their display value.
Spacing	Integer	An integer determining the space between categories in a graph.
Spin	Boolean	TRUE or FALSE indicating whether or not an Edit mask has spin control.
StdHeight	Boolean	TRUE or FALSE indicating whether to use standard horizontal scroll bar height (TRUE) or system horizontal scroll bar height (FALSE).

Window Control Attributes

StdWidth	Boolean	TRUE or FALSE indicating whether to use standard vertical scroll bar height (TRUE) or system vertical scroll bar height (FALSE).
Style	Long	Controls the appearance of the user object.
TabOrder	Integer	An integer that describes the tab order of the window control in relation to other controls.
TabStop[]	Integer array	A signed integer array containing the position of the tab stops in an Edit mask, List Box or Multi-Line Edit.
Tag	String	A string containing the tag value of the window control.
Text	String	The text associated with a window control.
TextCase	Enumerated (Case!)	A Case! enumerated variable denoting the case of a text field.
TextColor	Long	A long indicating the color of text in a field.
TextSize	Integer	An integer indicating the size of the text in a text field.
ThirdState	Boolean	TRUE or FALSE indicating whether or not a check box is in its third state.
ThreeState	Boolean	TRUE or FALSE indicating whether or not a check box has three states (TRUE) or only two states (FALSE).
Title	String	A string containing the title of the DataWindow or graph.
TitleBar	Boolean	TRUE or FALSE indicating whether or not the DataWindow has a title bar.
TitleDispAttr	grDispAttr object	A grDispAttr object defining the style of a title in a graph.
Underline	Boolean	TRUE or FALSE specifying whether or not the text in a control is underlined.
UnitsPerColumn	Integer	A feature that indicates the number of PowerBuilder units a user scrolls when clicking on the scroll left or right.
UnitsPerLine	Integer	A feature that indicates the number of PowerBuilder units a user scrolls when clicking on the scroll up or down.

(continues)

VI

References

Window Control Attributes   Continued

UseCodeTable	Boolean	TRUE or FALSE indicating whether or not an Edit mask will use code tables. This is useful for spin controls in non-numeric fields.
Values	grAxis object	A feature that sets the attributes of the values in a graph control.
Visible	Boolean	TRUE or FALSE indicating whether or not the window control is visible or not.
VScrollBar	Boolean	TRUE or FALSE indicating whether or not the window control has a vertical scroll bar.
VTextAlign	Enumerated	An enumerated data type specifying the alignment of text in a PictureButton control. Valid values are Bottom!, MultiLine!, Top!, and VCenter!.
Weight	Integer	An integer containing the weight (line thickness) of the text. Weight is in points. PowerBuilder suggests 400 for normal or 700 for bold.
Width	Integer	A number indicating the width of the window control.
X	Integer	The X coordinate of the window control in relation to the window.
Y	Integer	The Y coordinate of the window control in relation to the window.

DataWindow Control Events

Clicked	The user has clicked on the window control.
Constructor	The window has opened and the window control is being constructed.
DBError	A database error has occurred on the DataWindow control.
Destructor	The parent window is closing and the control is closing (being destroyed) with it.
DoubleClicked	The user has double-clicked on the control.
DragDrop	The user has dropped an object on the window control.
DragEnter	A dragged object has entered the window control area.

DataWindow Control Events

DragLeave	A dragged object is leaving the window control area.
DragWithin	The user is dragging an object within the window control area.
EditChanged	The user is typing into an edit control.
GetFocus	The window control has received focus.
ItemChanged	An item has changed value in the DataWindow control.
ItemError	An item has not passed its validation test.
ItemFocusChanged	The focus within the DataWindow control has changed.
LineLeft	An HScrollBar has just moved one line left.
LineRight	An HScrollBar has just moved one line right.
LineUp	A VScrollBar has just moved one line up.
LineDown	A VScrollBar has just moved one line down.
LoseFocus	The window control is about to lose focus.
Modified	A multi-line edit, single-line edit, list box, or drop-down list box control loses focus and has been changed (modified).
Other	A Windows 3.x event has occurred that is not specific to PowerBuilder.
LineLeft	An HScrollBar has just moved one page left.
LineRight	An HScrollBar has just moved one page right.
PageUp	A VScrollBar has just moved one page up.
PageDown	A VScrollBar has just moved one page down.
PrintEnd	The DataWindow control has finished printing.
PrintPage	A new page is about to start printing.
PrintStart	The DataWindow control is about to print.
RButtonDown	The right mouse button is clicked on the window control.
Resize	The DataWindow control is being resized.
RetrieveEnd	A retrieve has just finished.
RetrieveRow	A row has been retrieved.

VI

References

(continues)

DataWindow Control Events Continued	
RetrieveStart	A retrieve is about to start.
RowFocusChanged	A new row has received focus.
ScrollHorizontal	The DataWindow control is being scrolled horizontally.
ScrollVertical	The DataWindow control is being scrolled vertically.
SelectionChanged	The selection has changed in a list box or drop-down list box.
SQLPreview	A Retrieve, Update, or ReselectRow function call has just been issued, but the function has not yet been executed.
UpdateEnd	An update has just finished.
UpdateStart	An update is about to start.

Chapter 24

Message Quick Reference

No matter how well you design and implement your system, situations will come up in your application that need to be handled. You already have coded some error handling. This reference discusses ways to handle errors and lists the errors, the corresponding error message, and the meaning of the error.

Handling PowerBuilder Messages

PowerBuilder errors are usually handled through the SystemError event in the application object. The exact error that occurred is stored in PowerBuilder's Error object structure.

SystemError Event

You already have coded the SystemError application event. The SystemError event is executed when a serious run time error occurs. If you don't write a SystemError script, PowerBuilder attempts to handle the error by displaying a message box containing the error number, error message, and Yes and No buttons, so the user can either continue or stop the application.

If the SystemError event has a script, PowerBuilder executes the script instead of displaying the message box. In the script for the SystemError event, you usually access the Error object to determine the error and where the error occurred.

◀ See "Programming for Application Events," p. 179

If you want to handle specific errors, usually CHOOSE CASE or IF statements are used. To halt the application, a HALT or HALT CLOSE is used.

Error Object

In the application SystemError event, you can access the Error object to determine the error and where the error occurred. To access the error object, statements like the following are executed:

```
int answer
    If Error.Number = 1 then
answer = Messagebox("System Error", &
    + "You tried to divide by zero at line "  &
    + string(Error.Line)  &
    + " in the " &
    + Error.ObjectEvent &
    + " event of the " &
    + Error.Object &
    + "."
    End If
```

The Error object structure is defined in table 24.1.

Table 24.1 Error Object Structure		
Error Structure Variable	**Data Type**	**Purpose for Variable**
Error.Number	Integer	An integer identifying the PowerBuilder error.
Error.Text	String	A string containing the text of the error message.
Error.WindowMenu	String	A string containing the name of the Window or Menu object in which the error occurred.
Error.Object	String	A string containing the name of the object in which the error occurred. If the error occurred in a window or menu, Object will be the same as WindowMenu.
Error.ObjectEvent	String	A string containing the event for which the error occurred.
Error.Line	Integer	An integer identifying the line in the script at which the error occurred.

SignalError( ) Function

Sometimes you'll want to initiate an error in an application. To do this, use the SignalError( ) function. SignalError( ) invokes the application SystemError event. To use SignalError(), move values into the Error Object and use the SystemError event.

Note

The SignalError() function returns 1 if successful and -1 if an error occurs, but usually the return value is not tested.

Following is an example of the use of the SignalError function. First assume that a file that should exist on the system has been deleted. The signal error function triggers a custom SystemError event.

```
error.number = 99
error.text = "File not found!  Please Restore!"
error.windowmenu = "w_window"
error.object = "cb_openfile"
error.ObjectEvent = "Clicked!"
error.line = 5
SignalError ( )
```

Run Time Errors

Table 24.2 is a list of PowerBuilder errors, the corresponding message, and the meaning and/or probable cause of the PowerBuilder error.

Table 24.2   PowerBuilder Error Messages

Number	Message	Meaning
1	Divide by zero	You tried to divide by zero. Probably one of your variables was inadvertently set to zero.
2	Null object reference	You tried to access a variable or object that has not been declared or opened yet.
3	Array boundary exceeded	You have declared an array but have exceeded the upper limit. This happens often with variable length arrays which are set with the first access.
4	Enumerated value is out of range for function	The function requires an enumerated data type, but you have passed it a value that is out of scope for the enumerated data type.

(continues)

VI

References

Table 24.2 Continued

Number	Message	Meaning
5	Negative value encountered in function	This is a low level error that occurs when a function tries to reference a negative memory address.
6	Invalid DataWindow row/column specified	You tried a DataWindow row function on a row that doesn't exist in your DataWindow, or you tried to access a column (probably with a string) that does not exist. This happens often when you misspell a column name.
7	Unresolvable external when linking reference	Some DLLs can have multiple functions with the same name. If this happens, PowerBuilder will not be able to resolve which function to call.
8	Reference of array with NULL subscript	The offset integer you used with your array has been set to NULL. This happens often if an SQL call to fill your offset integer has failed.
9	DLL function not found in current application	You made a function call to a DLL but deleted the reference to it in the external references.
10	Unsupported argument type in DLL function	A function in your DLL requires an argument whose data type is not supported in PowerBuilder.
12	DataWindow column type does not match GetItem type	You issued a GetItem function, but the type of variable listed in the GetItem function is not the type of variable declared on the DataWindow.
13	Unresolved attribute reference	The attribute you are trying to set does not exist for this object. This happens when you use a PowerObject variable type to store an object, and then try to reference an attribute of that variable type.
14	Error opening DLL library for external function	The DLL you specified in your external definition does not exist or cannot be opened for some reason. A corrupted DLL will also cause this message.

Number	Message	Meaning
15	Error calling external function	You tried to link your program with a function inside an external DLL, but PowerBuilder could not find the function. This happens often when you misspell the function name. Also, some C and especially some C++ programs perform "name maligning" to support polymorphism. Name Maligning must be turned off for PowerBuilder to access your DLL.
16	Maximum string size exceeded	Strings can only be 32K in PowerBuilder. Somehow you have exceeded this. Look for a runaway loop.
17	DataWindow referenced in DataWindow object does not exist	You tried to define a DDDW (Drop Down DataWindow) in your DataWindow that does not exist.
50	Application reference could not be resolved	You have made a reference in your application which has one or more possible reference targets.
51	Failure loading dynamic library	You declared a dynamic library resource that does not exist.

Handling Watcom SQL Messages

Watcom SQL also has error messages. These messages are listed alphabetically in a quick reference format, as well as in a descriptive format, in your Watcom SQL book that comes with PowerBuilder. Table 24.3 gives you quick access to all your Watcom SQLDBCODE messages, and lets you limit the number of books you have to carry around with you.

Note

An '%s' in table 24.3 refers to a string in the message that Watcom passes back to the application.

VI

References

Table 24.3 Watcom SQL Messages	
SQLDBCODE	**Description of Message**
0	(no error and no message)
100	row not found
101	value truncated
102	using temporary table
103	invalid data conversion
104	row has been updated since last time read
105	Open or Resume has caused a stored procedure to execute to completion or a cursor to restart
200	warning
271	trigger definition conflicts with existing triggers
400	the supplied buffer was too small to hold all requested query results
-074	database is in an inactive state
-075	access was denied
-076	no loaded databases
-077	database name is conflicting with the name of another loaded database
-078	could not allocate dynamic memory
-079	bad switch has passed
-080	unable to start database engine
-081	invalid database engine command line
-082	unable to start specified database
-083	specified database not found
-084	specified database is invalid
-085	communication error
-086	not enough memory to start
-087	database name required to start engine

SQLDBCODE	Description of Message
-088	client/server communications protocol mismatch
-089	database engine not running in multi-user mode
-095	could not parse string parameter in a START command
-096	database engine is already running
-099	connections to database have been disabled
-100	database engine not running
-101	not connected to SQL database
-102	too many connections to database
-103	invalid UserID or password
-104	invalid UserID and password on preprocessed module
-105	cannot be started — '%s'
-106	cannot open log file '%s'
-107	error writing to log file
-108	connection not found
-109	there are still active database connections
-110	'%s' already exists
-111	index name '%s' not unique
-112	table already has a primary key
-113	column '%s' in foreign key has a different definition than primary key
-114	number of columns does not match SELECT
-116	table must be empty
-118	table '%s' has no primary key
-119	primary key column '%s' already defined
-120	'%s' already has grant permission
-121	do not have permission to '%s'

VI

(continues)

SQLDBCODE	Description of Message
Table 24.3 Continued	
-122	operation would cause a group cycle
-123	'%s' is not a user group
-125	ALTER clause conflict
-126	table cannot have two primary keys
-127	cannot alter a column in an index
-128	cannot drop a user that owns tables in run time engine
-130	invalid statement
-131	syntax error near '%s'
-132	SQL statement error
-133	invalid prepared statement type
-134	'%s' not implemented
-135	language extension
-138	tablespace could not be found
-139	more than one table is identified as '%s'
-140	UserID could not be found
-141	table '%s' not found
-142	correlation name '%s' not found
-143	column '%s' not found
-144	column '%s' found in more than one table—need a correlation name
-145	foreign key name '%s' not found
-146	no way to join '%s' to '%s'
-147	more than one way to join '%s' to '%s'
-148	unknown function '%s'
-149	column '%s' cannot be used unless it is in a GROUP BY
-150	aggregate functions not allowed on this statement

SQLDBCODE	Description of Message
-151	subquery allowed only one select list item
-152	number in ORDER BY is too large
-153	SELECT lists in UNION do not match in length
-154	wrong number of parameters to function '%s'
-155	invalid host variable
-156	invalid expression near '%s'
-157	cannot convert '%s' to a '%s'
-158	value '%s' too large for destination
-159	invalid column number
-160	can only describe a SELECT statement
-161	invalid type on DESCRIBE statement
-170	cursor has not been declared
-172	cursor already open
-180	cursor not open
-181	no indicator variable provided for NULL result
-182	not enough fields allocated in SQLDA
-183	cannot find index named '%s'
-184	error inserting into cursor
-185	SELECT returns more than one row
-186	subquery cannot return more than one result
-187	invalid operation for this cursor
-188	not enough values for host variables
-189	unable to find in index '%s' for table '%s'
-190	cannot update an expression
-191	cannot modify column '%s' in table '%s'
-192	invalid operation on joined tables

(continues)

VI

References

Table 24.3 Continued	
SQLDBCODE	**Description of Message**
-193	primary key for table '%s' is not unique
-194	no primary key value for foreign key '%s' in table '%s'
-195	column '%s' in table '%s' cannot be NULL
-196	index '%s' for table '%s' would not be unique
-197	no current row of cursor
-198	primary key for row in table '%s' is referenced in another table
-199	INSERT/DELETE on cursor can modify only one table
-200	invalid option '%s'—no PUBLIC setting exists
-201	invalid setting for option '%s'
-207	wrong number of values for INSERT
-208	row has changed since last read—operation canceled
-209	invalid value for column '%s' in table '%s'
-210	'%s' has the row in '%s' locked
-211	not allowed while '%s' is using the database
-212	CHECKPOINT command requires a rollback log
-213	SAVEPOINT was attempted without a rollback log
-214	table in use
-215	procedure in use
-220	subtransaction '%s' not found
-221	tried to rollback within an atomic compound statement
-222	SELECT without INTO or a RESULT CURSOR were attempted within an atomic compound statement
-230	sqlpp/dblib version mismatch
-231	dblib/database engine version mismatch
-232	server/database engine version mismatch
-240	unknown backup operation

SQLDBCODE	Description of Message
-241	database backup not started
-242	incomplete transactions prevent transaction log renaming
-243	unable to delete database file
-250	identifier '%s' too long
-251	foreign key '%s' for table '%s' duplicates an existing foreign key
-260	variable '%s' not found
-261	already a variable named '%s'
-262	label '%s' not found
-263	invalid absolute or relative offset in FETCH
-264	wrong number of variables in FETCH
-265	procedure '%s' not found
-266	database was initialized with an older version of the software
-267	COMMIT/ROLLBACK not allowed within ATOMIC compound statement
-268	trigger '%s' not found
-269	cannot delete a column referenced in a trigger definition
-270	cannot drop a user that owns procedures in run time engine
-271	trigger could not be created because of conflicts with an existing trigger
-272	invalid REFERENCES clause in trigger definition
-273	COMMIT/ROLLBACK not allowed within trigger actions
-274	infinite loop caused by a procedure or trigger
-297	stored procedure or trigger signaled a user-defined exception
-298	attempted two active database requests
-299	statement interrupted by user

(continues)

Table 24.3 Continued	
SQLDBCODE	**Description of Message**
-300	run time SQL error—'%s'
-301	internal database error '%s' transaction rolled back
-302	terminated by user transaction rolled back
-304	disk full transaction rolled back
-305	I/O error '%s' transaction rolled back
-306	deadlock detected
-307	all threads are blocked

Appendixes

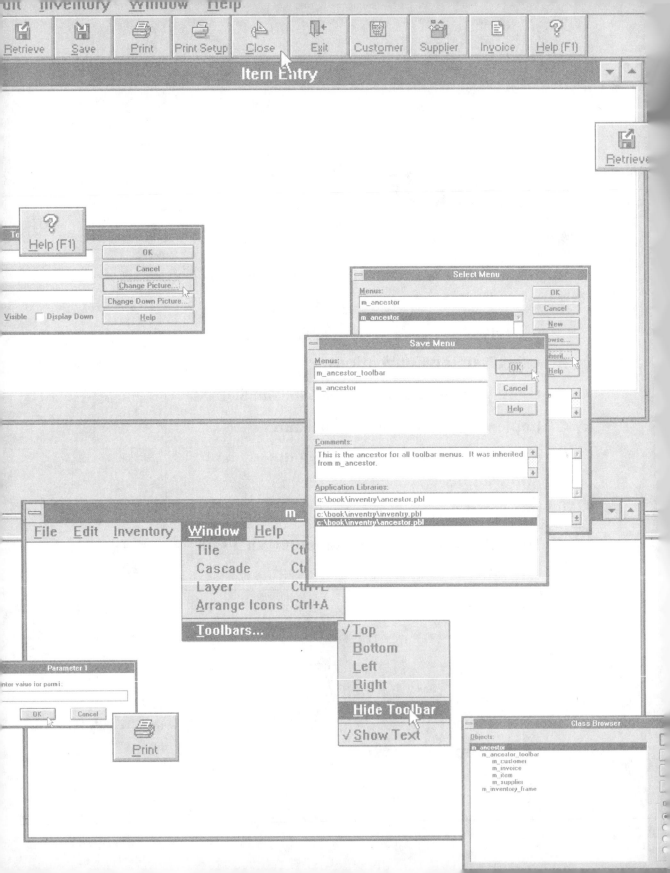

Appendix A

Using Naming Conventions

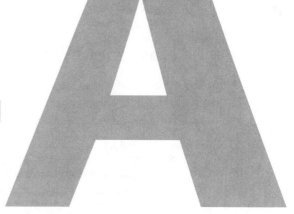

The naming conventions in this appendix are suggestions. Use the naming conventions that best suit your needs—the important thing is to use naming conventions while developing. Naming conventions makes maintenance and debugging much easier.

These naming conventions rely on a prefix that indicates exactly what kind of variable or data you are dealing with.

Naming Objects

PowerBuilder uses seven object types within an application to build its systems. Table A.1 shows the naming conventions for object types.

Table A.1   Naming Object Types

Object Name	Convention	Example
DataWindow Object	d_	d_client
Function (global)	f_	f_display_error
Menu	m_	m_client
Structure	s_	s_employee
Query	q_	q_clients_for_agent
User Object	u_	u_request
Window	w_	w_ancestor

Naming Window Controls

Every window can have several controls. These controls have default names, but should be renamed to be more descriptive and to make your application more manageable. Table A.2 shows the suggested window control prefixes.

Table A.2 Naming Window Controls

Control Name	Convention	Example
CheckBox	cbx_	cbx_draft
CommandButton	cb_	cb_OK
DataWindow Control	dw_	dw_data
DropDownListBox	ddlb_	ddlb_agents
Edit Mask	em_	em_phone
Window Function	wf_	wf_sqlerr
Graph	gr_	gr_income_per_agent
GroupBox	gb_	gb_output_choice
HScrollBar	hsb_	hsb_red
Line	ln_	ln_shortline
ListBox	lb_	lb_agents
MultiLineEdit	mle_	mle_comments
Oval	oval_	oval_team
Picture	p_	p_employee
PictureButton	pb_	pb_update
RadioButton	rb_	rb_construction
Rectangle	r_	r_rect
RoundRectangle	rr_	rr_screen
SingleLineEdit	sle_	sle_customer_name
StaticText	st_	st_customer_prompt
UserObject	uo_	uo_request
VScrollBarr	vsb_	vsb_percent_done

Naming Variables

Every variable has a scope (when it can be accessed) and a data type. The scope should always be as limited as possible. For example, don't use an instance variable when a local variable will suffice. Limiting scope will aid in encapsulation, release memory sooner and make the application easier to maintain.

In the variable scope, x indicates the data-type convention that follows the variable-scope conventions.

Naming by Scope

Table A.3 describes the conventions for naming by scope.

Table A.3 Naming by Scope	
Variable Scope	**Convention**
Local	l*x*_ or nothing (a prefix on local variables is optional)
Global	g*x*_
Instance	i*x*_
Shared	s*x*_
Argument	a*x*_

Naming by Data Type

Table A.4 describes the conventions for naming by data type.

Table A.4 Naming by Data Type	
Data Type	**Convention**
Window	w
MenuItem	m
DataWindow Control	dw
Structure	str
User Object	uo
Integer	i

(continues)

Table A.4 Continued	
Data Type	**Convention**
Unsigned Integer	ui
Long	l
Unsigned Long	ul
Boolean	b
String	s
Double	db
Real	r
Decimal	dc
Date	d
Time	t
DateTime	dt or ts (TimeStamp)

Naming Variable Examples

Table A.5 lists naming variable examples.

Table A.5 Naming Variable Examples	
Variable Name	**Data Type Description**
sstr_data_points[ ]	Shared Structure array
iul_client_id	Instance of an Unsigned Long
ss_name	Shared String
ii_count	Instance of an integer
loop_count	local variable (prefix not required)
li_loop_count	local integer (optional prefix added)
lw_window_instance	local instance of a window variable
as_error	argument string (passed)

Object Functions

Along with global functions, functions can be attached to individual objects. The object prefix should precede the function prefix to indicate a function that is tied to a specific object.

Table A.6 describes naming object functions.

Table A.6 Naming Object Functions		
Function Object Type	**Convention**	**Example**
Global Function	f_	f_sql_error
Menu Function	mf_	mf_exit
User Object Function	uf_	uf_request
Window Function	wf_	wf_update

Using Watcom Database and Watcom SQL

Watcom SQL is one of the many databases supported by PowerBuilder. In 1993, PowerSoft and Watcom merged companies. Now, a development copy of Watcom SQL is included in every version of PowerBuilder as well as other PowerSoft products like InfoMaker.

If you've used Watcom SQL in the past but felt the product wasn't meeting your needs, you may be in for a surprise! Watcom SQL Version 3.2 has added huge performance boosts. Watcom SQL Version 4.0 has also increased performance and added high-level features such as stored procedures, triggers, cascading updates and deletes, multiple database-single server support, and temporary tables.

According to the October 11, 1994 issue of *PC Magazine*, Watcom performance keeps up with other SQL server databases and, in fact, has the best response time for single-user ad hoc queries of any tested database. (Ad hoc query benchmarks test a product's effectiveness in a decision-support environment, like PowerBuilder.)

Watcom SQL's price per user is the lowest in the industry for SQL servers *for any number of users* compared to other mainstream SQL databases. Its price/performance ratio (as determined by *PC Magazine*) is the best for under-18 users and always competitive with other tested databases for any number of users!

Furthermore, their installation of Watcom SQL is the easiest in the industry. You can install the run time by running SETUP.EXE from the setup disk. The Watcom development environment is automatically installed when you install PowerBuilder.

If money is a factor or if you have a limited support staff coupled with a department-wide or peer-to-peer database or want to distribute a stand-alone copy of your work, Watcom should be your database of choice.

The Watcom SQL database is provided with PowerBuilder. There are many actions you can perform with Watcom SQL that are not included in the Watcom SQL documentation.

Understanding Watcom SQL Files

Watcom SQL uses DOS files to store data. These files include the .DB file, .LOG file, and several temporary files used for processing. The .LOG and .DB files are defined in this section.

Understanding the Watcom SQL DB (Database) File

All your tables go into a single database (DB) file on your hard drive. All the tables that are created in the database painter in Chapter 2 are stored in the INVENTRY.DB file. Your database file (INVENTRY.DB) should be backed up on a regular basis using backup software or the BACKUP command that comes with MS-DOS.

Understanding the Watcom SQL LOG (Transaction Log) File

Your PowerBuilder Watcom SQL application also generates a *log*, which is a file with a LOG extension. (The Inventory Tracking system described in this book uses INVENTRY.LOG.) This log file is called the *transaction log* or the *forward log* file. The transaction log is optional when the database is created, but if created inside PowerBuilder, the transaction log always exists.

The log is used to record transactions to the database. Without a log, Watcom is forced to perform a checkpoint every time you write to disk. (A *checkpoint* writes a copy of any updates you make to the hard disk into a temporary file.) Often, this can slow down database updates.

A transaction log is also used to make Watcom more stable. If the Watcom SQL database file was corrupted, the transaction log and the previous backup could be used to restore your database *up to the moment of failure*! This is because all database transactions are recorded in the transaction log.

If you have a machine with two physical hard drives, it's good to write the log to a separate hard drive from the database. If the disk with the database file crashes, the transaction log will remain intact on the other hard drive. The transaction log can then be used to restore the database.

Watcom SQL defaults to using a transaction log with the same file name as your .DB file but with a .LOG extension (for example, INVENTRY.LOG). You can change the default status of your log with the DBINITW program when you create your database. You can also change the log settings of a database with the DBLOGW program if your database is in existence, or convert your log to SQL using the DBTRANW program. These Watcom SQL programs are included with PowerBuilder, and are discussed in the next section.

Using Watcom SQL

The PowerBuilder version of Watcom includes several programs that can help you manage your Watcom SQL database—especially upon distribution. These programs are on your disk and are probably in either your PowerBuilder directory or your WSQL directory (depending on which one you installed first). Examples are given later in this chapter.

Watcom SQL programs will not run within the PowerBuilder environment. It is necessary to run the Watcom SQL programs by opening the **F**ile menu and choosing **R**un in Windows, or by clicking an icon and pressing Ctrl+R. Several of the programs take command line options, but you also can run them through an icon if you want to set one up.

This documentation will discuss the purpose of each program. If the syntax documentation provided by PowerBuilder is incomplete, a fuller syntax definition will follow. All of the programs are included with PowerBuilder, but are run outside of the PowerBuilder environment. However, many can be duplicated with the database painter from within the PowerBuilder environment.

Understanding Connection Parameters

Connection parameters have been changed in Watcom 4.0. Watcom SQL commands established connection to databases in previous versions (of course), but the commands were cryptic and hard to use. In Version 4, connection parameters are clearly marked.

Connection parameters are used when you want to connect to a database. Commands that use connection parameters are DBBACKW, DBUNLOAW,

DBVALIDW, DBWATCHW, and ISQL. (These commands are reviewed later in this section.) Table B.1 lists the verbose keyword, the short form of the keyword, an example of how to use the connection parameter, and a description of each.

Table B.1	Command Parameters		
Verbose Keyword	**Short Form**	**Example**	**Description**
Userid	UID	UID=dba	The user id defined in the Grant SQL statement.
Password	PWD	PWD=SQL	The password of the user id.
Connection	CON	CON=conn1	The name of the connection used to connect to the database (for multiple database connections).
EngineName	ENG	ENG=Sample	The name of the ODBC engine to start.
Database Name	DBN	DBN=Powersoft Demo DB	The name of the database assigned by the database configuration in the database painter.
Database File	DBF	DBF=\wsql\sample.db	The file of the database.
DatabaseSwitches	DBS	DBS=-d	Switches used in the database.
AutoStop	AutoStop	AutoStop	(In PB.INI, use AUTOSTOP=TRUE) Disconnects from the database after the command that's using the connection parameters is finished if there are no other connections to the database.
Start	Start	Start=DB32W	The name of the Watcom program used to start the database Engine.
Unconditional	UNC	UNC	(In PB.INI, use UNC=TRUE) Starts the database even if the log file cannot be used.

The following is an example of how to use a connection parameter:

```
UID=dba;PWD=sql;ENG=sample
```

You'll notice this line is similar to the CONNECTSTRING parameter found in the PB.INI file. You can also connect using positional parameters without qualifiers as was necessary in PowerBuilder Version 3.0 as follows:

```
dba,sql,sample
```

Using the old positional connection parameters will connect to a database engine, but using positional connection parameters will disable the use of multiple databases running on one server. (Running multiple databases on one server is a new feature of Watcom 4.0.)

Using DB32W.EXE, DBSTARTW.EXE, RT32W.EXE, and RTSTARTW.EXE

Watcom SQL programs DB32W.EXE, DBSTARTW.EXE, RT32W.EXE, and RTSTARTW.EXE are the Watcom SQL database engines. You choose one of the database engines when starting your database to describe the access your program will have when your database is running. The engines with a 32 in their name indicate 32-bit disk access will be used; 32-bit access should be used if possible.

> **Tip**
> 32-bit access takes advantage of the advanced architecture of the Intel 80386 chip (and later versions of Intel processors) to speed up your disk access.

The database engines are the only Watcom SQL program that you can run within PowerBuilder. To define your database engine, get into the database painter by clicking on the Database icon. Then click on **F**ile and choose Con-figure **O**DBC. The Configure ODBC dialog box appears. Click on the database driver for your database and choose your database (data source).

This pulls up the WATCOM SQL ODBC Configuration dialog box. In the **E**xecute text box (where the mouse is pointing in fig. B.1), type in the data-base engine with flags that you want to use.

The syntax for the WATCOM SQL start program is as follows:

```
program_name [flags] database_file
```

program_name. This can be DB32W, RT32W, DBSTARTW, or RTSTARTW. If you have a 386 or 486 machine, you should use RT32W or DB32W.

database_file. This is the name of the database file on your hard drive. (For the Inventory Tracking database, it is INVENTRY.DB.)

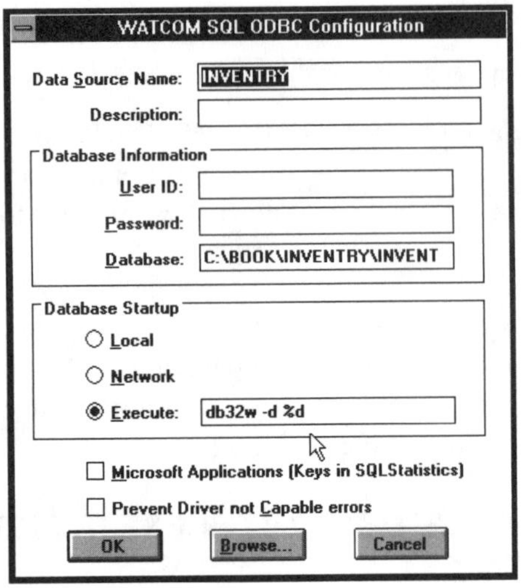

Fig. B.1
In the WATCOM
SQL ODBC
Configuration
dialog box,
instruct Watcom
to execute DB32W
to run your
database.

flags. The flags in use are as follows:

- **-b** Use Bulk mode. Although this is handy for large quantities of data at a time, it is not recommended for everyday use because it forces autocommit (which commits automatically after every SQL instruction) and only allows one user.

- **-c** Set cache size. This is a number that sets the size of the cache. Any cache size less than 10,000 is assumed to be kilobytes (K). If an M is placed at the end of the number, megabytes is assumed. By default, the database uses 2M cache.

- **-n** Set the name of the database engine. By default, the name is the name of the database file. (For the Inventory Tracking system, the default is INVENTRY.)

- **-q** Quiet mode. Don't print any messages.

- **-v** Log old values of columns on SQL Updates as opposed to only enough information to uniquely identify the key. This is useful if you are working on a copy of the database.

- **-a translog** Apply the transaction log named by translog. This option applies the log and then terminates.

- **-f** Force-start the database. This starts the database without a log, and immediately terminates. This is handy for clearing the database once the log has been lost.

- **-d** Use normal DOS input and output instead of direct BIOS input and output. When you have a small database (less than 3M), and you have disk-caching software running, DOS calls can be faster than BIOS calls. If your database is over 10M, don't use this flag.

- **-noems** Don't use expanded memory.

- **-noext** Don't use extended memory.

- **-nofar** Don't use DOS 640K for extra cache.

- **-u size** Use only size bytes of lower (640K) memory. This option is handy if your application takes up too much lower memory space, but can really slow down your database. Never set size any less than 200K.

Troubleshooting

My Watcom SQL program works fine on my computer and on all computers with PowerBuilder or Watcom SQL installed, but when I try to make a stand-alone version, I can't access the database. What should I do?

When you install PowerBuilder, your Watcom databases are configured to use DB32W as the starting program. The run time version does not have DB32W; it must run RT32W or RTSTARTW. Be sure you change it if you are distributing Watcom's run time SQL version with your program.

Using DBBACKW.EXE

DBBACKW makes a backup copy of all the files that make up a single database, which include all tablespaces and log files. From here, you also can erase and restart your transaction file. An example of the function call is as follows:

```
DBBACKW -c UID=dba,PWD=sql,ENG=inventry \book\inventry
```

In the DBBACKW command, you can specify the database and where it's located. For a complete description on uses of the DBBACKW command, see your Watcom SQL reference manual.

Using DBCOLLW.EXE

This extracts a *collation* (sorting sequence) from your database, suitable for use with DBINITW, to create a database using a custom collation. This is for the really advanced database power user. A *custom collation* is a sort order that is not ascending or descending. For instance, if you want city names to appear in ZIP code order when indexing your file, you can use a custom collation. DBCOLLW extracts that collation, if one exists.

The syntax for DBCOLLW is as follows:

```
DBCOLLW [flags] output_file
```

flags. The flags in use are as follows:

- **-c** [connection parameters]   Supply the database-connection parameters.

- **-e**   Include empty mappings. Normally, collations don't specify the actual value that a character is to sort to. Instead, each line of the collation sequence sorts to one higher than the last one. However, older collations have gaps between some sort positions. DBCOLLW skips these gaps unless the -e flag is specified.

- **-q**   Quiet mode. Don't print any messages.

- **-s** "cmd"   Specify the command line to start the database. This defaults to DBSTARTW.

- **-x**   Use hex for extended characters. Some sites support extended characters, especially for foreign languages. If an extended character goes above hex 7F, this flag converts the character to a two-digit hexadecimal number.

- **-y**   Replace the existing output file without asking for permission.

- **-z col-seq**   Specify the collating sequence label. Use this if the label is different than the one being used by the database.

output_file. This is the name of the file you want to place your collating sequence in.

Using DBERASEW.EXE

DBERASEW erases a database, log file, or write file. This is useful because Watcom SQL database and log files are marked read-only. The format for DBERASEW is as follows:

```
DBERASEW [flags] filename
```

flags. The flags in use are as follows:

- **-q**   Do not print any messages.

- **-y**   Erase database without confirmation.

filename. This is the name of the log file, database file, or write file you wish to delete.

Using DBEXPANW.EXE

DBEXPANW expands a compressed database created by DBSHRINW, which is a good method for distribution. The format for DBEXPANW is:

```
DBEXPANW [flags] compressed_file database
```

flags. The flags in use are as follows:

- **-q** Do not print any messages.

- **-y** Operate without confirming actions.

compressed_file. This is the name of the compressed file created by DBSHRINW. If no extension is listed, a .CDB extension is used.

database. This is the name of the database you want to create. If no extension is listed, a .DB extension is used.

Using DBINFOW.EXE

DBINFOW displays information about a database file or write file, including the options that were used to create the database, the name of the transaction log file, and other information. The database engine shouldn't be running when you run DBINFOW. The format for DBINFOW is:

```
DBINFOW [flags] filename
```

flags. The flags in use are as follows:

- **-c** [connection parameters]   Supply the database-connection parameters.

- **-q** Do not print any messages.

- **-s** "cmd"   Specify the command line to start the database. This defaults to DBSTARTW.

- **-u** Output page-usage statistics.

filename. This is the name of the database or write file that you want information about.

Using DBINITW.EXE

This creates a new database. An example of its use is as follows:

```
DBINITW INVENTRY.DB
```

The Watcom SQL manual provided with PowerBuilder does a fine job describing DBINITW, except that you can also use the -l flag to list available collating sequences.

Using DBLOGW.EXE

DBLOGW is used to display or change the name of the transaction log. Its format is as follows:

```
DBLOGW [flags] database
```

flags. The flags in use are as follows:

- **-n**   Do not use a transaction log.

- **-q**   Do not print any messages.

- **-t** *log_name*   Change the name of the transaction log file to *log_name*.

database. This is the name of the database you want to access.

Using DBSHRINW.EXE

DBSHRINW compresses a database that can later be expanded using DBEXPANW. This is a good method for distribution. The format for DBSHRINW is:

```
DBSHRINW [flags] database compressed_file
```

flags. The flags in use are as follows:

- **-q**   Do not print any messages.

- **-v**   Verbose output. Any additional status messages will be displayed.

database. This is the name of the database you want to compress. If no extension is listed, a .DB extension is used.

compressed_file. This is the name of the compressed file to be created. If no extension is listed, a .CDB extension is used.

Using DBTRANW.EXE

DBTRANW translates the log file into an ASCII SQL command file. An example of DBTRANW is as follows:

```
DBTRANW INVENTRY.LOG INVENTRY.SQL
```

This command translates the inventory transaction log file to INVENTRY.SQL.

Using DBUNLOAW.EXE

DBUNLOAW is used to unload a database into an ASCII file containing SQL statements called RELOAD.SQL (unless you use the flags described in the

Watcom SQL manual to change the name of your output file). An example of DBUNLOAW is as follows:

```
DBUNLOAW -c UID=dba,PWD=sql,ENG=inventry \book\inventry
```

This command creates RELOAD.SQL in the \book\inventry directory, which will contain SQL calls to duplicate the inventory database.

Using DBVALIDW.EXE
DBVALIDW validates all indexes on a table in the database. It is good to use in conjunction with DBBACKW. An example of DBVALIDW is as follows:

```
DBVALIDW  -c UID=dba,PWD=sql,ENG=inventry
```

The above statement validates the item table in the inventory database.

Using DBWRITEW.EXE
DBWRITEW is used to manage database *write files*, which are files that contain all the changes to a particular database, leaving the original database unchanged. An example of starting up a write file using DBWRITEW is as follows:

```
DBWRITEW \book\inventry\inventry.db \book\inventry\inventry.wrt
```

This statement creates a write file for the inventory database.

Tip
Write files are good to use for testing because they don't allow corruption or data manipulation of the database.

Using DBSQLW.EXE and RTSQLW.EXE
DBSQLW (and RTSQLW in the run time version) allows you to run ASCII files containing interactive SQL statements. Interactive SQL (or ISQL) is a broader set of SQL statements. The format for DBSQLW and RTSQLW is as follows:

```
command [flags] sqlfile/sqlcommand
```

command. The command can be DBSQLW or RTSQLW.

flags. The flags in use are as follows:

- **-c** [connection_parameters] Supply the database-connection parameters.

- **-q** Do not print any messages.

- **-s** "cmd" The command to start the database. Defaults to DBSTARTW.

- **-v** Verbose mode; output information on commands.

- **-x** Syntax check only; no commands are executed.

sqlfile/sqlcommand. This can either be a single command or an SQL file containing many SQL commands.

RTSQLW is really useful for installation programs—you can issue ISQL commands that aren't available to you in PowerScript.

Exploring Embedded SQL and ISQL

Embedded SQL is the SQL you can use within a programming language such as PowerScript. ISQL or interactive SQL is SQL that can be used from the DBSQLW and RTSQLW programs.

There are several ISQL commands that are useful, especially in installation programs (they aren't available in PowerScript). A listing of available commands can be reviewed in the Listing ISQL Commands section later in this chapter.

Comparing the Run Time Version and the Developer's Version

There are certain commands you can run in PowerScript or in DBSQLW that aren't available when using RTSQLW. Inconsistencies between the developer's version of Watcom SQL and the run time version of Watcom SQL can cause many problems if you're running under one environment but distributing under another.

Using the run time version, you can't issue any CREATE, ALTER, or DROP SQL statements. Although they work in your test environment, they no longer work when you distribute with the run time environment.

Using RTSQLW or DBSQLW, you can execute your own SQL. In a DOS editor, create your SQL statements in an ASCII file. The following command runs the SQL commands in sqlfil.sql against the Inventory Tracking database:

```
\pb3\RTSQLW.EXE -v -c dba,sql,\book\inventry\inventry
➥\book\inventry\sqlfil
```

In the above example, inventry is the database and sqlfil is the file with the SQL statements.

Listing Watcom ISQL Commands

No ISQL commands appear in the Watcom SQL. This section lists Watcom's ISQL commands available to you through RTSQLW and DBSQLW.

Using CONFIGURE

CONFIGURE allows you to design your database environment. The syntax for the CONFIGURE command is simply:

```
CONFIGURE;
```

The CONFIGURE command pulls up the ISQL Configuration dialog box (see fig. B.2), which allows you to configure your ISQL commands.

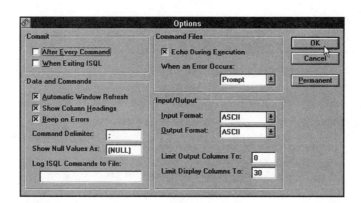

Tip
When using the RTSQLW program, if you leave off the extension on your database or your SQL file, .DB or .SQL are assumed.

Fig. B.2
The Options dialog box is pulled up by the ISQL CONFIGURE; command.

Using Variables

Variables can be used inside an SQL script. Where typically you need a programming language to use variables, Watcom gives the developer the capability to declare variables without resorting to programming in a conventional language like PowerScript. You can manipulate variables with the following Watcom SQL commands:

```
CREATE VARIABLE identifier data_type;
SET identifier = constant or identifier;
DROP VARIABLE identifier;
```

The CREATE VARIABLE statement creates a variable in SQL and specifies a data_type. The variable created contains a NULL until it is set by the SET command. The DROP VARIABLE command releases the variable. The variable is dropped at disconnect if no drop statement is made.

Tip
The -v flag on the RTSQLW command forces verbose messages. By typing **CONFIGURE;** at the end of your SQL file, you force the RTSQLW program to stop at the end until you're ready to go on.

Assume the following rows exist on the Customer table:

customer number	customer name	customer contact	customer address1
1	Zeppelins and Blimps	Robert Plant	123 4th St.
2	Silver Bullets and More	Bob Seger	231 123rd St.
3	Queen Headgear	Freddy Mercury	33 Bohemian Avenue
4	Grapes, Nuts, and Health Foods	Euell Gibbons	8 Pine Tree
5	Doors, Inc.	Jim Morrison	23 Stormriders Court

The following ISQL runs through RTSQLW:

```
Create Variable avg_cust int;
Set avg_cust = 3;
select customer_name
        from customer
            where customer_number > avg_cust;
output to \book\inventry\highcust.dat format ASCII;
configure;
```

The resulting output in \book\inventry\highcust.dat is:

```
'Grapes, Nuts, and Health Foods'
'Doors, Inc.'
```

All customer_names were selected whose corresponding customer number was greater than 3. You can see the resulting RTSQLW window in figure B.3.

Fig. B.3
With the verbose flag on (-v) in RTSQLW, you can see the results of your testing in the ISQL message box.

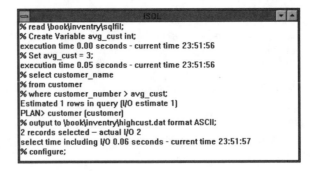

```
% read \book\inventry\sqlfil;
% Create Variable avg_cust int;
execution time 0.00 seconds - current time 23:51:56
% Set avg_cust = 3;
execution time 0.05 seconds - current time 23:51:56
% select customer_name
% from customer
% where customer_number > avg_cust;
Estimated 1 rows in query (I/O estimate 1)
PLAN> customer (customer)
% output to \book\inventry\highcust.dat format ASCII;
2 records selected — actual I/O 2
select time including I/O 0.06 seconds - current time 23:51:57
% configure;
```

Using INPUT

```
INPUT INTO {creator}.table
    FROM filename or PROMPT
    { FORMAT filetype }
    { BY NAME }
    { DELIMITED BY string  }
    { COLUMN WIDTHS (integer, ....)};
    { NOSTRIP }
    { (column_name,...) };
```

Tip

If possible, test your SQL function calls through RTSQLW using the verbose flag. As you can see in figure B.3, time for each statement is provided.

filename. The name of the input file. You can see the PROMPT clause instead of the FROM clause, and the user will be prompted for the file name.

filetype. The type of file format. Allowable formats are ASCII, DBASEII, DBASEIII, DIF, FIXED, LOTUS, SQL, TEXT, and WATFILE. If this clause is left out, INPUT tries to determine the file type on its own.

BY NAME. Allows you to input into a table, based on the name of the field, if your input file format is one that contains column names. If this is left out, INPUT will try to read the input file BY ORDER.

NOSTRIP and **DELIMITED BY.** For ASCII file formats only. Normally, space padding is stripped out by the INPUT command. The NOSTRIP clause leaves any space padding in. DELIMITED BY *string* will put a specified delimiter between columns. (The default is commas.)

COLUMN WIDTHS. Valid only for FIXED format. This specifies the width of each column. The default is computed for the data type for that column, and is large enough to hold any value of that data type.

column_names. Allows you to specify which columns will be input and in what order.

Using OUTPUT

```
OUTPUT TO filename
    FORMAT filetype
    { DELIMITED BY string  }
    { QUOTE quote_string {ALL}}
    { COLUMN WIDTHS (integer, ....)};
```

filename. The name of the output file.

filetype. The type of file format. Allowable formats are ASCII, DBASEII, DBASEIII, DIF, FIXED, LOTUS, SQL, TEXT, and WATFILE.

The DELIMITED BY and QUOTE clauses are for ASCII file formats only. The DELIMITED BY *string* will put a specified delimiter between columns. (The default is commas.) The *quote_string* specifies what quote symbol will be placed around string variables (default ' — single quote). It specifies all placed quotes around all columns, not just string columns.

COLUMN WIDTHS. Valid only for FIXED format. This specifies the width of each column. The default is computed for the data type for that column, and is large enough to hold any value of that data type.

See the CREATE VARIABLE example to view the OUTPUT command.

Using PARAMETERS

```
PARAMETERS parameter1, parameter2, ...
```

PARAMETERS. Allows you to specify input parameters coming in from the command line. If this command is invoked, and those parameters are missing, you are prompted for them.

Using the command PARAMETERS *parm1* with no parameter in the command line produces the screen output shown in figure B.4.

Fig. B.4
ISQL prompts the user for the missing parameter.

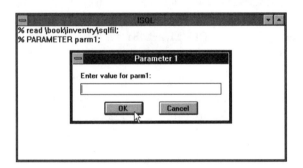

```
READ filename { parameters}
```

The READ command causes RTSQLW to execute a series of SQL commands *filename*. Parameters are needed if a PARAMETER clause is specified, otherwise they are ignored.

RTSQLW issues its own read when you pass it a file name, as shown by the verbose output in figure B.4.

```
SET { TEMPORARY } OPTION { UserId. or PUBLIC.}option_name = value;
```

SET OPTION. Allows you to set an option that the end user can set with the CONFIGURE command or during the Watcom installation.

TEMPORARY. Specifies that this option change is valid for the current database connection only.

UserId. Allows you to specify someone else's options. You must have DBA authority to use this.

PUBLIC. Allows you to specify a default option for any user who hasn't set their own options.

Tables B.2 and B.3 show the different options you can specify.

Table B.2 Watcom Database Options		
Option	**Values**	**Default**
BLOCKING	ON, OFF	ON
CHECKPOINT_TIME	number of minutes	60
CONVERSION_ERROR	ON, OFF	ON
DATE_FORMAT	string	'MM/DD/YYYY'
DATE_ORDER	'YMD', 'DMY, 'MDY'	'MDY'
ISOLATION_LEVEL	0, 1, 2, 3	0
PRECISION	number of digits	30
RECOVERY_TIME	number of minutes	2
ROW_COUNTS	ON, OFF	OFF
SCALE	number of digits	6
THREAD_COUNT	number of threads	0
TIME_FORMAT	string	'HH:NN:SS.SSS'
TIMESTAMP_FORMAT	string	'YYYY-MM-DD HH:NN:SS.SSS'
WAIT_FOR_COMMIT	ON, OFF	OFF

Table B.3 ISQL options		
Option	**Values**	**Default**
AUTO_COMMIT	ON, OFF	OFF
AUTO_REFETCH	ON, OFF	ON

(continues)

Table B.3	Continued	
Option	**Values**	**Default**
BELL	ON, OFF	ON
COMMIT_ON_EXIT	ON, OFF	ON
ECHO	ON, OFF	ON
HEADINGS	ON, OFF	ON
INPUT_FORMAT	ASCII, FIXED, DIF, DBASE, DBASEII, DBASEIII, LOTUS, WATFILE	ASCII
ISQL_LOG	file_name	'' (empty string)
NULLS	string	'(NULL)'
ON_ERROR	STOP, CONTINUE, PROMPT, EXIT	PROMPT
OUTPUT_FORMAT	ASCII, FIXED, DIF, DBASEII, DBASEIII, LOTUS, SQL, WATFILE	ASCII
OUTPUT_LENGTH	integer	0
STATISTICS	0, 3, 4, 5, 6	3
TRUNCATION_LENGTH	integer	30

Defining the best way to set each of the options listed in the tables is another book in itself. If you have a question about ways to configure your options, contact PowerSoft or Watcom technical support. You should also consider buying a full version of Watcom SQL for your Database Analyst (DBA).

From Here...

Hopefully there's enough Watcom information here to help you better manage the Watcom SQL database that came with PowerBuilder. If not, here are some other places you can go for help:

■ The best book on Watcom would have to be Que's *Using Watcom SQL with PowerBuilder* by Charles Wood due out early in 1995. Que Corporation and Charles Wood have brought together a team of experts to guide you through using and implementing Watcom SQL. Have your local bookseller order you a copy.

- You also can find some information in the Watcom SQL manual that comes with PowerBuilder.

- If you need more DBA type assistance, don't be shy about calling for technical support. Watcom's technical support is pretty good, and they have a knowledgeable staff.

- Finally, at least one person in your organization should buy a stand-alone copy of Watcom SQL, if that is the database you're using. The user's guide that accompanies Watcom SQL is a good reference book.

B

Appendixes

Appendix C

Implementing Advanced Procedures

There are some PowerBuilder features not covered in this book that you may want to be aware of. This appendix is designed to inform you of the existence of these features and to perhaps lead you in the right direction if you decide to use them.

After reviewing this appendix, you should be able to:

- Use queries and database views

- Use INI files in your PowerBuilder application

- Create user objects

- Design dynamic menus for your applications

- Implement OLE (Object Linking and Embedding) 2.0, DDE (Dynamic Data Exchange), and External DLLs (Dynamic Link Libraries)

Using Queries

Queries are used in place of SQL Selects when creating a DataWindow. You can even save your SQL select as a query in the SQL select painter that you get to from the DataWindow painter. Think of a query as a permanent SQL select that can be used with many DataWindows.

To declare a query, click on the Query icon. The Select Query dialog box appears, as seen in figure C.1. To start building your query, click on **N**ew.

Fig. C.1
The Select Query
dialog box lets
you modify or
create a query.

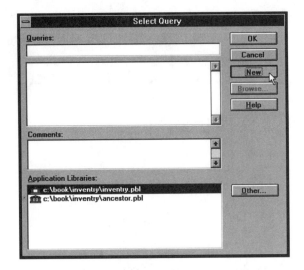

Now you will be allowed to choose which tables go into the query through
the familiar Select Tables dialog box, as seen in figure C.2. Choose the tables
you want and click on **O**pen.

Fig. C.2
The Select Tables
dialog box lets
you select tables
for your query.

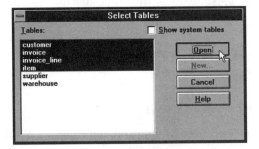

Now you are in the query painter, shown in figure C.3. (Look familiar?
It should! This painter is identical to the SQL select painter.)

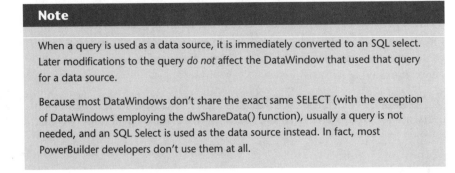

Note

When a query is used as a data source, it is immediately converted to an SQL select.
Later modifications to the query *do not* affect the DataWindow that used that query
for a data source.

Because most DataWindows don't share the exact same SELECT (with the exception
of DataWindows employing the dwShareData() function), usually a query is not
needed, and an SQL Select is used as the data source instead. In fact, most
PowerBuilder developers don't use them at all.

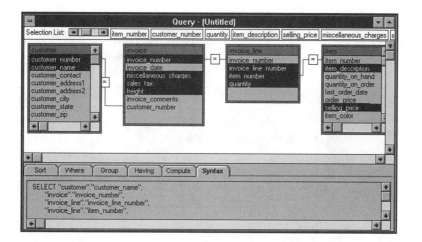

Fig. C.3
Choose the columns you would if you were creating an SQL Select DataWindow, and then save. You can use the finished query as a data source for a DataWindow.

Using Views

Often, database administrators (DBAs) like to limit access one has to both data and updatability. To accomplish this, they use views. Views are a cross section of the databases that are used primarily for display.

You need to be in the database painter to create a view. Once in the database painter, you can click on the View icon. The Select Tables dialog box opens and lets you select which tables you want for your view (see fig. C.4).

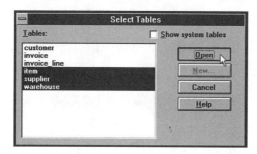

Fig. C.4
The Select Tables dialog box lets you select tables for your view.

When you're done selecting tables, you are returned to the view painter, as seen in figure C.5. Here you pick the columns you want for your view, and save your view using the Save View Definition dialog box, shown in figure C.6.

Fig. C.5

The view painter allows you to pick the columns for your view.

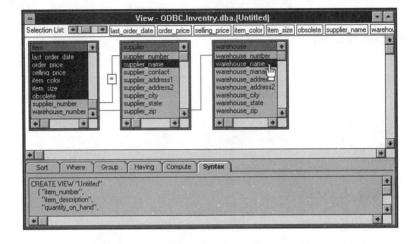

Fig. C.6

The Save View Definition dialog box allows you to name and save your view.

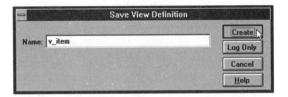

The view is immediately displayed in the database painter, as seen in figure C.7.

Fig. C.7

The view you created is now displayed in the database painter.

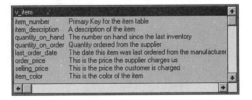

When you double-click on your view, instead of getting an Alter Table dialog box as you would with a table in the database painter, you get a Select statement (see fig. C.8), which describes the view you have just created.

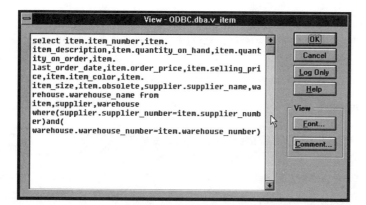

Fig. C.8
Instead of an Alter Table dialog box, you get a Select SQL statement when you try to modify the definition of a view.

> **TrackNote**
>
> The view was dropped after creation from the Inventory Tracking system, because the view was not used by the system.

Using INI Files

In the Inventory Tracking system, all access to the database was hard coded in the application open event. Many PowerBuilder programs instead use an INI file to give the power users greater flexibility. An *INI file* is an application initialization file that contains variables used by the applications and allows customization of an application by the user.

If an INVENTRY.INI file existed with the following lines:

```
[sqlca]
dbms=ODBC
database=inventry.db
userid=dba
dbpass=sql
logid=
logpass=
servername=
DbParm=ConnectString='DSN=Inventory Tracking;UID=dba;PWD=sql'
```

you could then access that INI file using the ProfileString() PowerBuilder function as follows:

```
sqlca.DBMS      = ProfileString("inventry.ini","sqlca","dbms","")
sqlca.database  = ProfileString("inventry.ini","sqlca",
                    ➥"database","")
sqlca.userid    = ProfileString("inventry.ini","sqlca",
                    ➥"userid","")
```

```
sqlca.dbpass       = ProfileString("inventry.ini","sqlca",
                     ➥"dbpass","")
sqlca.logid        = ProfileString("inventry.ini","sqlca","logid","")
sqlca.logpass      = ProfileString("inventry.ini","sqlca",
                     ➥"logpass","")
sqlca.servername   = ProfileString("inventry.ini","sqlca",
                     ➥"servername","")
sqlca.dbparm       = ProfileString("inventry.ini","sqlca",
                     ➥"dbparm","")
```

Syntax-at-a-Glance

ProfileString (filename, section, key, default)

ProfileString allows a PowerBuilder program to access a DOS file. Filename is the name of the file being searched; section is the name of a bracketed entry (for instance, [sqlca]). The key is the specific parameter under the section for which the program is looking, and the default is a string containing the value if no value is found.

In the Inventory Tracking system, you substituted flexibility for security and did not allow the use of an INI file. Many systems, however, include an INI file to allow the user to pass a large set of parameters to the application.

Creating User Objects

Every window or menu has events and object functions that are accessed when specific events occur. By coding at the event level, much time can be saved on development and maintenance.

Unfortunately, it's difficult to show two functions as being related when in a group of other functions. Furthermore, it's hard to encapsulate your functions from each other, since they all share common instance and shared variables. To address these problems, PowerBuilder developed user objects.

User objects are a collection of related events, functions, and instance or shared variables. A user object can also be defined as an object such as a DataWindow control that has many of its events coded and can be dropped onto a window, thereby saving a lot of coding time because it is reusable. User objects are never needed in an application. Sometimes, however, a developer will want to group different functions and variables together in a class-like, object-based structure. For this, you would create a user object. To create a user object, follow these steps:

1. To start a user object, click on the User Object icon. The Select User Object dialog box appears, as shown in figure C.9.

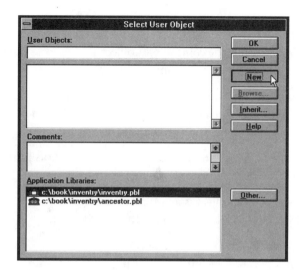

Fig. C.9
The Select User
Object dialog box
lets you modify or
create a user
object.

2. Click on **N**ew. The New User Object dialog box opens, as seen in figure C.10.

Fig. C.10
The New User
Object dialog box
lets you define the
type of user object
you are creating.

3. Now choose the type of user object you want to create. There are two non-visual user objects (custom, standard, and C++) and four visual objects (custom, external, standard, and VBX).

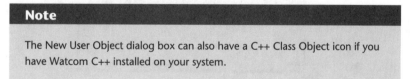

> **Note**
>
> The New User Object dialog box can also have a C++ Class Object icon if you have Watcom C++ installed on your system.

User objects are either visual or class (non-visual). *Visual* objects group objects together and are attached to a window via a window control. *Class*, or non-visual objects, group functions, events, and data together in an object-oriented construct.

The object types are defined as follows:

- *Custom*. A custom object is an object you build to perform tasks specific to your programming.

- *Standard*. A standard object is an object that is inherited from one of PowerBuilder's stocked user objects. Modifications can be made after you inherit the object.

- *External*. An external object can contain controls from the underlying Windows system.

- *VBX*. A VBX object is an object that is compatible with both Microsoft Visual Basic and with PowerBuilder.

- *C++*. A C++ object is an object whose functions consist of DLL calls to C++ functions. Using these can really speed up a PowerBuilder application, but you need to know C++ to use them. For more information, see Appendix E, "Using C++ in Your PowerBuilder Application."

4. When you're done grouping all the controls into the user object, save the user object by double-clicking on the user object painter control box and opening the Save User Object dialog box, as seen in figure C.11.

Fig. C.11
You name and save your user object in the Save User Object dialog box.

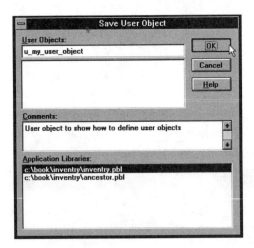

TrackNote

Since you don't use user objects in the Inventory Tracking system, this user object was not saved.

Designing Dynamic Menus

A frequently asked question on coding techniques is, "How would you provide menu customization at run time?" This question is not easily answered. As discussed in Chapter 4, "Defining Menus," PowerBuilder provides an easy-to-use menu painter for fast development of application menus, but provides only limited functionality to change a menu dynamically.

PowerBuilder menus are not true objects. They are rather properties of the parent window to which they are attached. Unlike other PowerBuilder objects, menus do not allow you to define user events. They are lacking the standard methods and attributes, and expose quirks in behavior when you try to modify them dynamically.

You can use a few well-described techniques to customize menus at run time:

- Switch the current menu to a completely different one, using the ChangeMenu() function. This method is useful when two menus have very little in common.

- Define (if applicable) invisible menu items in the original menu and switch the menu items' visibility, using the hide() and share() functions, or by setting the menuitem.visible attribute to either TRUE or FALSE. This method is useful when two windows share the same major set of menu items.

Please note that in both cases, you have to know all menu items and their locations at design time. This may be acceptable when you have just a few menu options you want to enable or disable during run time, but these methods will not be sufficient for the menuing needs of some applications.

Consider these other desired behaviors that cannot be effectively handled using static menus:

- An object or control that is activated on a window dynamically could attach a submenu to the Window's main menu.

- A security system can allow access to application menu options based on the user's profile.

The ultimate solution is to create and attach menu items dynamically. The following techniques demonstrate a proven method of designing menu objects dynamically.

Attaching Menu Item to an Existing Menu

For this example, assume that the menu you are designing is called m_main, and it contains c a top-level menu item, m_option. Now add a menu item with the text A dynamic item to the end of m_option's submenu list.

Step 1: Create a Menu Object, m_dynamic

This menu should contain only one menu item: m_Item.

Within m_dynamic, declare two instance variables:

```
window  iwCreator
string  isNotificationEvent
```

In the PowerScript for the Clicked! event for m_Item item, place the following code:

```
IF IsValid(iwCreator) THEN
    iwCreator.TriggerEvent(isNotificationEvent)
END IF
```

You'll change the value of isNotificationEvent to the name of the event which has to be triggered when the item gets clicked. You'll change the value of iwCreator to the window which has to be notified of that click.

Step 2: Add Your Item

In the window that will eventually process the dynamic menu item's function, declare a user event ue_dynamic_item_clicked. Then, in the clicked event of the "A dynamic item menuitem," place the following code:

```
m_main      mCurrentMenu
m_dynamic   mAdditional
int         ii
mCurrentMenu = MenuId
mAdditional = create m_dynamic
mAdditional.m_item.Text  =  "A dynamic &item"
mAdditional.iwCreator  =  this
mAdditional.isNotificationEvent = "ue_dynamic_item_clicked"
ii = UpperBound(mCurrentMenu.m_option.Item) + 1
mCurrentMenu.m_option.Item[ii] = mAdditional.m_item
```

Step 3: Force Menu to Redraw

A dynamic menu now is attached! However, the menu is not redrawn, and you can't see any changes yet. To force redrawing of the menu, add two more lines of code:

```
mCurrentMenu.m_option.Item[1].Visible = NOTmCurrentMenu.m_option.Item[1].Visible
mCurrentMenu.m_option.Item[1].Visible = NOTmCurrentMenu.m_option.Item[1].Visible
```

Removing Menu Items

Menu items are collected in arrays. Unfortunately, PowerBuilder does not allow you to reduce the bounds of arrays. If you need to delete an item(s) from an array, create an empty array of the same type, copy the entries you want to keep there, replace the new array in control sequence, and destroy the original one.

Designing a Menu Configuration System

This section will show you how to create menus at execution time based on user profile. It can be used as a part of a security system to allow control of the options available to each user. A complete set of functions and objects for creating and maintaining dynamic menus is included on the *Using PowerBuilder 4 Companion CD* in the DynaMenu Toolkit. The complete system allows you to do the following:

- Import existing (PBL based) menus and store them in a database

- Create new menu in the special menu painter

- Edit database-kept menu, providing user specific profile for each menuitem

Here you'll examine the structure and more important functions used in that system.

First of all, you need to establish tables to keep information about nodes and users who are granted permission to particular nodes.

The first table (t_menu_node_info) keeps all the information about all the nodes for all the menus (or applications) being used. The second table keeps IDs for those users who are authorized to use that system. The following example creates menu information for a particular user. Please note that users get access to nodes which are authorized for a group they belong to.

```
string sSQLStatement, sUserGroupName
int iiGroupUId
SELECT a.gid INTO :iiGroupUId  FROM sysusers a WHERE name = :sqlca.userid;
select name into :sUserGroupName  from sysusers where uid = :iiGroupUId;
s_SQL_Statement = "SELECT a.* FROM t_menu_node_info a, t_menu_users b "+ &
   "WHERE a.generated_id = b.generated_id AND a.appname_s = b.appname " +&
   "   AND a.appname_s = '"+gsMenuName+"' " + &
   "   AND ( b.user_id = '"+gsUserName+"' " or b.user_id ='" &
   +s_UserGroupName+"')"
f_array_from_database(sSQLStatement)
f_array_to_menu(w_test_menu_sheet)


global subroutine f_array_from_database (string is_sql_statement)
// Clean Out whatever they had before
s_MenuNode istr_EmptyConstructor[]
s_MenuNode istr_Node
   gstr_MenuNode = istr_EmptyConstructor
   DECLARE my_cursor DYNAMIC CURSOR FOR SQLSA ;
   PREPARE SQLSA FROM :is_SQL_Statement;
   OPEN DYNAMIC my_cursor ;
   int i = 1
   DO
      FETCH my_cursor INTO :istrMenuNode;
      IF (sqlca.sqlcode = 0) THEN gstr_menunode[i] = istr_node
      i += 1
   LOOP WHILE SQLCA.SQLCODE = 0
   CLOSE my_cursor ;
end subroutine


global subroutine f_Array_to_Menu ( window pwParentWindow)
menu m_out_menu
int j, i = 1
   if IsValid(UserWindow.MenuId ) then Destroy( UserWindow.MenuId )
   UserWindow.ChangeMenu(m_empty)
   m_out_menu = UserWindow.MenuId
   FOR j = 1 to UpperBound(gstr_MenuNode)
      IF  gstr_MenuNode[j].gen_Parent_Id =0  THEN
         m_out_menu.Item[i+1] = f_Create_Menu_Node_From_Array( UserWindow,&
                        gstr_MenuNode[j].itemorder )
         i = i + 1
      END IF
   NEXT
   m_out_menu.Item[1].Visible = NOT m_out_menu.Item[1].Visible
   m_out_menu.Item[1].Visible = NOT m_out_menu.Item[1].Visible
   m_out_menu.Item[1].ToolBarItemVisible = &
      NOT m_out_menu.Item[1].ToolBarItemVisible
   m_out_menu.Item[1].ToolBarItemVisible = &
      NOT m_out_menu.Item[1].ToolBarItemVisible
end subroutine
```

```
global function menu f_Create_Menu_Node_From_Array ( &
      ref window pwParentwindow, int nodeid)
   menu im_menu
   int i, j = 0
   im_menu  = create m_dynamic_item
   FOR i = 1 to UpperBound(gstr_MenuNode)
      IF  gstr_MenuNode[i].gen_Parent_Id = NodeId THEN
         j = j + 1
         im_menu.Item[j] =f_Create_Menu_Node_From_Array(iw_ParentWindow, &
                               gstr_MenuNode[i].itemorder)
      END IF
   NEXT
   f_structure_to_menunode(gstr_MenuNode[f_Index_from_Id(NodeId)], im_menu)
   im_Menu.ParentWindow = pwParentWindow
   return im_Menu
end function
```

Implementing OLE 2.0

Object Linking and Embedding (OLE) is Windows' way of running one application (or more) inside another. To insert an OLE object, click on the OLE 2.0 icon. The Insert Object dialog box appears, as seen in figure C.12.

Fig. C.12
The Insert Object dialog box allows you to insert an OLE 2.0 object into a window.

Here you choose which program you want to insert in your DataWindow. In figure C.12, Microsoft Works 3.0 Sheet is selected. When you return to your window, you can see that a spreadsheet-like interface is attached to your window (see fig. C.13).

Now when you run your program, anything in your spreadsheet is shown on your window. OLE is a powerful way to link two programs together.

Fig. C.13
Through OLE, the
spreadsheet now
appears with your
window.

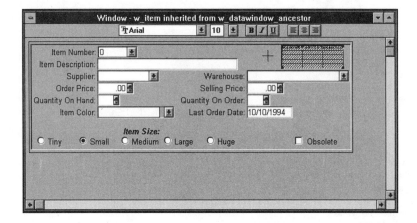

Caution

Using OLE 2.0 can really slow down an application because the application must fire off two interfaces—one for the application and one for the OLE program. This not only consumes system resources but can also slow down an application considerably.

OLE 2.0 is a really neat feature of Windows and PowerBuilder, but don't use it frivolously or you will sacrifice execution speed.

TrackNote

The imbedded Microsoft Works 3.0 spreadsheet was not saved into the final system.

Introducing DDE

Dynamic Data Exchange (DDE) is a quick way for two Windows programs to send each other data. Unlike OLE 2.0, DDE is not visible but tends to be a little quicker.

To use the DDE in your application, you need to perform the following steps:

   1. Open a PowerBuilder window if one is not already opened.

   2. Start communication with the client application using the OpenChannel( ) PowerBuilder function. (The client application is the application you want to access.)

3. Identify your application as a DDE server using the StartServerDDE( ) PowerBuilder function. (The server application is the application that invokes the client application.)

4. Execute the client functions by using the ExecRemote( ) PowerBuilder function for each client function you want to access.

5. When you're finished executing client functions, close the DDE channel with the CloseChannel( ) PowerBuilder function.

6. Close the PowerBuilder window opened in step 1 unless you want to keep it open for other processing.

Syntax-at-a-Glance

handle - OpenChannel (applname, topicname, {windowhandle})

OpenChannel opens a DDE channel to another application.

handle is an integer identifying the DDE connection.

applname is a string containing the DDE name of the DDE.

topicname is a string identifying either the data or instance of the program you want to use. If only one instance of the program is available, *topicname* is often the same as *applname*.

windowhandle is the handle of the window acting as a DDE client. Use this if you have more than one open window.

Syntax-at-a-Glance

StartServerDDE ({windowname}, applname, topic{, items})

StartServerDDE causes the application denoted by *applname* to begin acting as a DDE server.

windowname is the name of the server window. The default is the current window.

applname is the DDE name for your PowerBuilder application.

topic is a string containing the basic data grouping of the server application to be accessed by the client application.

items is a comma-delimited string list of what the DDE server will support.

Syntax-at-a-Glance

ExecRemote (command, handle{,windowhandle})

ExecRemote executes a remote function from the server application.

command is a string containing the name of the command you wish to execute. Although the format of the command depends on the DDE application you wish to access, usually the command is surrounded in brackets.

handle is the handle returned by the OpenChannel function.

windowhandle is the handle of the window acting as a DDE client. Use this if you have more than one open window.

Syntax-at-a-Glance

CloseChannel (handle{, windowhandle})

CloseChannel closes the DDE channel opened by OpenChannel and identified by handle.

handle is the handle returned by the OpenChannel function.

windowhandle is the handle of the window acting as a DDE client. Use this if you have more than one open window.

One good use of DDE is to create a Windows 3.x group and insert a Windows icon for your application during the install process. If you are making a stand-alone application for distribution, you'll also need to write an install program to make your application accessible from Windows 3.x without burdening the end user. In your install program, you can manipulate Windows 3.x groups and icons with the following PowerScript:

```
int handle // Define the handle for identifying the remote application

Open (w_dde)        // Open a PowerBuilder Window

// Now open a remote DDE channel to PROGMAN

handle = OpenChannel ("PROGMAN","PROGMAN")

// Define your app as a DDE server

StartServerDDE(w_dde, "dde", "System")
```

```
// Execute PROGMAN functions

// Add a group

ExecRemote("[CreateGroup(MyGroup)]", handle)

// Add an item to the group with a path and description

ExecRemote("[AddItem(C:\PROGPATH\PROGNAME.EXE, Description]", handle)

CloseChannel(handle) // Close the remote DDE channel to PROGMAN

Close(w_dde)         // Close the PowerBuilder window
```

To learn more about DDE, look up DDE in the on-line help that comes with PowerBuilder or read the User's Guide on Dynamic Data Exchange.

Using External DLLs

Before Windows, developers were expected to develop in only one language. If multiple languages were used in an application, calling modules and called modules usually required special processing to pass data back and forth between modules.

When Microsoft developed Windows, the company added a common interface for "sections" of code called *DLLs*, or *Dynamic Link Libraries*. DLLs can be generated by most compilers and called by most Windows programs without additional research and coding required to handle parameters. DLLs—or Microsoft SDK (Software Developers Kit) EXEs—are much like PBDs (PowerBuilder Dynamic Libraries) in that they are not linked into a program until run time.

PowerBuilder can interface with DLLs written in other languages like C++ or Visual Basic and EXEs used in the SDK.

To declare an external function inside a DLL to be accessible to PowerBuilder, choose Declare, Global External Functions. (The Declare option is available in most painters.) This opens the Declare Global External Functions editor. Here you can declare a function using the Function data type.

As you can see in figure C.14, you wrote a function to attach to another drive and directory. This function is one of many inside a DLL called CFUNCS.DLL. By this declaration, you are allowing PowerBuilder to access your function.

Fig. C.14
PowerBuilder is allowed to access CHANGEDIR inside CFUNCS.DLL.

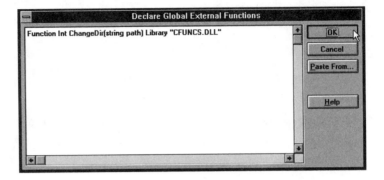

Customizing Your PowerBuilder Environment

PowerBuilder lets you customize your PowerBuilder environment by using one of two methods: through the preferences painter or by editing the PB.INI file.

PowerBuilder Preferences Painter

To get into the preferences painter, click on the Preferences icon on the PowerBar. The preferences painter opens, as seen in figure C.15.

One of the most common changes is to the source vendor of the library. If you're using PVCS as your source vendor, click on Library and change the SourceVendor variable to PVCS, indicating that PVCS will be used as your library manager, as shown in figure C.15.

Fig. C.15
The preferences painter can be used to change the default preferences in PowerBuilder.

PB.INI and the PowerBuilder Editor

If you're comfortable editing INI files, you can go straight to the PB.INI file in your PB4 directory using any editor and make modifications. Some people like editing PB.INI from the PowerBuilder editor because they have access to PowerBuilder on-line help if they have a question.

To access the PowerBuilder editor, press Shift+F6 or click on the Edit icon, and then choose a file to edit.

Each of the parameters in the file (see fig. C.16) sets a condition inside PowerBuilder. Use the on-line help to determine the proper values for each and which ones you want to change.

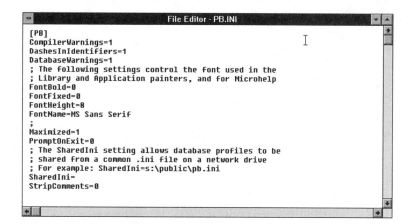

Fig. C.16
Although it's rather compli-
cated, the PB.INI file can be used to change preferences inside PowerBuilder.

Caution

There are two considerations to be wary of when editing your PB.INI file inside PowerBuilder:

- What you do will not affect your environment until you leave PowerBuilder and come back in. Then, if you made changes that are incorrect, you may have corrupted your PowerBuilder environment. It would be wise to make a copy of the PB.INI file before altering it to avoid this.

- You should not open the preferences painter at the same time as you're edit-ing your PB.INI. The preferences write to the PB.INI file, so changes to PB.INI made in one Windows/PowerBuilder session may be overwritten with changes in another Windows/PowerBuilder session.

Writing PowerBuilder Applications for Multiple Platforms

This book concentrates on developing PowerBuilder applications for the Windows 3.x environment only. However, the new version of PowerBuilder will eventually be able to develop completely transportable applications from Windows 3.x to other applications, including Windows NT, Windows '95, the Apple Macintosh, several "flavors" of UNIX, and OS/2.

Although applications are transportable, certain system specific functions like OLE and DDE will not work in a non-Windows environment. PowerBuilder lets you test for this with the new global parameter *g_platform*. You can use *g_platform* in a CHOOSE CASE statement to code for operating-system-specific script as follows:

```
CHOOSE CASE g_platform

   CASE Windows!

      .

      .

      .

   CASE Macintosh!

      .

      .

      .

   END CASE
```

Coding in this manner will let you take your complete PowerBuilder application and port it *without changes* to another platform! For the software developer, this could mean easy access to other markets with a minimal amount of effort.

Appendix D

Getting Help with Your PowerBuilder Applications

PowerBuilder is relatively easy to learn and use, once you understand "event driven," as opposed to "procedural" programming . However, every developer needs help and advice at one time or another. This appendix is designed to help you find the advice you need.

You can get many PowerSoft products and third-party PowerBuilder support products through most retail software outlets. If you need more than just software—like support and training—help is not far away. In addition to a robust on-line help system, PowerSoft has designated PowerBuilder Development Consultants and PowerSoft Authorized Training Partners.

Note

Are you having trouble finding information to help you when developing your PowerBuilder application? Before you seek assistance from other sources, try the on-line help system built into PowerBuilder. Just click on the Help icon and then search for your topic. PowerBuilder has very extensive on-line help. Such comprehensive help systems are rare in Windows 3.x development products.

Getting Help from PowerSoft

If you still can't find what you need, you can contact PowerSoft by calling 1-800-395-3525. You usually don't have to wait that long, and the call is toll free. Although this number can't give you technical support beyond installation assistance, the service representatives can often steer you toward a support plan that fits your needs and resources. If you have a bug you want fixed or an enhancement you want added, you can report it here.

Getting Free PowerBuilder Support

Many of your questions can be answered by PowerBuilder's FaxBack system. If you have access to a fax, the service is free. Call PowerBuilder's FaxBack system at 1-617-238-6800. (At the risk of insulting your intelligence, don't dial this number with your fax. That would just confuse both machines. Use a regular voice telephone.) PowerBuilder's FaxBack automated voice mail will guide you first through ordering a catalog of available faxes, and then (on a second call) ordering the fax help you need. You'll be surprised how helpful this is.

If you have access to CompuServe, you can access the PowerSoft forum by typing **GO POWERSOFT**. This free service (other than the normal CompuServe usage fees) is probably one of the better ways to eventually communicate with a live technical support person from Team PowerSoft (TEAMPS). Team PowerSoft is a worldwide web of independent developers who help those in need with their PowerSoft problems. It was organized by PowerSoft to answer the growing need for PowerBuilder technical support. Alternatively, PowerSoft also has its own Bulletin Board System (BBS) where you can leave questions and download patches and bug fixes. The BBS number is 1-519-884-2103, and the connection is 8-N-1 (8 data bits, No Parity, one stop bit).

Buying PowerBuilder Support

As easy as PowerBuilder is to use, sometimes you may find yourself needing a little extra support. PowerSoft has many programs available to meet your budget and needs. You find a price comparison listed at the end of this section in table D.1.

- If you need to purchase support but either have limited resources or have a small development shop with experienced PowerBuilder developers, the pay-per-issue plan is for you. This plan comes in packages of five issues (or problems) and can be purchased for the desktop or the enterprise editions.

- If you need a little extra support, PowerSoft provides annual support programs for PowerBuilder Desktop. The desktop annual support is limited to 15 issues, but you get support for PowerBuilder Desktop, InfoMaker, Watcom VX-REXX (for OS/2), Watcom SQL Single User Editions, Watcom C/C++, and Watcom FORTRAN 77. You also get the single user Infobase CD-ROM annual subscription and any bug fixes.

- If you have the PowerBuilder Enterprise edition, there's a PowerSoft Enterprise annual support program. The Enterprise annual support includes either unlimited issues or two contacts with 55 issues, and you support all products carried by the desktop annual support as well as support for PowerBuilder Enterprise and the Watcom SQL Network Server Editions. You also get the multi-user Infobase CD-ROM Server subscription, all the bug fixes, and two printed copies of the documentation.

- If you've bought the Enterprise annual support program but have used up your support, you can purchase the Add-on Enterprise Support, which allows you one additional contact or 25 additional issues.

- For the big corporations with large numbers of PowerBuilder developers, there's the PowerBuilder's Custom Annual Support program. This program allows you two contacts or 100 issues, guaranteed 15 minute response, monthly report of calls, Infobase Server Subscription, scheduled conference calls to cover the status of any open problem, two copies of documentation, and an annual technology briefing.

Table D.1 PowerBuilder Support Pricing (as of 12/15/1994)		
Product	**U.S. Dollars**	**Canadian Dollars**
Pay-Per-Issue Desktop Products (5 issues)	$ 375.00	$ 525.00
Pay-Per-Issue Enterprise Products (5 issues)	$ 500.00	$ 700.00
Annual Support Desktop Products (15 issues)	$ 950.00	$ 1,300.00
Annual Support Enterprise Products	$ 5,000.00	$ 7,000.00
Add-on Annual Enterprise Support	$ 2,500.00	$ 3,500.00
Custom Annual Support	$25,000.00	$35,000.00

D

Appendixes

Getting Help from Third-Party Sources

Tip

PowerSoft Training Partners can teach you PowerBuilder, and most of them also provide consulting services.

Finally, you could always take a class to increase your PowerBuilder skills. PowerSoft Training Partner instructors go through a thorough rigorous training process before they become qualified PowerBuilder instructors. Table D.2 is a list of the PowerSoft Training Partners ordered by state (or province) and name. (Canadian training partners follow the United States training partners.)

Table D.2   PowerSoft Training Partners

Partner	Address	City
MIDAK	2800 North Central Avenue, Suite 100	Phoenix
American Digital Technologies	3100 Bristol Street, Suite 380	Costa Mesa
IG Systems, Inc.	2800 28th Street, Suite 250	Santa Monica
Inventa Corporation	2620 Augustine Drive, Suite 225	Santa Clara
NetBase Computing, Inc.	3625 Del Amo Blvd.	Torrance
NexGen SI, Inc.	30 Corporate Park, Suite 410	Irvine
Panttaja Consulting Group	55 Francisco Street, Suite 300	San Francisco
Software Integration Consulting Group	2834 Wentworth Road	Cameron Park
Greenbrier & Russel	999 18th St. Denver Plaza, S. Tower, Suite 1590	Denver
Semiotix	10620 East Bethany Drive	Aurora
Computer Management Sciences, Inc.	200 Glastonbury Blvd., Suite 304	Glastonbury
Linc Systems	310 West Newberry Road	Bloomfield
MetaCorp Strategies International	325 Riverside Avenue	Westport
Computer Management Sciences, Inc.	8133 Baymeadows Way	Jacksonville

D

Appendixes

St	ZIP	Contact	Phone	Fax
AZ	85004	Lawana Diffie	(602) 266-9029	(602) 266-6252
CA	92626	Scott Shulga	(714) 433-1300	(714) 433-1312
CA	90405	Carol Taylor	(310) 396-0042	(310) 396-0061
CA	95054	Ashok Santhanum	(408) 987-0220	(408) 987-0230
CA	90503	Donna Reed	(310) 214-8181	(310) 214-9822
CA	92714	Laura Meisenbach	(714) 476-4097 x226	(714) 476-0201
CA	94133	Paul Hamberis	(415) 705-6868	(415) 705-6876
CA	95682	Jan Porter	(916) 676-0750	(916) 676-7735
CO	80202	Mary Delutri	(800) 453-0347	(708) 706-4020
CO	80014	Sonny Hendrick	(303) 743-1400	(303) 743-1410
CT	06033	Chuck Spewock	(203) 633-3608	(203) 633-3609
CT	06002	Kerry Leslie	(203) 286-9060	(203) 286-9023
CT	06880	Russell J. Nugent	(203) 222-6685	(203) 222-5872
FL	32256	Chuck Spewock	(203) 633-3608	(203) 633-3609

(continues)

Table D.2 Continued

Partner	Address	City
Computer Task Group	7650 Courtney Campbell Causeway, Suite 605	Tampa
PowerCerv	400 North Ashley Drive, Suite 1910	Tampa
PowerCerv	5890 S. Semoran Blvd.	Orlando
Systems Consulting Group	760 NW 107th Avenue, Suite 310	Miami
Greenbrier & Russel	300 Galleria Parkway, Suite 290	Atlanta
Omni Training Centers	1150 Hammond Drive, Bldg. A, Suite 1190	Atlanta
OSoft Development Corporation	6 Piedmont Center, Suite 303	Atlanta
Client/Server, Inc.	5701 N. Sheridan Road, Suite 160	Chicago
DC Systems	533 S. York Road, Suite B	Elmhurst
Greenbrier & Russel	1450 E. American Lane, Suite 1640	Schaumburg
Analytical Technologies, Inc.	6060 Castleway West Drive, Suite 233	Indianapolis
NewMedia, Inc.	200 South Meridian, Suite 220	Indianapolis
Analytical Technologies, Inc.	9401 Nall Avenue, Suite 100	Shawnee Mission
SoluTech, Inc.	Lighton Plaza I, 7300 College Blvd., Suite 165	Overland Park
CSC Partners	One Newton Executive Park	Newton Lower Falls
Waterfield Technology Group, Inc.	430 Bedford Street	Lexington
Client Servers	21 Governor's Court	Baltimore
The Orkand Corporation	8484 Georgia Avenue, Suite 1000	Silver Spring

St	ZIP	Contact	Phone	Fax
FL	33607	Mike Niemann	(813) 289-4471	(813) 289-6737
FL	33602	Marc Fratello	(813) 226-2378	(813) 222-0886
FL	32822	Marc Fratello	(813) 226-2378	(813) 222-0886
FL	33172	Marcia Datolli	(305) 225-3325	(305) 225-6789
GA	30339	Mary Delutri	(800) 453-0347	(708) 706-4020
GA	30326	Rhonda Sides	(404) 395-0055	(404) 395-1164
GA	30305	Michael Kelleher	(404) 814-6030	(404) 814-8401
IL	60660	Harvey Mayerowicz	(312) 275-2513	(312) 275-2513
IL	60126	Leslie Kuster	(708) 834-2095	(708) 834-2096
IL	60173	Mary Delutri	(708) 706-4000	(708) 706-4020
IN	46250	Lisa Aquino	(810) 540-4440 x24	(810) 540-4342
IN	46225	Joe Bains	(216) 481-7900	(216) 481-1570
KS	66207	Lisa Aquino	(810) 540-4440 x24	(810) 540-4342
KS	66210	Mary Freeman	(314) 947-9393	(314) 947-9898
MA	02162	Janet Wittenberg	(617) 332-3900	(617) 332-2864
MA	02173	Bill Heys	(617) 863-8400	(617) 863-8408
MD	21244	Michael King	(410) 944-3280	
MD	20910	Robin Froelich	(301) 585-8480	(301) 565-0828

(continues)

Table D.2 Continued

Partner	Address	City
Analytical Technologies, Inc.	30300 Telegraph Road, Suite 200	Bingham Farms
Visual Systems Development Group	100 W. Big Beaver Road, Suite 200	Troy
Benchmark Computer Systems	4510 W. 77th St., Suite 300	Edina
Connect Education Services	9855 West 78th Street	Eden Prairie
Fourth Generation	Galtier Plaza, Suite 763, 175 East Fifth Street	St. Paul
Insight Software, Inc.	23 Empire Drive	St. Paul
Grant Thornton	500 Washington Street, Suite 1200	St. Louis
SoluTech, Inc.	117 S. Main Street, Suite 111	St. Charles
Cedalion Education Services, Inc.	8401 University Executive Park	Charlotte
Cedalion Education Services, Inc.	79-4401 Alexander Dr., P.O. Box 13239	Raleigh Research Triangle
Financial Dynamics	3600 Glenwood Avenue, Suite 100	Raleigh
CSC Consultants	1200 U.S. Highway 22	Bridgewater
Indus Consultancy Services	140 East Ridgewood Avenue	Paramus
PC Strategies & Solutions	6 Century Drive	Parsippany
Trecom Business Systems	333 Thornall Street	Edison
Advanced Communication Resources	350 Fifth Avenue, Suite 7803	New York
DRT Systems International, Inc.	12 Corporate Woods Blvd.	Albany
Information Technologists, Inc.	100 Allens Creek Office Park, Suite 200	Rochester

St	ZIP	Contact	Phone	Fax
MI	48025	Lisa Aquino	(810) 540-4440 x24	(810) 540-4342
MI	48084	Debbie Yasenka	(810) 680-6650	(810) 642-6442
MN	55435	Kimberly Carlberg	(612) 896-6800	(612) 896-9728
MN	55344	Kathy Carroll	(612) 946-0210	(612) 946-0211
MN	55101	Chiam Titlebaum	(612) 224-9919	(612) 224-7754
MN	55082	Kelly Roddy	(612) 227-8669	(612) 227-8764
MO	63101	Banon Ellison	(314) 241-3232	(314) 241-3240
MO	63301	Randy Schilling	(314) 947-9393	(314) 947-9898
NC	28213	Debbie Martin	(704) 549-4765	
NC	27709 -3239	Walt Wintermute	(919) 549-8116	(919) 549-8693
NC	27612	Carolyn Caldwell	(800) 486-5201	(703) 820-2298
NJ	08807	Diane Mondoro	(908) 253-3229	(908) 253-3217
NJ	07652	Sandip Gupta	(201) 261-3100	(201) 261-1399
NJ	07054	Carol Lee	(201) 984-1000	(201) 984-7907
NJ	08837	Allison O'Neill	(908) 549-4100	(908) 549-4148
NY	10118	Maria Colavito	(212) 629-3370	(212) 629-3374
NY	12211	Cecil Elmore	(518) 434-0294	(518) 434-3697
NY	14618	Kristine Waters	(215) 832-1000	(215) 832-1010

(continues)

Table D.2 Continued

Partner	Address	City
Systar Technologies	1890 Palmer Avenue	Larchmont
Tangent International	30 Broad Street, 44th Floor	New York
ComputerPeople	50 Northwoods Blvd.	Worthington
McHale USConnect	31200 Bainbridge Road	Solon
NewMedia, Inc.	503 East 200th Street, Suite 202	Cleveland
Business Consulting Group	4500 South Garnett, Suite 620	Tulsa
Cutting Edge Computer Solutions	5 Great Valley Parkway	Malvern
Icon Solutions, Inc.	175 King of Prussia Road, Suite A	Radnor
Information Technologists, Inc.	555 North Lane, Suite 5040	Conshohocken
Information Technologists, Inc.	101 North Meadow Drive, Suite 113	Wexford
The Database Group	11 Technology Circle	Columbia
Analytical Technologies, Inc.	20515 SH 249 Trombell Parkway, Suite 330	Houston
B.R. Blackmarr & Associates	1950 Stemmons Freeway, Suite 3031	Dallas
BSG Education	11 Greenway Plaza, Suite 900	Houston
Coopers & Lybrand	2711 LBJ Freeway, Suite 312	Dallas
PowerSoft Latin America	2929 Briar Park, Suite 529	Houston
ScottSoftware	90 South Trace Creek Drive	The Woodlands
Software Integration Consulting Group	10000 Richmond, Suite 660	Houston

St	ZIP	Contact	Phone	Fax
NY	10538	Jeff Bernstein	(914) 833-0300	(914) 833-0399
NY	10004	Alelie Llabitan	(212) 809-8200 x32	(212) 968-1398
OH	43235	Ellen Saunders	(614) 433-0133	(614) 433-0114
OH	44139	Kathleen Binder	(216) 498-3550	(216) 498-3623
OH	44119	Joe Bains	(216) 481-7900	(216) 481-1570
OK	74146	Kim Strom	(918) 665-0883	(918) 665-0699
PA	19355	Tom Olenzak	(610) 648-3881	(610) 695-9752
PA	19087	Dennis Rehm	(610) 995-9000	(717) 731-5496
PA	19428	Kristine Waters	(215) 832-1000	(215) 832-1010
PA	15090	Tim O'Shea	(412) 934-5885	(412) 934-5889
SC	29203	Susan Moffitt	(803) 935-1100	(803) 935-1111
TX	77070	Steven McDermott	(713) 379-1006	(713) 379-5035
TX	75237	Vicki Heckle	(214) 746-4779	(214) 746-4780
TX	77046	Karen Martinez	(713) 965-1175	(713) 961-1430
TX	75234	Michelle Bode	(214) 243-1256	(214) 243-6956
TX	77042	Yolanda Berea	(713) 977-0752	(713) 977-7049
TX	77381	Richard Scott	(713) 367-2734	(713) 367-0596
TX	77042	Dwight Williams	(713) 977-6421	(713) 977-5048

(continues)

Table D.2 Continued

Partner	Address	City
Systems Evolution Incorporated	3023 Pecan Point Drive	Sugar Land
Techsys Computer Associates	1420 W. Mockingbird Lane, Suite 270	Dallas
The Austin Software Foundry	500 Capital of TX Hwy N., Bldg. 8, Suite 190	Austin
Erudite Software & Consulting	2474 N. University Avenue, Suite 100	Provo
Financial Dynamics	5201 Leesburg Pike, Suite 701	Falls Church
IPC Technologies	7200 Glen Forest Drive	Richmond
Noblestar Systems Corporation	3141 Fairview Park Drive, Suite 400	Falls Church
ServerLogic Corp.	2800 Northup Way, Suite 205	Bellevue
Greenbrier & Russel	13555 Bishops Court, Suite 201	Brookfield
Wisconsin Public Service Corporation	700 North Adams Street, P.O. Box 19002	Green Bay
Computronix Holdings Ltd.	Suite 1101, Exchange Tower, 10250 101st St.	Edmonton
DCS Systems	Bay 1, 4001A 19th Street N.E.	Calgary
B.P.R. Consulting	1205 Deeks Place	Victoria
DCS Systems	4170 Still Creek Drive, Suite 120	Burnaby
Online Business Systems	130 Scott Street	Winnipeg
Ajja Information Technology	457 Catherine Street	Ottawa
Visual Systems Development Corp.	One University Avenue, Suite 303	Toronto

D

St	ZIP	Contact	Phone	Fax
TX	77478 -4224	Karen Stephenson	(713) 265-7075	(713) 265-7075
TX	75247	Robert Chadwell	(214) 638-8324	(214) 638-8326
TX	78746	Don Hudecek	(512) 329-6697	(512) 329-6698
UT	84604	Gene Loveridge	(801) 373-6100	(801) 576-8815
VA	22041	Carolyn Caldwell	(703) 671-3003	(703) 820-2298
VA	23226	Jeffrey Brownstein	(804) 285-9300	(804) 285-4492
VA	22042	Marlin Schrock	(703) 641-8511	(703) 641-8517
WA	98004	Terry LeLievre	(206) 803-0378	(206) 803-0349
WI	53005	Mary Delutri	(800) 453-0347	(708) 706-4020
WI	54307	Chuck Belekevich	(414) 433-1550	(414) 433-1125
AB	T5J-3P4	Jeff Pfahl	(403) 424-1617	(403) 425-8536
AB	T2E-6X8	Debra Clark	(403) 291-5343	(403) 250-3629
BC	V8P-5S7	Derek Ball	(604) 391-0734	(604) 325-4137
BC	V5C-6C6	Lorraine Dame	(604) 291-1054	(604) 325-4137
MB	R3L-0K8	Sandra Foster	(204) 452-0614	(204) 452-0622
ON	K1R 5T7	Virginia Tough	(613) 563-2552	(613) 563-3438
ON	M5J-2P1	Suzanne Starr	(416) 368-5464	(416) 322-5907

Joining PowerBuilder User Groups

One of the best places to meet other PowerBuilder developers and figure out those hard-to-solve PowerBuilder problems is to attend a user group meeting. You'll usually get a good speech on some interesting technique and/or third-party software, and you can always discuss what PowerBuilder problems you have with the other members.

Table D.3 shows a list of all PowerBuilder user groups at the time of publication. If you can't find a user group near you, call PowerSoft. New user groups are opening all the time, and PowerSoft keeps an up-to-date list of user groups and how to join them. Also, kudos to PowerSoft for keeping the user groups relatively independent. PowerSoft truly acts as a resource—as opposed to a controller—for the PowerBuilder user groups.

Table D.3 PowerBuilder User Groups as of 11/5/1994		
Location	**Person to Contact**	**Telephone Number**
In State/ Province Order	**PowerSoft Employee in Parentheses**	
Alabama - Birmingham	Dave Seaman, Vulcan Materials	205-877-3045
Arizona - Phoenix	Jeff Colyar	602-554-4372
Baltimore, Maryland	(Ruth Howard)	508-287-1859
Calgary (Canada)	Glen Murphy	403-290-6515
California - Northern LA	Tony Tortorice, DRT Systems	310-590-8805
California - Orange County	Jon Bruce	714-436-4390
California - San Diego	Marie Gajo, San Diego City School	619-293-4489
California - San Francisco	Edie Harris, Harris & Associates	510-865-7417
Colorado - Denver	Scott Levin	303-783-0607
Connecticut	Muffie Fox-Dyer, Pitney Bowes, Inc.	203-351-7316
Florida - South	(Ruth Howard)	508-287-1859
Florida-Tampa Bay	Mike Nieman	813-289-4471
Georgia - Atlanta	Steve Benfield	404-813-1201
Illinois - Chicago	Jeff Barnes	312-727-4422

Location	Person to Contact	Telephone Number
In State/ Province Order	**PowerSoft Employee in Parentheses**	
Illinois-Decatur	(Ruth Howard)	508-287-1859
Indiana-Indianapolis	Paul Horan, Dome—Ernst & Young	317-780-1956
Iowa - Des Moines	Mark Herbsleb, Principal Financial Group	515-248-3349
Kansas	(Ruth Howard)	508-287-1859
Massachusetts - Boston	John Dacy, Waterfield Technology	617-863-8400
Michigan - Detroit	Debbie Yasanka, Anatech	313-540-4440
Minnesota - Minneapolis	Steve Anastasi, Insight Software, Inc.	612-227-8682
Missouri - St. Louis	Randy Schilling, SoluTech	314-947-9393
Nebraska - Omaha	Jerry Pape, Applications Design & Development	402-691-8774
New Jersey	Bob Champolian, Johnson & Johnson	908-524-3930
New York - Buffalo	(Ruth Howard)	508-287-1859
New York City	Mike Ryan	212-236-9359
New York State	Mark Balley	315-428-6504
North Carolina - Charlotte	Tanya Watkins	704-335-1200 x2213
North Carolina -Central	Phyllis Weldon, Burroughs Welcome Company	919-315-4984
Ohio - Cincinnati	(Molly Quinn)	708-706-9600
Ohio - Cleveland	Marleane Troxel	216-344-4760
Ohio - Columbus	Don Long, White Castle	614-228-5781 x709
Oklahoma - Oklahoma City	(Ruth Howard)	508-287-1859
Oklahoma - Tulsa	(Ruth Howard)	508-287-1859
Oregon - Portland	Doug Atterbury, City of Portland	503-823-7090

(continues)

D

Appendixes

Table D.3 Continued

Location	Person to Contact	Telephone Number
In State/ Province Order	**PowerSoft Employee in Parentheses**	
Ottawa (Canada)	Kevin Light, Department of Government Services	613-736-2906
Pennsylvania - Philadelphia	Bill Turocy, National Liberty	215-648-5473
Pennsylvania - Pittsburgh	(Ruth Howard)	508-287-1859
Regina (Canada)	(Ruth Howard)	508-287-1859
South Carolina	Joseph Grant, Graniteville Company	803-663-2235
Tennessee - Nashville	Greg Coe, DRT International	615-366-4074
Texas - Austin	Bill Reynolds	512-343-7964
Texas - Dallas	James Pujals, Client/Server Campaign	214-393-3586
Texas - Houston	Scott Heath, BSG	713-965-1330
Texas - San Antonio	(Ruth Howard)	508-287-1859
Toronto (Canada)	Stephen Kwiecien, LGS	416-492-3003
Utah	Doug Austin	801-373-6100
Vancouver (Canada)	Michael Li, Infocam Management	604-432-1709
Virginia - Richmond	Dan Black, Blue Cross	804-354-3316
Virginia/Maryland - Federal	Robert Williams, Mindbank	703-893-4700
Washington, DC	Stuart Hill, Noblestar	703-641-8511
Washington - Seattle	Mike Carney, Washington Natural Gas	206-521-5667
Winnipeg (Canada)	Susan Hogan, On-Line	204-452-0614

Appendix E

Using C++ in Your PowerBuilder Application

PowerBuilder 4 can generate Windows applications faster than most (if not all) other Windows development tools. As with many other development tools, however, its ease of use is compromised by slower execution speed. If you are truly devoted to building the fastest applications possible, or if you need to speed up a specific section of your PowerBuilder application, you should incorporate C++ into your PowerBuilder code.

You could always write C++ code in your favorite Windows C++ compiler, compile it into a Windows Dynamic Link Library (DLL), and incorporate it into your PowerBuilder application. In previous versions of PowerBuilder, this process was tedious and difficult, and usually required a developer who was an expert in both C++ and PowerBuilder.

Version 4 of PowerBuilder has changed all of that—with the Enterprise Edition of PowerBuilder, you also receive a scaled-down version of Watcom C++. Once installed, you can define a C++ user object. This user object lets you write C++ code functions, and sets up the header files (H or HPP files) and the DLL calls for you. Using C++ user objects not only is an easy way to speed up your application, but also takes away much of the complexity previously found in coding C++.

In this appendix, you learn about the following:

- How to define a C++ function inside PowerBuilder

- How to generate C++ code from PowerBuilder

- How to add your own functionality to the C++ code generated from PowerBuilder

- How to access your C++ function from inside PowerBuilder

- The difference between C++ shared and instance variables versus PowerBuilder shared and instance variables.

> **Note**
>
> PowerSoft and Watcom have joined forces to integrate a Watcom C++ compiler into PowerBuilder Enterprise Edition. Incorporating C++ into your PowerBuilder application has the potential to dramatically speed up the execution time of your application with considerably less effort than was used in previous PowerBuilder versions.
>
> However, C++ is still considered a difficult language to master, even with PowerBuilder doing much of the setup for you. C++ is extremely obscure in array processing and string manipulation.
>
> This appendix is not designed to teach the developer C++, but rather to show a C++ programmer how to easily incorporate C++ into the PowerBuilder application. It would benefit the programmer to develop good C++ skills before incorporating C++ into an application, except with simple, math-oriented tasks.
>
> Que offers several excellent books that can teach you C++. For starters, you might want to look at *Special Edition Using Watcom SQL*.

Installing Watcom C++ for User Objects

If you purchased PowerBuilder Enterprise Edition, you have nine disks containing the Watcom C++ for User Objects. Install the program from the Windows 3.x environment by putting Disk 1 into your drive, clicking on **F**ile, **R**un and typing **a:setup**. This takes you through the installation process. Watcom C++ for User Objects requires about 18M of hard disk storage.

E

Appendixes

> **Caution**
>
> The Watcom C++ development environment that comes with PowerBuilder takes over 19M of disk storage. Be sure you have the disk storage available before you install Watcom C++.
>
> After installing Watcom C++ on your PC, be sure to reboot so that your changes to your environment variables and to your path take effect. Otherwise, using Watcom C++ will have unpredictable results.

Defining a C++ Object

You must use a user object to incorporate C++ into a PowerBuilder application. Click on the User Object icon to pull up the Select User Object dialog box seen in figure E.1, and then click on **N**ew.

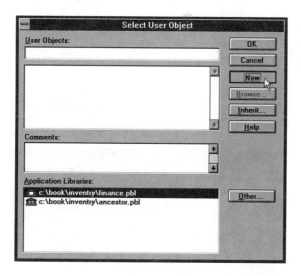

Fig. E.1
You can create or modify a user object with the Select User Object dialog box.

You now see the New User Object dialog box shown in figure E.2. Click on the C++ icon in the Class area and then click on OK.

Fig. E.2
The New User
Object dialog box
is used to define
the type of user
object you wish
to define.

Troubleshooting

I don't have the C++ icon shown in figure E.2. Why not?

If you can't find your C++ icon in the New User Object dialog box, you have not installed the Watcom C++ for User Objects compiler that comes with the Enterprise Edition.

If you have the Desktop Edition, you don't have the Watcom C++ for User Objects compiler.

The Select C++ DLL Name dialog box is displayed (see fig. E.3). In this dialog box, choose the name and directory for your DLL. Type the name and directory of the DLL associated with this user object, and click on OK.

Fig. E.3
Choose the name
and directory of
your DLL using
the Select C++ DLL
Name dialog box.

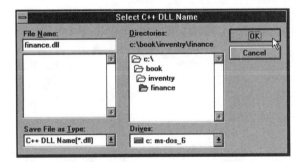

E

Appendixes

> **Note**
>
> The directory choice is an important decision. Eventually, Watcom will build a project file containing all C++ modules needed to build the DLL. It will then place (for better or worse) *all* C++ modules that currently exist in the directory you have chosen, into the project file. If you have some existing C++ functions you want to include, simply place the C++ modules and header files in the directory you have chosen to automatically incorporate them into the DLL you are creating.

Now you have to define the user object functions. These are eventually translated into C++ functions. To define the user object function, choose Declare, **U**ser Object Functions, as shown in figure E.4.

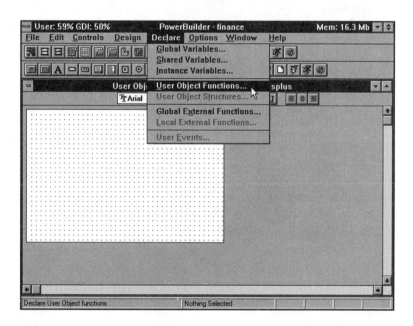

Fig. E.4
Click on Declare, **U**ser Object Functions to start defining functions for your C++ user objects.

You now see the Select Function in User Object dialog box shown in figure E.5. Click on **N**ew.

You now see the New Function dialog box as shown in figure E.6. Type the function name and function parameters in this dialog box. Because there are no financial functions in PowerBuilder, you can write two C++ functions to get a monthly loan payment and the percentage of a loan principal left to pay after a given number of years. Click on OK after typing in the function name and function parameters.

Fig. E.5
The Select
Function in User
Object dialog box
allows you to
choose whether to
create or modify
an existing user
object function.

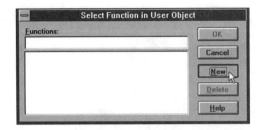

Fig. E.6
The New Function
dialog box
specifies the name
and parameters
defined in a new
function for your
User Object.

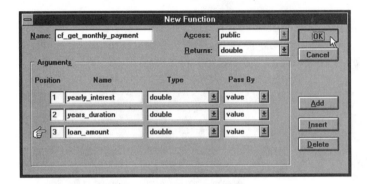

> **Note**
>
> Not all PowerBuilder data types are supported by C++. When defining your return value and your parameters in the New Function dialog box, you are limited to those data types supported by C++.

 Now click on the C++ icon. This does three things. First, the message box shown in figure E.7 is displayed. This informs you that the name you save your user object under serves as the class name for the C++ library, but the user object is not saved until you are finished with your C++ definition. Click on **Yes**. Second, PowerBuilder sets up the header (.HPP) files for you. Third, PowerBuilder sets up a C++ shell in a .CPP file. This allows the developer to code only the C++ function without all the extensive setup required with a C++ program.

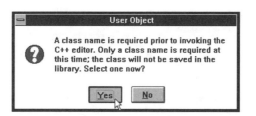

Fig. E.7
The User Object
message box
explains that a
class name is
needed.

Now the Save User Object dialog box is displayed (see fig. E.8). However, as
was mentioned in the message box in figure E.7, typing a name and clicking
on OK (which you have to do) does not save the user object but rather names
the C++ class.

Fig. E.8
Usually the Save
User Object dialog
box saves a user
object. In this case,
it is used to define
a C++ class.

> **Note**
>
> Notice that there is a cpp suffix on all C++ user objects. Also, the user object func-
> tions are defined with a cf to denote a C++ function as opposed to the normal uf
> that denotes a user object function.

You are now ready to use the Watcom IDE C++ development environment.

Using the Watcom IDE Environment

When the Save User Object dialog box closes, the Watcom C++ Integrated
Development Environment (IDE) opens, as seen in figure E.9. Watcom C++ is
a separate program from PowerBuilder. (PowerBuilder is still running in the
Windows 3.x background.)

Fig. E.9

The Watcom IDE is used to maneuver when programming in Watcom C++.

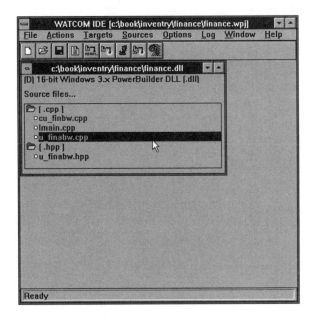

PowerBuilder has already formatted all your C++ header files and program setup for you except for the actual function code. These functions are located in the u_ C++ program module (u_finabw.cpp). Double-click on this module. This pulls up the WATCOM Windows Editor (see fig. E.10), which is a text editor for Windows 3.x. Your module should also be inside the editor when it is pulled up.

Fig. E.10

Type your C++ code in the WATCOM Windows Editor.

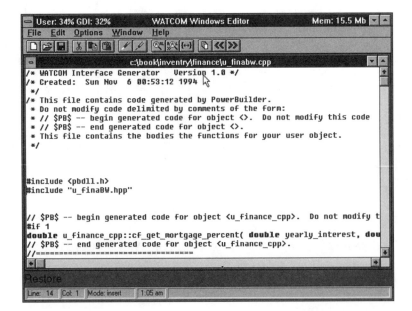

All the C++ code generated by PowerBuilder will look something like this:

```
/* WATCOM Interface Generator    Version 1.0 */
/* Created:  Sun Nov  6 00:25:44 1994
 */
/* This file contains code generated by PowerBuilder.
 * Do not modify code delimited by comments of the form:
 * // $PB$ -- begin generated code for object <>.  Do not modify
      ➥this code
 * // $PB$ -- end generated code for object <>.
 * This file contains the bodies the functions for your user
   ➥object.
 */


#include <pbdll.h>

#include "u_fina_BW.hpp"


// $PB$ -- begin generated code for object <u_finance_cpp>.  Do not
   ➥modify this code
#if 1
double u_finance_cpp::cf_get_monthly_payment( double
yearly_interest, double years_duration, double loan_amount ) {
// $PB$ -- end generated code for object <u_finance_cpp>.
//===================================

    /*
     * PUT YOUR CODE HERE
     */

    return( 0 );
}
#endif // PowerBuilder code, do not remove


// $PB$ -- begin generated code for object <u_finance_cpp>.  Do not
   ➥modify this code
#if 1
double u_finance_cpp::cf_get_loan_percent( double yearly_interest,
double years_duration, double years_paid ) {
// $PB$ -- end generated code for object <u_finance_cpp>.
//===================================

    /*
     * PUT YOUR CODE HERE
     */

    return( 0 );
}
#endif // PowerBuilder code, do not remove
```

The following lines that are in bold were added to the two C++ functions to have access to some financial functions.

```
/* WATCOM Interface Generator    Version 1.0 */
/* Created:  Sun Nov  6 00:53:12 1994
 */
/* This file contains code generated by PowerBuilder.
 * Do not modify code delimited by comments of the form:
 * // $PB$ -- begin generated code for object <>.  Do not modify
     ➥this code
 * // $PB$ -- end generated code for object <>.
 * This file contains the bodies the functions for your user
   ➥object.
 */



#include <pbdll.h>
// math.h was added by Chuck Wood - 11/6/1994 -- Can't do pow()
   ➥without it!
#include <math.h>
#include "u_finaBW.hpp"


// $PB$ -- begin generated code for object <u_finance_cpp>.  Do not
   ➥modify this code
#if 1
double u_finance_cpp::cf_get_mortgage_percent( double
yearly_interest, double years_duration, double years_paid ) {
// $PB$ — end generated code for object <u_finance_cpp>.
//===================================

    /*
     * PUT YOUR CODE HERE
     */
// Added by chuck wood - 11/6/1994
//
// cf_get_mortgage_percent returns the percentage left of a loan's
   ➥principle
// when given the interest, duration (years), and number of
   ➥durations
// (years) the loan has been paid.
//
// Adjust the yearly interest by dividing it by 12 to get monthly
   ➥interest.
// Calculate the months left using the formula
//              months_left = 12.0 * (years_duration - year)
// Adjust the yearly duration by multiplying it by 12 to get
//        months of duration.
// Then use the formula:
//        loan_percent_left = (1 - ((1+interest)^(-months_left)))
//                            / (1 -
((1+interest)^years_duration)))

    if (yearly_interest) {                    // If interest rate is
                                              ➥not 0
      return (double) ((1.0 - pow(1.0 + (yearly_interest / 12.0),
        -12.0 * (years_duration - years_paid)))
        / (1.0 - pow(1.0+(yearly_interest / 12.0), -12.0 *
```

```
years_duration)));
    }
    else {
      return (double) (years_paid / years_duration);
    }

}
#endif // PowerBuilder code, do not remove


// $PB$ -- begin generated code for object <u_finance_cpp>.  Do not
    ➥modify this code
#if 1
double u_finance_cpp::cf_get_monthly_payment( double
yearly_interest, double years_duration, double loan_amount ) {
// $PB$ -- end generated code for object <u_finance_cpp>.
//=====================================

    /*
     * PUT YOUR CODE HERE
     */
// Added by chuck wood - 11/6/1994
//
// cf_get_monthly_payment returns the monthly payment of a loan
    ➥when given
// the loan interest, loan duration, and loan amount
//
// Adjust the yearly interest by dividing it by 12 to get monthly
    ➥interest.
// Adjust the yearly duration by multiplying it by 12 to get
//       months of duration.
// Then use the formula:
//       monthly_payment = amount * interest / (1 -
((1+interest)^duration))

    if (yearly_interest) {                      // If interest rate is
                                                ➥not 0
        return (double) ((loan_amount * (double) yearly_interest /
12.0)
                        / (1.0 - pow((1.0 + ((double) yearly_interest /
12.0)),
                                     (double) years_duration * -12.0)));
    }
    else {
        return (double) (loan_amount / (years_duration * 12.0));
    }

}
#endif // PowerBuilder code, do not remove
```

When you're done, choose File, Exit to return to the Watcom IDE.

Assuming you've coded everything properly, you can generate your DLL by clicking on the Make All Targets in a Project icon. This compiles and links all your C++ modules into one DLL. Exit from the IDE to return to PowerBuilder.

Tip

Be sure to comment your C++ code extensively, because many PowerBuilder developers don't know C++.

Accessing Your C++ User Object Function

Now you can use this C++ user object function like any other object function. To access this function, you must first instantiate (declare) the user object and then use dot notation to call the function:

```
uf_finance_cpp mortgage_info
    .
    .
    .
payment = mortgage_info.cf_get_monthly_payment(interest, duration,
➥amount)
    .
    .
    .
```

Defining C++ Class Variables from PowerBuilder

Although you didn't use class variables in the example, you can define instance and shared C++ class variables in the PowerBuilder C++ User Object painter. Click on **D**eclare to declare a variable type and choose either **I**nstance Variable or **S**hared Variable.

When declaring C++ instance class variables, as seen in figure E.11, type in the variable name, choose a C++ data type, and give the variable either private or protected access. Use the same process when declaring shared variables, as seen in figure E.12, but remember that shared class variables are protected (not private) when defining them through the PowerBuilder C++ user object painter.

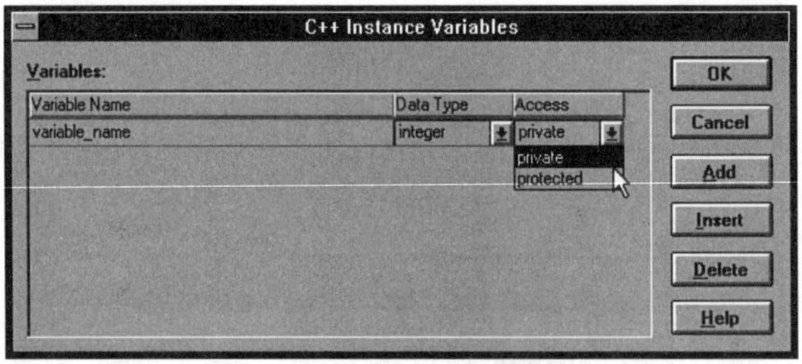

Fig. E.11
Instance variables are declared using the C++ Instance Variables dialog box.

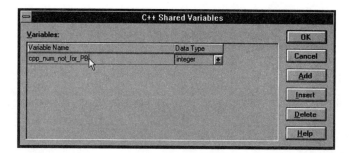

Fig. E.12
Shared class
variables are
declared using
the C++ Shared
Variables dialog
box.

Note

C++ instance and shared variables can't be accessed through PowerScript. They are
for C++ use only.

In a similar vein, C++ functions can't access PowerScript variables. Both systems
can communicate with each other through return values and passing variables by
reference.

Final Thoughts on C++

Programming in C++ has always resulted in efficient execution speeds that
rivaled assembler coding, but the code was hard to write, hard to maintain,
and prone to run time errors. Conversely, PowerBuilder programs were easy
to write and maintain, and usually had very few run time errors, but lacked
the execution speed found in C++ programs.

PowerSoft has merged the two technologies to combine the ease of use of
PowerBuilder with the execution speed of C++.

Appendix F

Third-Party Products and Support (What's on the CD?)

In this appendix, you learn about the software included on the *Special Edition Using PowerBuilder 4 Companion CD*. These products may be useful when developing and managing PowerBuilder development projects.

You'll also find a listing of the current CODE Partners—PowerSoft-certified resources around the country that you can contact for consulting and training.

Installing the CD Software

The CD-ROM that accompanies this book contains over 100M of applications, tools, and demonstration products. Using an easy installation program, you can install the entire disc or just a few items at a time directly from your Windows environment.

The disc has two major sections:

- The Inventory Tracking System sample application files that you build throughout the book.

- A collection of demonstration applications, scaled-down software, and shareware that all work with (or around) PowerBuilder.

> **Note**
>
> When you run your Inventory Tracking system through PowerBuilder, you may get a message that the Inventory Tracking system is not Version 4, and must be migrated. If this happens to you, read the README.TXT that comes with the Inventory Tracking system if you need help migrating from the beta version to the production version of PowerBuilder 4.

To start the installation program, run INSTALL.EXE from the Program Manager or File Manager. The self-explanatory screens will guide you through the individual application installations.

Third-Party Products

Following is a brief description of the products and demos you'll find on the disc from third-party vendors.

> **Note**
>
> Most of these products were designed to work with PowerBuilder 3. It was uncertain at press time whether they will run under version 4 without modification. If you have problems using the demo, contact the vendor for an updated version.

EasyCASE System Designer

Evergreen CASE Tools Inc.
8522 154th Ave NE
Redmond, WA 98052

Description

EasyCASE is an easy-to-use, low cost, highly functional Computer-Aided Software Engineering (CASE) tool that supports a wide range of methods for process event and data modeling. It is used primarily during the analysis and design phases of system development. It can be used for logical and physical data modeling, which results in the generation of SQL database creation scripts, and supports forward and reverse engineering of xBASE databases.

Price

$1,295

Key Features

Ease-of-use, high functionality level, low price, value for money, wide range of supported methodologies, flexibility, schema generation.

ER-Modeler

Chen & Associates
4884 Constitution Ave, #1E
Baton Rouge, LA 70808

Description

The Chen PowerBuilder Companion is a CASE tool for optimal database design. The user can launch a PowerBuilder script to implement the design on the host DBMS. Schema changes are supported. Also supported are links to the CHEN ER-Modeler Workbench, which includes data and process modeling, and reverse engineering for more than 30 DBMSs. Migration/conversion is supported. Dictionary reports are produced. The sophisticated Chen Normalizer can decompose records/relations into more desirable formats, including 3NF. Links to major data dictionaries and CASE tools are provided. Stand-alone and network operations are supported.

Price

Call for details

Key Features

Launches PowerBuilder scripts from a Chen data model.

Essbase Analysis Server

Arbor Software, Corporation
325 Chesapeake Terr.
Sunnyvale, CA 94089

Description

Essbase Analysis Server is premier workgroup software system optimized for business reporting and analysis applications. Essbase enables end-users to combine large volumes of diverse, enterprise-wide data and analyze it from any perspective and at any level of detail directly from a spreadsheet.

Price

Begins at $35,000

Key Features

Essbase improves corporate decision making by converting mountains of raw data into information. It complements spreadsheets, relational databases, SQL tools, executive information systems, and financial and vertical applications by adding powerful analytical capabilities in an open, easy-to-use environment.

Formula One

Visual Tools
15721 College Blvd
Lenexa, KS 66219

Description

Formula One is the first and only real spreadsheet tool available for various Windows development environments. Formula One is an Excel-compatible spreadsheet that enables developers to embed a fully functional Excel compatible spreadsheet into their application. Formula One has over 126 spreadsheet functions, supports Virtual Mode for editing and reporting of any size database, and is royalty free.

Price

$295

Key Features

Excel Compatible Spreadsheet, Royalty Free

GUI Guidelines

Corporate Computing
2549 Waukegan Road #108
Bannockburn, IL 60015

Description

GUI Guidelines consists of on-line help software explaining GUI design guidelines for all components of GUI application design. It provides corporate programmers with immediate access to quality information to facilitate the successful design of GUI applications. GUI Guidelines is necessary for any company that wants to produce consistent, successful, cost-effective GUI applications.

Price

Pricing ranges from $1,995 for 30 users, 1 site through $16,495 for worldwide unlimited users, unlimited sites.

Key Features

GUI Guidelines provides techniques for creating consistent GUI components, popup illustrations of GUI design standards and terms, rules and recommendations that are easy to follow and administer, and forms for maintaining and enhancing GUI Guidelines. GUI Guidelines dramatically reduces randomly designed GUIs due to lack of reference documents, inconsistent dialog boxes, menus and buttons, and costly trial and error in GUI design.

Info Modeler

Asymetrix Corporation
110 110th Ave. NE #700
Bellvue, WA 98004

Description

Info Modeler is a set of CASE/Methodology visual design tools for database professionals. InfoModeler uses conceptual modeling tools based in ORM (Object Role Modeling) that help to communicate and automate the process of building sound relational database management systems. Designers and end users use English business rules and sample data to build the information model. Info Modeler then generates a correctly normalized database automatically.

Price

$495

Key Features

English business rules; sample data modeling for communicating database designs. Automatic normalization and DDL creation.

ObjectStart

Greenbrier & Russell
1450 E. American Lane Suite 1640
Schaumburg, IL 60173

Description

RPC Painter provides a transparent interface between PowerBuilder and the three-tiered architecture of Encompass from Open Environment Corp. Three-tiered architecture overcomes the scalability problems of traditional two-tiered client/server environments by using standard Remote Procedure Call technology. This allows business logic to be implemented in server procedures using any available language. By partitioning business logic from both the Windows GUI front-end and the relational database back-end, three-tiered architecture is able to exploit the capabilities of high performance servers programmed in a compiled native language. RPC Painter will allow the PB developer to develop for a three-tiered architecture with the same level of simplicity and transparency that the two-tiered architecture supports today.

Price

$19,120 per developer (includes OECs Encompass); $3,120 if company has Encompass.

Key Features

RPC Painter integrates the DataWindow technology with Remote Procedure Calls; easily migrates from TCP/IP three-tier architecture to a DCE architecture; reuses existing COBOL, CICS, PB, and C Code programs. Functions include: graphical tool for preparing and editing remote procedure interface definition, automatic generation of RPC stubs for the PB client, automatic generation of RPC objects in a PB Library for application developer, generation of DataWindows for population with RPC results, compatible with ObjectStart Toll Kit technology.

OPEN/image

Wang User Objects
One Industrial Way
Lowell, MA 01851

Description

OPEN/image User Objects are image-enabling tools designed specifically for the PowerBuilder programming environment. They integrate with standard PowerBuilder user objects to easily and inexpensively image enable PowerBuilder applications.

These imaging user objects provide for the scanning, printing, and displaying of images; image annotation and manipulation; image document management; and OCR, fax, and client/server image access across multiple platforms. Image-enables applications can run in standalone, redirected, or client/server environments. For client/server environments, applications access Wang's NetWare and UNIX image servers.

Price

$395 list (US dollars)

Key Features

Image-enabling User Objects for image scan, print, display, annotate, image document management, fax, OCR, and Client/Server Image access.

PowerClass

ServerLogic Corp
2800 Northup Way, Suite 205
Bellevue, WA 98004

Description

PowerClass is a PowerBuilder class library that can reduce the amount of code and time needed to create PowerBuilder applications by 40-60%. It provides a foundation for application standards, a consistent look and feel to an application, reduces application maintenance, and includes a 700-page user manual, tutorial, and sample applications.

- PowerLock is a PowerBuilder security library and administration tool that provides access control down to the DataWindow field level.

■ PowerObjects is a collection of stand-alone PowerBuilder objects that include a tabbed folder, configurable toolbar, calendar, and several multi-media objects.

Price
Several pricing packages are available.

Key Features
Code reusability; fully integrated object functionality

PowerFrame Application Security Library Version 2.0
MetaSolv Software, Inc
14900 Landmark, Suite 240
Dallas, TX 75240

Description
PowerFrames's Application Security class library provides a comprehensive application security system which can secure PowerBuilder applications, at runtime. Applications can be secured at a window, window control (menu items, command buttons, data window, etc.), and database column level. Security authorizations may be granted at a user and/or group level.

Price
$1,495 per production server

PowerTOOL
PowerCerv
400 N. Ashley Dr. #1910
Tampa, FL 33602

Description
PowerTOOL is a library of reusable PowerBuilder objects. These objects embody a powerful, standardized methodology for the development of PowerBuilder applications. This methodology provides developers an

accelerated foundation for large scale, client-server application development. PowerTOOL promotes a standard use of inheritance and provides a proven method for navigational control and application security. PowerTOOL saves the PowerBuilder developer time usually measured in months.

Price

$8,995 unlimited developers; $4,995 for 5 developers; $1,200 single developer. For PowerBuilder Desktop: $249 list price, with an introductory promotion in place with some resellers.

Key Features

Complete support for MDI Applications, Object-Oriented Class Library, Application Template, Window Ancestor Hierarchy, DataWindow Ancestor Hierarchy, Naming Conventions, Database-driven Navigation/Security Methodology, Intersheet Communication, Comprehensive Tutorial.

RoboHelp Version 2.6

Blue Sky Software
7486 La Jolla Blvd. #3
La Jolla, CA 92037

Description

RoboHelp turns Microsoft Word for Windows into a hypertext Help authoring system capable of producing help systems as easily as plain text. Create topics, popup definitions, hypertext jumps, and more, simply by pointing and clicking. No programming experience is needed. RoboHelp automatically generates all source files (.RTF files), which you may compile using the help compiler (included with RoboHelp). Great for documentation departments, technical writers, and Windows developers/programmers.

Price

$499.00

Key Features

Generates .RTF files automatically with no programming experience required.

S-Designor

SDP Technologies
One Westbrook Corporate Ctr., Suite 805
Westchester, IL 60154

Description

S-Designor database modeling tools empower users to draw entity-relationship diagrams, create scripts, reverse engineer, and produce quality documentation for over 40 databases. The two-level design process starts with the user's conceptual model. Then, S-Designor generates the physical model where one can enhance tables, references, integrity rules, indexes, and PowerBuilder extended attributes. The bidirectional PowerBuilder bridge transfers column formats, validation rules, and edit styles. Other features include seamless reverse engineering through ODBC, alter table commands, integrity triggers, and sub-models. The network version, S-Designor Corporate, couples work-group management with a SQL-based central dictionary, allowing team members to share complete design information.

Price

$1,795 to $3,295 per license

Key Features

Two-level design, reverse engineering

Spinlist

OSoft Development Corp.
6 Piedmont Ctr, Suite 303
Atlanta, GA 30305

Description

Spinlist provides a simple and elegant solution to the creation of complex reports under Windows. It is a dynamic link library that can be called from PowerBuilder and other languages. Spinlist allows a report to be laid out in Word for Windows, Ami Pro, WordPerfect, or Ventura Publisher. The report layout can be of any complexity and can include multiple result sets, complex forms such as invoices, mailmerge, newsletters with snaking columns, database publishing with presentation markup, and any other kind of report that can be designed in a word processor.

Price

$329.00. Call for volume pricing.

Key Features

Spinlist enhances existing windows report writers by providing a solution for complex and unusual reporting requirements.

Visual Speller

Visual Tools
15721 College Blvd
Lenexa, KS 66219

Description

Visual Speller is a Visual Basic custom control that allows you to add spell checking to a Visual Basic or Visual C++ application with a minimum of programming. It also has a built-in DLL interface, which means you can use Visual Speller by making direct calls from C, C++, Microsoft Access, Powerbuilder, and so on.

Price

(Not listed.)

Key Features

Multiple standard and custom dictionaries, ignore/replace lists, word or block checking, automatic suggestions generation, shared memory for dictionaries, extensive customization capability, standard dictionary maker.

Finding PowerSoft CODE Partners

The PowerSoft CODE (Client/server Open Development Environment) partners all have products designed to work with PowerBuilder. Current CODE partners are listed in table F.1—along with their product, the product's category, and a telephone number and fax number where they can be reached. Table F.1 lists CODE partners by name.

> **Note**
>
> The information on table F.1 is effective 9/20/94. For a more updated list, contact PowerSoft.

Table F.1 CODE Partners Sorted by Name

Company	Product Name	Category
Arbor Software	Essbase Analysis Server	Executive Info System
Arcland	DesignPad	Diagramming Productivity Tools
Asymetrix Corporation	Info Modeler	CASE/Methodology
Attachmate Corporation	Extra!	Host Connectivity
AutoTester, Inc	AutoTester	Automated Testing
Bachman Information Systems, Inc.	Generator for PowerBuilder	CASE/Methodology
Banyan Systems, Inc.	ENS	Connectivity
Blue Sky Software	RoboHelp	System Development Tool
Born Software Development Group	ODBC for the AS/400	Database/ODBC
BrownStone Solutions	DataDictionary / Solution	Repository
CASE/MATE	Power-Aid	CASE/Methodology
Chen & Associates	ER-Modeler	CASE/Methodology
Cincom	Supra	Database/ODBC
Computer Associates	CA-QbyX	Database/ODBC
Control Data A/S	The NIAM Suite	Data Modeling Tool
Corporate Computing	GUI Guildelines	Class Libraries & Custom Controls
Datawatch Corporation	DataSync	Database Services
DCA	Irma	Host Connectivity
Dharma Systems, Inc.	SQL Access	Database/ODBC
Digital Equipment Corporation	Rdb	Database/ODBC

Contact	Phone	Fax #	Start Date
Matt Slavik	(408) 727-5800	(408) 727-7140	11/93
Alex Ramsay	(215) 993-9904	(215) 993-9908	12/93
Bruce Linn	(206) 637-2488	(206) 637-2435	4/94
Mark Leff	(203) 325-0066	(203) 325-1216	4/93
Larry Goldsticker	(214) 368-1196	(214) 750-9668	4/94
Kelly O'Rourke	(617) 273-9003	(617) 229-9904	9/92
John Fratus	(508) 898-1713	(508) 836-2880	4/94
Roger Zucchett	(619) 459-6365	(619) 459-6366	2/94
Rob Velasco	(507) 280-8083	(507) 280-6555	9/93
Flint Lane	(212) 370-7160	(212) 867-7820	6/94
Garland Favorito	(404) 448-0404	(601) 437-2146	3/94
Dave Hewins	(504) 928-5765	(504) 928-9371	3/94
Ed Lennon	(513) 573-3434	(513) 459-0612	12/93
Bill Pollack	(201) 592-0009	(201) 585-6745	
Bjorn-Harold Sjogren	47-22-892389	(472) 215-9821	7/93
Christine Comaford	(708) 374-1995	(708) 374-1124	10/93
Peter Kusterer	(919) 549-0711	(919) 549-0065	4/94
Bob McGowan	(404) 442-4556	(404) 442-4397	8/93
Swaroop Conjeevaram	(603) 886-1400	(603) 883-6904	9/93
Mike O'Connell	(603) 881-1627	(603) 881-0120	7/93

(continues)

Table F.1 Continued

Company	Product Name	Category
Ernst & Young	Navigator	CASE/Methodology
Evergreen CASE Tools Inc.	EasyCASE System Designer	CASE/Methodology
FileNet	WorkFLO	Imaging & Document Mgmt
FileT Software Corp	FileT/PC	Data Access Library
Folio Corporation	Folio VIEWS	Text Processing
Frustram Group	TransPortal PRO	Host Connectivity
Fulcrum Technologies, Inc.	Ful/Tex	Text Processing
Greystone Technology	GTM	Database
Gradient Tecnologies Inc.	Visual-DCE	Distributed Computing
Greenbrier & Russell	ObjectStart	Class Libraries & Custom Controls
Information Engineering	IE: Advantage, IE: Advisor	CASE/Methodology
Hewlett Packard Company	ALLBASE/SQL, IMAGE/SQL	Database
IBM Corporation	DB2/2, DB2/6000	Database
IBM Corporation	DDCS/2 to DB2, SQL/DS	Database/ Connectivity
Information Builders	EDA/SQL	Database/ Connectivity
Informix Software	Online Dynamic	Database Server
Integre France	Powertalk	Prototype Generator
Intersolv	Excelerator	CASE/Methodology
Intersolv	PVCS	Version Control
IRI Software	EXPRESS	Imaging & Document Mgmt
Lante Corporation	Lotus Notes	Groupware

F

Appendixes

Contact	Phone	Fax #	Start Date
David Bonner	(214) 444-2100	(214) 444-2102	
Rob Pritt	(206) 881-5149	(206) 883-7676	9/93
Michael Piti	(714) 966-3400	(714) 966-3490	3/94
Glenn Englund	(719) 661-8371	(719) 576-0832	1/94
Mike Judson	(801) 344-3671	(801) 344-3787	
Chris Davis	(212) 338-0721	(914) 428-0795	5/93
Colin McAlpin	(613) 238-1761	(613) 238-7695	11/93
Robert Shear	(617) 937-9000	(617) 937-9022	3/94
Dave Zwicker	(508) 624-9600	(508) 229-0338	
Deb Turkot	(708) 706-4000	(708) 706-4020	1/94
Cathy Begley	(703) 739-2242	(703) 739-0074	4/94
Todd Hirozawa	(408) 447-5705	(408) 447-4597	
Larry Chan	(416) 448-4291	(512) 823-2110	
Larry Chan	(416) 448-4291	(416) 448-4439	
Gary Goldberg	(212) 736-4433	(212) 564-1726	4/93
Susan Nurse	(415) 926-6688	(415) 322-2805	
France Thebault	33-1-40911060	33-1-4011032	5/94
Kelle McConnell	(301) 230-3349	(301) 230-2883	
Kelle McConnell	(301) 230-3349	(301) 230-2883	
Dave Meninger	(617) 672-4689	(617) 672-4660	4/94
Jeff Weinberg	(312) 236-5100	(312) 236-0664	

(continues)

Table F.1   Continued

Company	Product Name	Category
LaserData	DocuData	Imaging & Document Management
LBMS - System Engineer	System Engineer	CASE/Methodology
Legent Corporation	Endevor	Version Control
LexiBridge Corporation	LexiBridge Transformer	CASE/Methodology
Logic Works, Inc.	ERwin/ERX	CASE/C72 Methodology
Lotus Development Corporation	Notes	Groupware
Magna Software	MAGNA.X	DCE
MapInfo Corporation	MapInfo	Mapping
MediaWay, Inc.	MediaDB	Database
MetaSolv Software, Inc.	PowerFrame	Class Libraries
Mercury Interactive	Win Runner	Automated Testing
MicrodecisionWare	Database Gateway	Database/Connectivity
Microsoft Corporation	SQL Server	Database
Microsoft Corporation	Microsoft Test	Automated Testing
Millennium Corporation	PowerBase	Reporting
Mortice Kern Systems, Inc.	RCS	Version Control
Netwise, Inc.	TransAccess DB2/Integrator	Database/Connectivity
NobleNet	WinRPC	Distributed Computing
Open Environment Corporation	POWERextender	Distributed Computing
Open Horizon, Inc.	Connection/DCE	Connectivity/DCE
Oracle Corporation	Oracle Server	Database
OSoft Development Corp.	Spinlist	Class Libraries & Custom Controls

Contact	Phone	Fax #	Start Date
Rich Grady	(508) 649-4600	(508) 649-4436	8/93
Jim Fatiuk	(800) 231-7515	(713) 623-4955	12/92
Bruce Hall	(508) 870-1900	(508) 836-5992	3/93
Fred Holahan	(203) 459-8228	(203) 459-8220	
Barbara Bogart	(609) 243-0088	(609) 243-9192	3/93
Jeff Brown	(617) 693-4875	(617) 229-8678	
Ross Altman	(212) 727-6719	(212) 691-1968	2/94
Geoff LeBloud	(518) 266-7289	(518) 272-0014	6/94
Debbie Gronski	(408) 748-7402	(408) 748-7405	7/94
Dana Brown	(214) 239-0692	(214) 239-0653	1/94
Inbar Lasser-Raab	(408) 987-0100	(405) 982-0149	9/93
Chris Matney	(303) 546-1228	(303) 546-1110	4/93
Brian Lania	(617) 487-6450	(617) 487-7925	
Bob Saile	(206) 936-3468	(206) 936-7329	6/94
Kent Marsh	(206) 868-3029	(206) 868-5093	6/94
Chuck Lownie	(519) 884-2251	(519) 884-8861	12/93
Bill Jacobs	(303) 442-8280	(303) 442-3798	4/93
Bill Bogasky	(508) 460-8222	(508) 460-3456	1/94
Peter Foster	(617) 562-5852	(617) 562-0038	8/93
Kurt Dahm	(415) 593-1509	(415) 593-1669	6/94
Gini Bell	(415) 506-6337	(415) 506-7225	
Michael J. Gora	(404) 814-6030	(404) 814-8401	9/93

(continues)

Table F.1 Continued

Company	Product Name	Category
PARADIGM Computer Solutions	PowerPlate	Class Libraries
Pegasus Imaging Corp	PIC View	Imaging/Graphics
Popkin Software Systems, Inc.	System Architect	CASE/Methodology
PowerCerv	PowerTool	Class Libraries & Custom Controls
Praxis International	Connect*	Database/ODBC
Promark Inc.	Rhobot/Client-Server	Automated Testing
Quadbase Systems, Inc.	Quadbase SQL	Database/ODBC
Red Brick Systems	Red Brick Warehouse	Database/ODBC
SDP	S-Designor	Database Design
Sietec Open Systems	ViSietec	Imaging & Document Mgmt
Select Software Tools	Select OMT	CASE/Methodology
Segue	QA Partner	Automated Testing
Server Logic Corp	PowerClass	Class Libraries & Custom Controls
ShowCase Corporation	ShowCase ODBC	Database/ODBC
Softbridge, Inc.	Automated Test Facility	Automated Testing
Soft-tek International	GRAFSMAN	Graphics
Software Quality Automation	Team Test	Automated Testing
Sterling Software	Answer Testpro	Automated Testing
Strategic Mapping, Inc./TerraLogics	TerraView	Mapping
Stylus Innovation, Inc.	Visual Voice	Voice Processing
Sybase	SQL Server	Database
Tandem Computers	NonStop SQL	Database/ODBC

Contact	Phone	Fax #	Start Date
Gary Cook	(800) 593-5106	(403) 256-8398	3/94
Chris Lubeck	(813) 875-7575	(813) 875-7705	3/94
Ron Sherma	(212) 571-3434	(212) 571-3436	
Bernie Borges	(813) 226-2378	(813) 222-0886	12/93
Joan Kaminski	(617) 492-8860	(617) 497-1072	2/94
Daniel Rosen	(201) 540-1980	(201) 540-8377	6/94
Frederick C. Luk	(408) 738-6989	(408) 738-6980	
Sylvia Waelter	(408) 354-7214	(408) 399-3277	10/93
Serve Levy	(708) 947-4250	(708) 947-4251	11/93
David Macklem	(416) 496-8510	(416) 496-8524	4/94
Terri Rodriguez	(714) 957-6633	(714) 957-6219	2/94
Christina Kasica	(617) 969-3771	(617) 969-4326	3/94
Terry LeLievre	(206) 803-0378	(206) 803-0349	1/94
Amy Johnson	(507) 288-5922	(507) 287-2803	4/93
David Stookey	(617) 576-2257	(617) 864-7747	1/93
Michael Christensen	(316) 838-7200	(316) 838-3789	4/94
Eric Schurr	(617) 932-0110	(617) 932-3280	3/93
Douglas Turner	(818) 716-1616	(818) 998-2171	2/94
David C. Snow	(508) 656-9900 x909	(508) 656-9999	7/93
Michael Casidy	(617) 621-9545	(617) 621-7862	2/94
Tom Barrett	(510) 922-8534	(510) 922-4747	
Allyn Beekman	(408) 285-8550	(408) 285-6004	12/93

(continues)

Table F.1 Continued

Company	Product Name	Category
Tangent International	Distributed Computing Integrator	Distributed Computing
Techna International	SEMREC	Reengineering
TechGnosis, Inc.	SequeLink	Database/Connectivity
Text Systems International	SYSQL, ADAQL	Connectivity
The Ask Group	Ingres	Database/ODBC
Thinking Machines	Decision SQL	Database
Transarc Corporation	Encina	Distributed Computing
Trinzic Corporation	Infohub, Infopump	Database/Connectivity
UniSQL, Inc.	UniSQL/M	Connectivity
UniSQL, Inc.	UniSQL/X	Database/ODBC
Visible Systems Corporation	Visable Analyst Workbench	CASE/Methodology
Visual Tools	First Impression, Formula One,	Class Libraries & Custom Controls
Vmark/Constellation	HyperSTAR	Database/Connectivity
Walker Richer & Quinn	Reflection	Connectivity
Wall Data, Inc.	Rumba	Host Connectivity
Wang Laboratories, Inc.	Open Image	Imaging & Document Mgmt
WATCOM	WATCOM SQL	Database
Watermark Software	Watermark Discovery Edition	Imaging & Document Mgmt
XDB	XDB	Database

Contact	Phone	Fax #	Start Date
Enzo Greco	(212) 809-8200	(212) 968-1398	5/94
Dave Ghosh	(408) 982-9131	(408) 982-9132	9/93
Don Plummer	(617) 229-6100	(617) 229-0557	6/94
Itzhak Margolis	(203) 637-4549	(203) 698-2409	12/93
Barbara Skrbino	(510) 769-1400	(510) 748-2546	
Franklin Davis	(617) 234-2060	(617) 234-4444	3/94
Peter Oleinick	(412) 338-4368	(412) 338-4404	
Eric Egertson	(617) 891-6500 x2963	(617) 622-1544	4/94
Robert Albach	(512) 343-7297 x137	(512) 343-7383	6/94
Robert Albach	(512) 343-7297 x137	(512) 343-7383	6/94
Stewart Nash	(617) 890-2273	(617) 890-8909	10/93
Tom Debaaco	(913) 599-6500 x102	(913) 599-6597	
Barry Cushing	(508) 620-0200	(508) 620-7443	2/94
Leonard Bargellini	(206) 217-7100	(206) 217-0292	4/94
Rob Spence	(206) 883-4777	(206) 861-3175	4/93
Wang Telesales	(800) 639-WANG	(508) 967-0828	6/93
Chris Kleisath	(519) 886-3700	(519) 747-4971	
Kevin Lach	(617) 229-2600	(617) 229-2989	6/93
Kathy Magenheim	(301) 317-6800	(301) 317-7701	4/93

Index of Common Problems

If you have this problem...	You'll find help here
Application Design & Programming	
C++ icon does not appear	p. 616
CREATE, DROP, or ALTER don't work after program is distributed	p. 197
Foreign keys attached to primary keys message appears when attempting to change or delete a row on a table	p. 71
Local variable gets reset, but does not go out of scope	p. 136
Local variable in script keeps resetting to 0 or ""	p. 132
Numbers in format string do not print	p. 238
PBL just created in the library painter can't be found	p. 20
Want to hide ColorBar or StyleBar to get more viewing area	p. 40
Data Entry	
Error messages continue to appear after incorrect value is fixed	p. 257
Expression is not valid error message appears	p. 311
Invalid entries are allowed even though validation rules are set	p. 257
Sort order was not set before previewing report	p. 317

(continues)

If you have this problem...	You'll find help here
Debugging & Delivery	
Cannot connect to database after executable is distributed	pp. 395, 563
Characters in string variable do not all display when debugging	p. 379
Nothing happens when line is clicked on during debugging	p. 371
Script containing enumerated data type will not compile	p. 510

Index

Symbols

J-K

X-Y-Z